John Esten Cooke

The Virginia Bohemians

A Novel

John Esten Cooke

The Virginia Bohemians
A Novel

ISBN/EAN: 9783337028398

Printed in Europe, USA, Canada, Australia, Japan

Cover: Foto ©Thomas Meinert / pixelio.de

More available books at **www.hansebooks.com**

THE VIRGINIA BOHEMIANS

A Novel

By JOHN ESTEN COOKE

AUTHOR OF

"STORIES OF THE OLD DOMINION" "MR. GRANTLEY'S IDEA" "HENRY
ST. JOHN, GENTLEMAN" "PROFESSOR. PRESSENSEE"

NEW YORK

HARPER & BROTHERS, FRANKLIN SQUARE

1880

CONTENTS.

8 . CONTENTS.

VIRGINIA BOHEMIANS.

I.

BOHEMIA was in all its glory: not the Bohemia of the Austro-Hungarian monarchy, but the valley of that name under the shadow of the Blue Ridge in Virginia.

It nestled, this Virginia Bohemia, down between two ranges—the main great crest of the real "Blue Ridge Mountains" rolling off to the blue distance in long surges —tipped with the foam of the snow in winter; the fleecy charm of the white clouds when the summer sun was shining; and a much lower range, a chain of wooded hills, which hemmed it in on the west. Clasped by the two, Bohemia slept like a bird's-nest cradled in a rift of foliage.

Northward the valley had its *embouchure*, and the view sweeping far beyond Front Royal, where the branches of the Shenandoah melt together, lost itself on the infinite horizon of the Maryland mountains. Southward, Bohemia stole away into a wooded gorge—shadowy, silent, full of mysterious gloom. It was the Virginia Hartz, this gorge and mountain—for above it was the "Hogback" peak, a bristling crest whose name describes it, where the country people said that witches gathered in the midnights, bent on unknown ceremonies. Standing in the mouth of this fantastic gorge, Bohemia is mysterious, almost sinister. The sun scarcely enters. Yonder is the battlement he rises over late, and the other battlement he sets beyond, soon. A glimpse, and then night descends.

But if you turn your back upon the gorge and enter the valley, travelling northward, all is changed. Bohemia smiles and holds out caressing arms in the summer days and the moonlight nights; in the summer days, when the little stream of Falling Water running yonder laughs under its sycamores with the mottled arms; in the moonlight nights, when the dreamy splendor sleeps on the tulip-trees and the winds whisper. The hills sloping to the Shenandoah assume feminine outlines: the wheat rolls its long amber waves in the wind; and the frou-frou of the corn mingles with the silence. Then you follow this path through the long grass of the meadow, and down the stream to the wooden bridge where the stage-road crosses—the stage-road coming from the west across the hills, and winding up the mountain yonder, like a yellow ribbon with an emerald border, through the Gap, beyond which, on the eastern slope, lies the village of Piedmont.

The scene is wild, but that only makes it lovelier. Few houses are in view— those you see perched on the heights, or in the little gorges, are the lodges of hunters. Bohemia has nothing whatever to do with the stupid outer world. It is not a part of that real world at all. It is Dream-land, and the Dream-land is awaiting something or somebody.

II.

A LOITERER.

THE stage—old-fashioned and deep-laden, which ran, or walked, between the railway station and Piedmont—was going eastward one September afternoon, and stopped on the western range of hills to rest its horses. As the horses had just dragged it through the Shenandoah and then up the steep road, they were entitled to that.

A young fellow with brown eyes, in a brown travelling suit, and carrying in his hand a breech-loading carbine and jointed fishing-rod strapped together, got down from the stage. After looking down into the valley, he said,

"I think I'll stop here, driver."

The driver, who was stooping to examine his linchpins, raised a head and neck encased in an ancient felt and voluminous bandanna, and responded in a friendly way,

"You say you'll stop, sir?"

"Yes; I'll tell you good-bye here."

"I thought you were booked for Piedmont—"

"So I was; but I am a sort of bird that lights on the first tree. I am a hunter by trade. I'll take lodging at some house in the mountain here, and stay a few days. I might get a shot at a buck."

The driver nodded, and the traveller said,

"You can leave my valise at Piedmont, and I'll send for it. If no one will lodge me, I'll call for it on my way back to New York."

"All right, sir."

"I see a house yonder on the side of the mountain; that would suit me. Can you tell me who lives there?"

"Oh yes—Daddy Welles is his name."

"Is he a hunter, and the sort of man I would be apt to like?"

For some reason best known to himself, the driver of the stage uttered a short laugh. The traveller, who had a pair of bright, roving eyes set in a ruddy face, looked at him with curiosity.

"You don't answer me," he said.

"Oh, the Daddy's a great hunter," the driver said, with the same laugh.

"And you think I'd like him?"

The driver again nodded.

"Oh yes, you'd be certain to like the Daddy," he said. "He's one of the best-natured men you ever met, and if people tell queer stories about him, that's neither here nor there. It's none of *my* business."

"Queer stories? What do you mean?"

"Well, I don't mean anything in particular; and p'rhaps I've said too much. Oh yes! you'll like the Daddy.—Here you are, gentlemen, will you get in?" he added to the passengers, who re-entered the stage.

"You think you'll stop at Daddy Welles's, sir, do you?" said the driver to the young traveller."

"Yes."

"Well, don't let him know I said people told queer stories about him. It might bring me bad luck."

"I won't."

III.

A MOUNTAINEER.

THE stage went on its way, and the traveller, with fishing-rod and carbine swung over his shoulder, followed it down toward the bridge.

His appearance was that of a city man—his walk was very different. He had the long, swinging gait of the mountaineer or pedestrian in rough countries. At the foot of the hill he came on the bridge, and stood still for some minutes looking at the landscape. A light wind stirred the magical colors of the foliage on the slope of the mountain; a translucent mist descended slowly: from a field of corn beneath came up a low, faint rustle, like the rustle of a woman's dress. It was nearly sunset, and long shadows ran across Bohemia, or lay motionless, rather, in the grass and on the leaves. They whispered like the corn, and then were silent again. Not a breath stirred. Bohemia had re-entered into Dream-land.

The young man nodded to the valley —it was his salute—and said, " You will do." He then shifted his rod and carbine to the other shoulder, and, striking into a path obliquing to the right from the bridge, entered the valley beyond, followed the path through a meadow, and, crossing a brush fence, found himself upon a country road winding southward in the direction of the gorge. About a hundred yards farther another path went up the slope. Into this the traveller turned. As the ascent was gradual, it did not tire him in the least, and in a quarter of an hour he reached a plateau, on which stood a small mountain house.

The house was within fifty yards of him, when a pack of deer-hounds rushed out, baying furiously. The traveller advanced to meet them, and patted them on the head, whereat they changed their minds, and leaped up to be caressed. He then looked at the house. It was of wood, with a veranda in front, whose roof was an extension of that of the building. The yard was enclosed with split palings, and a small gate with a horse-block in front gave access to it. In rear of all was a stable, and a building probably used as a kitchen.

This was plain and home-like. It seemed to please the new-comer. He went into the enclosure, and walked up to the house. As he reached the small porch, the host, a man of tall stature, with long gray hair falling on his shoulders, and clad from head to foot in homespun, made his appearance.

The traveller seemed to have travelled: he was off-hand.

"Are you Daddy Welles?" he said.

"The same, friend."

The voice uttering these words was cordial, and a guileless smile went with them; but the visitor inwardly decided that he never had yet seen a more piercing pair of eyes.

"My name is Brantz Elliot, and I am on my way to New York," said the visitor. " I saw your house from the hill yonder, and liked its looks. People tell me there is a great deal of game here; I thought I'd try to get a shot at it before I went back."

The voice communicating these particulars was frank and straightforward. It evidently made a favorable impression, but the master of the mansion as evidently hesitated.

"I've all the money I want, and of course I expect to pay," said the traveller.

Still the old mountaineer seemed dubious, though it was plain that the allusion to a money payment had strengthened his good opinion of his visitor.

"Well, well, friend, we'll have time to talk about things to-morrow," he said. "You'll stay to-night—plenty o' room."

He went in, followed by his guest, to a small, low-pitched apartment on the right of the entrance. Here everything was very plain, but very neat. On the narrow mantel-piece stood a wooden clock, and there were some cheap prints on the whitewashed walls. The furniture was simple enough; a few stiff "split-bottomed" chairs stood against the wall, and two others, with rockers, at the corners of the fireplace. In the middle of the room was a round table of stained pine, holding a family Bible, a copy of the "Pilgrim's Progress," "Short Sermons to Believers," and a temperance work in handsome binding, entitled "Fly the Bowl."

"Sit down, friend," Daddy Welles said, drawing forward one of the rocking-chairs. "You must be hungry, but my old 'oman's busy at supper, and here she is to say it's ready, I ruther think."

This was followed by the appearance of the old woman, a motherly dame in a snuff-colored gown and a frilled cap, who came in, smiled in a friendly way, and welcomed the visitor.

"Supper's ready, Daddy," she said.

IV.

DADDY WELLES EN FAMILLE.

DADDY WELLES led the way across a narrow passage, decorated with a pair of deer's antlers supporting a rifle, a hand-

12 VIRGINIA BOHEMIANS.

net, and some fishing-rods, into the room opposite, where a table was spread with an excellent supper. All about this room was plain, like the former, and the table-service was as unassuming. The plates and cups were of cheap white china, and the knives and two-pronged steel forks had buck-horn handles. The table was of pine, and the chairs had split bottoms; but then there was smoking venison, and wheat and corn bread, and good coffee with rich cream, and the chairs looked extremely comfortable.

Mr. Brantz Elliot, traveller, evidently took this view of things and congratulated himself. He was probably accustomed, if an opinion could be formed from his dress and general appearance, to much more imposing *ménages*, but possibly liked this better.

As they were sitting down, a girl came in and made a shy courtesy to the stranger. She was very poorly clad, but very pretty. Her dress was a checked linsey, confined at the waist by a black patent-leather belt with an imitation silver buckle, worth only a few cents, and her shoes and stockings were of the commonest material. In spite of these drawbacks, the rustic beauty of the girl impressed the visitor. She had a fine suit of dark hair which fell upon her shoulders behind, and very large eyes, which were half hidden by long eyelashes. Her shyness made her awkward; but the young man said to himself that some of these days this mountain maid was probably going to be a beauty.

He had not much time to look at her at the moment. There is something even more attractive than a pretty face to a hearty young fellow, who has breakfasted early and had no dinner: this is a good supper. Mr. Brantz Elliot, therefore, concentrated his attention on the venison and coffee, and subsequently retired with Daddy Welles to the room opposite, to which a lamp had been taken, as it was night now, in a state of perfect physical and mental satisfaction. He was evidently pleased with his quarters, and, drawing a cigar-case from his pocket, asked if any one minded his smoking.

"Oh no," said Daddy Welles, with the guileless smile which seemed to be the habitual expression of his features; "I mostly smoke myself after supper, friend. I s'pose you don't keer about this sort of thing?"

He went to a corner and produced a box containing smoking-tobacco, and red-clay pipes with long stems of reed root.

"You are mistaken," said Brantz Elliot, promptly depositing his cigar-case on the table and filling one of the pipes. "I like a pipe a great deal better than a cigar. Cigars are rather sloppy."

He then sat down, and they began to smoke, falling into easy conversation.

"I think I've come to the right place," said Elliot. "This looks like a good neighborhood for game—they told me I'd find a plenty around Piedmont."

"Well, Bohemia beats the Piedmont neighborhood for that a long way, friend," Daddy Welles said, smoking tranquilly. "You see, around Piedmont's thickly settled. Bohemia's wilder, as stands to reason, being mostly mounting."

The word "Bohemia" thus used twice by his host plainly excited the curiosity of his guest.

"What do you mean by Bohemia?" he asked.

"Well, I mean here in the mounting," said Daddy Welles. "People call the deestrict here *Bohemia*, as they call another deestrict in these parts *Arabia.** I don't know why it is, but hereabouts was called Bohemia as far back as when I was a boy."

"Well, that's odd enough," said Elliot. "It's not a bad name, and I rather think I'm something of a *Bohemian* myself. I like to rove around better than living in cities. The houses are bigger and finer in town, but I don't care much for that. Every man follows his own taste, you know."

* "Arabia" is the name given to one of the neighborhoods, or precincts, in Clarke county.

"Jest so, friend, that's reasonable," said the host, much pleased with his guest.

"I've been to the Springs," Elliot explained further; "but there's too much of town even there—it's pretty much all dress and show. I'd rather go deer-stalking—I have done a good deal of it in Scotland; so I thought I'd stop here for two or three days, or a week, and try my luck. My valise has gone on to Piedmont, but that's no great matter. What puzzles me is to know where you are going to put me."

"Never you mind about that," Daddy Welles said. "There'll be no trouble, and if we can accommodate you, I'll go for your baggage to-morrow. I'm going over to Piedmont, any way, as my darter Nelly—that's her you saw at supper—says she wants to see the circus."

"Is there to be a circus at Piedmont?"

"They say it's to be there to-morrow."

"Well, if there's anything I like, it's a circus!" Elliot said, with animation. "It's ahead of the opera, in my opinion. I reckon, as you say in Virginia, there'll be no trouble about taking me as a lodger for a few days, and we can all go for the valise, and then to the circus."

The manly delight of the circus-lover evidently pleased Daddy Welles.

"To be sure," he said. "I've got a spring-wagon that'll take us all—I mean you and me and Nelly; the old 'oman mostly stays at home."

"The wagon's the thing, Daddy Welles," said Mr. Brantz Elliot, with great satisfaction; and as he yawned soon afterward, his host rose and said he reckoned he was sleepy. Elliot replied that he *was* a little tired, and so he was conducted up-stairs to his bedroom.

The chamber into which Daddy Welles led the way, lamp in hand, was a small room, with a dormer-window in front and another in rear. A single glance showed Elliot that the chamber belonged to a woman or a girl—probably to Nelly Welles. There was a small white bed with one pillow, an old toilet-table with a cracked looking-glass, and on the mantel-piece stood two cheap jars with colored pictures pasted upon them, and holding some autumn flowers. There were more flowers at one window—creepers in a rude box. Cheap white curtains hung in front of the windows, and on a small table in the middle of the room were a few tattered old books, and a girl's work-basket, which had probably been overlooked. It was not the sleeping-room of a man, evidently, but a sort of bird's-nest, and the bird was evidently a female.

"This is your daughter Nelly's room, Daddy Welles," Elliot said, stopping at the threshold, "and you are turning her out on my account. That won't do! I can sleep anywhere."

"Never you mind about that, friend," returned his host. "Yes, this is Nelly's room, but there's her bed in our room where she slept when she was little—though she's not so big yit."

Elliot shook his head doubtfully, and said,

"I really can't think of that. She'd have no opinion of me if I deprived her of her room."

"Who—Nelly? Bless you, you don't know Nelly. *She* never thinks about herself. You couldn't please her better."

"Are you certain she won't mind?"

"To be sure she won't."

"Well, it will be for only a few days at most. Everything's so neat and nice here that I begin to think more than ever that I had a streak of luck when I turned into the path to your house, Daddy Welles."

The off-hand and friendly manner of the speaker evidently had its effect on the Daddy. He bade his guest good-night, and on rejoining his family delivered a mild eulogium upon him.

———◆———

V.

A STARTLING INCIDENT.

BRANTZ ELLIOT retired promptly, stretching himself luxuriously in his small bed, which was only a straw mattress—but then the sheets were as white as snow, and fragrant from the rose-leaves in which, after the country fashion, they had been packed.

This attention was due, of course, to the old woman or to Nelly; and that made him think of the girl whose bed he had invaded so unceremoniously—sending her away to sleep where she slept "when she was little." She was a very handsome child, indeed, he informed himself—for she was no more than a child. He never had seen finer eyes, though she was so shy that he had scarcely been able to obtain a good look at them; and her features were delicate and lady-like, by no means such as he would have expected in a rustic maiden of the plainer class. Altogether, she was an agreeable feature of the mountain establishment, and adorned her somewhat rude surroundings like the flowers on the mantel-piece and in the window.

"I hope she won't feel any malice against me for turning her out of her room," he muttered, smiling a little and yawning. "I would rather be friends with everybody—and decidedly I like Daddy Welles and his old 'oman; and I mean to shoot a buck and express it to the club, and when I go back they'll pass resolutions, and give me a reception!"

A delighted extension of the limbs, followed by another yawn, succeeded these words. It then became plain, as Mr. Brantz Elliot's eyes began to close, that he was thinking in a vague sort of way of the scenes of the evening.

"*Bohemia!*" he muttered; "that's a queer name! And then the *queer stories* about Daddy Welles. He seems to be a plain enough old fellow, with nothing mysterious about him. Is he a brigand of the mountains? He don't look like it, and his old 'oman is not in the least my idea of a 'brigand's bride.' And then Nelly: she's an honest-looking sort of a maiden; can't read or write, I suppose—yes she can, there are the old books on the table; but—her eyes—shy, but there is nothing at all sly about her—*queer stories?* The driver said—'queer stories'—I wonder—"

Mr. Brantz Elliot was fast asleep.

He was waked by a wild and startling cry, which rang through the whole establishment, and made him rise suddenly in bed and listen.

Now to be aroused at midnight—it was about that hour—by a shrill and piercing shriek, apparently, in a strange house in the lonely solitude of a mountain, is not agreeable. It tries the nerves. In one's dwelling-house or hotel in a city there is the bell to ring, or a burglar alarm to sound; or other resource against housebreakers and possible murder. On the present occasion the surroundings of Mr. Brantz Elliot were quite different. He was in a secluded fastness of the Blue Ridge, in the midst of strange people, of whom "queer stories" were told; and he had suddenly been aroused at dead of night by a piercing cry—was it one of pain or menace? What did it mean?

Sitting up in bed, the young man listened. The moon had risen above the mountain, as a long yellow bar of light upon the floor of the room indicated. He could hear the melancholy sigh of a low wind in the foliage without. With this exception, there was profound silence.

All at once, within a few feet of him, apparently, the wild cry rang out again—a cry shrill, piercing, and filling the night. Brantz Elliot started back; then he burst out laughing. The cry was articulate now. It was "whip—poor—will!" In fact, a harmless member of that fraternity, which loves the vicinity of human dwellings, had lit in an oak nearly brushing one of the dormer-windows, and uttered its startling cry. As the young man, according to his habit, had raised the sash to admit the fresh air before retiring, the sound had rung in his ears like the notes of a clarion.

"Well—that's not in the least like Broadway or Fifth Avenue, at least!" he muttered, laughing. "I suppose that night patrol will retire pretty soon."

A dusky shadow flitted across the window as he spoke. The whip-poor-will had already flown elsewhere, as a distant complaint a moment afterward indicated, and Elliot was about to drop asleep again when he heard voices beneath his window. He lay still for some moments listening—there were the voices. This was curious—it was at least midnight. Who was abroad at so late an hour? He got up and went to the window. As he reached it and looked out, he saw two dusky figures disappearing in the shadow of some evergreens near the house.

Interested more and more by this incident, Elliot remained at the window, and soon saw a figure come back through the moonlight and re-enter the house. This was the figure of Daddy Welles. From a hospitable desire, no doubt, not to disturb his guest, he entered noiselessly. Then a slight sound on the staircase indicated that the Daddy had cautiously mounted to the room opposite that occupied by his visitor, the door of which was heard to close quietly.

Brantz Elliot went back to bed in a state of great curiosity. What did it mean? Old rustics like Daddy Welles did not go to bed at nine o'clock, and then hold business interviews subsequently with people at midnight. Then the voices had been low and guarded. What could it all mean?

"I don't know," Brantz Elliot muttered, as if somebody had asked him the question; "but I'll try and find out the mystery before I go back."

He then fell asleep.

VI.

PIEDMONT WAKES UP.

PIEDMONT was an ancient and stereotyped village lying east of the Blue Ridge, a mile or two from the Gap.

The place had been finished for a number of years, and life had gone to sleep there. The arrival of the daily stage was the one event of the twenty-four hours. As this lumbered up to the antique tavern, with the battered sign-board hanging at an angle of forty-five degrees from a bough of the aged elm in front of the hostelry, Piedmont nearly opened its eyes;

the loungers on the tavern porch were almost interested. They were not at all interested in the outer world or its people; but then human nature must absolutely have something to stare at, even to speculate about. Travellers afforded this solace. Peace or war, in Europe or elsewhere, were not matters of interest, but the arrival of the stage was an event. In the absence of this distraction from ennui they attended to the business of their neighbors. This was done with assiduity and almost with energy, and a scandal aroused in these worthy people a sort of mild excitement. If it was a slight and feeble scandal, they nursed it and set it to grow, until it attained creditable proportions; if it was strong and full-grown, they patted it on the back and made the most of it, smiling and whispering about it under the breath. In other words, the human mind was cramped at Piedmont. There was no public library; and, after reading the newspapers, there was nothing else to do but discuss, in a feeble and vacuous manner, the affairs of their neighbors. The days succeeded and resembled each other. Piedmont and the Piedmontese were asleep.

It was very much like other towns. In the suburbs were two churches, belonging to the Episcopalians and Methodists. The main street was broad, and there were several shops and private residences upon it, some of the latter quite handsome, with lawns and large trees in front. The town-pump stood at a corner, with a warning to drivers not to water stock at it. Near one extremity of the main street was the blacksmith's shop, where small boys watched with delight the grimy bare-armed smith hammering out sparks to the anvil chorus. In front of the stores were boxes with rolls of dry goods upon them; and the smug clerks, afflicted with ennui, were generally seen standing in the doors, watching maidens with an attack of the "pull-back" mania lifting their skirts as they crossed the dusty or muddy street.

The tavern was near the middle of the

village, and was the favorite resort of idlers. These were occupied generally in laboriously killing time. Some smoked, and others chewed tobacco, expectorating thoughtfully at intervals. An observation from any one went a great way, and occasioned meditation. When weary of the burden of thought, they dropped into an apartment where a personage, generally in his shirt-sleeves, disseminated liquids behind a counter. Having thus refreshed existence, the idlers came back to the benches on the porch of the tavern, and resumed the sleepy talk until dinner-time, when they dispersed — for an hour or so. Then Piedmont subsided into its sleep of sleeps. Even the banging of the anvil chorus sunk to silence; not a cur was heard to yelp; not a hoof-stroke resounded on the streets. The silent Blue Ridge leaned above, with the stage-road descending through the Gap, as if it led from Drowsy-land to a country of the same description. The wind had not even strength to move the leaves of the trees; and the long shadows crawled, evidently not at all in a hurry, toward evening and the representative of Piedmont—sleep.

One morning, however — it was the morning after the day upon which this narrative begins — a great change came over the village of Piedmont. From mouth to mouth passed the startling intelligence, "The circus is coming!"

The fact had been announced by gigantic posters on the walls and fences, containing highly-colored representations of flying-trapeze performers; flying horses in splendid caparisons; flying bare-back riders, male and female, for the most part nearly destitute as to clothing; and a superb Mr. Merryman in party-colored costume, who jumped and grimaced at the crack of the ring-master's whip. There were also pictures of imposing wild animals, for it was a circus and menagerie combined that was coming. Elephants, nearly of natural size, stepped carefully over their prostrate masters on the posters; and sea-lions, giraffes, rhinoceroses,

and other wonders of more than life-size filled the bosoms of small boys with wild enthusiasm. The procession was to enter the town that morning, and perform in the evening — at which the village of Piedmont opened its eyes and grew wide awake. The tavern porch was crowded with loungers, who expectorated fearfully. The bar within did a tremendous business. If intelligence had arrived at the moment that the empire of Russia had been incorporated with the British dominions, the announcement would have been received with complete indifference.

———

VII.

A TRIFLE LEADING TO A GREAT DEAL.

THE triumphal entry was a triumphant affair. The cages containing the wild animals were in rear of all; preceding them were the elephants; in front of all came a mighty car of blue and gold, filled with the performers of the troupe, with excited musicians, and drawn by twenty-four party-colored horses.

The drums roared; the trombones groaned; the French bugles split the air; the immense crowd of small boys and negroes who accompanied the procession uttered cheers; and the only portion of Piedmont which did not relish the ceremony was the horse-flesh tied to posts here and there on the street. There was danger to bridles as the pageant drew on, and the riders hastily looked to their property.

One person did not seem under any apprehension in reference to his own horses. This was a gentleman in a light carriage, with a young lady beside him. He drove two very fine animals, and seemed to have no difficulty in controlling them, as he drove past the long line of party-colored animals, in a direction opposite to that taken by the procession. But the moment came. He was not to pass. The carriage had just reached a point opposite the front wheel of the chariot of the circus men, when a deaf-ening crash from a combination of brass instruments burst into their faces. Terror maddened them. They reared, wheeled, caught the delicate wheel of the vehicle in the huge mill-burr affair of the chariot—and then horses, gentleman, and young lady seemed to disappear in one confused mass beneath the wheels.

The dust, no doubt, produced this confused impression. They were not really beneath the wheels. The gentleman and his daughter were standing unhurt, a moment afterward, upon the sidewalk.

One of the circus men had swung from the high perch in front of the car, and caught the young lady in his arms as she was about to fall under the wheels. This act of agility could only have been performed by an acrobat; but who the person was, or what was his place in the troop, no one knew, inasmuch as he had immediately taken away his arms when the young lady was safe on her feet, remounted the car, and the whole had disappeared in the dust-cloud.

The gentleman and his companion were looking somewhat ruefully at the fractured wheel of their vehicle—the horses had each been brought under control again—when a family carriage, containing two ladies, drove up and stopped.

"Good heavens! my dear Colonel Cary! an accident?"

It was the elder of the two ladies in the family carriage who uttered this pretty exclamation.

"A slight one—it really is of no importance, my dear Mrs. Armstrong. It was my fault; but my horses are so excellently broken that I am imprudent. An hour's detention will be all."

Meanwhile the gentleman's companion had fraternized with the younger occupant of the carriage, whom she evidently loved very much, as she kissed her with enthusiasm, though the syllogism may appear doubtful to the cynics.

"Do go home with us, or at least let us take dear Frances!" exclaimed the elder lady.

And when Colonel Cary declined this invitation with smiles and great courtesy,

the lady shook her head, as if she really could not consent to leave them in their extremity. Persuaded at last that things were not so bad, as the carriage was led away to the shop by a servant, she made more pretty, friendly speeches, and smiled anew; and then, bowing with fascinating grace to the gentleman and his companion, she directed her respectable old black coachman to drive on.

VIII.

A BEAUTY WHO YAWNS.

She was a very handsome person indeed, this elderly occupant of the family carriage, which — returning apparently from a shopping expedition—now drove out of Piedmont in a southern direction.

She was fifty, and had the air of thirty-five; but it did not impress you as in the least in bad taste, any more than her dress, which certainly was *very* rich for a morning dress. You realized, however, at a single glance that this lady could do what others could not. She had taste, and whatever she put on became her. Even her French vivacity did not impress people as insincere. She was fascinating, indeed, in her dress and address, and won people. As to the possibility that under the caressing smile of the exquisitely dressed young-middle-aged beauty there were traits not precisely as fascinating as the smile—to inquire thus were to inquire too curiously. Don't go below the surface if you wish to get on in the world. A great deal lies beneath surfaces. Mrs. Armstrong of "Trianon" was quite charming—and was not that enough?

It was her daughter Juliet, aged twenty-three, with superb dark hair, superb dark eyes, and an air of queenly composure, who leaned back in the cushioned seat beside her. Juliet was unquestionably a beauty. She was tall, with a figure of extreme grace in every movement, and an apparent indifference to everybody and everything around her which was piquant, if not engaging. She was looking out of the window when her mamma said, with light annoyance,

"My *dear* Juliet! I really don't believe you've heard a word I have said. You certainly have not asked where we are going."

"Going, mamma? I thought we were going home, as we have finished shopping—"

"And nearly been finished by that *horrid* Miss Grundy ourselves!" exclaimed Mrs. Armstrong. "Good heavens! was there ever such a chatterbox! She positively paralyzes me! And you go away after meeting her with the fearful conviction that she will tear your character to pieces for the amusement of the next friend she meets!"

"It is very probable. I suppose she is fond of talking, as Piedmont is a very dull place," returned Miss Juliet, in an uninterested tone.

"Frightfully dull, and the arrival of the circus must be a blessing to them. Would you like to go?"

"To the circus?"

The young lady stopped before the word "circus" for an instant to indulge in a slight yawn.

"My dear child!" her mother exclaimed, "you are positively yawning! This life in the country, with no resource but riding out now and then, is wearying you to death."

"It is tiresome enough, mamma," Miss Juliet said, candidly.

"Fearfully so, and that is the reason why I asked if you would not like to go to the circus. I took you once when you were a child, and you seemed to enjoy it."

"Go to the circus? I don't know. Do ladies go? I really don't care. Yes —no—that is, just as you please."

The elder lady sighed. It was very plain that Miss Juliet was considerably bored, and in a very indifferent state of mind, indeed.

"The trouble would be about an escort," said the young lady, looking out of the window. "You know the night air gives you the rheumatism, and I should not like to go by myself with Uncle William"—this was the old driver.

Her mother smiled with the air of a person who has already provided for things.

"Well, perhaps you might find some one to escort you—a good many persons will no doubt be going. What a lovely day, and just see what superb corn! General Lascelles is an excellent manager."

Miss Juliet contemplated the far-reaching expanse of corn, with its ripe tassels and broad blades, rustling in the light breeze, and said,

"Why, this is the road to Wye, mamma."

"Yes, my dear, I thought I would call on our way home. It really is an age since we have been to see Mrs. Lascelles; she is a most agreeable person, and General Lascelles and myself are great friends."

"I like Mrs. Lascelles very much," said Miss Juliet, composedly, "and Anna Gray. She is one of the sweetest people I have ever met."

"Well, my dear, I am glad I thought of calling, as it seems to please you. We shall find Mrs. Lascelles and Anna at home, I have no doubt, as they rarely go out. It is not so certain that we shall see the general or Mr. Douglas Lascelles."

"Very doubtful, I suppose," the young lady said, with indifference.

"Do you like Mr. Douglas?"

"I scarcely know him. There have been no parties lately, you know, and he never comes to see us."

"He very seldom goes into society, I hear, which is a pity, as he is very handsome, and a young man of excellent manners. He ought not to be so unsocial. I am informed, however, that he reads a great deal, and is very intellectual."

"Is he?" said Miss Juliet, serenely.

"People say so, but he is very reserved, though that is frequently a good sign. He will improve, no doubt, when he is married. He must be nearly thirty, and at that age a young man should think about matrimony—don't you think so, my dear?"

"I should suppose it would depend

upon whether he wished to marry or not, mamma."

"But he *must* marry some one, my dear," said Mrs. Armstrong. "He is an only child, and will inherit the whole Wye property; and as General Lascelles is old, he may do so at any moment. Then, how *could* he remain unmarried in so large an establishment, with the great estate attached to it, my dear Juliet? It would be absurd. There would be no one but his mother to receive company. The income from the property must be thirty thousand a year, and how could he ever spend it, unless some one assisted him! It is at least thirty thousand."

"Is it, mamma?" Miss Juliet said, composedly.

"At least, if not more; and thirty thousand a year is a very pleasant sum, indeed, to have at one's disposal, my dear. Perhaps you do not know what it means. It means travel in Europe, winters in Paris, and the opera, and suites of apartments elegantly furnished, and many other agreeable things. Just think of having a magnificent equipage and footmen, of diamonds, and entertainments, and a superb wardrobe, and—desirabilities generally!" said Mrs. Armstrong, at a loss for a climax. "Upon my word, if I were a young lady, I am not sure I should not set my cap at the fortunate youth myself, and try to become Mrs. Douglas Lascelles!"

Miss Juliet again yawned slightly, and said, with great composure, that she supposed Mr. Lascelles *would* be very wealthy at some time; and as she made this observation the carriage rolled into the grounds around "Wye," the abode of the prospective Crœsus. These grounds were quite extensive—a sort of park with a rolling surface covered with green turf, and dotted here and there with groups of very old oaks. A flock of sheep dotted the greensward in the distance, and some very fine young heifers, evidently of choice breeds, grazed in the shadowy glades between the trees. The carriage-road wound through this peaceful scene to the house, which stood on a hill, and was a large building of lead-colored brick, with a flat top surrounded by a heavy balustrade, above which rose an octagonal observatory. On both sides were extensive wings, in rear of which were the servants' quarters, with the stables beyond. In front of the main building was a broad porch with a flight of stone steps, much worn, and the large front-door folded in the middle, and had an antique iron knob which you pressed upon to open the door. Above was a semicircle of triangular panes. In front of the house stood an ancient sun-dial. Everything about the place was plain and unassuming, and took visitors back in thought to "old times."

Mrs. Armstrong and her daughter were shown, by a silent and respectful old negro servant in black, through a large hall, wainscoted in oak, into a room on the right of the entrance. This was a large apartment, with a matting of white and ashes-of-roses on the floor. The furniture was antique and ugly, but would have delighted a lover of *bric-à-brac*. Some newer arm-chairs had been added, however, and a modern mantel-piece of gray marble, flanked by fluted columns at each side of the wide fireplace, in which stood a pair of huge old-fashioned brass andirons. The former mantel-piece, which was of wood, and very high and narrow, had been left, the newer one supported a little bijou of a clock, very unlike the tall white-faced old affair, rising like a ghost in the hall; and at each end was a vase full of roses. Above the wooden mantel-piece the wall was wainscoted to the ceiling, and around the room hung some family portraits, slowly fading from age.

IX.

MR. DOUGLAS LASCELLES.

As Mrs. Armstrong subsided into an easy-chair, she said to Juliet,

"It is always a pleasure to me to come to Wye—everything is so quiet and solid. I invariably feel, when I enter a room like this, that the family belong to the best people. It is much better than to have money only," added the lady, succinctly, "though money is a very good thing, indeed."

"It makes people very disagreeable," said Juliet, with indifference; "that is, it is the disagreeable people who generally seem to have it."

"There is no general rule," responded the elder lady, with a little smile; "it hides a great deal—and there is often a great deal in people that is best hidden; but here you have both wealth and charming people too, and—"

What Mrs. Armstrong was about to say will, in all human probability, never be known. The door opened and two ladies came in—one of them tall and about sixty, in a black bombazine dress and a white cap, with a placid smile upon her thin lips; and the other a plump little personage of about twenty, in a simple but scrupulously neat morning toilet, smiling as cordially as her companion.

Mrs. Armstrong received them with effusion. Her face beamed, and she uttered exclamations of pleasure.

"My *dear* Mrs. Lascelles," she said, "how very glad I am to see you! We have not met before for a century. I am so much engaged at home with dear Juliet, and looking after things, that I never see my very best friends."

Mrs. Lascelles greeted this apology with her sweet smile, and replied, in a soft voice, that she was very glad indeed to see her visitor. She had brought with her a leathern key-basket, in which she had thrust a stocking which she had been knitting, and now glanced at it from habit; but she probably thought it would be a little unceremonious to resume her knitting—so she did not do so. Meanwhile Juliet and Miss Anna Gray, a niece of Mrs. Lascelles, were talking by the window, through which there was a fine view of the mountain, and the rich extent of open land at its feet. They were evidently friends, and enjoyed each other's society. Miss Juliet's eyes grew bright and her face animated. She was smiling now, not yawning, and looked quite charming.

While thus eng[...] she sat with her b[...] at once she heard h[...] "My dear Mr. [...] tainly are not go[...] come in and see m[...]

These words we[...] son who was pass[...] He had come dow[...] ently bent on reacl[...] site the drawing-ro[...] drawing-room door[...] strong sat facing i[...] clamation followed.

Mr. Lascelles—l[...] Mr. Douglas Lascel[...] had spoken durin[...] turned round, exh[...] and pleasure, and[...] ing-room, bowing l[...] the ladies. Mr. La[...] about thirty-five,[...] neatly dressed in t[...] features were delic[...] some, his manner[...] his air a little fore[...] press strangers as [...] acter—rather, perh[...] ter awhile, as peop[...] closely at him, th[...] There was somethi[...] seemed to show th[...] terior there were tr[...] were very far ind[...] monplace. Now [...] weariness fell on tl[...] impression that M[...] good deal of life in[...] springs of enjoyme[...] lost their elasticity.[...] ous, but wanted th[...] People never got [...] certain distance of [...] time thrown away [...] intimate with him.[...] not the material to [...] those who caught [...] eye which characte[...] pretty certain that [...] good enemy. He [...] however; if you n[...] it would be your o[...]

"This is an unexpected pleasure; you really are such a hermit!" said Mrs. Armstrong, graciously extending one of her jewelled hands.

Mr. Lascelles gently pressed it, bowing above it, and smiling deferentially as he did so.

"It is quite natural, you know," said the lady, laughing, "that one should become excited at meeting a recluse! Is it not, Mr. Douglas?—pardon my want of ceremony! I am an old woman, and detest formality!"

"I am very much flattered, indeed, to have you drop it in my case, madam," said Mr. Lascelles, with his most cordial smile, "and I feel that your words are a reproach. It is my own fault that I am such a stranger to you, but I have contracted the habit of shutting myself up at home, even when society the most charming is near at hand. I am aware that it is a bad habit. I wish I could break myself of it."

"Oh!" said Mrs. Armstrong, with an affected pout which ended in a smile, "that is very easy to say. But do you know, I think you are not quite frank!"

"Not frank, madam! How could I be otherwise with *you?*"

"I am very much obliged; but you cannot have a very high opinion of us poor country people."

At this accusation Mr. Lascelles counterfeited sincere astonishment.

"What could possibly induce you to take up such an erroneous impression, my dear Mrs. Armstrong?" he said. "Is there any society better than our country society in Virginia? I do not know where it is."

"That is very easy to say, sir; but if you appreciate us so highly, why do you fly off to Paris every year or two, and retire to your holy cell on your return?"

"You adhere, I see, madam, to the hermit illustration! As to Paris, I have not visited it for some years, and rarely travel at all. It is very tiresome."

"Tiresome? You cannot be in earnest! I really adore travelling—there is so much pleasant novelty and incident. Country life is fearful, and I do grow so *very* tired sometimes of its sameness. I feel tempted to set the house on fire, or do something desperate."

"That is truly dreadful," said Mr. Lascelles, smiling.

"Is it not? This morning, after a visit to Piedmont and hearing Miss Grundy's chatter, I became quite wild! It was one monotonous, fearful, steady flow, and prostrated me so that I nearly resolved upon an act of desperation."

"What was that, madam?"

"To go to the circus at Piedmont tonight. Are you convinced now of my desperate condition of mind? The circus! and at my time of life, and subject as I am to neuralgia!"

"But no doubt your force of character enabled you to resist, madam."

"Barely; I felt very much as our great-grandmamma Eve must have done, with the apple before her. I thought of the lights, the music; think how charming it will all be! But it is impossible! my dreadful neuralgia—I can't venture out at night. And worse than all, dear Juliet cannot go without an escort."

At these words Miss Juliet turned her head and looked at her mother with sudden displeasure and a contraction of her brows. Mrs. Armstrong was not, or pretended not to be, aware of this. She gazed with an expression of dove-like innocence through the window, and seemed about to direct the conversation to another topic, when Mr. Lascelles said,

"If the want of an escort is all that prevents Miss Juliet from going, I shall be only too glad if she will accept my own."

"Yours!" Mrs. Armstrong exclaimed, with extreme surprise, before Juliet could speak. "No, indeed! I could not hear of such a thing. What would you think of me?"

"I should retain my present opinion, madam," Mr. Lascelles said, gallantly. "I will not tell you what that is, as you would accuse me of flattery."

"No, indeed—impossible! To pick you up with so little ceremony, and make use of you in such a shockingly free-and-easy manner! You really must not mention it. I cannot imagine what I was thinking of, and shall never learn to hold my tongue and not say the first thing which comes into my poor head. If Juliet wishes to go, there will be no trouble at all about it. The night will be clear, and the distance is so short. Old William is entirely reliable, and can escort you, my dear," she said, turning to the young lady; "and when you reach Piedmont you can join some party of friends. A number will, no doubt, be going."

"I am sure I do not care in the least to go, mamma," said Miss Juliet, with extreme stiffness and hauteur. The young lady did not toss her head, but looked very much as if she would have been relieved by doing so.

"Why, you said this morning that you would like to go, my dear!" her mother said.

"Indeed, I did not!" said Miss Juliet; "you must have quite misunderstood me."

Mr. Lascelles interfered to still the rising storm, and said, earnestly,

"I hope you will change your mind, Miss Juliet, and accept my escort. I go from home so little, that the circus has the charm of novelty. I am sure I shall enjoy it, and I think you will. You will have a canter on horseback, at least—I know you will enjoy that."

Mr. Lascelles touched a responsive chord, for Miss Juliet Armstrong was almost passionately fond of horseback riding, and had a small mare nearly thorough-bred, who ran as swiftly as a bird flies. But in spite of the temptation Miss Juliet persisted in politely declining. This, however, only made Mr. Lascelles more pressing. Might he not be permitted to call at Trianon, say at half-past six on that evening? The night would be pleasant; there would be a moon; and a ride by moonlight was enjoyable—to him, at least.

Miss Juliet's eyes sparkled a little, and after awhile she yielded, though not with a very good grace. Her enthusiasm in the direction of Mr. Lascelles was evidently much more moderate than her mamma's, and it was probably the prospect of a ride on horseback which decided her. She consented to go, and it was arranged that Mr. Lascelles should be at Trianon by half-past six in the evening; and soon afterward the ladies took their departure.

Mr. Lascelles escorted them to their carriage, and assisted them to enter it. He then made a smiling and deferential bow, and the vehicle drove away.

For some moments Mr. Lascelles stood on the porch looking after it with a peculiar smile.

"I have heard of the cool of the evening," he said, "and here is *Madame Crépuscule* in person. She was in want of an escort for mademoiselle, and quietly made use of me—I never saw a thing done better! Well, a man seldom makes anything by opposing a woman when she has mapped out her programme. Madame wanted somebody to go with mademoiselle, and he is going! It's not so dreadful a bore either. That girl is superb—I never dreamed she was so handsome; and she had nothing to do with this little comedy—I could see from her eyes that madame's proceedings outraged her. I never saw a finer pair in my life!"

These latter words apparently referred to Miss Juliet Armstrong's eyes, and not to herself and her mamma. After his soliloquy Mr. Lascelles went into the house, looking into the drawing-room as he passed; the ladies had gone up-stairs. He then decided, apparently, upon going into the library, where General Lascelles was writing his letters, and took some steps in that direction; he, however, changed his mind, and proceeded to an apartment in rear — the dining-room. Here he drew a small key from his pocket, yawning as he did so, and opened an old-fashioned mahogany cellaret in a corner. From this he drew a square decanter of brandy, poured some into a cut-glass tumbler, which he took from the sideboard near, mixed some water with it, and drank it.

"Dry work!" he said, as if apologizing to the brandy.

X.

THE LADY-BIRD'S NEST.

"TRIANON," the somewhat fanciful name of Mrs. Armstrong's residence, was a handsome cottage orné, embowered in foliage, not far from Piedmont. All about the place was feminine and attractive, for this lady was a person of excellent taste, and knew very well how to surround herself with what gratified the eyes—above all, with what made a good impression upon visitors. The veranda was supported by light fluted pillars, and surrounded by scroll-work. The greensward, dotted with ornamental shrubs, was close trimmed, and guiltless of a single leaf or twig to mar its beauty. The carriage-drive was of white gravel, and swept round a diminutive circle, in the midst of which stood a large wicker-work basket overflowing with green creepers in full bloom. And in the small, neat hall of the house a glimpse was caught through the open door of delicate bookcases and aerial stands—the former containing handsome volumes in gilt binding, and the latter a profusion of flowers, which filled the air with fragrance. If Wye was a good type of the old "solid" class of houses, and the ancient regime in general, Trianon represented the new regime; which you preferred was a matter of taste. One was antique and substantial, and had memories about it; but the other was very pretty and attractive.

Trianon, in its *ensemble*, was the result of a conviction on Mrs. Armstrong's part that when one has an unmarried daughter home ought to be made attractive — to visitors; and these visitors must be persons of a certain class. The Armstrongs were people of excellent family. They had lived in an adjoining county, but had been forced to remove from it some years before. Mr. Armstrong had been a gentleman of great elegance and jovial instincts, who liked society, and had run through a large estate by entertaining the very best company in the very best manner to the very last day of his life. Then the crash came. The skies had been cloudless, but suddenly a snow-storm of "writs" began to fall. The estate was quite insolvent, and his wife and daughter were left penniless.

But Mrs. Armstrong was a woman of energy. She had an old bachelor uncle who was very well off, and had enjoyed a great deal of good wine at her table. He was fond of Juliet; and the homeless lady promptly appealed to him for a temporary refuge—she could then look about her, she said. They went to live with the old bachelor uncle, and Mrs. Armstrong paid him charming attentions. When he died, not long afterward, he left her a good legacy, and with this legacy the lady purchased the small estate of Trianon, and built the house upon it. After paying for the land and cottage, there was very little of the legacy left. A portion remained, however, and Mrs. Armstrong exhibited her good-sense in the disposition of it. She did not spend it in trifles to gratify her tastes, though no one had a greater fondness for the elegant nothings which money purchases. She invested it in good stocks, which brought her a moderate but certain income; and with this and the proceeds of her estate, which was managed for her by a reliable person living in a small house on her land, she lived in comfort — her neighbors said in luxury.

In fact, Mrs. Armstrong was one of those persons who give to a little the appearance of a great deal. Everything about her small establishment was in perfect taste. Her silver was the old family plate, which she had managed to rescue from the wreck, and her table-service was of snowy china, thin to transparency, and decorated with moss-rose-buds. As to her napkins and table mats, they were the despair of her lady acquaintances; the falling snow was not whiter. In the drawing-room there were loves of easy-chairs, with ornamental tidies on their backs. The table in the centre was of carved walnut, and supported the goddess Vesta in bronze, holding aloft a superb lamp. On the table lay volumes containing the poems of Mr. Tennyson, Mrs. Browning, and others — English copies, bound in embossed leather. The paper on the wall was fawn color, with a small gilt figure at intervals. The matting was white. The elegant couches everywhere made you indolent, they looked so comfortable. From all this there resulted a conviction on the part of visitors that Mrs. Armstrong "had investments," which investments would, of course, one day fall to Miss Juliet.

It is possible that this was the impression which Mrs. Armstrong desired to produce. If it was an illusion she did not attempt to dispel it. On the contrary, she encouraged it. It would do no harm. She was in the habit of alluding incidentally to the rise and fall of stocks, to the good-sense of people who preferred safe investments at a moderate rate of interest, to those promising larger dividends, but which could not be depended upon. After thus expressing her financial views Mrs. Armstrong would sigh, and, rustling her rich silk, trimmed with Valenciennes lace, deplore the pecuniary straits to which she, in common with everybody, was reduced. This, of course, had convinced her listeners. Mrs. Armstrong, of Trianon, was evidently as easy in her circumstances as she was charming. And that dear Juliet! how fortunate she was, in having such a future of ease and comfort before her!

Now, Mrs. Armstrong knew perfectly well that this carefully-nursed impression in the community was quite illusory, and that Juliet would be placed in a very embarrassing situation, indeed, at her own death. This event she hoped would not take place for a long time to come; but then life was uncertain, and it was incumbent upon her as a good mother to prepare for contingencies. She was a very good mother, for she was devotedly attached to Juliet, and a sudden chill always followed the reflection that the girl might be left unprovided for. At her death Juliet would be practically homeless, for it would be impossible for her to live at Trianon; and without her own careful

management the estate and their small income from the investments would not go very far; Juliet would at once become a poor and unprotected girl; and at this idea Mrs. Armstrong positively shuddered. Juliet must marry.

It was a bitter thought that she might one day be separated from her daughter; but then it would be far better for the daughter to marry and settle down, and this worldly person did not hesitate. She determined to effect a brilliant match for Juliet—it must be brilliant, and her child should be surrounded with every luxury. This pearl of pure water should have a golden setting; and for two or three years now Mrs. Armstrong had been in search of this setting. She and Juliet had spent their winters in the cities, and their summers at the watering-places. A number of admirers had appeared, and the young lady had not wanted offers; but the suitors were not eligible in the mother's eyes, and she quietly dissuaded her daughter from encouraging their attentions. Juliet had done so with apparent alacrity, and there it ended.

Miss Juliet Armstrong, indeed, seemed not to have the least desire to marry anybody. But she was very reserved; her mother had never understood her precisely; and it seemed impossible that she should not desire to make a brilliant match. She was not much pleased, she confessed, with their humdrum life at Trianon. What more natural than that the young lady should be willing to exchange it for new scenes, the pleasure of travel, and all the incident and novelty attainable by persons of ample means? She had often suggested this attractive future to Juliet, clearly intimating that all depended upon the discovery of the Crœsus. As Mrs. Crœsus she would enjoy all the delights of life. It would be better to look out for him, and not repulse him when he appeared.

Juliet assented with an air of extreme indifference to her mother's views, and then they seemed to pass entirely out of her mind. She was a peculiar person, with a quiet air which probably expressed her character. She was very composed and pleasant in society, and read a great deal; but the one passion of her life seemed to be music — unless horseback riding could be added. Her voice was a clear soprano, and she sang the most difficult passages from her favorite operas with the greatest ease. At such moments she seemed to become another person: her indifferent air disappeared; her cheeks became flushed; and her tall figure seemed about to rise from the piano and act the scene which she was singing. One day her mother said to her, as she was executing a passage after this fashion from Bellini, " Well, my dear, if you are ever cast on your own resources, you can become a prima donna." The excitement lasted, however, for a few moments only. When she shut down the lid of her piano the young lady's face grew composed again, and resumed its air of indifference.

This was the state of things at Trianon when the present narrative opens. Crœsus had not appeared, or at least the particular one whom Mrs. Armstrong desired. An aged millionnaire at the —— Springs had plainly been ready to lay his wig and money-bags at Miss Juliet's feet, but she had quietly turned her back upon him. Mother and daughter were once more at Trianon, and it seemed doubtful whether they would leave it for a long time. Their travelling expenses had been large, and the dividends from the investments were not due until the ensuing January. Seclusion at home was thus rendered necessary, and, with a sigh, Mrs. Armstrong gave up the thought of further pleasure excursions — and Crœsus — for that year.

This was sorrowful to think of, but suddenly a brilliant idea occurred to the lady — it was wonderful that it had never occurred before. There was Mr. Lascelles, of Wye, who was a very good *parti* indeed! Why should not Juliet marry Mr. Douglas Lascelles, and become the mistress, in due time, of that desirable establishment? Having conceived this idea, Mrs. Armstrong proceeded to give it careful reflection. The more she thought of it, the more attractive it appeared. The estate was a large one, and the Lascelles family were among the very best people of the country. Everything connected with Wye was agreeable — more than agreeable. As Mrs. Douglas Lascelles, of Wye, Juliet would be established in life in a manner which suited her mother's aspirations.

Various points, however, remained to be considered. Would Juliet accept Mr. Lascelles? Would that gentleman ask the young lady to accept him? And was his personal character such as to warrant her in intrusting her daughter's happiness to him? Upon this latter point there seemed to be no reasons for distrust. Mr. Lascelles was a very quiet and gentlemanly person, against whose good character no one had ever breathed a word; and when a man reached thirty or more thus exempt from criticism, Mrs. Armstrong reflected that it was a very favorable sign indeed. Young enough for Juliet, without vices of any description, intellectual, good-looking, domestic in his habits, and evidently a cordial and amiable person as his demeanor showed, Mr. Lascelles had positively no drawbacks whatever that she could think of. Juliet might not agree to all this — but then, again, she might. If Mr. Lascelles laid his heart and hand at her feet, she might accept them. But would he do so? Would it be possible to bring the young people together even? Mrs. Armstrong knit her brows and reflected.

It would be difficult to manage; Mr. Lascelles had paid a few short and formal visits to Trianon in past times, but he had not been at the house for a very long while now. Indeed, he seemed to go nowhere, since his return from Europe some years before, and remained quietly at Wye, preferring books, apparently, to ladies' society. He was rarely seen abroad, and only then seated in his elegant drag, which was driven by his servant, on his way to dine and spend the evening with a bachelor friend a few miles distant. This bachelor friend, it was true, bore an indifferent reputation, and it was whispered that his dinners generally terminated at two or three in the morning, with packs of cards and empty bottles scattered around. But this was probably a mere scandal. At all events, Mr. Lascelles certainly took no part in the drinking and gambling. He was much too correct a person to indulge in such proceedings, and, no doubt, visited his friend to enjoy his jovial society after protracted study at Wye.

Mr. Lascelles thus led a life of great seclusion, and it would probably prove a very difficult undertaking to bring Juliet and himself together. It would be a delicate affair, and every precaution must be taken to conceal her design. Nothing would be easier than to defeat it completely in the very beginning by a single false step. Juliet was extremely proud, and Mr. Lascelles, at his age, had probably made the acquaintance of many matchmaking mammas. Energy in the prosecution of her design would be essential; but another thing would be more essential still—not too much energy.

The result of these reflections had shown itself in the visit to Wye. Mrs. Armstrong knew Mrs. Lascelles very well, and nothing certainly could be more natural than that she should make a morning call. When she left Wye she had succeeded in her object, and taken the first step. Mr. Douglas Lascelles would escort Juliet to Piedmont on horseback; the night promised to be fine, with bright moonlight, and Juliet looked superb on horseback. Thence consequences might ensue. She had been compelled to be a little too plain in the matter of the escort — but then that was unavoidable. The fact had to be suggested in some manner, and she had done so as delicately as possible. Juliet had evidently been displeased, and Mr. Lascelles might have had his private views — but then this would soon pass. If Juliet's beautiful eyes made the impression which she hoped they would make, Mr. Lascelles would be the first person to thank her —when he became her son-in-law.

Mr. Lascelles made his appearance at Trianon punctually; and Juliet, who never kept anybody waiting, had on her riding-habit. In this dress she was very handsome; it exhibited her figure to perfect advantage, and the small riding-hat set off her erect head admirably. It was plain that Mr. Lascelles was much struck with her appearance, but evidently wondered a little at the stiffness of his reception. This resulted from the fact that Miss Juliet had been much outraged by her mother's proceedings at Wye, and, in fact, had sulked all the way back to Trianon. If she had been able to do so, she would have broken her engagement;·but as this was impossible, she solaced herself with a mild continuation of the sulks.

Tea was served on the brilliant little table in the *bijou* of a supper-room, which was fragrant with the perfume of flowers. Then Miss Juliet's small mare was led up to the veranda, and her ill-humor disappeared—her eyes sparkled. She had her foot in the stirrup before Mr. Lascelles could assist her, and, arranging her skirt with a single movement, looked over her shoulder to signify that she was ready. She was a beauty, sitting lightly thus on her spirited little animal, with her cheeks glowing, and Mr. Lascelles silently informed himself of the fact.

"Take care of yourself, my dear! do be careful — you ride so recklessly!" exclaimed Mrs. Armstrong, "and don't stay late, Mr. Douglas."

"You need not be afraid, madam, I will bring Miss Juliet back in good time," replied Mr. Lascelles.

He then mounted his own horse, which was a very fine one, and they set out at full gallop in the direction of Piedmont. The moon had just risen, and Mrs. Armstrong, standing upon the portico, could see Juliet's long hair waving in the mellow light. She stood for some moments musing, and quietly smiling. She then said, in a low tone,

"*Mrs. Douglas Lascelles, of Wye!*—it does not sound badly."

She then turned round to go into the

house, when a sort of shadow flitted across the passage.

"Who is that?" said Mrs. Armstrong. There was no reply to this.

"Was that you, Miss Bassick?"

The words were addressed to a young lady who was hovering in an assiduous manner over the tea-table, arranging the cups.

"Me, ma'am?" said the young lady, in a cooing voice, and turning her head with an innocent look.

"At the door! You certainly were there, with your shoes of silence! You were listening!"

"Oh, ma'am!"

"I have called your attention before, miss, to my views upon that subject," said Mrs. Armstrong, haughtily; "and you will please remember them—give me my tea!"

XI.

THE UNRIVALLED COMBINATION AND ITS MANAGER.

THE circus opened in its great tent, full of dazzling light, to a crowded audience.

The huge canvases had risen in an open field in the suburbs, as if by magic. One of the tents was for the cages containing the wild animals, and the other for the bare-back performances. From the summits floated proudly the national flag. Around were grouped smaller tents for the exhibition of "side shows." On these were pictures of women with beards —glued on; of men weighing five hundred pounds, or any weight you chose— stuffed out with pillows; of three-legged pigs, five-legged dogs, and woolly horses; the price of admission being fifteen cents. There was also a merry-go-round, where rustics gyrated rapidly on a wooden horse. Insinuating personages with sweet smiles exhibited revolving wheels, where one could bet with a tolerable certainty of losing. Cakes, candy, and lemonade were for sale in every direction; and the crowd moved to and fro, laughing, jesting, and in extreme delight.

It was a motley crowd, and had been arriving all day. At an early hour the streets had begun to fill with persons from the surrounding country—old farmers in homespun, with their motherly dames; rustic beaux, who munched gingerbread, and saluted their sweethearts on the street with loud laughter; and with these mingled many gentlemen of the neighborhood on horseback, for the circus was dear to all classes. From this it resulted that the main street of Piedmont presented quite a holiday appearance. The sidewalks were full of pedestrians, and the shops overflowed. The old rustics cheapened the goods, and hesitated long before purchasing; or they repaired to the tavern and mildly refreshed themselves with drams, while their "old women" waited in the porch.

The tavern porch was the centre of things. The circus men had "put up" at the place; and they were a very peculiar-looking set of people, as they stalked about slowly, drank at the bar, and contemplated the crowd with the air of animals belonging to another species. They wore citizens' clothes, but you could see that they were not citizens. Something about them produced the impression that it would not be advisable to quarrel with them. They would be dangerous people, probably, in a brawl. They were not rude or threatening in the least, but looked a little ferocious, which may have resulted from a familiarity with the animals in the menagerie. A man accustomed to enter the cage of a lion when he is tearing raw meat, acquires the habit, perhaps, of looking a little stern, not to say fierce, as that gives warning; and there was an expression in the faces of these men, whose muscles were plain under their clothes, which said, "It would be best for you not to get into any difficulty with me." There seemed a probability at one time that such a difficulty would take place, as one of the busybodies thronging the tavern accidentally trod upon the toes of a heavy-browed and powerful individual imbibing liquids at the bar, and was treated to a ferocious scowl, accompanied by a growl, which made him recoil and look outraged. But a friend took the busybody aside, and said to him, "You had better let these fellows alone—their trainers put too much muscle on 'em ;" and a portly individual in a suit of black, a white waistcoat, and a tall "stove-pipe" hat, went up to the Hercules, and tapping him on the shoulder said, in a low tone, with a significant look, "No making trouble with citizens!" Then the gentleman with the stove-pipe hat approached the offended busybody and said, in honeyed tones,

"I hope, my dear sir, you'll not think hard of my boys. They are a well-meaning set, and as peaceful as lambs, but they are overworked sometimes, and that tells on the nerves, you know! We shall have the pleasure, I trust, of seeing you to-night."

Here he slipped an admission ticket into the hand of the mollified citizen, and they parted with mutual bows and smiles.

He was, in fact, a very good judge of human nature indeed, this Mr. Brownson, manager and proprietor of Brownson's Unrivalled Combination of Attractions. The object of his existence was dollars, and he was devoted to it. He had maxims by which he regulated his conduct, and would have them respected. One was, "Never have any difficulty with citizens;" another, "Don't give the legal authorities a hold on you ;" and a third was, "Receipts are the great thing." He had his explanation always ready, showing the good-sense of these maxims. Difficulties produced "rows," and arrests followed, and there was a scandal—and nothing injured a circus more than to acquire the reputation of having a quarrelsome and disagreeable set of performers. Citizens would not stand that. They would not attend the performances, and as receipts were the great thing, that would be disastrous.

Beyond this Mr. Brownson did not insist. He was a patriarch mildly ruling his band of wild animals, and if they only performed to his satisfaction, he made not the least objection to their enjoying themselves. Everything was permitted that was not forbidden—private life was sacred. Cards? Certainly; where was the harm in social relaxation in hours of leisure? Drink? Why not? Wine cheered the heart of man, and he himself, at intervals throughout every day, retired to indulge in that solace. But it must never be forgotten that receipts were the great thing. Drink to any extent, so there was no quarrelling and the nerves were steady. That must be understood. These conditions complied with, no questions would be asked, for he, Mr. Brownson, was not a police-officer or a detective, to be shadowing gentlemen and interfering with them in their private relations. But—no rows, and the nerves must be up to time. If anything unfortunate happened it was unfortunate, and the matter ended. If the performer on the flying-trapeze broke his neck in consequence of being drunk, it was his misfortune, and his sorrowing comrades would drop a tear. It would be an inconvenience, and subject the management to loss—the victim might even have obtained an advance on his salary. But then accidents would happen in the best-regulated companies, and there was the element of compensation which mingles with all human affairs. For a performer to break his neck was a superb advertisement. It was "thrilling!"— crowds flocked to the next performance in hopes that another neck would be broken —and he, Mr. Brownson, clad in a white waistcoat and irreproachable black coat, had the opportunity of making a feeling address: "It was his painful duty to announce that since his last visit to his friends at ——, the distinguished Señor Gomez, in executing his great feat of throwing himself fifty feet backward on the flying-trapeze had missed the ropes, and, falling, had broken his neck! His fate had moved the sternest of his comrades to tears. He was mild and amiable, and exempt from every vice, especially from the great curse of intemperance. His friends mourned his loss, but consoled themselves with the reflection that he had died on the field of honor, a bright example to all; and the same feat would now be performed by Mr. Welby Brown, after which Mr. Donald Melville, the foremost bare-back rider of the world, would exhibit his daring um-um-um, and the performance would now commence."

After making this little address Mr. Brownson was accustomed to wave his stove-pipe hat and bow respectfully to the audience, after which he retired with his head erect and an air of the highest respectability. When the next accident happened the same speech was taken out and aired, and the same lament was uttered over the comrade who had fallen on the field of honor. It was the commander-in-chief issuing his order of condolence, and giving voice to the general grief. Dead, the fallen one was mourned—living, he had not been shadowed or interfered with. The attention of his surviving comrades was called to that fact. No interference with the private affairs of gentlemen off duty. Drink and cards? Certainly. Liberty to cut each others' throats? If they chose. But no difficulties with citizens; and, drunk or sober, the nerves must be up to time. The performance advertised must be performed. No shirking. Business was business, and receipts the great thing.

This slight sketch of Mr. Brownson is a digression; but then the worthy manager of the "Unequalled Combination" was a type—and types are always worth looking at. In addition, Mr. Brownson is destined to appear in a few scenes of this narrative; hence this brief sketch in passing of the excellent man.

Night came at last, and the crowd flowed toward the ground where great domes of light—the tents, "lit from the inner"—were seen glowing. The tent containing the wild animals was already crowded. There was general enthusiasm. Men, women, and children, absorbed in the spectacle before them, moved to and fro over the green turf forming the floor of the canvas house, laughing, jesting, exclaiming, and enjoying to the utmost what is one of the greatest enjoyments of this world—the being ardently interested in something.

It was a very good menagerie, and the animals, ranged in their cages against the canvas walls, looked with languid interest at the ridiculous creatures with two legs who were inspecting them. There was a huge rhinoceros, who could have crunched half a dozen of them at one mouthful; lions, tigers, and leopards, who could have torn them to pieces; and a grizzly bear, one of whose hugs would have sufficed for the strongest man present. Why were they put in cages? they may have asked themselves sometimes. They were stronger, swifter, keener of sight, keener of ear: did the little contents of the brain-cavity make such a difference? They were there at least, and the rustic beaux poked at them with their sticks, and made the rustic belles laugh; and the children shouted over the monkeys, and drew back from the elephant's trunk; and the sea-lions splashed, and a young hippopotamus yawned portentously; and altogether it was a very interesting menagerie.

An opening led into the next tent, where the performances of the ring were about to take place. The spectacle here presented was the familiar one of a circular space covered with sawdust, and enclosed by a low barrier. Clusters of lamps encircled the large pole rising in the centre, and rows of benches extended from the ground to the canvas eaves. Opposite the entrance was another opening leading into a third tent, containing the performers and horses. Near this opening the band was seated—they were already tuning their instruments, and stray notes mingled now and then with the hum and buzz of anticipation.

The benches were already filled nearly to overflowing. On the left were the sons and daughters of Africa, a wild-eyed, grinning mass of bright colors and ebony, who always start with delight at the announcement that a circus is coming. On the right was the white audience, composed of persons of every class and both sexes. The rustic and urban mingled in harmonious union—the Caucasian facing the African; the Mongolian was not there yet, though he may make his appearance some day in spite of Mr. Dennis Kearney. In some seats divided off from the rest, and comfortably cushioned, sat Brantz Elliot and Nelly Welles, and not far from them Mr. Lascelles and Miss Juliet Armstrong.

It was really a very dazzling spectacle with its brilliant lights, and there was an *aura* which excited and raised the spirits. A great crowd exerts a certain magnetic effect. You may be a philosopher, and smile serenely at the general excitement, but you end by sharing it. And this crowd was very much excited, as crowds at circuses almost always are, for the circus is one of the great popular institutions of the modern world. It replaces the Olympian festivals of antiquity, and with its lights, resounding music, splendid dresses, and wonderful feats, exactly satisfies the demand of the *populus.* The eye and ear are enormously delighted, if not the mind. It is not *Lear* or *Hamlet,* where the human soul is dissected, and there is nothing resembling the sweet charm of Juliet's love-dream. But then there is Mr. Merryman, the clown, who supplies the place of Touchstone, if not of Falstaff; and fine horses, and superb bare-back riders and athletes, all in wondrous costumes, climbing, leaping, and flying, and chasing the flying hours, under dazzling lights, to the sound of rejoiceful music. At this the *populus* thrills. Look at the faces packed together on the benches yonder. There is no trace of *ennui* there. You of the *élite* may go in kid gloves and opera cloaks to your city theatres, to enjoy Mr. Booth in tragedy or Mr. Jefferson in comedy. You may listen with critical ears to the music of Mr. Thomas or the notes of Madame Patti; your enjoyment is æsthetic, but the *populus* does not even understand the meaning of the word. It flocks to the circus, as the *Populus Romanus* once thronged to the amphitheatre to see the tigers and the fighting of the gladiators.

Suddenly the music burst forth, and the wonderful wonder began.

XII.

SOME CHILDREN OF THE RING.

It was a very good circus. Six Hungarian horses, jet black, with silver-plated trappings, and rosettes on their heads, darted into the ring, driven by long silken reins in the hands of a woman. She was a brilliant young creature with flashing eyes and rosy cheeks, and her costume chiefly consisted of stockinet, and a very scant gauze skirt. She drove, standing on the point of one satin slipper, on the horse in rear, and the other foot was pointed at an angle behind her, as if the laughing maiden had just spurned something. This was Mademoiselle Clare de Lune, as any one could see from the handbills. She was a light-hearted girl, who evidently enjoyed life, and thought pirouetting before a crowd charming amusement. Having flashed around the ring, kissing her hand, and changing from one foot to the other on her steed, she began to exhibit the accomplishments of her Hungarians. At the signal they stopped suddenly and wheeled in circles, and were mixed up hopelessly; then they promptly untangled themselves, and resumed the gallop in a long, streaming line. Then Mademoiselle Clare de Lune placed her extremities upon two horses and drove the rest. Then the rush became more furious; the plated harness clashed, the steeds broke into line again, and, kissing her hand amidst applause, Miss de Lune was borne away out of the ring.

Mademoiselle Zephyr succeeded her on a milk-white steed without saddle or bridle, and clad in a costume scanter even than Miss de Lune's. Then the unequalled male performers of the Unrivalled Combination came on in their turn; the ring was one great *mêlée* of flashing costumes and rushing steeds. Then they vanished as they came, at a furious gallop, and the audience burst into shouts of applause and laughter.

The applause was meant, no doubt, for the unequalled bare-back riders, but the laughter was caused by Mr. Merryman.

That gentleman rose apparently from the earth beneath the feet of the horses, and came forward, bowing and grimacing.

He was a singular figure in stockinet and short pantaloons, surrounded by red stripes. His legs were as thin as pipestems, and he wore a fool's-cap with a tassel. His cheeks and lips were daubed with carmine, and his corked mustache curled toward his ears. This was the figure which came forward grimacing with intense enjoyment, and bowing until his frame described an exact right angle.

Mr. Merryman made an address, in which he congratulated the audience upon seeing him again. "His own feelings," he said, "were inexpressible, and he would therefore not express them. This very large and intelligent congregation of miserable sinners had a great pleasure before them. They had seen the animals, their first cousins according to Mr. Darwin—the Syrian jackass, the tiger, and the monkeys. They would now have a rarer enjoyment than this, or his own society even—the wonderful feats of the celebrated Señor Karl."

The brass band burst forth, and a man came slowly into the ring on foot. Having reached the middle of the ring, he made the professional salute by raising one hand to a level with his face and letting it fall. As the assistants had not arranged some weights which he was to lift, he stood looking at the audience and they at him. He was broad-shouldered and powerful. As he wore no clothing but stockinet, and velvet pantaloons reaching from his waist to the middle of his thighs, the huge muscles of his chest and limbs could be seen plainly. His head was striking. A heavy black beard and mustache nearly concealed his face. His forehead was broad, and there was a great space between the eyes. His eyebrows were black and heavy, and had the peculiarity of nearly uniting in the middle, which had the effect of giving his whole physiognomy a stern, almost savage expression. Otherwise the face was a frank and honest one, and the man's glance not

at all fierce. His complexion was ruddy, apparently from drink, but excess had not yet undermined his immense physique. His walk was firm, and his carriage erect. He was evidently as hard as iron from head to foot—a Titan trained and developed to the highest degree of physical force by the prospect of two hundred dollars a week, probably spent for the most part in drink.

When the weights were arranged on the platform, supported on two carpenters' benches, the Señor Karl placed his shoulders beneath the platform, braced himself by resting his hands on his knees; then his muscles rose in ridges, and the mass ascended about a foot. As the weight was two or three thousand pounds he could not support it long. When he allowed the platform to fall back with a crash, and came out drawing a long breath, the audience testified by their loud applause that they were satisfied.

Feats on the trapeze followed, in which performers of both sexes took part. Some of these were very curious, and seem to nullify the Newtonian principle of gravity—almost to reverse it. When Mademoiselle Clare de Lune wrapped the instep of one of her feet around a rope hanging from the summit of the trapeze frame, and, hanging head downward, kissed her hand, it was a mystery how she supported the weight of her person in that position; and how, when she fell, she managed to light upon her feet.

The Señor Karl, it seemed, had another performance to go through with, and, after an interlude of bare-backers, he reappeared in the ring. His performance, like the first, was to be an exhibition of strength. One of the leopards of the menagerie had been trained to participate in it, and it consisted in ascending the trapeze ropes with the animal perched on the performer's shoulder.

He advanced to the middle of the ring, looking toward the opening into the first tent, and the keeper there loosed the animal, which bounded into the arena. He was a large and very beautiful leopard, with fur as soft as velvet, streaked and spotted with black and yellow. The cat-like eyes sparkled, and the leopard sprung at the man growling—it was apparently a part of the performance: a glance at his face, however, made this doubtful. He had caught the leopard by the throat as if to defend himself, and was looking at the animal with an expression of some surprise, his black eyebrows nearly joined in the middle.

For nearly a minute the man and the animal preserved their statuesque atti-tudes, the leopard growling, and the man apparently only preventing him by main strength from fixing his teeth in him. His eyes were fixed on the animal's, and seemed to have a magnetic effect. The leopard ceased to growl, at length, crouch-ed down with a sidelong and submissive glance, and at the order sprung and perched himself on the man's shoulder.

Then the performance began, and the man raised himself slowly, hand - over-hand, by a single rope, ascending to the summit of the trapeze. Once there he paused. A moment afterward a furious growl was heard from the man and the animal in unison, and they descended rapidly, and reached the sawdust. What had happened? Was the whole a part of the performance? If so, the performer was a very excellent actor. He seized the leopard by the throat at the moment when the animal was apparently attempt-ing to escape from him, and, throwing him upon the ground, placed one knee on his breast.

The audience burst into applause, but the performer seemed in no mood to ac-knowledge it—he was plainly furious. His black eyebrows had made the straight line across his face, and the gasps and struggles of the animal left no doubt that the performer's object was to strangle him. All at once the worthy Mr. Brownson rushed into the ring. His face was red and his eyes flashed. The good man had quite lost his self-possession, and discharged a volley of oaths, winding up with a demand what all this meant.

The performer rose to his feet. The leopard lay still. "He bit me and I strangled him!" he said, in a deep voice with a foreign ac-cent. "That is the meaning of it."

"Strangle my best leopard, that cost me two thousand dollars!" came in a howl of wrath and anguish.

"He nearly cost me my life; but I've done for him, and I'm glad of that."

Having made this response in a phlegmatic and unimpressed voice, the athlete made his professional salute to the audience and went out of the ring. "What is the matter, Lefthander?" said Clare de Lune, running to him.

The Lefthander—which seemed to be the Señor Karl's designation in private life—put his finger under the rosy chin of Miss de Lune, and laughed slightly. "I choked the leopard to death for biting me, and old Brownson is furious," he said.

"Choked the leopard!"

"The vermin sunk his teeth in my left shoulder. You can see it."

Mademoiselle de Lune had been laugh-ing, but suddenly cried,

"Oh me! you are hurt, Lefthander; you are bleeding!"

Before he could prevent her she took her white gauze skirt and pressed it to the bleeding shoulder.

"There, you've ruined your dress—just look at it!" said the Lefthander. "I'm not hurt in the least: you are a good girl, pétite."

They then parted. As to the leopard, he had been dragged out of the ring, and the bare-backers had rushed in. The in-cident was apparently forgotten.

It was not forgotten by one person—Mr. Lascelles—and had impressed Miss Juliet Armstrong.

"A very strange incident," she said. "Was it real, or a part of the perform-ance?"

"I think the incident was a real one," said Mr. Lascelles, suddenly recovering, apparently, from a fit of the deepest ab-straction.

"The leopard must have bit him.

What a singular-looking person!" said Miss Juliet.

"Very singular," said Mr. Lascelles, with a peculiar expression upon his face. It was hard to read the expression — it seemed one of vague astonishment; and it had been there from the moment of the Lefthander's first entrance.

"What is his name? I mean the leopard-slayer," said Miss Juliet, with mild interest.

"His name? I do not know. How should I—"

Mr. Lascelles stopped suddenly. What was he saying? He laughed, and begged his companion to pardon his rudeness— he was growing so absent-minded that he felt really ashamed of himself. The performer's name? He would ascertain. And having procured a bill from the attendant stationed at the entrance to the reserved seats, he brought it back, and presented it with a bow to the young lady.

"He is called the Señor Karl," he said, with an air of indifference.

And as the acrobats at this moment entered, the subject of the Señor Karl quite disappeared from Miss Juliet's mental horizon.

XIII.

MOUSE.

Having parted with Clare de Lune, the Lefthander — to adopt the private name of the Señor Karl—went to a slit in the canvas, opened it slightly, and fixed his eyes on Mr. Lascelles, who sat in the full light of a circle of globe lamps. For some moments he scrutinized him closely, with a very moody expression on his face. He then muttered,

"It is the man or his ghost! I am sure of him. What is he doing here?"

After a few minutes he walked away and went into a side compartment of the large tent. Here he sat down on an empty box, upon which lay a short meerschaum pipe and a pouch of smoking tobacco, which he had probably placed there when he went into the ring. He filled the pipe, lit it from a match taken from the pouch, and, leaning one of his ponderous elbows on his knee, began to smoke — looking thoughtfully, as he did so, at the finely caparisoned horses without, with their riders standing beside them, which he could do through the opening. At a signal the horses and riders passed at a swift gallop and darted into the ring. The Lefthander then concentrated his attention upon two figures seated upon some bags of oats opposite his box, smoking his pipe tranquilly with an air of enjoyment, and looking at them with interest.

They were a picturesque little group— a slender young fellow of about twenty, clad precisely like the Lefthander in close-fitting stockinet and velvet pantaloons; and a child, apparently about ten, dressed as a ballet girl. This dress consisted of a blue satin body, and a white muslin skirt reaching about to her knees, where it was joined by flesh-colored stockinet, ending in red morocco boots fitting tightly to her tiny feet. All about the child, in fact, was tiny—her slender limbs, her delicate arms, which were bare, and her features. Her hair was of a dark auburn, and fell on her bare shoulders in short curls; when she raised her eyes you saw that they were large and blue, and had a very earnest little-womanish expression. At the moment she was seated upon one of the bags, with her left foot over her right knee, chalking the sole of her boot —a proceeding which both the young man, who was leaning back on his elbow, and the Lefthander, who was smoking his pipe, contemplated with interest. As, after rubbing away with the chalk for a moment, the child uttered a slight sigh, the Lefthander, taking his pipe out of his mouth, said,

"Tired, Mouse?"

The voice which asked this question was not the same which had said briefly, "He bit me and I strangled him!" to Manager Brownson. It was quite different, and had something caressing about it.

"No, I am not much tired; but it's a tiresome sort of business, this dancing and prancing," said the small lady addressed as Mouse; "but I suppose I'll have to put up with it."

"I don't know. I don't altogether like it. You ought to be at school, Mouse."

"*Me*, at school? Away from *you?* What in the world would become of you?"

Having reflected on this, the Lefthander said,

"Well, you are right, perhaps. I couldn't very well get along without hearing my Mouse squeak sometimes, and would feel a little lost, probably."

"And Gentleman Joe, and Harry, what would *they* do? What would you *all* do, if I was not here to take care of you?" Mouse said, with a business air.

"Really, I never thought of that," said the Lefthander, lost in reflection; "the fact is, we would all probably go to the dogs, which is not a very good place to go to."

He smoked for a moment, and then added, "But we might all tramp off somewhere together."

"Oh, that would be grand, poppa!" exclaimed Mouse, with enthusiasm. She called it "pop — ah," emphasizing the first syllable, and gesticulated with the hand holding the chalk as she spoke.

"Would you like to give up dancing on the tight-rope, Mouse?"

"Give it up! I'd get down on my knees and bless the day! I'm all the time thinking my foot's going to slip and I'll fall; and the crowd always looks at me as if I was—well, a whole menagerie, including the rhinoceros and the grizzly bear!"

The Lefthander uttered a slight grunt, which might have indicated either amusement at or sympathy with this view of things.

"And, then," he said, "the way of living is not so very good a way of living for a small body like you. The life of circus men and women is not an easy life —it is a very hard life."

"I should say it was!" Mouse returned, with aristocratic scorn; "sleeping in hay-stacks half the time, and prancing about

from one place to
boxes to sit on inst
being Mademoiselle
stead of a body's r
spectable!"

Mouse was evide
other things her de
bills, which was "]
Delavan," as she ir
miliar appellation
she was known am

"Well," the Lef
and looking with a
smoked, at the ch
curls, "the fact i:
body, Mignon, to
You were made for
big doll, about the
to be tucked in be
hay-stacks. You le
operas: I have a
first wind would
blew tolerably har
hard. You ought
tight-rope busine
much."

"Well, I don't
consequential Mov
money, as I don't a
anything to do wit

"Your poppa de
thing to do with i
you call invested."

"What's *invested*
let me give it away

"Yes, to poor pe
suffer. That's *in*
hander, smoking.
do the rope busin
plaguing me till I
were tired idling,
you to be idle."

Mouse shook he
test, but the Left
view.

"What business
to work for mone
meant you to foll
for nothing else m
ent. I've stuck a
set in the groove
wagon-horse, and

out—hew to the line; but I'm rather tired of it."

"Are you really?" Mouse said, earnestly.

"Rather, Mignon; and sometimes I think I'll take you and go off and live quietly somewhere. You'd have the flowers and the sunshine, you see, and go to sleep when the birds do, instead of hopping up and down on a tight-rope till midnight. I think I'll take you."

Mouse was chalking her boot, but at these words she stopped. Her eyes sparkled.

"Do you think you will?" she exclaimed.

"I really do. I don't see what better I can do than look after my young one. I'm a big fellow, and can lift heavy weights, and when animals fall out with me, as one did to-night, I can do for 'em—but that's not much. The best thing to do is to look after the young ones."

A wonderful expression of softness came to the rugged face as he looked at the child. It quite changed its whole appearance.

"Yes," he added, with a nod; "I think I'll retire from public life before long."

"Do you really — really, poppa?" Mouse repeated, in ecstasies.

"Yes, and you and I will go off to the country, and live in a quiet way. I'll put on a plain suit of clothes, and you will have a little frock reaching down below your knees, and good black shoes—not a gauze skirt and fancy boots like that, made of red morocco — and go to school, and see the grass and the flowers grow, and hear the birds sing from morning till night."

The Lefthander stopped to utter his grunt of mild enjoyment.

"I think I could stand 'em, and keep away from the bar-rooms," he said, "on your account, Mignon. Yes, I could stand that, and I could work for you like a good poppa; and smoke my pipe and live respectably, as you said just now — didn't you? But then there's a difficulty."

Mouse, cast down from her eminence of joy, turned her head suddenly.

"What would you do without Harry?" said the Lefthander, nodding toward the third member of the group. This was the young fellow in stockinet who was leaning back on one elbow on the bags of grain, and had listened to the whole conversation with a smile.

"There's Harry to think of," the Lefthander said.

"And Gentleman Joe," said a melancholy voice behind them.

At this all looked up and saw Mr. Merryman. He had just come out of the ring, and the expression both of his face and figure had completely changed. The tumbling, dancing, grimacing Mr. Merryman had given way to a rather melancholy old fellow, who stood calmly erect, and looked quite sad. Looking at him you were apt to recall the legend of the poor jester on the stage who threw the crowd into ecstasies, and then retired behind the scenes to the bedside of his dying child.

He was given to such changes of mood, even in private, this eccentric old Gentleman Joe. His comrades said there was a "crack" in him somewhere—a screw loose in his mental machinery. He alternated between extravagant mirth and depressing sadness. The least circumstance made him laugh or brought tears to his eyes. Sighs and smiles chased each other over his thin old face; and there really did seem to be something the matter with him. His memory was very unstable, and he could not tell the name of the last place which he had performed at after an interval of two or three days. As to his past life, it seemed to be a blank to him, and nothing more was known of him than that he had been connected for a long time with the company, and that his name was Vance. He and his son Harry, the young fellow leaning on the bags of oats, were both very popular with their comrades. Gentleman Joe was an especial favorite. He was so amiable, and so ready to do an act of kindness, that everybody was his friend. He was treated with the utmost regard, but never with undue familiarity, in spite of his undignified position in the troupe, for there was something about Gentleman Joe which completely discouraged intrusive people. He was very easy and friendly, but no one had ever been known to slap him on the shoulder or indulge in liberties with him. Even Manager Brownson, who was a dictatorial person, never spoke imperiously to Gentleman Joe—a name which had evidently been bestowed upon him from the mild courtesy of his manners.

"And Gentleman Joe — what would poor old Gentleman Joe do without you, Mouse?" he said now to the child.

Mouse seemed equal to the occasion, and promptly replied:

"Why of course you and Harry would go with us, Gentleman Joe. You don't for one minute think that I could get along without you and Harry, any more than you could get along without me?"

"It would be a hard business, a very hard business, indeed," said Gentleman Joe, shaking his head; "and as to Harry's not having you to tease, he would lose his good spirits and pine away."

"I certainly would, Mouse," said the young fellow, laughing. "I'd miss my grandma every hour."

"Would you, really, you good-for-nothing plague?" Mouse said, affectionately. "Well, I can tell you one thing —it would be bad for *you*. If ever there was a young man who required looking after, and to have somebody to keep him straight, it's *you!*"

"Listen to grandma!" was the response. "The old lady's begun her discourse. It's a weakness with her."

"Never you mind, sir. You'll come to a bad end if you don't take care—mark my words."

"I hope not," the young fellow said; "and you oughtn't to be thinking of going away, Mouse, if I require moral lecturing so much."

"You and Gentleman Joe can come with us. What is to prevent you, sir?"

"I don't think that would suit; would it, father?"

"I'm afraid it would not," Gentleman Joe replied, shaking his head; "not that I like being Mr. Merryman. I do not like it at all; but I am growing old now, Mouse, and old people find it hard to give up their pursuits and follow different ones. I was not a clown always—though I can't say I remember exactly *what* I used to be. My memory is not so good as it was. I lived somewhere—I forget precisely where—and was not a clown. It amuses me to laugh and make the crowd laugh—sometimes. I don't think I should like altogether to give up the old trade."

"But we'd be so happy, Gentleman Joe!" Mouse persisted, with great earnestness. "Think of the birds and the flowers; and then, we needn't give up everything. We might come to it by degrees, you know. We might make up a little troupe of our own, and go about the country, and perform in a quiet way."

"Really, I never thought of that," said Gentleman Joe.

"Nor I," said the Lefthander; "that's not a bad idea, Harry."

"Not a bad idea at all," said the young man.

"It's a very good idea," said Gentleman Joe.

Mouse saw that she had made an impression, and this always stimulates one to further eloquence.

"I am glad to find that you lords of creation have some good-sense left after all," she said. "If I *am* a mouse I can squeak what's reasonable, and not nonsense such as I generally hear from that good-for-nothing young man there, who is looking at my ankles while he is picking his teeth with a straw!" said Mouse, severely. "Of course it's a good idea! Think! Poppa could lift weights and perform on the ropes, and you and Gentleman Joe could do the juggling, Harry!"

"And the Mr. Merryman business," said Gentleman Joe, reflecting.

"And I could play the tambourine!" said Mouse, "and take around the hat! And we could get a hand-organ and a little monkey — a small one with a red coat, and a feather in his cap!"

"Really, that sounds like business, Mouse," said the Lefthander. "We could buy a light wagon and a horse to carry the properties, and a small tent and the rest — and there you are. We'd be a troupe of Bohemians, which is not a bad thing to be. We would have no more to do with this beastly old Brownson, and you would not have to pirouette any more—"

"Before common people and servants," Gentleman Joe said, with the air of an aristocrat. "That is the best of all—isn't it, Mouse?"

"Oh yes! yes, indeed!" exclaimed the delighted Mouse, "and we will be free—free! We needn't act unless we want to. We can stop anywhere we choose — on the side of the road in the grassy fence corners, or under the trees; and I'll boil the pot, poppa, and cook for everybody; and you shall smoke your pipe, and Harry shall be just as good-for-nothing as he pleases; and you and me, Gentleman Joe, will walk off and hear the birds sing, and you'll pet me, and maybe take me up and carry me if I am tired, as there's not much of me—for you know you always liked me better than anybody in all this wicked world!"

Mouse stopped, out of breath. Suddenly a sort of growl was heard near them, and turning in the direction of this sound they saw Manager Brownson. He was very red indeed in the face, probably the result of recent potations, and scowled fiercely, striking his stick upon the ground as he did so.

"What does this mean? What are you trifling here for?" cried Mr. Brownson. "Don't you hear the audience howling, and getting the devil in 'em?"

"I have just returned from the ring," said Gentleman Joe, with dignity; "and I will add that your tone of voice is unpleasant, sir."

"Curse my tone of voice—hear 'em! they're breaking down the benches!— There's nobody in the ring!"

He turned furiously to Mouse and said,

"This is your private parlor, eh? You're entertaining your friends when it's your turn to go on!"

Mouse shrunk a little from the inflamed eyes.

"Get up!" cried Mr. Brownson.

"I haven't chalked my shoes — I will soon be ready, sir," the child said, with alarm. She then hastily rubbed her shoes in a nervous manner, and rose hastily to her feet.

"Hear 'em!" exclaimed Mr. Manager Brownson, digging his cane into the ground with fury as the prolonged thunder of impatience came from the main tent. "Hear 'em — they'll split the benches!"

These words were addressed to the Lefthander, who had continued quietly to smoke his pipe, while Mouse, Gentleman Joe, and Harry hastened off.

"Do you hear?" cried the manager.

"Hear what?" said the Lefthander, tranquilly.

"That infernal row—the audience are wild."

"Yes, I hear it—it is loud enough for that," said the Lefthander, with great composure.

"And that girl's the cause of it—it's her neglect!"

"Neglect of what?"

"Her business!"

"That is a lie!" said the Lefthander.

Manager Brownson stood for a moment looking at the personage who uttered these calm words, with a species of stupor. The world was plainly coming to an end. Could he believe his ears? He, Manager Brownson, proprietor of the Unrivalled Combination of Attractions, had been informed to his face that a statement which he made was "a lie!"

"Wh—what do you mean?" he gasped.

The Lefthander rose erect slowly, having first knocked the ashes from his pipe and laid it upon the box beside him.

"Well," he said, in a calm and matter-of-fact voice, "I mean that what you say about Mouse is a lie — she was not called; she's always ready, and brings you in double what you pay her. As for you, I will tell you what I think of you: you are an old beast! And I will give you a little advice. Let Mouse alone; it will be better for you."

There was no doubt at all about the meaning of these words, and the expression of the speaker's face was not encouraging. The black eyebrows had united in the middle, and the ponderous left hand slowly closed. Manager Brownson changed color; a personal collision with the athlete seemed imminent; when a cry was heard from the main tent, where Mouse was going through her performance. Something had evidently happened. Had Mouse met with any accident?

The Lefthander turned his back on Manager Brownson, and hastened to the opening in the canvas through which his figure disappeared.

XIV.

AN ACCIDENT.

MOUSE had, in fact, met with an accident. After the angry colloquy with the manager, she and Gentleman Joe had hastened into the ring, which was unoccupied at the moment by any of the performers — hence the impatience of the audience. It was a fixed habit with old Gentleman Joe to thus act as the child's escort. He was very much devoted to her, and saw that the sight of the great sea of heads and eyes generally frightened her a little; so he always "went on" with her, and thus diverted to himself a part of the public attention. This was a proof of Gentleman Joe's delicacy of sentiment, as well as of his affection for Mouse. This thin-faced old clown was not a mere merry-andrew; you could see that. He had about him the indescribable something which indicates elevation of character; and his manner, and the tones of his voice, when he was speaking to the child, had that suavity which marks highbred persons.

As they entered the ring, Gentleman Joe's expression changed at once. He executed a grimace, and, bending his body forward at a right angle, extended his left elbow horizontally toward Mouse, who took the arm offered. He then stepped out with his right foot, putting it down cautiously, as if he were walking upon eggs, and escorted Mouse to the spot where a tight-rope was stretched over forks about ten feet from the ground.

"Ladies and gen-tle-men," said Gentleman Joe, "I have the honor to introduce to you my young friend, Mademoiselle Celestine Delavan, who will perform for your amusement upon what is called, by the common people, the tight-rope."

In the midst of applause, Gentleman Joe then released his arm from Mouse's grasp, knelt on one knee, and held out his hand. The child placed her small foot in it, and Gentleman Joe tossed her up to the tight-rope, and handed her the long balancing-pole; he then smiled, retired backward, looking at her admiringly as he did so, fell over a wooden block behind him, turned a somerset, and lit upon his feet, grimacing. The performance then began.

It was evident that the child was ill at ease, and a little afraid to begin her performance. This was so plain that Miss Juliet Armstrong, who seemed to be much interested in her, said to Mr. Lascelles,

"It is very wrong to make such a poor little thing perform in public. She is afraid of falling; I hope she will not fall."

"There is probably no danger," Mr. Lascelles replied; "these people are always well trained."

"But she is such a wee body," said the sympathetic Juliet very earnestly for so calm a person, "and quite a little beauty too."

"Do you think so?"

"Don't you?"

"Well," said Mr. Lascelles, rather indifferently, "I really had not looked at her. Yes, she is tolerably good-looking, and a mere child, as you say, Miss Juliet."

"She is too young. Look, she certainly is frightened — she is clinging to the rope with her feet like a bird."

This was true. Mouse's boots were not sufficiently chalked, which is essential in performances on the tight-rope.

Alarmed by the angry expression and rough address of the manager, the child had hastened in to go through her performance before she was ready to do so. The smooth soles of her boots made her foothold insecure, and her feet were wrapped around the tight-rope in the manner noticed by the young lady—as a bird grasps the bough of a tree.

Nevertheless, Mouse attempted to execute her part. She advanced nervously, moving her long balancing-pole up and down—her foothold was evidently uncertain, and once or twice her feet slipped, but she regained her equilibrium.

"The poor little thing! look at her face," exclaimed Juliet; "she is frightened, and is going to fall!"

Mouse fell—her foot had slipped, and she was precipitated from the tight-rope. As she fell she endeavored to grasp the rope, but only bruised her arm, causing the blood to flow. She struck the sawdust heavily, and lay still, moaning.

Gentleman Joe had rushed forward to catch her in his arms as she fell, but he was too late. The child was lying with one of her tiny limbs doubled beneath her, and her bleeding arm above her head, as if to ward off a blow. Some of the blood from it had fallen on her light curls. At sight of this Gentleman Joe had uttered the cry, and the audience had risen to their feet with exclamations of sympathy. It was an affecting sight to see Gentleman Joe, with a sudden rush of tears washing the paint from his cheeks, kneel by Mouse's side, calling to her. But he was all at once thrust aside, and the Lefthander caught the child in his arms.

"What's the matter, Mignon?" he exclaimed. "Are you hurt? Your arm is broken. You fell!"

"Yes, I fell, poppa. My shoes were not chalked," faltered Mouse, trying to smile.

"Your arm is broken! It was his fault—I'll kill him!"

The tone of these words frightened the audience, who distinctly heard them. The Lefthander's voice and face were, in fact, ominous. His black brows had made the straight line. Another person probably heard him, and saw the eyebrows, through the opening of the tent—Manager Brownson, who was observed to retire hastily to his private apartment, away from the general confusion.

The Lefthander raised Mouse in his arms, growling as he did so like one of the wild animals. He was evidently, indeed, a very dangerous animal at the moment, and it was probably just as well that Mr. Brownson had business which occupied him elsewhere. Mouse was quite pale, and her white skirt was stained with the blood flowing from the wound upon her arm. The Lefthander had clasped her close to his breast, as a mother holds a baby, and was talking to her. He then rose, with Mouse in his arms, and went out of the tent, muttering, "If he gets in my way I'll kill him!"

The audience did not hear these words, but they looked after the big athlete carrying the tiny being in his arms, and could see the yearning expression of his face as he leaned over the child and repeatedly kissed her. A murmur rose at this sight—it was the 'touch of nature which makes the whole world kin.' Miss Juliet Armstrong quietly passed a small white handkerchief over her eyes, and then restored it to her outside pocket, where it was convenient to pick-pockets.

"He must love her very much," she said, half aloud.

"Yes," said Mr. Lascelles, "or pretends to. There is never any certainty with these people that what they do is not a part of the performance."

XV.

THE DRESSING-ROOM.

If it was a part of the performance the Lefthander performed his part to the life, and continued to do so when out of sight of the audience. Gentleman Joe had hastened after him with a piteous expression. The fact that no one was left in the ring seemed a subject of profound indifference to the poor clown. Manager Brownson might rage if he chose. There was Mouse to think of.

The circus men, standing by their horses, ready to go on, flocked about the Lefthander inquiring what had happened. The rough fellows in their glittering costumes were not the sort of persons to look for womanish sympathy from, one would have supposed; but there was the sympathy, and it was plainly strong and real.

"What's the matter with Mouse, Lefthander?"

"Poor girl!"

"Broke her arm!"

These evidences of feeling came from the crowd, but the Lefthander did not stop. He only said, as he passed, "If he gets in my way I'll finish him!"

He went on, carrying Mouse close to his breast, to a small compartment on the left, which was divided from the main tent by a breadth of canvas. This he pushed aside and went in. In the room was a mattress, covered with an old counterpane, a small pine table, two chairs, and a cracked looking-glass hanging by a string tied through two holes in the canvas. On one of the chairs was a pile of female clothing, evidently discarded recently by its owner or owners for the scantier costume of the ring. The place was evidently a dressing-room for the female performers, and if there had been any doubt of this the presence of Clare de Lune and the Zephyr would have established the fact. The Zephyr was engaged at the moment in tying the ribbon of her slipper, and Clare de Lune was standing in front of the cracked looking-glass rouging her cheeks with one hand, while the other hand held a powder-puff with which she had just been powdering her shoulders. Both were in full ring costume, and their appearance was airy and sylph-like.

The Lefthander entered without ceremony. As the Zephyr went on with her occupation, and Clare de Lune at first did not turn her head, it was obvious that the intrusion was not at all resented — the new-comer was probably only "one of the family." As Clare de Lune finished rouging her cheeks, however, at the moment, and had secured the smile which she had been practising for some moments in front of her mirror, she turned her head with mild curiosity, and looked at the intruders. Then she suddenly cried,

"What has happened?"

"Well, I'll tell you what has happened," said the Lefthander, in his bass voice; "Mouse was made to go on, before her shoes were chalked, by that beast Brownson, and she's broke her arm, I think; she slipped and fell."

He laid Mouse on the old mattress, and passed his large hand over her arm.

"Only bruised," he said. "Where are you hurt, little one?"

"It's only my foot. I think it's sprained, poppa," said Mouse, in rather a faint voice; "but I don't think it's much, and it's not worth making a fuss about—it only hurts a little."

Mouse tried to say this in a matter-of-fact tone, but she uttered a slight moan, which indicated very plainly that she was in pain.

The sound seemed to act upon the ballet-girls like magic. Clare de Lune forgot her rouge and the Zephyr her slipper, and ran to Mouse, throwing their arms around her and crying. One laid her head easily on an old pillow and drew the tattered counterpane over her. The other ran for a stone pitcher with a broken spout, and began to bathe the sprained ankle in cold water. Mouse looked up, smiling — the Lefthander's arm was around her neck. The group, with the circus girls on their knees in the sawdust, and covering the child with caresses, made quite a picture.

They were not wrong, perhaps, these worthy ballet-girls, in supposing that caresses and petting were good for people in Mouse's condition. Kisses soothe, and tones of love and sympathy heal the wounds of the body as well as the mind. They are wholesome. So Mouse smiled as she received the caresses of these young

Amazons of the ring, whom their hard life had not hardened.

"There, girls, that will do!" said the Lefthander; "let the young one be quiet now and rest a little."

He looked at them from under his shaggy eyebrows and muttered, "Good girls!"

A boy appeared at the opening of the dressing-room as he was speaking, and called out, "Lefthander!"

"Well?" he growled.

"It's your turn, Lefthander. The barebackers are off."

"Go to the devil!" said the Lefthander.

The boy's face filled with delight, and he chuckled.

"Must I tell old Brownson that?"

"Yes, tell him! I'll probably send him there before the night's over."

The boy disappeared, apparently overwhelmed with delight at these words. He was a call-boy, of a humorous turn, and probably did not like "old Brownson." As he let the flap fall, the faces of Gentleman Joe and Harry were seen watching and waiting anxiously to hear if Mouse was really hurt. There was no time to tell them at the moment. They and Clare de Lune and the Zephyr were successively "called." The two girls, obeying the inexorable summons, went out of the dressing-room; and the Lefthander was left alone with Mouse.

She was lying quite easily, and did not seem to be suffering. Her paleness had disappeared, and the delicate lips were smiling. She had closed her eyes, apparently to shield them from the light of a cluster of lamps high up upon the large pole supporting the tent; and the Lefthander, half stretched upon the old mattress beside her, looked at her quietly. It was a great contrast, the huge athlete with the ponderous chest, and limbs rugged with muscle, leaning on his elbow near the child, who seemed, as he had said, light enough to be blown away by the first wind. While he was looking at her with a tenderness which made the rough features wonderfully soft, Mouse opened her eyes.

"Well, old lady," said the Lefthander, quietly, "how is the foot?"

"It's easy," said Mouse, "and it really don't amount to much, I do assure you, poppa."

"How about the arm?"

"Well, it's the least bit bruised; I wonder it bled so, and it doesn't hurt now. Here's a rumpus," added Mouse, "all about a small body that could be put in a thimble."

"You may be a small body in the eyes of other people, but you are a big body in mine, Mignon," the Lefthander said. "I'd rather see the whole Unrivalled Combination sunk to the depths than have your little finger hurt."

"The Combination sunk?" Mouse rejoined; "that would be a bad thing to happen; for you know, then, Clare de Lune and the Zephyr would be sunk too."

"Well, that would be bad," the Lefthander acknowledged.

"And there's Gentleman Joe and Harry. They oughtn't to be sunk instead of playing away yonder—just listen to that music and the applause. I think Long Tom must be turning his back somerset."

Long Tom was Mr. Donald Melville, chief of the bare-back riders, and a friend of Mouse.

"No, it wouldn't do to sink Gentleman Joe and Harry," she said, shaking her head. "I don't think I could get along without them; and then you know we couldn't go off and make up that troupe I was telling you about."

"The travelling company? So it's all arranged?"

"Of course it's all arranged. I am now considering about the monkey," said Mouse; "he is to have a red jacket trimmed with gold braid, and a blue velvet cap. I will train him to play the tambourine and carry round the hat."

"And you'll look after the flowers and the sunshine?"

"In my moments of leisure, when I've nothing else to do."

Mouse spoke with a matter-of-fact air, but her eyes sparkled at the thought of the flowers and the sunshine. The Lefthander evidently saw the expression and said,

"Well, I think I've about made up my mind, Mignon; and we'll go off and get up the company."

Mouse started with joy.

"Are you really in earnest, poppa?" she exclaimed.

"I really am."

"And Gentleman Joe! and Harry! Do you think they will go with us?"

"I think I can talk both into it — I don't know; I think I can. Harry's ready, and old brute Brownson's getting Gentleman Joe in a bad humor with him."

Mouse forgot her foot, and clasped her small hands with delight.

"It's too good to be true! it is not going to happen!" she exclaimed. "There's no such luck to be expected, and I'll never see that monkey—no, never!"

"You would like to?"

"Like to? I'd take him on my back and carry him all day, only to have him! Oh, poppa! we'd be so happy. Think! —there'd be no more tight-rope dancing, and falling down and getting hurt—we'd act in the daytime—and the sun would shine so, and the grass, and flowers—just think of it all! You'd be happier than you ever were, and I'd take *such* good care of you!"

"I really believe I would be happier, Mignon — and I'd keep away from the bar-rooms. And there's another thing; if I stay here I'll put an end to old Brownson some day."

"Oh, no! that would be sinful. You know what I read you in my Bible, poppa?"

"Yes, I know, and that's why I want to get away before I do him any damage. I'm not a bad sort of fellow if people let me alone; but I'm rather hard to manage when I'm trifled with. I begin to see red! Some day or other old Brownson will provoke me; then I'll give him one of my left-handers that will do for him. What noise is that?"

"Somebody's quarrelling," Mouse said, listening.

A loud hubbub was heard without, and

the sound of voice
Curious to know w
Lefthander got up,
and telling Mouse
in a moment, went
room.

———

X

OF THE HEAVY BLO
UNRIVALLED   CO
MANAGER.

THE accident to
forgotten by the au
after its occurrence
ment interrupted fo
its full force. Thi
life and the world
ring, are much the
speare told us that?
private tragedy, and
haps; but then it
theirs.   It makes a
but ripples soon dis
goes on, for the au
be amused, not to s
is broken?   Your l
is very sad.   Your
the slippery arena o
poor fellow!   But f
will break.   There
sympathize with yo
ryman making on
Ha! ha!—ha! ha!
grimace?   What a
without a care in t
come the bare-back
dresses!   The ligh
roars;   the great a
and splendor and i
blood is oozing ou
curtain.

So the gay perfo
the jugglers tossed
Clare de Lune and
their velvet saddles
ville, *alias* "Long
did back somersets
comrades bounded
horses abreast; and
a heavy heart, grim

cating the very height of human enjoyment.

He was very heavy-hearted, indeed, this poor old Gentleman Joe, in his striped costume, exploding with jests, and doubling himself up in the ecstasies of his mirth. He was thinking of Mouse the whole time. The child was very dear to him, as he had no one of his own—only Harry, who was grown now — and he could not bear the thought that she was lying there in pain, a few feet from him. This thought made Gentleman Joe extremely unhappy; and as he had an opportunity at length of temporarily absenting himself from the ring, he went out, and directed his steps toward the corner where the colloquy had taken place between himself and his friends just before the child's accident. Perhaps the place recalled her, and he thought that he would go there for a moment before proceeding to inquire into her condition. He was wiping his face on his arm, and unconsciously removing some of the paint, when a voice behind him said,

"What is the matter, father? Something troubles you."

It was the voice of Harry. He had just finished his leaping performance, and seeing the figure of his father disappear in the direction of this corner, had followed him.

"What makes you look so sorrowful?" he added.

"Mouse," said Gentleman Joe, sighing deeply.

"She is not much hurt," replied the young man. "Clare de Lune said so. Only a sprain and a slight bruise."

Gentleman Joe shook his head despondently, and put his hand to his forehead—a common gesture with him—as if something was wrong there.

"I can't bear it, I can't bear it!" he said, in a piteous tone. "She ought not to be here. It is not suitable for a little slip of a thing like Mouse to live in such a rough world as this—I mean, to be a circus girl. She is a bud with the dew on it. The dust and heat will dry up the dew. I can't bear it!"

It was really a piteous sound that issued from the lips of Gentleman Joe. The sigh which he uttered seemed to be sufficient to "shatter all his bulk." The young man looked troubled at his father's trouble, and seemed to be thinking of Mouse too, for he said,

"You are right, father. I wish she was off somewhere, living easily and in quiet, as a child should, as much as you do. It is strange how much Mouse makes everybody love her. I don't know how I would get along unless I heard her laugh and tease me—and it is all pretence; she is devoted to all of us."

"She has a warm heart — too warm for this hard business," sighed Gentleman Joe.

His eyes grew dreamy as he said this, and he added, in a thoughtful tone,

"A hard business, a very hard business. I have been at it now for—let me see—for—well, for nearly three years, and I know all about it."

"For *three* years, father!"

"At least that, my boy. Maybe for twenty or more. You see my memory fails me a little, sometimes. I can't fix the exact time; but it has been a very long time indeed, and I have seen a great many things as I travelled about."

Harry looked a little sorrowful at this aberration of his father's memory, although he was used to it.

"Some things were very sad," Gentleman Joe said, with sudden tears in his eyes. "There was little Charley, Long Tom's nephew. They were training the child. You know they hold them by a cord through a ring as the horse gallops. One day the cord broke, and little Charley fell under the horse's feet and was trampled to death. He was bleeding from a wound on his forehead made by the hoof of the horse. When they took him up he was dead."

Gentleman Joe uttered a sob.

"That was enough to make people cry —poor little Charley! he was very fond of me."

"Well, father," said the young man, "I wouldn't think of these sorrowful things. There is enough of trouble in this world without looking it up."

"That is very true," said Gentleman Joe, resuming his equanimity.

"There are bright things and scenes as well as sad ones. You must think of the bright ones."

"I do, Harry, I do," said Gentleman Joe, cheerfully. "I remember a great many of that sort, too. I could make you split your sides laughing if I told you about some things I have seen. There was the old farmer in Ohio, who waddled into the ring and squared off to fight me for pointing at him, and asking him if he 'wanted to be a Granger, and with the Grangers stand ?' "

Gentleman Joe smiled with sudden delight at the recollection.

"He was angry, I suppose," said Harry, humoring his father.

"Angry ? He was wild !" exclaimed Gentleman Joe, in immense enjoyment. "He doubled up his fist and struck at me; but I stooped down and ran between his legs, and sent him sprawling in the sawdust—ha, ha !"

The speaker shook from head to foot in ecstasies of mirth, after which he executed a series of grimaces from the force of habit.

"That was amusing enough," he said, at length, assuming an air of dignity, as though ashamed of his outburst; "but everything I have seen was not so comic as this. We can't always laugh."

" 'It is better to laugh than be sighing'—you know what the song says, father ?"

"Well, I'm not so certain of that," was the thoughtful reply. "A man who is always laughing is like an empty gourd with pebbles in it. You grow tired after awhile of the empty rattle, and long for quiet and an opportunity to think. But then thinking hurts the head. You remember things, too, when you think, and that hurts the heart."

He looked at the young man dreamily. It was a sorrowful, absorbed look, and his mind was evidently busy with thoughts of other persons or places.

"I often think of Ellen when I look a you, my boy," he said.

"My mother ?" Harry said, in a low tone.

"Yes. She is dead now—it has been a long time. I wish I was dead, too !"

"Don't talk so, father."

"Why not ? It is true," Gentleman Joe said, with a sad dignity in his face and voice which was wonderfully in contrast with his clown's dress. "Do you think it so very strange that a man should wish to die when he has lost his wife ?"

"But what would have become of me ?" said the young man.

"True; I ought to think of that. In fact, I did think of it," said Gentleman Joe, calmly. "You were a little one then, and put your arms around my neck and kissed me, and I saw what was to be done. My place was to live and take care of you."

As Gentleman Joe spoke, he looked at Harry with such tenderness that the young man's face flushed and his lip trembled a little.

"When did mother die, and where was it, father ?" he said.

"Hush !" said Gentleman Joe in a low voice, with his eyes swimming suddenly in tears; "it was a long time ago — don't remember the place, but I remember how she looked," he added, piteously.

The young man did not speak again for some moments; he was plainly endeavoring to regain command of his voice At length he said,

"Well, well, father, as it distresses you so I will not ask any more questions You will tell me some of these days, when we are quietly settled down somewhere I wish that was now. You ought to give up this business."

"I'm afraid that will never be, my boy,' Gentleman Joe said, shaking his head "You can't teach an old dog new tricks.'

"But it is wearing you out, father And such a life does not suit your character in the least. You are entirely different from these people—it may surprise you to hear me talk so, when I have nev er known any other sort—and they are good friendly fellows too. But they are different from *you*. You have no idea how I feel when I see you in this clown's dress, making fun for negroes and common people!—I hate it! And I hate my own trade of a circus-man. I'd rather live by digging ditches!"

"But what are we to do—we are so poor, Harry!"

"I will work for you, father. It is my duty—you have worked for me. It is a very small return for all your love and care since I was a child."

"No, no—the fathers must do their part. When they are old and weak, the children can take care of them then."

"You are getting to be both, father, and I mean to take care of you," said Harry. "You may think I am a thoughtless boy, and I am thoughtless enough, but I am not bad-hearted. It is my place to watch over you, and keep you from wanting anything. I never had a want that you did not supply when you could, and you have never been anything to me but the very best father that a boy ever had. Now I am a man, and I intend to try and make you some return for all you've done for me. Only say the word, and we'll leave the company and settle down quietly, and I'll do the working for both of us—you couldn't please me better."

"Leave the company, Harry? Leave the Lefthander, and Long Tom, and Clare de Lune—she's a good girl—and Mouse, worst of all? I don't think I could do that, my boy. No, I never could leave Mouse."

"We might talk the Lefthander into the idea of going off with us. I don't think he's very much pleased of late with the business and Manager Brownson. He was drinking at the tavern this morning, and a man trod on his foot, which made him angry, and Brownson spoke roughly to him. He wouldn't have liked the Lefthander's look if he had seen it as he turned his back."

"Well, he is getting more ill-tempered —I mean Mr. Brownson. Still he is not discourteous to you or me, Harry, and—"

"What the devil are you doing idling when you ought to be on?" cried a voice near them. They looked up—there was the gentleman of whom they had just been speaking.

Manager Brownson was not in a good-humor, that was very plain from his face. Indeed, several circumstances had combined to mar the worthy man's serenity on this day, and during the performance. In the morning the Lefthander, while engaged in the discreditable proceeding of drinking at the village tavern, had nearly gotten into an altercation with a citizen, which was prejudicial to receipts, and had cost him, Manager Brownson, an admission ticket, by way of salve to the citizen's feelings. Then, since nightfall other things had irritated the good man. The performers had not been as prompt as he expected. Things had gone wrong generally. The Lefthander had in mere wantonness, and evidently from personal malice, strangled the African leopard, one of the finest animals in the menagerie, which was a dead loss of more than two thousand dollars. And even that was not all: this big bully had dared to tell him, Manager Brownson, to his very face, that what he said was *a lie!* and when he was "called" to his performance, subsequently, had sent him word that he, Manager Brownson, might *go to the devil!* Was this the manner in which the manager and proprietor of the Unrivalled Combination of Attractions was to be treated by one of his subordinates? What he said was *a lie!!* and he might *go to the devil!!!*

Instead of going to the devil, Manager Brownson went to his private retreat in the rear and solaced himself with brandy. He had solaced himself repeatedly before, and his face became redder, and his temper more irascible. He was ready to confront all the Lefthanders on earth by this time; and, going toward the ring, his heavy cane striking the ground as he walked, he chanced to see Gentleman Joe talking with Harry. As the phrase "go to the devil" was rankling in his mind, he naturally uttered the words "what the devil," etc., as above. He then grasped his large walking-cane about a foot from the head in a threatening manner, and scowling at Gentleman Joe, who was nearest to him, said,

"What do you mean, I say, by this fooling here? Look yonder! Not a soul in the ring—and hear the audience growling and howling like a whole menagerie!"

Gentleman Joe's frame stiffened, and his face assumed an expression of wounded pride which was very striking.

"I was only conversing with my son for a few moments, sir," he said, formally. "I am not aware that I am your servant, to be addressed in a manner so very unpleasant."

But the dignity in the tone of the speaker was quite thrown away on Manager Brownson. If he noticed it, he paid no attention to it.

"Don't try to be palming off your excuses on me!" he exclaimed, wrathfully. "You and that fellow, the Lefthander, and his daughter, cut down your business one-half. It's robbing me!—no better than taking my purse!"

Gentleman Joe colored with indignation, and said,

"It is not true that I neglect my part, sir."

"What do you mean?" cried Mr. Brownson, raising his heavy stick.

"I mean I am an honest man, and not a worm for you to tread upon, if I am a clown in your company," said Gentleman Joe.

"Give me another word and—go on, I say, or—"

"You have been drinking, sir. I will not go on. I will leave your company!" exclaimed Gentleman Joe, in a firm voice.

These words excited Manager Brownson in the highest degree, and uttering a volley of oaths, he raised his stick and struck at Gentleman Joe. As he did so, the young man, who had listened to this colloquy with a flushed face, sprung straight at him.

There was no personal collision, however, between Harry and Manager Brownson: a third person interposed. After leaving Mouse in the dressing-room, the Lefthander had looked in the direction of the sounds of angry discussion which had attracted his attention, and a glance was sufficient to explain everything. Manager Brownson had raised his heavy walking-stick above the head of old Gentleman Joe, uttering a volley of oaths as he did so. This made the situation of affairs quite plain, and the Lefthander acted promptly. It took him only a moment to reach the spot. Just as the manager's cane descended, something resembling a falling sledge-hammer passed through the air, and Manager Brownson staggered, reeled backward, and fell at full length on the sawdust. The Lefthander had delivered what he called his "left-hander," and the manager, struck between the eyes, had gone down under it like an ox under the axe of the butcher.

A crowd of the performers, leaving their horses standing, hastened to the spot. The manager was lying on the sawdust, with his face bleeding, and growling out curses.

"I have intended to let him have that for some time," said the Lefthander. "It will be good for him."

As Manager Brownson rose to his feet almost without assistance, it was obvious that his injuries were not serious. He directed a single look at the athlete, in which the venom of all the serpents in his menagerie was concentrated, and then retired without speaking, probably for the purpose of washing the blood from his face.

The Lefthander had stood by quietly, without saying anything more. He now took Gentleman Joe by the arm, and, pushing through the crowd, went to a retired corner, and talked with him for a few moments. They then separated, and the Lefthander returned to the group of circus-men, who had resumed their places by the horses, and shook hands with them one after another. It was evident that he was taking leave of them, and that the men regretted the fact—their faces showed that. The

Lefthander then went back to the dress-ing-room, where he found Mouse lying quietly on her old mattress.

"How's the foot now, Mignon?" he said.

"Well, it's nothing to give a body any anxiety," said Mouse. "A sprain's not much. Was there anybody quarrelling, poppa?"

"A small difficulty—not much. I say, Mignon, would you like to go away with me to-night?"

"Go away—to-night!"

"We are going away—it will be bet-ter. I'm getting in a bad humor with old Brownson, you see. I might do him some harm, and it is best to avoid that. Do you think you would like to go and see if we can't try to find the flowers and the sunshine?"

"Oh yes, poppa! Yes, yes! I can easily walk."

"You'll not have to walk. What's a big fellow like me worth if he can't carry a young one like you? It's like carrying a leaf, or a puff of smoke blown on the wind."

"But Gentleman Joe, and Harry!" Mouse exclaimed, suddenly.

"That will be all right—I've seen about it."

"Will they go, poppa?"

"Yes, they will go. Now, if Clare de Lune was here—you'll have to dress—"

"Here I am, Lefthander!" cried a voice at the opening. "What's this badness of yours?—quarrelling with that dear old darling, Brownson! You ought to be ashamed of yourself. I heard about it!"

Clare de Lune showed a fine set of teeth as she said this, and laughed in a way which indicated enjoyment of the manner in which the old darling had been treated. Behind her appeared the Zephyr, still flushed with her exertions in the ring; and the Lefthander proceeded to inform them that he and Mouse were "going to take French leave." At this announcement exclamations and wailing ensued. The prospect of seeing Mouse and the Lefthander leave them evidently upset these excitable beings; and one could see from the tears in the eyes of Clare de Lune, and her heaving bosom, that she was ready to burst out crying.

"Can't be helped," the Lefthander said, concisely. "Engagement wound up, and receipts signed and delivered. We are going on our travels—get Mouse ready, girls. I'll soon get these circus things off and come back for her."

"Yes, indeed, she shall be ready!—You're not really going?—She can't walk! —The idea of going!"

This combined wail arose from Clare de Lune and the Zephyr at the same mo-ment. The Lefthander paid no attention to it, and went out of the dressing-room. Thereupon the girls promptly set about getting Mouse ready for her expedition. This was not difficult. The child was ac-customed to sleep indifferently at public-houses or under the circus tent with the young women; and a small travelling-satchel containing her few clothes was ly-ing on the sawdust at the head of the old mattress. From this Clare de Lune now drew out a neat child's dress, a pair of black morocco boots, a small felt hat, and other articles of Mouse's wardrobe. She and Zephyr then removed the child's dancing-dress and replaced it with that taken from the travelling-satchel, tying her light curls behind with a ribbon, and the strings of the hat under her chin. They then retreated a few steps and look-ed at her critically as she leaned upon the old mattress. Mouse presented a very attractive appearance thus dressed, and resembled a child just ready to set out after breakfast for school—a resemblance which was assisted by the satchel lying beside her. After contemplating her with admiring eyes for a short while, Clare de Lune and the Zephyr rushed at her, burst into sobs, and covered her face with kisses. In the midst of this the Lefthander reappeared. He had discard-ed his stocking and velvet, and wore a plain brown citizen's suit, in which it was difficult to recognize him. The athlete had vanished, and the citizen had taken his place.

"Come on, Mignon," he said, "we are burning daylight. It's time to go."

Thereupon new wails arose, and new sobs and kisses.

"Don't take Mouse away, Lefthander!"

"How can we do without you and Mouse?"

"Needs must, girls," the Lefthander said; "who knows? we might meet again some of these days. But nobody ever knows about that. You are good girls—"

He went up to them and put his arms around them and kissed them.

"Good-bye!" he said. "You don't wear long frocks, and they're cut low in the neck, but there's something under them that fine ladies don't always have—a heart."

He took the satchel, and then lifted Mouse in his arms. Clare de Lune came and kissed her, crying, and then fixed her eyes on the Lefthander.

"I thought you would not leave *me*," she said in a low voice, sobbing.

"It is hardest of all," said the Lefthander, in the same tone; "but remember what I said. You are a good girl now—be a good girl still. Then some day—that will arrange itself."

He touched the cheek of Clare de Lune with his lips and went out of the tent, leaving the girl covering her face and sobbing.

When Manager Brownson woke on the next morning his head felt exceedingly uncomfortable, but far greater was his mental depression at certain intelligence which was promptly conveyed to him. The Lefthander, Gentleman Joe, Harry, and Mouse had all vanished; at one fell swoop he had been deprived of the pride and glory of the Unrivalled Combination—its athlete, its Mr. Merryman, its tight-rope attraction, and one of its best acrobats. Manager Brownson groaned; not even his morning bitters revived his spirits.

By sunrise the tents were struck, and the Unrivalled Combination of Attractions disappeared from Piedmont for parts unknown.

XVII.

GENERAL LASCELLES.

THE library at Wye was a pleasant spectacle on the evening of the circus. The family had assembled there after tea, and spent the time in pleasant talk, as people were accustomed to do in the cheerful little Piedmont neighborhood. For it was a very friendly and pleasant little neighborhood. Once the families had lived in affluence, and the houses had overflowed with company, and carriages stood at the doors at any and all hours of the day, apparently waiting for somebody to come and ride in them. There was a plenty of hospitality still, but few servants were seen now; and the wolf was at the door much oftener than the coach. Still this did not seem to matter much. The good people in the old country homes accepted their reduced fortunes cheerfully, and kept up their kindly association with each other as before. Certain persons, it is true, called them aristocratic and "exclusive;" which means, "You consider yourself better than I am." This was not just, however. They simply preferred the society of their own people and their blood relations; for which reason they were sneered at and styled ridiculous. They had not been sneered at once, when they rolled in their coaches and had plenty of means. If they had ever been an aristocracy, they were a very poor aristocracy now, and it is well known that little can be looked for from that sort of people. A rich aristocracy ought, of course, to be saluted respectfully—certain advantages may be derived from conciliating it. With a poor aristocracy it is very different. It is an offensive anomaly, and has no right to exist—certainly not to be holding its head up, as if it were somebody. You can laugh at it, and despise it even—no inconvenience will result—since nothing is to be expected from nothing.

The worthy people saw the difference, but did not care much. They had always saluted every one, and saluted still with friendly courtesy, whether anybody returned their salutes or not. The "freedmen" always returned them, with more respect even than when they were slaves. This was singular but true, and was even commented upon. The old regime was gone, but the old ways lingered. The suave old gentlemen and the serene old ladies, with their sweet smiles, were the same people. The very boys and girls were the same boys and girls, and one could see that they respected good morals and good manners. Youth raised them above fortune, and they were as bright as the spring sunshine. You cannot change nature, and the bright days return in defiance of everything. The grass and flowers will bud and bloom in spite of the ruts made by cannon-wheels. And here in the little neighborhood nature had come to heal the old wounds. Her face smiled and her great heart throbbed under the desolation; and old and young smiled too, making the best of things.

In the small neighborhood, here and there, however, were a few families who were comparatively very well off. Among these was the Lascelles family, living at Wye, at the head of which was General Lascelles — a title of courtesy merely, derived from his former rank in the militia. Wye was a very good estate, indeed, and covered more than three thousand acres. In old times several hundreds of Africans, nominally slaves, had enjoyed the proceeds of the estate. These were now free, and enjoyed the franchise, which they were quite willing to dispose of for a glass of whiskey; but the ancient establishment went on in something resembling the old style. The chief difference between the old and new regime was that the freedmen were paid — a fact which did not seem, however, to impress very deeply the gray-haired "uncles," who shook their heads, and made no scruple of intimating that, since no home was to be provided for them in their old age, freedom was a snare and a delusion; but they were free, and must make the best of it. The main thing was to be allowed to remain at Wye, and look to the family for things. So they remained, and looked to the family.

General Lascelles made a good deal of money. It is true, he spent a great deal. He was an excellent manager, and what went in at the spigot nearly made up for what gushed out at the bung. He sowed annually nearly a thousand acres in wheat, and raised vast crops of corn on his low grounds, chiefly for his stock. He was extremely fond of stock-raising. His cattle, sheep, and hogs were his pride, and no one was more successful with them. He gave large prices for fine cattle, but said that it paid. He had a small bull, much less imposing than Paul Potter's, for which he had given fifteen thousand dollars, and congratulated himself upon purchasing him so cheap. He had the purest breeds of Southdowns, Cotswolds, and Leicesters, and carefully crossed them, experimenting how to produce the finest mutton and the heaviest wool. His hogs were as carefully managed. Crossing the big white Chester and the small black Essex he produced a species like the Berkshire, which he said was the best hog of all. For his calves, lambs, and pigs he received very large sums, and stock-breeders came from all parts of the country to purchase them. All this pleased General Lascelles very much, apart from any question of profit; but his supreme passion was for horses. He could begin and tell you one after another the points of a good horse, from his pasterns to his ears, and looked at a thorough-bred as a bridegroom looks at his bride. His young stallion Roland, he said, was the very finest colt ever sired by Revenue, and everybody knew that Revenue had not a drop of blood in his whole body that was not thorough-bred. The general's colts were a little fortune to him, and were in training in all parts of the country. He had nothing to do with the turf now, and rarely attended even his dear Maryland races at Baltimore; but it would never do not to train such horse-flesh. He would not sell his best colts to anybody. He called them

4

his "beauties," and kept them for the pleasure of looking at them. It was his habit, generally after breakfast, to hobble out, leaning on his old body-servant—for the rheumatic gout had attacked him of late years—and have the beauties in glossy coats led up and down for his inspection. This was his pastime, and nearly all the personal part which he took in matters at Wye; for it was a somewhat singular fact that General Lascelles spent the whole day nearly in writing letters or reading the newspapers, and had very little to do with farming operations personally. It is true that he controlled everything to the minutest details; but he did so through an old and reliable manager, who had been with him for thirty years or more. He saw this personage every morning and gave his directions, and the instrument performed what the brain planned and ordered.

This slight sketch of Wye, and the ways of things there, may leave the impression that everything was prosperous and the family wealthy. "Wealthy" is a very general term. Persons who receive and spend a great deal of money are not always wealthy. Large sums flowed into the general's exchequer from his agricultural operations and his stock breeding; but he employed a great deal of labor, and his outlay was in every way very large. To raise grain is expensive. The cost cuts down the profit immensely, especially when a railway is mingled with the equation. There was such a railway with which General Lascelles and his neighbors were mixed up—the B. M. R. R. (Big Monopoly Railroad).

The Big Monopoly Railroad was conducted on strictly business principles. Every one was to look out for himself. You were informed that you were not obliged to send your grain over the Big Monopoly Railroad. You were free to transport it to market in wagons if you preferred. It was true you could not do so without incurring a ruinous expense, and that you were absolutely compelled to do business with the Big Monopoly Railroad. They were ready—but the "way freight" must pay for the "through freight." This was one of the great principles of moral philosophy. There was competition in the matter of the through freight—there was none as to the way freight. It was therefore plain, from the nature of things, that the Virginia grain-grower must be charged an amount which would be a fair division of his profits with the railroad: half to himself for raising the grain—half to the Big Monopoly for transporting it to market. That was just. They were bringing grain thousands of miles from the West at a dead loss; for there was active competition with other lines of railway. There was none in this case. It was way freight, and they transported it at least one hundred miles. If the profits on grain at Wye were ten thousand dollars, was not the Big Monopoly Railroad fairly entitled to one-half that sum?

This was one thing which prevented General Lascelles from becoming rich. There were two other obstacles. He spent a great deal of money, and owed a great deal. His mode of living all his life had been profuse; and then he was generous to everybody. He had endorsed for many friends in difficulties, and had been called upon to pay. This he had not been able to do in many instances, and the debts remained unpaid: people had not pressed him. He was very popular and very well off, which quiets creditors. So the general went on paying heavy interest, and making a great deal of money, and spending it generously; living, in a word, like a fine old Virginia gentleman, who is going to die some day with his affairs probably "tied up into a double bow-knot." It might not prove so bad in the case of the worthy general; but there was the fact. Wye was a fine estate, and the proceeds from the land were large—but the general owed a great deal of money.

He was the head of everything at Wye, although he rarely left his library—the fact has been mentioned. To say this is to say that he was a man of ability. This was conceded by everybody, and, indeed, he had filled a prominent place in public affairs. He had always been influential from his early manhood, and had promptly gone into politics — served a term in the State Legislature — represented his district in Congress — and filled out the unexpired term of a member of the Federal cabinet who had died suddenly. He was then offered the post of minister plenipotentiary to one of the first courts of Europe, but as the Civil War was plainly imminent at the time, he declined it. He returned to Virginia, and the war followed; but General Lascelles took no part in it. This was due, people said, to the scant respect with which he was treated by some of the Confederate officials, from which a bitter quarrel had resulted. Whether this was true or not, the general returned to Wye in great dudgeon. He simply announced, in a curt manner, that there seemed to be no place for a worn-out old dog like himself in the Confederate councils: he would go into the army if he was able to do so; as he was unable, he would stay at home — they could do without him, he supposed. So he stayed at home, and sent every surplus barrel of flour and pound of meat to the army; and fed the soldiers by hundreds at his table; and scowled haughtily at the blue-coats when they intruded on him. When peace came there he was still, with a great torn-down establishment, and scarcely a fence upon the estate; but he and his old manager had set to work and labored with combined energy — and here was Wye, at last, looking a little like its old self.

Personally the general was a rather imposing but a most agreeable old gentleman. He was tall and gray-haired, with a face ruddy from good living; for his appetite was still excellent, and he drank good wine at his dinner, as he had done throughout his life. He dressed in the old fashion, in a broadcloth coat and black satin waistcoat, with a lofty stock and standing shirt-collar. He wore his watch in his pantaloons pocket, and from the chain hung a bunch of seals, one of them a blood-stone, on which was the Lascelles coat of arms. When he walked the seals jingled: this jingle was a part of General Lascelles. As to his walk, it was the walk of the Senator, but he was not in the least stiff—very far from it. He was not only a most courteous person to everybody, high and low, but his manner was easy-going, and put people in a good-humor. He was perfectly unpretending, and the model of a plain old planter. He jested, had his humorous views of things, and the humblest man felt at his ease with him. It is true that he probably had a very good opinion of himself, for we all have our weaknesses—except ourselves. But this trait in the general did not offend people. He was entirely simple and friendly, and shook hands heartily with the humblest person, as he would probably have done with the Emperor of Germany or Russia if he had been presented to him. He was a communicant of the Episcopal Church, and helped a great many poor people. Critical persons laughed at him, but they were obliged to respect him. Here was a genuine man, whatever might be his foibles.

Such was Wye and the head of the establishment. It was quite an old house, built by the general's grandfather or great-grandfather, the Sieur Lascelles, of Touraine, in France—a Huguenot refugee. The old Sieur Lascelles had escaped to England, after privately disposing of his landed estate, and married an English lady, with whom he had afterward come to live in Virginia. Here he had erected this old house, giving it the name of "Wye," his dear wife's English home, and the ancient mansion had duly descended to the present representative of the family. The antique character of everything about it has been noticed. The oaks in the grounds, through whose vistas you had a fine view of a rich country, with rolling fields and belts of woods, with the mountain in the background, had evidently been there a long time, for they were gradually dying at the top. The old post supporting the sun-dial in the circle was leaning from age. The old steps leading up to the portico were nearly worn away. The ponderous folding-doors and iron knob took you back to old times. In fact, many generations of the Lascelles family had lived here, and the place had about it an air of births, christenings, and marriages — it was too cheerful to make you think of funerals. In the time of the present head of the house there had been a large family there. The mansion had overflowed with children, but they had died, or married and gone elsewhere. Besides General Lascelles there were now only three persons in the family — the aged Mrs. Lascelles, her trim little niece, Anna Gray, whom she had adopted some years before, on the death of the young lady's parents, and Mr. Douglas Lascelles, only surviving son, who was approaching middle age, and had spent several years of his life in Europe.

Such was this agreeable old Virginia country-house of Wye at the time of the present narrative. It was not precisely like its old self under the past regime, but as near an approach to it, perhaps, as the last half of the inexorable nineteenth century will tolerate. It tolerates a great many things that it would be better for it to put its heel upon, but the ancient regime is not one of them.

XVIII.

ELLIS GRANTHAM.

IT is time to come to the pleasant group in the library at Wye. This was the habitual resort of the family, for General Lascelles was not at all solitary in his tastes; indeed, just the contrary. He conducted a large political correspondence with his former associates, and read endless newspapers, but this did not interfere with anybody's coming and going. Some persons are unable to write if they are interrupted. The general seemed rather to like it. His children had invaded his sanctum in old days when there were children at Wye—he would have liked to have had them there

still — and he had not repulsed them in the least. Instead of frowning he had smiled, and laid down his pen. Then the little one would be on his knee, and would be encouraged to express his wishes. If these were a piece of candy, the general unlocked a drawer in which he always kept a supply of that child-luxury, and produced some. If it was a toy horse which required a string around his foreleg to pull him by, the general got up and looked for a string. If the young one was suffering from ennui, which afflicts children in common with adults, he relieved it by telling a story, after which the visitor retired, and the ex-statesman resumed his correspondence and discussion of public affairs.

The children had gone away now, and there were no more little pattering feet to produce a pleasant interruption; but General Lascelles made the best of it. He would have everybody understand that the large drawing-room, or "upstairs," was not the proper resort of the family. The library was the point of reunion. When Mrs. Lascelles was not engaged with household affairs, here was a cool refuge in summer and a cosy fireside in winter to bring her knitting and sit by. If Mr. Douglas wished to read and smoke his cigar, why not come and do so in the library? Or Anna Gray might seat herself on the opposite side of his writing-table, and flow on interminably in epistles to her female friends. It was not a bad thing to have her there. He was very fond of her, and if he wished to ejaculate denunciations connected with contemporary politics, it was rather pleasant to have a bright face rise up and a pair of smiling lips say, "Did you speak to me, uncle?"

It was a very good place to hold family reunions in, this snug library at Wye. It was surrounded by oaken bookcases full of volumes, ranging from dignified histories and collections of public documents to the last books of travel, literary essays, biography, and fiction — for the general was an omnivorous reader. The walls were painted in oak, and in the centre of the room was a heavy writing-table of carved walnut with a green cloth top, on which were pens and ink, a portfolio, a bronze lamp at night, and the last magazines and paper-bound novels. As to newspapers, they pervaded the room—chiefly the window-sills. The fireplace was large, and had in it a pair of old brass andirons. On the wooden mantelpiece were vases, behind which letters were thrust. Where the walls were not hidden by bookcases there hung some old portraits, delineating people of the Lascelles family in the times of Louis XIII. and XIV., in huge flowing wigs and lace doublets, or steel hauberks. Everywhere were seen easy-chairs, chiefly of the "Sleepy Hollow" pattern. There was a neutral-tinted carpet on the floor, which remained there throughout the year. Everything in this room seemed to ask you not to look at it, only to be content with it.

On this evening the bronze lamp was lit, and diffused a mild light through its ground-glass shade. The general was leaning back in a large Sleepy Hollow chair, reading his newspaper just brought from the post-office; Mrs. Lascelles was seated near him, knitting the stocking which never seemed to be finished, and Anna Gray was on the opposite side, talking with a young man of about twenty-five, who had made his appearance at Wye just before tea. This was Ellis Grantham, only son of the Rev. Mr. Grantham, the aged rector of the Piedmont parish. He was the picture of health, with black hair, ruddy cheeks, very fine black eyes, and manners full of cheerfulness and modesty. There was a great charm in this unaffected candor and sweetness. It was very plainly unaffected, and expressed his real character. In fact, Ellis Grantham was an exceptional person; he belonged to that very small class of human beings who seem to be born good. With most persons it is a terrible effort to remain pure in the midst of temptation, especially when youth heats the blood, and the mouth is not broken to the bit; but Ellis Grantham really

seemed to have kept himself pure without any difficulty. This was strange but true. It was natural to him to be good. He had avoided what was vicious, and loved what was pure, from native impulse. He had no vices whatever. A cynical person said of him one day that there must be some hidden depravity about him, as every young man had a certain amount of badness in him, and that if it did not come out in one way it would in another. If Ellis Grantham had any, it had never come out up to this time. He had been a good child and a good boy, and was a good young man. The result was that good people loved and respected him, and that certain other persons, finding that they themselves inspired a different sentiment, sneered at him. He was simply "goody," "milk-and-water," a hypocrite, and had, under all his mock-modesty, a very high opinion of himself, they said. One day he heard of these criticisms; one has always kind friends to communicate agreeable things that are said of us. He listened with the greatest surprise, but said nothing. He had a very poor opinion of himself; rated his intellect, indeed, much below its just value, and had never acted a part in all his life; what his critics meant was, therefore, a mystery to him. He never concealed anything, but said plainly what he thought of vice—namely, that it was hateful. As to vicious people, he did not hate *them* in the least; very far from it. He was going to enter the Christian ministry soon, and to begin by hating people would have appeared to him a very bad beginning indeed. He was, in fact, full of sweetness and charity, and had in his heart a broad love for humanity in all its phases, which disregarded dogmas and the worldly view of things. This country youth had discovered one great truth — that the human heart is never wholly debased, and that it is never too late to try to touch it and make it throb. The same heart, he said to himself, beats under the squalid rags of the outcast and the criminal as under the neat black coat and spotless linen of the clergyman and the "highly respectable" person. The difference was in circumstances. Some men took the right path and others the wrong one. His business was with the latter. It was quite as important to move the heart under the rags as that under the broadcloth. If it was the heart of a thief or a prostitute, all the better. One who had walked about preaching in Judea, eighteen hundred years before, had preached from preference to that sort of people.

As Ellis Grantham was going to return to the Theological Seminary on the next morning to finish his last session there, he had come to tell his friends at Wye good-bye. They had had a very long and familiar talk with each other — he and Mrs. Lascelles and Anna Gray—which was very natural, as he was a great favorite with both; and his mother, now dead, had been an intimate friend of Mrs. Lascelles.

"Well, my dear," the lady said, with the sweet smile which made her thin face so attractive, "I am very sorry you are going to leave us; but young men must prepare for their duties in this world, and ought not to forget that youth is the spring-time, when the seed must be sown. If we do not sow we cannot expect to reap. The fall and winter will come after awhile, and seed-time and harvest will be past, and then we will want bread. Old age is like night, and when that comes, you know, none of us can work. I am very glad, indeed, my dear, to see that you are resolved to do your duty."

"I mean to try, Aunt Maria," he said, cheerfully, using the title by which he had always addressed her from his childhood, although there was no relationship.

"I am certain you mean to, Ellis, and I am just as certain that you will be a good and useful man."

"Well, you could not wish me better than that, Aunt Maria; I know you wish me well in everything."

"Indeed I do; it would be strange if I did not," said Mrs. Lascelles, knitting tranquilly. "Your mother was a very dear friend of mine—she was a saint on earth—and I have always loved you as a son. We shall miss you very much, and I don't know what Anna will do without you. You are very much indeed like your mother: she was very dear to me."

The expression of the speaker and her tone of voice went to his heart; a slight color came to his cheek. Indeed, the voice of this lady moved people, touching a secret chord. Here was a thoroughly good woman, whose presence was a blessing to all around her; one with a wise mind intent on common duties, and a warm heart thinking of the happiness of others. An exquisite sweetness and resignation made the thin face beautiful. She had suffered a great deal in her time. Many of her children had died; others had married and left her; but she had not become at all gloomy. She was evidently looking beyond. As to controversial points connected with the relations between man and the Beyond in question, they seemed not to interest her in the least. If you cited Dr. Calvin or Bishop Butler, she said, "My dear, they knew no more than you and I do—the Bible is enough." If you discussed the Mosaic account of creation from a geological point of view, or propounded Mr. Darwin's or Mr. Spencer's theory of development, Mrs. Lascelles smiled tranquilly, and said that there were a great many difficult questions which we could not be expected to understand — but we could understand the Sermon on the Mount. She was always extremely cheerful, and smiled as she came back from the Holy Communion. When you were in trouble she did not sigh and quote texts, as many excellent people do. That was a very good medicine, but perhaps not the right medicine at the time. "You will find after awhile that it is all the same, my dear," she said, with her placid smile; "there is a place where people who are separated from each other see each other again." The thin finger moved slightly, pointing upward when she said this, and you knew what she meant. She herself had looked in that direction for consolation, and had found it. She, therefore, advised you to do so in your turn. Of such human beings it may be said that they are the salt that keeps a sorrowful world from the decomposition of despair.

"Are you going in the morning, my dear?" she now said to Ellis Grantham.

"Yes, after breakfast, Aunt Maria; there will be time enough to catch the train."

"And when will you be back?"

"Before Christmas, I hope, for a few days. I have never spent Christmas away from home, and would not like to miss one with father."

"It would be a very serious matter with him, I am sure, Ellis. You are the apple of his eye, and he would feel very lonely."

"I will certainly be back, if possible."

"And some of these days you will return not to go away any more, I hope. If you could only be your father's assistant, after you are ordained, I am certain it would please every one. Then you could think about being married, and settle down with us."

A slight color came to the already ruddy cheeks of the young man, and he looked for just half an instant toward Anna Gray, who, in mild unison with the employment of Mrs. Lascelles, was crocheting a table-mat. The young lady did not meet this glance, and Ellis Grantham said,

"I am too young to think of that just yet, Aunt Maria, and you know I am not competent to be father's assistant—I hope I will be some day."

Further discussion of the subject was interrupted by the sound of horse's hoofs without. The rider was then heard coming in, and Mr. Lascelles entered the library, politely saluting its occupants. In reply to a question from his mother, he said that he had passed a very pleasant evening, and Miss Juliet seemed pleased with the circus performance—they had, however, come away before it had ended. Having made this communication, Mr. Lascelles said to Ellis Grantham,

"Mrs. Armstrong mentioned a visit which you paid them this afternoon, and I presume you are well acquainted with the family at Trianon."

"Yes, I know them very well," Ellis said.

"Can you tell me who Miss Bassick is?"

"She is a young lady who lives with Mrs. Armstrong."

"In what capacity?"

"I do not know, precisely."

"A relative?"

"I think not."

"Then she is probably a house-keeper or lady's companion," said Mr. Lascelles.

Mrs. Lascelles here interposed, and said,

"Miss Bassick is a young lady who assists Mrs. Armstrong in her house-keeping, and is a confidential friend and companion, I believe. She rarely leaves home, I have heard, and seldom comes to church. You might have seen her there."

Mr. Lascelles did not, apparently, consider it necessary to call attention to the fact that he rarely went to church. He said,

"Well, I was a little struck by Miss Bassick; she is handsome enough, but rather peculiar in her appearance. When we came back from Piedmont Mrs. Armstrong was probably up-stairs, and Miss Bassick opened the door, when I was introduced to her by Miss Juliet, with a simple—'Mr. Lascelles, Miss Bassick.' There certainly was nothing in Miss Juliet's manner — not the least *nuance*, as the French say—to show that Miss Bassick was not her social equal in every particular."

"Juliet is much too well-bred for that," Mrs. Lascelles said. "She is very proud, and has a great deal of feeling, too."

"She is certainly very fine-looking, and Miss Bassick, the companion, is decidedly handsome, too. It strikes me she is rather hiding her light under a bushel. I was particularly struck by her eyes, and don't know whether to call them diabolical or angelic," said Mr. Lascelles, smiling, and lighting a cigar, after politely offering one to Ellis Grantham, who declined it.

"She must be a perfect little devil!" came, in a sort of explosion, from General Lascelles. Every head turned quickly, but it was evident that this exclamation had nothing whatever to do with Miss Bassick. The ex-statesman, during the conversation between Mrs. Lascelles and Ellis Grantham, had been absorbed in his newspaper. In this occupation the entrance of Mr. Douglas Lascelles had only interrupted him for a moment. He had been reading the Washington letter in his New York journal, from which it appeared that those who differed with the political opinions of the writer were all rogues, and wretches of the deepest dye; and, as the general was personally acquainted with some of the individuals thus characterized, he acknowledged that there was a grain of truth in the correspondent's strictures. He had then passed to another paragraph, in which the letter-writer drew the likeness of a certain female lobbyist then haunting Washington. The picture was bit in with acid, and was not unlike the portrait of Mr. Thackeray's Becky Sharpe, except as to personal appearance — the fair lobbyist being much handsomer. Her "tricks and her manners" were drawn with much gusto, and an amusing story was told of her attempt to black-mail a prominent statesman. Hence the appreciative exclamation of General Lascelles—"She must be a perfect little devil!"

Mr. Lascelles smiled with an air of enjoyment.

"Do you mean Miss Bassick, sir?" he said.

"Miss Bassick?" the general said, raising his head with a bewildered air.

"You say she is a little devil."

"Miss Bassick a devil? I really do not know in the least what you mean. Who is Miss Bassick?"

Mr. Lascelles explained, and much amusement was caused by the general's *apropos* or *malapropos* interjection.

"I am sure I did not mean to express any opinion of Mrs. Armstrong's friend, Miss Bassick," he said, laughing with the rest. "I was reading an account of a person in Washington—but, really, I will not introduce the ladies to such bad company. And I owe you an apology, my dear Ellis, for my absorption in this pestiferous journal. I fear reading the newspapers is becoming a mania with me. Are you really going to-morrow, my boy? I am sincerely sorry to hear that you are going to leave us."

And then the conversation proceeded until Ellis Grantham rose and bade the family good-bye. Mrs. Lascelles drew him to her and kissed him affectionately, and then he shook hands with the two gentlemen, and lastly with Anna Gray. As he went out of the room she rose quietly—a movement which Mr. Douglas Lascelles noted out of the corners of his eyes, after a somewhat sarcastic fashion— and followed him into the hall. She and Ellis Grantham conversed there together for a few moments in low tones, and the young lady went with him to the door. Then the front-door closed, and Anna Gray came back with a slight color in her cheeks and moist eyes.

"Why, my dear, you are crying," said Mrs. Lascelles.

"I am sorry Ellis is going, aunty," Anna Gray replied, in a low voice. She then rose quietly and went up-stairs.

XIX.

THE REVEREND MR. GRANTHAM.

In a room on the right of the front-door of a small house, in the suburbs of Piedmont, a man was seated at a table on this same night writing.

It was a very pleasant-looking little establishment within and without. The yard was covered with greensward, and some zinnias, petunias, chrysanthemums, and other flowers of autumn, were still in bloom. A honeysuckle was trained upon one of the pillars of the small porch, and a madeira-vine upon that opposite. Both were in flower, and you thus entered under a fragrant arch. A neat railing divided the house from the street, and with its lilacs and overshadowing trees it was nearly embowered in verdure.

The room mentioned was evidently a study. The walls were nearly covered with book-shelves containing leather-bound volumes, some of them ponderous folios. In one corner was an old mahogany secretary, with drawers opened by brass handles. Opposite the single window was a hard and narrow lounge, which looked very uncomfortable. The table which stood in the centre was covered with books and papers; and at this table sat the student—a man past sixty, with gray hair, and clad in black, with a white neck-cloth. His face was one of strong character, but had the mild expression peculiar to those who pass their lives in a round of simple duties, out of the great whirlpool of the world. Such, in fact, had been the life of Mr. Grantham, rector of the Piedmont parish.

He was an altogether excellent person, and had officiated at Piedmont for more than thirty years. He had frequently received calls elsewhere, for he was a very good preacher and one of the ablest theologians of his diocese, but he had declined them all. He would not sever his connection with the parish of his affections. The bait of a larger salary and "a more extended sphere of usefulness" had not moved him. As to the salary, he did not want it, he said, as he had daily bread—which was more than half the world, and many better people than himself, were certain of when they got up in the morning; and in regard to the more extended sphere of usefulness, there was a sufficient sphere for anybody in a parish with a dozen families. If he could look after that number of people, and keep them from stumbling, he would be satisfied. So Mr. Grantham had declined with friendly acknowledgments all the calls. His work was here. He had gone on marrying and christening and burying the people of his little parish year after year, and doing his best to console the heavy-hearted in their trouble. He was a very good preacher indeed—earnest and persuasive rather than given to chill logic, and habitually avoiding the discussion of eternal torment as a means of touching the heart. His theology began and ended, apparently, with the parable of the Prodigal Son. His wife had died some years before, but he was very calm and cheerful. He had bent for a moment, but risen upright again like a tree with a sound heart. He preached as usual on the Sunday succeeding her death. It is true that he had fainted as he entered his house, on returning from church, but nobody knew about that.

Mr. Grantham was a Low-Churchman. Almost all Virginia Episcopalians are. Sometimes high-church friends from other dioceses said to him, "You people in Virginia are not Episcopalians; why not call yourselves Methodists, or by any name that suits you, at once?" When such things were said to Mr. Grantham, he smiled and shook his head. His reply was mild but incisive: "It was better to be *low-church* than *on the way to Rome*," he said. "Rome was seductive—she knew human nature, and how to appeal to it. He would like to be a Romanist himself, if he could be, conscientiously — it was a tempting theory that we could be washed clean from sin by confessing and doing penance. That was alluring—it was better to be on our guard. The only safe rule to follow was, 'Touch not, taste not, handle not.' If you touched it you would probably taste it, and then handle it; and if you handled it, you would be apt to end by fondling it, which would be unfortunate—and he was afraid many good people were beginning to fondle it. As to the charge that the Virginia Church was low-church, that was true, but it was a very good Episcopal Church for all that. Its bishops claimed no 'mysterious sanctity' for themselves — there were Articles XXIII. and XXV. But they were apostolic, if not Romanist, and were all the better for it. In fact, Rome was schismatical, and heresy and schism were denounced in the prayer-book. In Virginia, however, people did not lean on ordinances but on the Word; they were evangelical, and not sectarian. It did not matter very much what Church you belonged to or what dress you wore. The important question was whether you were travelling the right road; if you were, by God's help you would arrive."

This good man went a step further: he had a lurking sympathy even with the "Reformed Episcopal" movement, though he did not approve of it. Under all the circumstances it was unnecessary. The word "regenerated," and other expressions in the prayer-book, ought not to hurt anybody's conscience: *regenerated* meant "grafted into the Church"—see Article XXVII. When you grafted on a young scion you did not change its nature, but you placed it where the new life could course through it. And then there was the point of linguistics. If you altered *regenerated*, you would have to go on and alter a great many things. It was unnecessary to reform the whole English language. Certain terms had changed their meanings. There was "the Lord *preventing* us;" which, nevertheless, was not a prayer to be hindered in our good deeds. The letter killed; it was the spirit that gave life.

A warm personal friendship for Bishop Cummins, the leader of the Reformed Episcopal movement, may have had its influence upon Mr. Grantham. It was difficult to believe that any views which *he* espoused were unfounded. Bishop Cummins, he often said, was "a heavenly man. His appeals were addressed too much to the mere feelings, perhaps. He was not wanting in strength, for no man had a clearer or sounder intellect; and he broke down the sceptical objections of the infidels who came to hear him by sheer force of logic—but then he did not keep to that. He appealed too passionately to the emotions, which should not be looked to so exclusively. This apart, Bishop Cummins was a man of the apostolic type, with no thought but his work, and resolved to wear out his life in it. He was also a man of kindling enthusiasm, and devoted to what was pure and of good report. He had the utmost

sweetness of temper. Children came to him unconsciously. His heart was exceedingly soft, and his hand open to distress. He liked humble people, and smiled sweetly upon them; but did not smile so readily at young ladies and others who made a clerical 'lion' of him, and sent him delicacies, and burnt incense before him. He had no time or desire to be made a celebrity of, and did not want the delicacies—there were the poor. He lived his life as seeing the end." This was what Mr. Grantham was accused to say of Bishop Cummins. One day he read a few words with black lines around them in a newspaper; he dropped the paper, and said aloud,

"Take him for all in all, we shall not look upon his like again."

On this evening Mr. Grantham had come into his study after tea to reflect and work. As Ellis had gone to call on his friends before his departure for the Seminary, which would take place on the next morning, the good man felt very lonely and depressed. Since the death of his wife, all his love for her had concentrated itself upon his son. The thought that he was going away was very sorrowful indeed. Life was uncertain, and he himself was growing old now—might not this be their last parting? He leaned his forehead on his hands, and his hands on the table. The light of the two candles, in old-fashioned candlesticks, fell upon his gray hair, and a deep sigh followed—it was very sad, indeed, to think of parting with his beloved Ellis.

After awhile the forehead rose, and Mr. Grantham got up and walked up and down the floor. He was thinking of some parish affairs demanding his attention on the next day. He could not neglect these. There was the poor family near the Ridge, who were terribly in want of clothing; and as he had appealed to some of his lady parishioners, he hoped to be able to supply them before the cold weather set in. There were also some orphans in a wretched cabin which he had visited. It had made his heart bleed to see how destitute they were. Something must be done for them. Whatever his private troubles or labors were he could not neglect "his poor"—a name he called them by: that indicated his personal concern with them. Other people had their own, no doubt. These were his.

Having reflected maturely upon the wants of his poor, and resolved what he would do at once to relieve them, he sat down, and opening an old portfolio began to write. He was evidently composing a discourse, or perhaps a treatise, as from time to time he rose, consulted a volume on the shelves, laid it open on the table before him and made quotations, and otherwise demeaned himself as a historical or polemical writer. In fact, the composition on which the good man was engaged was very polemical indeed. It was his "History of Ritualism," upon which he had been at work for many years—a crushing and vindictive *exposé* of the Tractarian movement in the Anglican Church, with trenchant and by no means complimentary references to its influence on the misguided clergy in certain portions of the United States of America. To this congenial occupation the mild Mr. Grantham applied himself with ardor. His face glowed — some reverend divine was probably receiving a severe thrust. All at once Ellis came in; then there was an end of further work on the "History of Ritualism," since it is impossible to compose when one is looking at another person, and can scarcely see the person through tears.

The low conversation between father and son continued until nearly eleven, when Mr. Grantham said that it was time for the young man to go to bed. What they said to each other was personal to themselves and ought not to be repeated; for the words and looks of certain human beings on certain occasions have a species of sanctity about them. Are there any more sacred than those of a father and son who are going to part from each other?

"Yes, you must go now; young people require rest," Mr. Grantham said; "it is very late for children to be up."

He smiled, but it was a very sorrowful smile.

"You will always be a child to me, Ellis. It seems only yesterday that your mother held you up in her arms for me to kiss!"

He placed his arms around the young man's neck and said, in a faltering voice, "Good - night, my boy!" kissing him as he spoke. Tears were in the eyes of both. Without speaking, Ellis Grantham went to his chamber; his voice had quite failed him.

XX.

MR. GRANTHAM'S GUESTS.

MR. GRANTHAM did not feel in the least like working any more, and resolved that he would not do so. He went back to his seat, however—from habit, no doubt —and, sitting down, assumed the same depressed attitude, his forehead resting upon his hands, and his hands on the table, or rather on the page he had been writing in the "History of Ritualism."

He remained immovable in this attitude for some time. Then he raised his head and listened; he had heard a knock at the front-door of the house.

"Some one needs me who is in greater trouble, perhaps, than myself," he said, in a low voice.

He took one of the candles from the table, and going to the front-door opened it. A man with a heavy black beard, holding a child in his arms, was standing in the moonlight on the little porch; and as the man at first looked at him without speaking, the incident was a little startling. Mr. Grantham did not appear, however, to regard it in that light, and said mildly,

"Come in, friend: can I be of any service to you?"

"You are the priest of this village?" said the man.

"I am a pastor, my friend—though priest is a very good word."

"I heard you never turned away anybody in distress."

"I have never done so; I trust I never shall."

"I am in distress. My child here is sick; her foot is sprained, and her arm hurt."

"Come in, friend."

"I am a common man—a circus-actor—and have my reasons for not going to the tavern to-night. Will you lodge us?"

"Yes."

"You know nothing about me. I may be a tramp or a thief. You are not afraid?"

Mr. Grantham placed the candle on a chair in the passage, and took Mouse in his arms.

"No, I am not afraid," he said.

Worn out by the many incidents of the evening and night, Mouse had fallen into a doze in the Lefthander's arms, and Mr. Grantham took her into his own so gently that she did not wake.

"If you will take the candle," he said, "I will show you your room."

He then went slowly up the narrow staircase, followed by the Lefthander, and opened the door of a chamber over the study, containing a bed, a table, an old sofa, and a few chairs. He laid the child upon the bed, drawing the counterpane over her, and as he had carried her with precaution she did not wake up.

Mr. Grantham stood looking at her for a moment, and admiring her delicate features.

"What a little snow-drop!" he said; for he was fond of flowers, and often used them as illustrations. He added,

"It is getting chill, and there is no fire here. Your child ought not to suffer for want of it."

He looked round him and saw some light wood in one corner, which had probably been there for a long time. With this and an old newspaper he kindled a cheerful fire, and then rose with a gratified expression as the blaze began to lick the sticks. The Lefthander was standing in the middle of the room, looking at him from under his straight black eyebrows. He had placed the candle on the table, and one of his large hands rested beside it.

"I have money," he said. "I will pay."

As he spoke he took a roll of bank-notes and some gold from his pocket. Mr. Grantham put them aside gently.

"Are you hungry?" he said; "you or your child? You see I come to the point. What we want most of all, sometimes, in this world, is food and sleep."

"I am not at all hungry, or Mignon—that is her name," said the Lefthander. "I see that what I heard about you was true. I was afraid you would turn us away."

"I do not turn away people, friend. I have a son. Perhaps he may want a shelter some of these days—I should not like to have him turned away."

Mr. Grantham went to Mouse and smoothed the hair gently back from her forehead, looking at her with a smile.

"Poor little one!" he said; "it is sad to think she should want a shelter." He added to the Lefthander, "If you should require anything during the night, friend, you will find me in the room under this. Wake me without any ceremony. There is no bolt on the door."

"You are not afraid of my robbing you?" repeated the Lefthander.

Mr. Grantham shook his head.

"There is no danger of that," he said. "Men who look at their children as you look at your little girl never rob people."

He went out and closed the door behind him. As he passed the room opposite he stopped, hesitated, and then turned the knob softly and went in. This was Ellis's chamber, and he was sound asleep. As the moon was shining brightly, his father could see him very plainly, and bending over his narrow bed he kissed him on his forehead.

"How can I live without him!" he said.

After gazing at the sleeper for some moments in silence, he sighed and went out of the room, down-stairs to his study. Here he looked round him, and seemed to be searching for something, which seemed to be an old buffalo-robe, used in his light carry-all in winter; it was lying in a corner, and Mr. Grantham brought it and spread it upon the narrow and uncomfortable lounge opposite the window. He then put out his remaining candle, and stretched himself upon the hard lounge, drawing the buffalo-robe around him. It was not a very pleasant couch, but then Ellis's bed was too narrow for two persons. As to his own chamber, his guests had that.

People do not sleep late in the morning in beds as hard as the lounge in Mr. Grantham's study. He woke a little after daylight, and, remembering the incident of the preceding night, listened to discover whether his guests were yet stirring in the chamber above. The whole house was perfectly still, and as Mr. Grantham did not wish to wake any one sooner than they desired, he lay wrapped in his buffalo-robe, engaged in reflection. After awhile the first rays of sunrise came in through the window, and the old servant of the household was heard going up-stairs. Mr. Grantham then reflected that his guests would be aroused, in any case, so he rose and went up the staircase, to ask if they needed anything. There was no reply to his knock, and he knocked again. Still no answer came, and he quietly opened the door.

The room was empty.

Mr. Grantham looked round him with an air of great surprise. What had become of the wayfarers? It was a proof of this good man's confidence in human nature, that it never even occurred to him that perhaps the rough-looking man with the singular eyebrows had gone off in this cautious manner, in order to take something which did not belong to him away with him. Having made his estimate of the man by the look bestowed upon his child, he held to it—this was not a thief. But what had induced him to go off during the night?

He scanned the appearance of things. The bed had been slept in, but not by the man, who had probably spent the night on the old sofa. The impression of the child's head was still on the pillow. All at once he saw a slip of paper lying on the table by an old inkstand and pen which generally stood on the mantelpiece. The paper was folded, and as Mr. Grantham took it up a gold eagle dropped upon the floor. The paper contained the following words, in the handwriting of a man apparently not accustomed to penmanship, but not illiterate:

"You took a poor man and his child into your house without asking any questions. You would not take money for yourself, but you will take this gold piece for some poor people who may want it."

Mr. Grantham read this paper with a bright smile upon his face, and picked up the gold piece and put it in his pocket. But why did his guest go away so quietly? He looked round him—there was nothing to throw light upon the subject. He was just on the point of leaving the room when something on the bed attracted his attention. It was a dark object, half covered by the counterpane, which seemed to have been accidentally thrown over it. He drew it out, and found that it was a travelling-satchel of black leather, which the wayfarers had probably overlooked in the haste of their departure.

Mr. Grantham stood for some minutes looking at the satchel, which was about the size of an ordinary carpet-bag. Should he see what it contained? It would be easy to do so. The satchel was unlocked—the key had been lost, or its small mistress might have it in her pocket: there would be no trouble, therefore; but, for all that, Mr. Grantham hesitated. He was a conscientious man, and did not like the idea of opening people's satchels. He could see through the opening that the bag contained some articles belonging to a child's wardrobe, and thought that he felt a book and a package of papers at the bottom; but he had no right to look at people's papers. He would keep the satchel; no doubt the owner of it would call and ask for it; if he did not, it might be defensible to examine its contents and endeavor to ascertain the ownership, with a view to its restitution. There would be time enough for that.

As he heard Ellis come out of his room at this moment, he put the satchel under his arm and went down-stairs.

XXI.

BRANTZ ELLIOT.

ONE morning Brantz Elliot came out of the front-door of the house in the mountain with a fishing-rod on his shoulder; and the dogs, who were his intimate friends by this time, greeted him with joy, leaping and frisking around him.

It was a clear crisp day of late September, and the rich sunshine bathed the foliage of the valley and the slopes burning away under the fiery finger of autumn. You could see a long way through the transparent atmosphere, but over the far headlands hung a dreamy smoke, rounding and idealizing them. October was near, and October in Virginia is the month for dreams, if you fancy wandering into the beautiful woodlands to indulge them.

Brantz Elliot had not left Daddy Welles's at the end of three days—in fact, more than three weeks had passed since his arrival. This had resulted from two circumstances. He had found the life of the mountains precisely to his taste, and his presence seemed to be a satisfaction to everybody. Nothing further had been said by the master of the mansion implying hesitation as to lodging the young sportsman; on the contrary, he was treated as a permanent guest. Daddy Welles evidently wished to have him remain as much as he himself desired to do so. They were huntsmen, and each recognized a comrade.

Hunting was the master-passion of Brantz Elliot. He had not wanted opportunities to substitute other pursuits for it. He was the only son of a merchant of New York, and as Elliot, Sr., was wealthy, the young fellow had pursued the career of youths with rich fathers who are devoted to them. He had gone to college and afterward to Europe, to think what he would do in the world, when the news reached him that his father had suddenly died. An uncle had taken charge of the estate, however, and managed it for him, and the young fellow remained in Europe, endeavoring to assuage his grief by travel: it was a distraction, but gave him little pleasure, and nothing afforded him much satisfaction but open-air sports. He did not wish to be a lawyer, or a politician, or a merchant; and looked forward with no pleasure to returning to his home on the Fifth Avenue, where an aunt still kept up the establishment for him.

He was essentially a rustic in his tastes, and cities bored him. Neither Paris nor Rome aroused any enthusiasm in him. While strolling along the boulevards, looking at the crowd and the brilliant equipages, he was generally thinking whether he could not get up a hunt somewhere in the country, and have woods and water and peasants around him, instead of shops with plate-glass windows, and *flâneurs* with waxed mustaches. If the peasants were poachers it would be all the better; but anything was better than kid gloves and the opera. He had hunted a good deal in Scotland and the Alps, and liked the Mer de Glace and the lakes. The Bernese Oberland was an attraction. He spent some weeks in the Tyrol; then he came back at last to New York, to reflect more maturely as to what he would do in life.

He could not decide. It was really very sad indeed, but New York, his native place, bored him just as much as Paris and Rome. It was a terrible struggle to get through his day. The club helped him a little—there were a great many good fellows there, laboriously engaged in the same employment of killing time. They were horse-men for the most part, and spoke of organizing an amateur coaching-club, to drive four-in-hand, and run regularly a day's stage from the city.

The coaches were to be strictly English—also the costumes, the equipments, above all, the demeanor and pronunciation of the gentlemen coachmen. "Strictly English" was to be the motto of the club, and everybody was to be a coachman of the strictest sect as to apparel, and passengers were to be "booked" and called for, and there was a horn that was to be blown, and the whole affair was to be a lark of the first magnitude, indulged in by the very best fellows of the club, in a fashion strictly English. As the details were not yet arranged, however, Mr. Brantz Elliot, who was fond of horses, put on the drab costume of a groom, and directing his real groom to ride behind him, drove his drag in the Central Park—the real groom looking on with folded arms to see that it was properly done. Even this, however, was slow. After all, he was "in town," and to be in town was his abomination. Cities were all sameness in his eyes. He was accustomed to express his views with great frankness to his intimates. Men who lived in crowds, he said, were all rubbed down to a fearful uniformity; there was no character about them. You could pick out any one hundred city men, and lay one of them down on pasteboard and cut out his figure, and it would fit the other ninety-nine. They all wore the same clothes and hats, and in the same way. They all walked with their arms at exactly the same angle. They all took off their hats alike; said "really!" suppressing the r, in the same tone; and were painfully like each other. What he wanted was people with angles and individuality. If they were rough, it did not matter much. After saying this, he generally yawned and lit a cigar.

In fact, what has been called "the wild side" was strongly developed in Brantz Elliot. Not that he was a lawless or reckless person, unobservant or careless of the proprieties of life, or at all wanting in culture; on the contrary, he was a very exemplary young man in his daily life. He had never soiled himself with the vices which lie in wait to entrap youth, when the possessor of this dangerous luxury is absent from home and exempt from family restraints, with plenty of money in his pocket. He had no taste for ignoble indulgence, and was very far from being deficient in literary culture. He had improved his time at college, and read French and German quite fluently; but, in spite of all, this innate "wildness" predominated. He liked hunting, fishing, and rambling in the woods a great deal better than reading or "good society." His tastes were robust. He preferred the open air to the atmosphere of the study. He would have been delighted with the company of Cooper's Leatherstocking, and the acme of enjoyment to him would have been to hunt lions in Africa. Not finding these luxuries within his reach, he looked round for substitutes, and had enjoyed an expedition to the Adirondacks. Afterward, hearing from a friend who had visited the White Sulphur Springs in Virginia that the mountains of the region were full of deer and old hunters, he had determined to try his fortune in that direction.

He had, accordingly, visited the Virginia springs in the summer of this year, and had made some satisfactory forays into the neighboring wilds. On his way back to New York now, he had taken the fancy to stop for a few days and pursue his favorite amusement under the auspices of Daddy Welles, who seemed to be a little of everything—hunter, agriculturist, principal or agent in some mysterious business, or what not; and thus it was that Mr. Brantz Elliot had become an inmate of and lingered day after day in the mountain house in the secluded little valley, cut off from the rest of the world, and known by the eccentric name of "Bohemia." This, he said to himself, was really a coincidence. He was something of a Bohemian himself—for there were Bohemians of the woods as well as Bohemians of the purlieus of cities. It was, therefore, perfectly appropriate that this young Bohemian of the fields and forests should set up his rest in the small vale of "Bohemia." He had not regretted doing so for a moment. There was no doubt at all about the fact that he was enjoying himself. There were a plenty of pheasants, wild turkeys, and deer, too, in the mountains; and the small stream traversing the narrow valley afforded excellent fishing. Now, to ramble along the grassy banks of a watercourse, fishing-rod in hand, or go out before sunrise and "drop a buck" at eighty yards, was to this young gentleman the height of human felicity. He had dropped several, and shot countless pheasants and turkeys. He could easily have paid for his board and lodgings with the game he had killed. When he was not hunting or fishing he was smoking a pipe, and reading the last magazines sent him, or talking with Daddy Welles on topics mutually congenial to their tastes.

XXII.

DADDY WELLES SURPRISED.

This serene old Daddy Welles was a great puzzle to Brantz Elliot. He was made up of piquant contrasts, and afforded a study in human nature. He was hospitable and liberal to his household, but evidently loved money. His guest had a supply of gold; and, when he paid Daddy Welles, the mountaineer's face indicated unmistakable pleasure at sight of the glittering coin. But he was not close in his dealings. He simply loved the sight of money, apparently. Then, for other contrasts: the guileless smile of the Daddy plainly concealed an acute and observant mind. He was uneducated in books, obviously—it was doubtful, even, if he could write his name—but, as obviously, he was very well educated in the book of human nature. He uttered observations which were apothegms, and inclined now and then to the epigrammatic. The oil, he said, that made a woman's tongue run glib was scandal; and the axle-grease that carried a man downhill very fast was whiskey. He called lawyers "the l'yers;" and when one day Nelly was paring some

apples to make apple-butter, he said, "You're not looking well, Nelly; go and take a walk and let the apples alone—pity old mother Eve hadn't." For Daddy Welles had his quiet humor.

What particularly struck Brantz Elliot, however, was the fact that something mysterious was going on around him; and that of this something Daddy Welles was evidently the mainspring and master-spirit. He had frequently recalled the words of the stage-driver that "queer stories" were told about his host. There really seemed to be some ground for the stories in question, whatever they might be. At certain times Daddy Welles would disappear, and remain absent for two or three days. When the good man returned on his old raw-boned steed, he would smile in his guileless way, and casually let fall the observation that business took him away oftener than he liked; but as to the precise character of the business in question, he apparently considered it unnecessary to enter into any explanation. Then certain roughly-clad persons frequently called to see Daddy Welles, and they held confidential interviews—looking round them now and then, apparently from a desire to satisfy themselves that they were not overheard. Once they were overheard. Brantz Elliot had gone out to hunt one morning, but, finding no game, had returned, and gone into the sitting-room, where he leaned back in one of the split-bottomed chairs to look at the engravings in a new magazine. While thus engaged, he had heard voices, and observed Daddy Welles pass by the house toward the rear in company with a visitor. This visitor was a scarecrow figure in a ragged felt hat, with a sarcastic smile on his tobacco-stained lips.

"I don't altogether like it, Daddy," said the owner of the ragged hat, in a low tone.

"No danger, no danger, Barney," Daddy Welles replied.

"Well, if you say so, it's so, Daddy," the visitor responded; "but strangers are mighty onsartain, and it's jest as well to be on the lookout. I wouldn't like to have to empty my double-barrel at anybody in the mounting."

Brantz Elliot could not see the face of the speaker, as he was walking away from him, but the tone in which he spoke seemed to indicate that a grin accompanied his words. Thence food for thought. The stranger who was mighty uncertain was apparently himself, and he it was who might have a double-barrelled gun emptied at him in the mountain. All this was more interesting than agreeable. What did it mean? After asking himself that question, without receiving a reply, he determined to propound it to Daddy Welles himself. One morning, therefore, he joined his host in the vicinity of the cow-shelter, and said, in his straightforward way,

"What's going on here, Daddy Welles?"

A sweet smile illumined the countenance of Daddy Welles, and he said, innocently,

"Goin' on, friend?"

"Yes," said Elliot; "there's no doubt of the fact that something *is* going on."

"Why, what makes you think so?"

"A friend of yours came to see you yesterday morning, didn't he?"

"Yistiddy mornin'? Oh yes;—you mean Barney Jones."

"Well, what were you and Barney Jones whispering about, like two conspirators? I was in the house and heard you, as you went by."

"Whisperin'? Me and Barney!" said the Daddy, with surprise. "Oh no; he was only talkin' about things in general, as neighbors will, you know, when they drop in to chat."

"So you talk about *strangers*, and their being *onsartain*, do you, Daddy Welles?— and of *emptying double-barrels at 'em in the mountain?*"

"Well, I do declare!" Daddy Welles said, with guileless smiles; "did anybody say that?"

"Yes, they did—your friend Barney said it."

"Well, well! but that Barney always *was* given to foolish ways of talkin'.

You see there's a catamount was met in the mounting last week—not a common wild-cat, but a regular painter—the first seen in these parts for a long time. He's a stranger hereabouts; and if you got a good look at one, you'd think a fight with him was mighty onsartain, indeed, unless you got a chance to empty both barrels at him before he got to you!"

"Come now, Daddy; you know your friend Barney Jones didn't mean a catamount.—Last week? was there one seen? I mean to have a pull at him!"

"We'll go after him, if you say so, friend."

The conversation was apparently passing to other topics, which did not seem to displease the Daddy.

"Agreed!—but about Barney Jones," persisted Elliot; "what were you and he talking about? It's none of my business, but—"

"Talkin' about? Oh yes; he did mention he had killed two wolves. They're mighty skeerce now, and nothin' hardly brings 'em but a dead horse."

Brantz Elliot fell into the trap. The connection between wolves and a dead horse evidently excited his curiosity in the highest degree. Forgetting all else, he said,

"A dead horse! What has a dead horse to do with wolf-hunting, Daddy Welles?"

"Law bless you!" the Daddy said, with an air of innocent surprise, "don't you know? Well, that shows you are city-raised, friend, much as you do know about huntin'. That's the way we hunt wolves. Only last year we got four that way. You ought to 'a been here."

"Tell me about it!" said Brantz Elliot, with a hunter's ardor.

"Well, you see, a wolf's a mighty cunnin' varmint, and hides all day, and only comes out at night. He won't go in a bear-trap. He jest smells around it, and shakes his head and goes away. In the mornin' he ain't in the trap, and there's your twenty dollars gone!"

Elliot, intent on thoughts of wolves, forgot all about Barney Jones.

5

"Twenty dollars!" he said.

"Didn't you know about that? The law pays twenty dollars for a wolf's hide and sculp—they kill all the sheep and calves they can find, and are worth it. Well, we set a dead horse last year, and made nigh on to a hundred dollars by him."

"A dead horse!" repeated Elliot, now highly interested; "tell me all about it, Daddy."

"Well, this is the way we did it: You see, snow was on the ground, and every mornin' you could see the wolf-tracks around the sheep-pens; and if a cow and calf strayed away in the mounting, the cow came back but the calf was missin'. This went on some time, and at last it was onsupportable. So me and some neighbors bought an old horse for five dollars, and took him up in the mounting and cut his throat."

"What on earth was that for?"

"Well, you see he was the trap. When he was done kickin', we slit him open from his forelegs along his belly and put strychnine in him, and went back home."

"Strychnine! Oh yes; I begin to understand."

"That's the way we do when dogs worry our sheep, and the owners won't keep 'em at home, spite of a civil request. We put strychnine in a dead sheep, and on the next day there's a pile o' dead dogs by that sheep."

Here Daddy Welles laughed cheerfully.

"And your horse-trap answered?"

"You ought 'a been in the mounting when we went up next mornin'! There was four big wolves, and a wild-cat, and crows, and hawks, no end of 'em, all lay-in' around dead in the snow nearabouts! They were the very biggest wolves you ever laid your eyes on, and we got eighty dollars for the hides and sculps."

"Well," said Elliot, "that's a new kind of trap, Daddy Welles. But you have not told me about those people going and coming—Barney Jones and the rest."

"Goin' and comin'! Why you must 'a deceived yourself, friend."

Elliot shook his head.

"There is something going on, Daddy! But then it's no business of mine, and I don't care. You are not counterfeiters, are you? If you are, it's nothing to me; but I am pretty certain you are not. If you are, go ahead; I'm not an officer of the United States Mint. I'm a hunter, and I have come here to drop a buck when I can, and see the sun come in at my window and tell me good-morning. I don't belong to the detective police, and I've got nothing to do with it. Things in this direction suit me exactly, and I mean to stay at least a week longer. The men of cities delight me not, nor the women either—see Shakspeare. All I ask is that Broadway will attend to its own business and let me attend to mine."

"Well, that's right, friend," said Daddy Welles, cheerfully. "I can't say I've got much notion of towns and sech like my-self. I'm mostly country-raised in my ways."

Which Brantz Elliot, looking at his gaunt old host in his homespun, regarded as a just statement.

"So am I," he said. "Shall we have a tramp, to-day?"

"I'm rather afeerd I can't go with you this mornin', friend," the Daddy respond-ed. "I've got to ride over to Piedmont to see the land-sharks on some business. That's what we call the l'yers."

"The lawyers, eh?"

"The same. The court people grind us poor folks every chance they git. But I s'pose they have to live, like the rest of us," added the Daddy, philosophically.

He then mounted his raw-boned old charger and set out for Piedmont, where he really did seem to have important busi-ness—either there or elsewhere—for he did not return until the evening of the next day. Mr. Barney Jones, on a horse as much of a scarecrow as himself, had parted with him at the foot of the path, and ridden on to his own home farther up the valley.

———

XXIII.

NELLY.

"NELLY!" said Mr. Brantz Elliot, on this morning, patting the head of one of the dogs who sprung up to be caressed. He turned his head and looked into the house.

"Sir?" said a voice.

"There it is again, — eternally *sir!*" said the young man, laughing. "You will never break yourself of that stiff monosyllable, Nelly!"

Nelly had come out to the door; she was smiling a little, and blushing a good deal. In her linsey dress, secured around her slender waist by the cheap black belt, and her hair falling behind, tied with a ribbon, she looked attractive; and the smile and blush did not interfere with the general impression which she produced.

"I say, you will not drop that formal 'sir,' in spite of all I can say," Elliot added. "Now I like to be at my ease with people, and have them at their ease with me."

"Why, what am I to say—sir?" Nelly replied.

"No, you are not to say *sir*, unless it is necessary to your personal comfort or convenience, in which case I have no more to say. I know I am an ancient and dignified sort of person, and ought to be treated with respect by a child like you; but then it's a bore, Nelly, and, if it goes on, I've made up my mind what I will do. I will address you as *Miss Welles*."

Nelly laughed at this: it was a brief, shy laugh, but not a rustic giggle; very far from it. There really was very little that was really "rustic" about Nelly, and Brantz Elliot had not heard her "giggle" once since they had been acquainted.

"I meant to ask you if you would go fishing with me," he said. "It's a great bore to spend a whole morning by one's self—there's nobody to say anything to if you wish to talk. I'm not much in the way of talk, and no great hand at making myself agreeable in ladies' society. In fact, I don't care much for them in general—but you are an exception!"

The statement in reference to himself by Mr. Brantz Elliot was perfectly correct. He cared little or nothing for the society of the opposite sex, and gave them very little thought. He had admired them now and then after a lazy sort of fashion. Sometimes a pretty face on the Parisian boulevards, or in passing equipages in the Bois or Cascine, had pleased him. He had looked, too, with indolent satisfaction at the graceful slips of girls promenading Broadway or Fifth Avenue in the afternoons, with taper waists, nicely arranged curls, and dainty feet peeping out from their painfully pulled-back skirts, as the gallant policemen escorted them safely through the tide of vehicles. But they were scarcely real people to him. They were simply a gallery of pictures, all these feminine faces and figures; and the young fellow had looked at them as at paintings—admiring them as pleasant objects, but forgetting them at the next moment. He had never been the least bit in love with any of them. In fact, what pleased him about Nelly Welles was the fact that she was not at all like them.

It was a little unceremonious, perhaps, in him to address the girl as "Nelly"—but then there were reasons for that. They had been thrown together hourly for nearly a whole month; and when we associate with persons familiarly for that length of time, they become friends—if they do not become enemies. Then everybody called her "Nelly," and almost unconsciously Brantz Elliot had come to do so, too. A last explanation was the fact that Nelly Welles was very young for her age, which was about seventeen. Some girls of seventeen are children, and others women. Nelly was a mixture of the two, but more of the first. She had the shyness and simplicity of girlhood—nothing of womanhood at all, in fact, but a certain sweet seriousness at times which strongly attracted him. The wonder was where she had acquired that expression of countenance and her real refinement. There was very little in her surroundings to account for it. Daddy Welles and his motherly helpmate were excellent people, but then they were not what is called high-bred. Nelly was really high-bred, in spite of her poor dress and all about her. She was a little awkward, but that evidently arose from youth and inexperience. She had none of the "ways" of rustic belles, who look sidewise at you and deploy their unpleasant wiles. She was very quiet, and even dignified. Her mind was almost a blank, indeed, as to education—a *tabula rasa* nearly, Brantz Elliot said to himself, but then she, too, seemed to know that, and to quietly lament it.

As to Nelly's personal appearance, she was certainly pretty. This fact had gradually dawned on Brantz Elliot, who was not curious in such matters. But youth is youth, after all. A young fellow may like to rise at daylight, and go and hunt deer, far better than to whirl in the waltz or German at the same hour with an armful of satin in his grasp. He may care very little for the smiles and wiles of such chance partners, in chance moments, when the object of each is only amusement. But there is always a heart somewhere in a young man's breast. It thus happened that Brantz Elliot had begun to follow Nelly Welles about with his eyes. She really was very pretty, he said to himself. Her figure in its linsey drew his attention, and was more graceful to him than the satin-encased corsages of the beauties he had seen in cities. There was something in her dark eyes, and hair gathered behind and tied with the cheap ribbon, which pleased him. Sometimes he realized that fact, and it made him laugh. Was he going to fall in love with the "mountain maid?" The idea struck him as rather absurd. To be in love with a girl meant to wish to tell her so, and to ask her to marry him. Now, to ask Nelly Welles to become Mrs. Brantz Elliot was a wild idea. Daddy Welles would not do in the least for a father-in-law. Such a *paterfamilias* would create a sensation in Fifth Avenue drawing-rooms. He might bring his long rifle with him and shoot somebody!— Having permitted his thoughts to roam idly in this fanciful direction, Elliot ended by laughing quietly and dismissing the whole subject as a chance vagary of the brain, engendered by idleness. He did not go away, however; either Nelly or the delights of deer-hunting detained him. And as there really was nothing of much importance to take him back to New York, he thought he would stay a little longer.

Nelly had gone fishing with him in the stream which ran through the narrow valley at the foot of the mountain more than once. This had been in consequence of his solicitation. Brantz Elliot had the tastes of a sportsman, but not those of a recluse. He liked company. Daddy Welles was generally engaged, and could only spare time now and then for a good tramp after deer: in the idle divertisement of rambling along the stream and fishing in the bright autumn days, his associate had thus come to be Nelly. They got on very well with each other. He could talk in a friendly way — she was company. She did not take much part in the conversation. Her shyness had worn off, in a measure, and she was much more at her ease with him; but she was still diffident, and apparently ashamed of her ignorance.

Having further urged, on this bright morning, his desire for company, Brantz Elliot succeeded in persuading Nelly to go fishing with him, and they set out together down the path toward the stream. Nelly had a brown chip hat, of very plain material, on her head, and had thrown an old cape around her shoulders. Her shoes and stockings were coarse, but she walked with a grace which attracted the admiring glances of her companion.

"Nelly," he said, "I have meant for some time to ask you a question, only I was afraid you would consider it rather impertinent. May I ask it?"

She turned her head and looked at him rather shyly, but smiling, and said "Yes."

"Well, it's this. How in the world did you ever come to be born here in this mountain?"

"In the mountain? Why shouldn't I be born here, sir?"

"There is that hateful *sir* again! I wish you would drop it."

"I will try, but I don't think I can."

"Well, at least try. It's really like a bucket of cold water! If we are ever going to become acquainted we ought to be now. It makes me feel as if I was eighty and you were eight—I am only twenty-five, and you must be at least *double* eight."

"I am seventeen," said Nelly.

"Well, I am told that is an agreeable age; I thought you were younger. Have you lived all your life in the mountain? That seems strange to me."

"Strange! Why should it be strange?"

"Because—and now we are coming back to the point—it is the greatest puzzle to me to understand how—but you will think I am ill-bred if I say what I was going to say."

"I am sure I will not," Nelly said.

"Well, I'll go on, then. I meant to say that you are *a lady*, from head to foot, and people in this world are influenced in their appearance and character by their surroundings. But really the thing is too low," said Brantz Elliot, as if addressing himself; "I can't go on."

Nelly blushed quickly, and said,

"I know what you mean; but I am not a lady."

"I swear you are!—excuse me, Nelly."

"I am a poor girl without education—my father and mother are poor people. I was born here in the mountain, and I will live and die without going anywhere—"

A chord had evidently been touched which Brantz Elliot had never even suspected. Nelly's bosom heaved.

"I am not a lady!" she said, with a quick sob. "How can I be? How could I be anything but what I am? I never had any education, and nothing will ever change my life here! If I had not had a few old books, and learned what I could, I would not know how to read or write. Oh, it is so hard! I am nearly grown up, and I am so ignorant! I don't know what to do sometimes when I think of it!"

The words were uttered in a voice which went to Brantz Elliot's heart.

"Why were you never taught!" he said.

"I don't know," Nelly sobbed; "there's a free school, but it is at Piedmont, and I was ashamed to go with the children. Father is as good to me as he can be, but he thinks very little of books, and says I can teach myself. But I never will be able to!"

Nelly turned her head to one side and indulged in a quiet cry, which seemed to relieve her, as she became calmer and said no more. As to Brantz Elliot, he seemed to be completely at a loss what to say. The girl's voice, full of passionate sadness, had strongly affected him. Not finding any reply to make at the moment he walked on in silence. At length he said,

"It is a pity—a very great pity, indeed."

Nelly did not reply for a few minutes; she then said, in a low voice,

"I did not mean that I was really discontented or not happy. I have a great deal to be thankful for, and I would not care to leave home for pleasure; but I can't help wishing sometimes that I was not shut up here in the mountains all my life. All I wish is that I could improve myself, and have books to read, and not live and die so ignorant of everything."

Brantz Elliot looked into her face and said, after a moment,

"You will be married some of these days, then you will go away."

At this Nelly shook her head.

"I would not like to be married to anybody."

He had begun to take a strong interest in analyzing the girl's thoughts and motives now, and said,

"You mean that you don't intend to marry one of the rough young mountaineers here—and you are right."

"I do not mean to marry anybody," Nelly said, quietly. "I ought not to have talked so much about myself, but it is very hard to think of living all my life as ignorant as I am. I ought not to have learned to read. It has only made me unhappy."

XXIV.

UNDINE.

NELLY plainly wished to change the topic, and Brantz Elliot said no more, but he remembered this conversation for a long time. The occupation of fishing afforded a diversion, and to this they proceeded.

Falling Water, as the small stream was called, was a picturesque watercourse, well stocked with bass, of which the Shenandoah is full. It ran between grassy banks, widening here and there over sandy bottoms, and at other points narrowing between cedar-fringed bluffs. A skirt of evergreens defined its outline through the little valley, and with these were mingled some large sycamores with huge hollow trunks and mottled arms, drooping in many places far out over the current, washing beneath the gnarled roots shaded with green water-flags. Along the grassy banks ran a well-defined path, made, no doubt, by cattle. Here and there a mossy rock jutted out above the current. On these rocks Brantz Elliot and Nelly Welles took their stand and began to fish.

They had very bad luck. This fact was due to heavy rains a day or two before, which had swollen the stream and made the water muddy. Such a condition of things is unfavorable to the pursuits of the angler. After an hour's fishing they had caught nothing, and Brantz Elliot proposed that they should go farther up the stream. Nelly assented, and they went along the bank until they reached a point where the current grew narrow and rushed swiftly between two bluffs. A felled tree, used as a bridge, reached from bank to bank; and thinking that the ground on the other side would prove more favorable for throwing the lines, they ventured cautiously on the log-bridge, which seemed rather insecure. It was more so than they supposed. Just as they reached the middle it gave way, and they fell into the water.

Brantz Elliot fell so suddenly that he went completely under. When he rose to the surface, he saw that Nelly had been swept off by the rapid current, which was bearing her along like a leaf. Elliot was an excellent swimmer. In half a dozen strokes he reached the girl, and taking one of her hands, placed it upon his shoulder. She made no effort to grasp him, as drowning persons frequently do, and he struck out vigorously toward the bank. The current was, however, even stronger than he had supposed, and, more unfortunate than all, Nelly's clothing, especially her cape, became heavily clogged with water. Elliot felt the weight on his shoulder increasing every moment; and seeing the fatal cape wrapping its wet folds more and more closely around the girl, he endeavored to tear it away from her. The effort only resulted in the disappearance of both beneath the surface. They rose again, but Elliot could see that the girl's strength was deserting her. His own was giving way. The water in her clothing and his own made the weight upon him terrible. With a sinking heart he calculated the probability of reaching the shore. It seemed slight. The current swept them along, and Nelly became weaker and weaker. With half-closed eyes she leaned more and more heavily upon him, but even then did not attempt to grasp him. Looking at her pale face, Elliot groaned. What could he do? In a few moments at most they would probably sink for the last time. The thought passed through him as a bullet passes through a man's breast.

"I will die with her!" he muttered.

As he said this a wave passed over them. They rose once more, and then something struck his face. This was a drooping bough of one of the sycamores growing on the bank. The bough extended at least fifteen feet out into the stream, and Elliot caught it with one hand, supporting the girl with his left arm.

"Nelly!" he said.

She looked at him, and her head leaned toward him as a child's toward a protector in trouble. She was smiling faintly.

"Do you think you can hold to this

bough for a few minutes? If you can, I'll save you."

"Yes," she said.

She raised her arms, caught the bough, and clung to it. Elliot found himself free, and forcing his hand into his soaked pocket drew out his knife, opened it with his teeth, and cut the string of the cape, which was at once swept away.

"Hold fast now, Nelly!" he said, "for a minute only. There is but one way of saving you."

Half a dozen strokes carried him to shore, and he ran to a large wild grape-vine near, from which he cut a long vine. With this he hastened back to the sycamore, climbed up, and, following the bough out into the stream, reached the spot where Nelly was clinging by both hands. The water was up to her shoulders, and her body swayed to and fro. He could see that she was nearly exhausted, but the same faint smile was on her face as she looked at him—a smile whose expression he had never seen before, and which he always remembered afterward.

"Do just as I tell you, now, Nelly," he said. "I am going to tie this grape-vine around you, and bring you to shore. It is the only way to save you. When I say 'Ready,' let the bough go, and trust to me."

"Yes," she said.

Elliot passed the vine around her under the arms, twisted it into a secure knot, tested the knot, and said,

"Ready!"

Without an instant's hesitation Nelly let go.

"Hold the vine tight," he said.

She obeyed, and proceeding slowly along the broad bough, Elliot gradually drew the girl, whose head just emerged from the water, to the shore. She was so much exhausted, however, that it was impossible for her to ascend the steep bank. Elliot saw this at a glance, and wrapped the vine around the bough, twisting it into a knot. He then swung himself to the ground, ran down the bank, and, catching the girl in his arms, carried her to dry ground.

"Saved! you are saved!" he cried, holding her in his arms, and smoothing her dripping hair from her forehead. Her arm was resting upon his shoulder in the natural posture of a person supported by another. It was almost around his neck, and her cheek was near his own. Brantz Elliot then did what perhaps he ought not to have done, but he did it almost unconsciously: he kissed the cheek.

Nelly blushed to the roots of her hair and the tips of her ears, and turned away her head: owing to the fact that she was in the young man's arms, this was all she could do.

"Don't mind me, Nelly!" he exclaimed, laughing joyfully. "Your face was so near that I kissed you without thinking. You mustn't be too hard on a fellow!"

He wrung the water as well as he could from her skirt and sleeves, which were drenched.

"Your arms and hands are like ice," he said. "That is from nervous exhaustion. Come on, and make haste home!"

He looked round him, and for the first time became aware of a fact which he had quite overlooked in his excitement. The sycamore which had been the means of saving Nelly's life stood on the west bank of the stream. There was the current galloping between them and home, and the log affording the means of crossing it had disappeared! There was a bridge on the stage-road about a mile below, but that would make their walk back at least two miles; and Nelly was trembling from head to foot.

"You have a nervous chill!" Brantz Elliot exclaimed. "You never could walk round by the bridge. And then I'd have to carry you up the mountain afterward, Nelly, like the boy that carried the princess he was to marry if he got to the top with her!"

He laughed ruefully. What was to be done? He was considering the matter when two persons came out of a clump of pines near them and walked toward them.

XXV.

THE two persons were a gentleman of forty-five or fifty, clad in black, and a slim girl of eighteen or nineteen, with brown hair, blue eyes, and a light shawl thrown over her shoulders. They came to the spot where Elliot and his companion were standing, and the girl exclaimed, addressing Nelly,

"Why, what is the matter? You are drenched from head to foot!—you are trembling all over. Did you fall into the water?"

Nelly's teeth were chattering so that she was unable to reply, and Elliot replied for her.

"Yes, miss," he said. "We tried to cross on a log, which broke, and we fell in, and were nearly drowned. This is Miss Nelly Welles, and my name is Brantz Elliot. I am from New York, and am staying here."

The young lady bowed in reply to this straightforward introduction of himself and Nelly, but at once concentrated her attention upon the latter. She had taken Nelly's hands in her own, and now exclaimed,

"Your hands are almost frozen! How cold you are, and your teeth are chattering! You ought to go home at once—but it is too far. I know where Daddy Welles lives. Come home with us!"

"We can go back—by the bridge," Nelly murmured, playing the castanets with her teeth. She really did seem to be about to have a nervous chill.

"No, indeed! You must come with us. We live only a short distance. Is this Nelly Welles? I have heard of you, Nelly, and am very glad to make your acquaintance. We were walking out. I am so glad we met you!"

There was something delightfully frank and affectionate in the girl's voice, and her companion, the gentleman in black, added his word, in a voice of mild courtesy.

"Your young friend ought to change her clothing at once, sir," he said to Elliot.

"My name is Cary, and I live almost in sight."

"Yes, indeed, papa! Make her come," said the tall girl.

And as Nelly had no means of resisting, she yielded, and they all walked up the hill through the evergreens. The path wound downward on the other side and entered a meadow. Beyond, on a rising ground, was an old-fashioned country-house of moderate size, standing in the midst of a lawn dotted with locusts and Lombardy poplars, a favorite tree with the old-time Virginians. The house was ancient and built of stone, covered with brown stucco. In front was a small porch reached by a circular carriage-drive. Here and there in the grounds rose white trellises, which seemed to indicate a love of flowers in the master or mistress of the mansion. The general appearance of things suggested plain comfort rather than ample means—an idea of tranquillity and home.

The slim young lady, who had introduced herself to Nelly as Frances Cary, at once disappeared up-stairs with her drenched companion, and Mr. Cary conducted Brantz Elliot into a room on the left of the entrance, which seemed to do duty as drawing-room and library combined. There were two or three bookcases filled with volumes, and some old pictures on the wall. In the centre stood a writing-table covered with books and papers—among the latter, some upon which the owner of the house seemed to have been engaged, as a pen was lying upon them. Two large arm-chairs covered with brown leather stood on each side of the table, and were apparently heirlooms. The apartment was in keeping with these antiquated pieces of furniture. Above the tall mantel-piece the wall was wainscoted in panels, and the whole appearance of things was antique. Some of the first settlers who crossed the Blue Ridge in the last century had probably built this house.

As his host had begged Elliot to excuse him for a moment, and had left the room, the young man had a good opportunity to look around him. It was quite plain, from the appearance of the apartment, that Mr. Cary was a man of literary tastes, and lived quietly among his books. An atmosphere of the past seemed to pervade the room — there was only one object which looked fresh and modern; this was a portrait of cabinet size, over the mantel-piece, representing a girl of about eighteen, with her hair in bands on the temples, and secured by a bow of ribbon behind. In the face of the picture there was an exquisite sweetness and modesty. The lips were virginal, and smiled. It was possible that this was the portrait of Miss Frances Cary, as it was an excellent likeness of her; but the hair was worn in a different manner.

Brantz Elliot was looking at it when Mr. Cary came back.

"I have just seen my daughter," Mr. Cary said; "and Miss Nelly will be able to come down to dinner, Mr. Elliot. If she wishes to return home this evening I will send her in the carriage."

They fell into conversation, and at length an old servant appeared and announced that dinner was served. Mr. Cary led the way into the opposite room, and there stood Miss Frances Cary and another person awaiting them. The tall young beauty looked at Mr. Brantz Elliot with a smile and an expression of curiosity — she was evidently expecting something. Suddenly she laughed—the something had happened. Brantz Elliot had taken three steps into the room when he stopped. He was looking at the figure beside Miss Frances Cary.

This figure was that of a young lady in a dress of light-blue silk, with a fringe of lace around the neck, and a train. The dress was cut in the pull-back fashion of the time, and, therefore, exhibited the whole contour of the wearer's person. Small black morocco slippers, decorated with ribbon knots, appeared under the elegantly trimmed skirt; lace cuffs emerged from the falling sleeves, and the young lady's dark hair was elaborately dressed in curls on the temples, with a string of pearls interwoven. The explanation of

all this was that, as her own clothes were drenched, Nelly Welles had been dressed up by Miss Frances Cary in a suit of her own—the best she had — and was now exhibited in triumph by her hostess.

"I thought you would be surprised, sir!" Miss Frances Cary said to Elliot, laughing. "Nelly has on one of my dresses, and it fits her to perfection, though I am taller than she is."

"It certainly does," Elliot said. He looked at Nelly with admiring eyes. The magic of dress had made her what he had said she was—a lady from head to foot. There was nothing in her air to detract from this; no *gaucherie* at all. She wore her elegant costume with the air of a person who had never put on linsey in her life, and the small feet in the morocco slippers seemed to have found the covering suited to them.

"By George!" said Elliot to himself, "who would ever have thought that dress would make such a difference in a girl! And yet there is really no difference."

"I have neglected my own toilet from want of time, gentlemen," Miss Frances Cary said, with a courtesy; "but I hope you acknowledge that Nelly is a beauty!"

Mr. Cary smiled and said,

"Certainly, and you seem to be becoming great friends."

"Friends, papa!—why not? Nelly's coming to see me. Mercy! do you think girls are as stiff as you lords of creation? Indeed, we are not. We become acquainted before you great people have finished shaking hands!"

Everybody then sat down, and dinner went upon its way, ended, and Mr. Cary and Elliot returned to the library, the young ladies going up-stairs again. The carriage had been ordered to be ready in an hour.

They entered into conversation, and he found Mr. Cary a quiet, friendly person, who made an agreeable impression by his air of simplicity and courtesy. There was absolutely nothing of the soldier about him, and yet Elliot knew, from what Daddy Welles had told him, that his host had passed through four years of terrible campaigning and all the battles of Virginia. This interested him; and seeing on the wall an engraving of a Confederate flag rising through a belt of clouds, with stars in the background, and a low moon on the horizon beneath, he said,

"That picture, no doubt, brings back old times, Colonel Cary—I mean the war times; and that reminds me that I ought to make you an apology for not addressing you by your military title."

Mr. Cary shook his head and said,

"I much prefer to be addressed as plain Mr. The war is a sad subject, and I like to forget it. I do not mean that it is sad otherwise than from sorrowful recollections connected with it. I should never have taken part in it if I had not regarded it as a just war—the resistance of the South to political oppression. But I do not recall it with pleasure, and prefer not being addressed by my military title, which brings it back to my mind. You are from New York, Mr. Elliot?"

This question was plainly meant to divert the conversation into a new channel.

"I am from everywhere and nowhere—but New York is my native State," Elliot said. "I lit like a bird in Broadway last year, but I have been flying over Europe. The truth is, Mr. Cary, I am a rather good-for-nothing sort of person. I am only fit for a life in the woods. Nothing wearies me like streets, and what people call society."

"That is not a proof that we are good-for-nothing, I hope," his host said. "I am not very fond of society myself. Indeed it wearies me, as it seems to do you."

"Weary me!" exclaimed Brantz Elliot. "It prostrates me, and drains the very life out of me! The one eternal chatter, chatter, chatter, takes away my senses. I know women whose tongues run like mill-clappers, and the worst of it is they grind no grist. It is one flow of froth—the whipped syllabub of talk beginning and ending nowhere—an eternity of gabble!"

It was not often that Brantz Elliot rose to the height of denunciation. He was a quiet and good-natured young fellow, but his pet dislike made him eloquent.

"I would much rather split rails than listen to it," he added.

"Well, I think our views agree tolerably well on that subject," Mr. Cary said, quietly; "but we find, as we go on in life, that we have to endure a great many things."

"I will never learn to endure gabble," Elliot said. "I am twenty-five, and it is harder to stand than when I was fifteen."

"Twenty-five is not very old; life is in the bloom at that age. I am nearly fifty, and the leaves begin to drop then."

"At fifty?" said Elliot. "I think a man is only in his full vigor at fifty."

"The mind may be," Mr. Cary replied, "and the body, too, perhaps, sometimes; but our illusions begin to leave us, which is a great misfortune. Life is like a coach; the springs may not break all at once, but they lose their elasticity. When the coach is new, it is elastic as well as strong, and will bear a great deal of wear and tear. As time passes, it loses its stamina as well as its gloss. It still keeps the road, perhaps, but some day it breaks down suddenly, and is consigned to the dust of the coach-house. Dust to dust, you know, Mr. Elliot."

Mr. Cary paused for a moment, and then added:

"This may seem melancholy talk; but, after all, is not life a melancholy affair? Old age comes soon enough, and happy is the man who does not linger out his last years."

Elliot listened in silence. The reasoning of his host imposed a certain gloom on his volatile nature.

"But would any one agree to have his life end because he is no longer young?" he said. "I doubt it."

"I am sure you would find very few who would agree to that. But the fact remains that old age is sad when the days pass with a dull pain at the heart, which is often the case. Death is better—and yet that will not come sometimes. The pulses go on beating, slowly and faintly, but they will not stop. Did you ever consult a Biographical Dictionary to find the date of some celebrity's death? You say to yourself, 'In such a year he made his great speech, or published his great book; half a century ago he was already famous—so he must have died many years since.' And then you look into your dictionary, and find that he is still living! He is not dead—only forgotten! not his fame only, but his very name. It was in every mouth once, and the world hailed him as one of the *éblouissemens*, as the French say, of the age. Now no one even remembers him —and yet he is living still. Living!— but how? Ecclesiastes will tell you: With his head bowed down, and his knees trembling. He was a giant once, and carried the world on his shoulders. Now the very grasshopper is a burden to him!"

The firm voice uttering steadily this sorrowful philosophy of life ceased. Elliot struggled against it in vain.

"Well," he said at length, "I suppose all that is true, Mr. Cary; but we must take things as they come, and make the best of them."

"Certainly," said his host, "it is well to make the best of things; and, after all, there is something worse than old age— it is the loneliness that comes to men at any and all ages."

Did the speaker glance toward the picture over the mantel-piece?

"I must apologize, Mr. Elliot, for inflicting such a melancholy lecture upon you," he said. "There are a great many pleasant things in life—to those who can enjoy them. One of them is your pursuit of hunting, to which you alluded. I am not myself much of a hunter, which springs, no doubt, from the fact that I am physically indolent. I am very much of an idler and dreamer, which may strike you as singular in an old soldier; but so it is. I walk or ride with my daughter frequently; afterward my resource against ennui is here in my library."

"I was looking at the books—they seem to be of every description."

"Yes, I read at random. My taste is for miscellany, old and new; I read my favorites over and over, even the old novels."

"Then you don't like the novels of the day?"

"I confess I do not—as much as other persons seem to. We have nothing now but analysis and realism, and the fashionable atmosphere is what a painter would call gray. I like neutral tints where the subject demands them. I can't say I like them in every case. There are other tints that have their *raison d'être* in art, as well as gray. But we are growing literary. You must excuse me—I am a mere bookman. Do you like Virginia?"

"I like it very much. It is a friendly sort of country."

"That is a compliment, and I take my little part in it. I shall be very glad if you will come and see me, Mr. Elliot. I seldom visit myself, but am truly glad to see my friends."

The carriage drove to the door as Mr. Cary was speaking, and a few moments afterward Frances Cary and Nelly Welles came down-stairs into the library. Nelly had taken off her friend's silk dress, but put on another of a plainer description, in which she presented a very neat and attractive appearance. A maid-servant had brought down a small travelling-valise in which Nelly's damp clothes were packed, and this was taken out to the carriage.

Elliot and Nelly then took leave of their host and hostess, and got into the carriage, which was a plain family equipage, driven by an old servant.

"Be sure you keep your promise, Nelly," said the young hostess, "and come and see me. I shall come and see you."

"Yes, indeed, I will come," Nelly said, as the door of the carriage was shut. It was then about to drive away when Miss Frances Cary uttered a piercing cry. Everybody started.

"Mercy! I've not kissed you!" exclaimed the young lady, rushing wildly to the carriage window.

A fervent embrace followed, and then the vehicle went upon its way.

XXVI.

THE CATAMOUNTAIN.

FOR some days after the accident on the stream, Brantz Elliot seemed to have something upon his mind. He would ramble away into the woods, and, instead of hunting, sit down and fall into fits of musing. Was he thinking of the kiss he had pressed upon Nelly's cheek as they came up out of the water? Such things return to the memory when we are twenty-five. He remembered everything very clearly, and could feel the girl's heart beating against his own again.

He continued to be haunted by recollections of his adventure, until one day every other thought disappeared from his mind but one. Daddy Welles announced that the catamount had been seen again; this time by Barney Jones, whose eyes were much too keen to be "fooled by a common wild-cat." The animal was a real "painter," or "catamounting," as the Virginia hunters called them. He had been seen higher up in the Blue Ridge, but now he had got to Bohemia —there was no doubt about it. Barney Jones had seen him near his house and shot at him, but missed him.*

Hearing this, Brantz Elliot lost sight of all else in the world. One thing only was now necessary to his happiness—to go on a panther-hunt. He had grown a little tired of shooting pheasants and wild turkeys, and even deer-stalking began to lose some of its attractions. What we require in this world is variety and contrast. The palate inured to rich sauces asks something richer still; and the new sauce which Mr. Brantz Elliot craved was a shot at a real catamount.

"We'll try him in the morning, Daddy Welles," he exclaimed, with excitement; "and if you won't go, I will! I mean to see your distinguished stranger and have his blood—that is, his skin—to take back to New York with me."

Daddy Welles smiled sweetly. The ardor of his guest seemed to please him.

"There won't be any trouble about my goin'," he said. "I'm most as cur'ous to see the varmint as you are. I'll jest send Barney Jones word to be ready by daylight, or a leetle before, and we'll look up the calf-eater."

"He eats calves, then?" said Elliot.

"To be sure," Daddy Welles responded. "That stands to reason, as a wild-cat will, and a catamounting is a sort of wild-cat, only bigger and stronger. This varmint has cleaned 'em out, they tell me, farther up. So I'd like to put a bullet in him myself as he is comin' this way."

Daddy Welles was thus evidently intent on the hunt from a business view of things, as well as for his private satisfaction, and all the arrangements were made. Some ragged offspring of Mr. Barney Jones, who were fishing on the banks of

---

* Even if unsupported by further developments, there would be no reason to doubt the accuracy of Mr. Jones's eyesight. The cougar, panther, or catamount, as it is variously called, is still occasionally met with in the Blue Ridge. This fact is shown by the annexed slip from the Culpeper (Va.) *Times*, in the autumn of 1878: "A great deal of excitement has recently been created in the neighborhood of Mount Poney, about three miles from here. It is reported that strange cries, resembling a man hallooing in distress, have frequently been heard of late on the mountain, but nothing had been seen to cause any fear among the inhabitants until last Sunday, when some persons who were on the mountain saw a wild and ferocious looking animal, which, it was thought, had been making the terrifying demonstrations, and which is supposed to be a panther. It is said to be about five feet in length, of a yellow color, and very large, and when seen was making its way through the woods toward the top of the mountain, where there is a mass of rocks which afford it a hiding-place. The inhabitants of that section are very much alarmed at the sudden appearance of this carnivorous animal, and will not venture outside of their houses after dark in consequence of it. Several years ago a huge catamount was killed on the same mountain."

the stream below, were told to notify their parent that Daddy Welles and Mr. Elliot would be at his house by daylight on the next morning to go after the catamount; and then Elliot went to bed, and dreamed that he was engaged in a breast-to-breast struggle with an animal of huge proportions, in the midst of which Daddy Welles tapped at his door and informed him that it was time to be moving. They breakfasted by candle-light, and took their arms—Daddy Welles his long rifle, and Elliot his carbine. Both carried hunting-knives, used in cutting the throats of deer. Thus equipped, they mounted two raw-boned horses, sole equine possessions of the Daddy, and, followed by the hounds, rode down the mountain, turning to the left when they reached the foot, in the direction of Barney Jones's.

It was a superb autumn morning, and the bracing air brought the blood to the young man's face. The leaves were of every color of the rainbow. The least possible trace of frost lay like silver on the grass, and a light breeze rustled the foliage—blood-red where the maple and dog-wood were in the ascendant, and like molten gold where the hickory-trees predominated. Such a scene always made the pulses of Brantz Elliot throb with delight. It brought out the "wild side" in him in full force. He would probably have laughed at you if you had hinted that Fifth Avenue or the Boulevards were anything in comparison to the valley of Bohemia at that moment.

They rode on through the dusk of morning up the valley, from which a white mist was slowly rising, as the dawn began to glimmer above the mountain. Later in the autumn this mist was going to turn into a long, dense cloud of milk-white vapor, defining the course of the Falling Water. Now, however, it was a light smoke only which the dawn was chasing. Soon the sun would come up over the Blue Ridge, and it would completely vanish.

They found Mr. Barney Jones waiting in front of his habitation—a weather-board establishment, of moderate size, nestling down in a gash of the mountain. Bohemia gradually narrowed here, terminating in a deep gorge. Mr. Jones's mansion, which was unassuming but looked thrifty, was a sort of sentinel at the mouth of the gorge.

He was standing by his horse, which closely resembled those ridden by his visitors, and held a rifle in his hand. He was not an imposing figure in his old faded hunting-coat, his ragged brown felt hat, and his patched pantaloons thrust into his boots. But then Mr. Barney Jones did not seem to care much for that. His expression of face was humorous and sardonic. He expectorated with an independent air. He was very much of a scarecrow in apparel, but plainly regarded himself as one of the sovereigns.

"Well, here you are at last, Daddy," Mr. Jones said. "I'd a'most begun to give you out."

The speaker bestowed a side movement of the head upon Brantz Elliot, and at once mounted his horse.

"The rep-*tile* was seen yistiddy in the Hogback," said Barney Jones. "Here, pup!—here, pup!"

This summons was responded to by half a dozen tawny hounds, who ran joyfully in front as the three hunters rode up the gorge toward the Hogback, a ridge parallel with the main range.

Barney Jones promptly communicated all the intelligence which he had received in reference to the catamount. He had come over from the "Three Sisters"—a spur of the mountain—some days before, and had been seen by Jimmy Wood and Tom Wilkins on two occasions. They had followed and shot at him, but he had got off unhurt, and made his way to a pile of rocks on the Hogback, where he seemed to have his den. Afterward he, Barney Jones, had got a sight of him near his house and fired at him, but missed him. It was jest between hawk and buzzard in the evenin', and he couldn't see plain, but there was no doubt about it—he was a genu*ine* catamounting. He was after sheep and calves, and he, Mr. Jones, meant to give him a lead pill to swaller, which he ruther thought would settle his hash for him.

Mr. Jones's dialect was not classic, but Brantz Elliot did not mind that. His pulse thrilled, and as they rode on up the gorge toward the Hogback his face glowed. This gorge was narrow, and heavily wooded. Falling Water ran through it, and over it hovered a cloud of mist. On the left rose the shaggy battlements of the Ridge, and on the right the steep range called the Hogback, probably from its bristling pines. On the very summit towered a huge pile of rocks, lying as though emptied from a gigantic wagon. In the crevices grew evergreens, and even from a distance, through the fog, Elliot could make out the cavernous apertures beneath them. In one of these caverns the catamount had his den.

The hunters pushed on rapidly up the steep and rocky bridle-path. Their object was to reach the top, dismount, conceal themselves, and wait until the catamount, after his night-prowling, returned to his den — which would probably be about sunrise. Nocturnal animals — of the cat species, above all—see best in the night: the opal eyes expand; in the day the iris contracts. Like the burglar, the night-prowler takes the time when the world is asleep to attain his sinister ends.

They reached the summit of the Hogback just as the rosy flush began to deepen beyond the battlements of the Blue Ridge, whose sombre outline was clearcut against the coming sunrise. They dismounted, hid their horses behind a thicket of cedars rising in beautiful cones, with bases resting on the rocks in which they grew, and every one took his stand, Brantz Elliot crouching in the tufted head of a fallen pine. From his post he had a full view of the pile of rocks, which was not more than a hundred and fifty yards distant, and of the gorge beneath.

He watched the changes in the wild landscape with admiration. The course of the stream was clearly defined by a mass of vapor, the upper edge of which was traced boldly, without the least blur, against the dense growth of evergreens on the opposite mountain. This lasted for a few moments only. As the flush on the summit of the Ridge changed from delicate rose to red, the mist seemed to grow uneasy. Then it shifted, undulated, and as a fiery spark like a distant beacon appeared above the fringe of evergreens, the upper edges of the mist grew ragged and began to drift upward. Then the sun soared up, suddenly flushing the wild gorge, and the mist fled before it. The outline grew more ragged, flitted off in shreds, and in a few moments the whole mass became translucent — you could trace the outlines of the gigantic pines now through it, and every object in the gorge.

All at once an almost imperceptible sound, like a distant growl, came up from the gorge, and Daddy Welles, who was not far from Elliot said, in a low tone,

"Did you hear that?"

"Yes," said Elliot, his heart beating; "remember, you promised me the first shot."

"To be sure," Daddy Welles said, in the same low tone; "but you'd best keep quiet now."

Elliot nodded, and cocked his carbine, kneeling on his right knee, and completely concealed from view.

The dogs had been called in, and were lying in rear of their masters, plainly understanding that it was not time for them yet. The hunters, crouching down, remained silent, waiting. The air was perfectly still. Not the least sound disturbed the solitude of the Hogback. Suddenly a twig snapped in a mass of brush in front of them, and a moment afterward the catamount came out into the open space, crawling stealthily, with his body nearly touching the ground, toward his den.

There could no longer be the least doubt. He was a full-grown panther or American cougar, nearly six feet in length, with reddish-brown fur, white under the body, and dashed on the throat and chest with black and white. As he advanced with his stealthy crawl he turned his head from side to side suspiciously, as if his instinct led him to scent danger, and the glitter of his yellow eyes could be seen. A stray beam of the sunshine falling on them seemed to turn them to fire.

One of the blissful moments of life had come for Brantz Elliot. His heart throbbed and his pulse galloped — his hand shook a little with excitement and full delight, as a lover's trembles when he draws the head of the one he loves to his breast. But the tawny head of the catamount was at that moment an object of infinitely greater attraction to the young hunter than could have been the curls and roses of the fairest fair with golden hair that ever lived.

He waited until the catamount had reached a point midway between the undergrowth from which he had emerged and the mass of rocks. Then, resting on his right knee, and taking deliberate aim at the animal behind the fore-shoulder, he fired.

It was plain that he was struck. He uttered a wild scream, wholly unlike the low growl which had heralded his coming, and bounded into the air. As he descended two other shots rang out, but evidently did not touch him. He wheeled, cleared a pile of brush behind him with a bound, and disappeared in the gorge.

"He's tetched, but he ain't much hurt," cried Barney Jones; "whoop! here's for him!"

With this war-cry, Mr. Jones leaped on his rawboned charger, shouted to the dogs, and rode headlong down the rocky slope of the Hogback, followed by his companions, who had hastened also to their horses. Reckless of danger, and wild with the excitement of the hunter, they plunged down the breakneck road, intent only on following up the game.

After that it was more like a deer-chase than a panther-hunt. The dogs followed their foe by the scent, never losing his trail for a moment, as their furious baying showed. The game was obviously very far from being disabled by Brantz Elliot's bullet; it had no doubt inflicted a flesh wound and no more. The tireless running of the animal showed that.

Barney Jones even led Daddy Welles and Elliot. He seemed to have made up his mind to administer the fatal leaden pill, or break his own or his horse's neck in the attempt. With heels dug into his Rosinante, and long rifle flourished above him, he hallooed on the dogs, and went after them like the Wild Huntsman.

His companions were at his heels, and they ran, scrambled, tumbled over the rocky mountain-paths for several hours. The dogs were plainly still on the trail, for the baying was as furious as before. But the game was not giving out yet. He doubled from one end of the gorge to another, and then mounting to the top of the Blue Ridge, followed the summit southward.

Daddy Welles drew rein and said, looking at his horse,

"Well, old Tom's nigh gi'n out, Barney. The varmint's off."

"Not by no means!" exclaimed Mr. Jones; "he'll double agin; I'll swear to it—if I ken only git a chance to empty my gun at him."

He dug his heels into his steed, uttered his warwhoop, and plunged on, followed by Daddy Welles and Elliot—for great is the moral influence of enthusiasm. The three hunters disappeared southward, following the dogs as before, and taking the chances that the animal would double once more.

He was going to double again, and that fact was to lead to a somewhat startling incident.

The sun had mounted high by this time, and it was nearly noon. The valley of Bohemia looked very pretty in the fresh light, and what made the landscape along the banks of the Falling Water more attractive was the presence of what painters call human figures. These were the figures of Mr. Cary and his daughter, who were riding along quietly, admiring the rich coloring of the leaves, and conversing. As Mr. Cary had informed Brantz Elliot, one of his few diversions, outside of his library, was to walk or ride with his daughter; and on this morning they had set out on horseback to enjoy the fresh air and the autumn scenery. There was a picturesque route along the western bank of the stream, which they could cross by a ford above, and then return along the eastern bank, in sight of Daddy Welles's. They accordingly followed this road, splashed through the ford where the water was scarcely above the horses' knees, and, turning back, were riding slowly along the bank, in order to return home by the bridge on the stage-road leading to the Gap.

For some time Mr. Cary had heard a distant baying in the gorge toward the Hogback, and had called his daughter's attention to it.

"Some one is hunting," he said; "probably Mr. Elliot. He is a very agreeable young man, and quite a Nimrod."

"He is very agreeable, indeed," Miss Frances said, with her habitual mirth. "I would set my cap at him if he was not already engaged!"

"Is he engaged?"

"Well, I don't mean engaged, exactly, papa; but it is perfectly plain."

"What is plain, dear?"

"That he is in love with Nelly Welles."

"Do you really think so?"

"I am sure he is. Mercy! you didn't see how he looked at her when she came down in my blue silk. There is not the least doubt about it," said the astute young lady.

"Very well, dear," Mr. Cary said; "I am sure little Nelly will make him a good wife if they are married. She has a charming face."

"Hasn't she? I have fallen in love with her, and I wish you would stop and let me see her to-day."

"Certainly, if you wish, France," Mr. Cary said, bestowing his pet name on the girl—"but take care of your horse. You know he is skittish, and I hear the baying in the mountain coming nearer. The dogs might frighten him."

"There's no danger, papa."

"Still, it is just as well to be on your guard, and to keep your reins well in hand. With a skittish horse there is always a certain amount of danger."

There was danger, and a very considerable amount of it, indeed. They were passing through a dense belt of woods, not far from the stream, when a crashing sound was heard from the slope on their right, the foliage parted, and the catamount which the hunters had been pursuing bounded into the path within a few yards of them. He was panting, and covered with blood. His red tongue hung from his lips edged with froth, and his sharp teeth were visible. As much frightened as the horses, he uttered a deep growl, and seemed about to adopt the plan of cowards—that is, spring toward the object of which he was afraid.

The growl was followed by an exclamation from Mr. Cary. His daughter's horse, wild with fear, had bounded ten feet, and snapped his rein. The catamount crouched, apparently with the intention of springing, when a rifle-shot rung out, and the animal rolled over on the ground, tearing up the earth with his claws and teeth. He was shot through the body; and as he writhed, a gush of blood stained the carpet of pine tags.

Mr. Cary had seized the bridle of his daughter's horse close to the bit, and held him with a grip of iron.

"Can I help you, sir?" said a voice.

He looked round, and saw a young man in plain clothes, who had come out of the woods to the spot, and was leaning on a rifle.

"Did you fire that shot?" Mr. Cary exclaimed.

"I am glad to say I did, sir," the young man said.

"Then I have to thank you for saving my daughter from what might have proved a fatal accident!" Mr. Cary said, grasping his hand. "My name is Cary, sir, and I shall never forget the service you have done me to-day."

"You rate it too highly, Mr. Cary," said the young man. "My name is

Vance, and I am very glad I came up at the moment."

"Do you reside in this neighborhood, Mr. Vance? If so, I hope you will come and see me, and let me thank you at my leisure."

"In your near neighborhood," the young fellow said. "Thank you, Mr. Cary."

With this non-committal reply the young hunter went to the spot where the panther was lying. He was quite dead by this time, and lay with his mouth open and his red tongue hanging out. The upper lip was raised, and revealed the sharp teeth.

"It is a real panther," said the young man. "We had a superb one in the Un-rivalled Combination of Attractions."

He laughed as he said this. A moment afterward the dogs rushed upon the scene, and the three huntsmen on their jaded horses followed, halting suddenly, and looking with astonishment at the group.

"So he's dead!" Brantz Elliot exclaimed; and turning round, he said, "Why, Miss Cary! is that you?"

"In person," she said, laughing, and making him a little bow.

"So you are in at the death."

"It was nearly my own," the girl said.

Then explanations followed, and the general satisfaction was increased by the war-dance, accompanied by whoops, which Mr. Barney Jones executed around the dead animal.

"So I am not to take his skin to New York and show it at the club, after all!" Brantz Elliot said, ruefully.

"Do you want it? You may have it if you wish—I suppose it is mine, as I shot the owner of it," said the young man with the rifle, amiably.

"May I?" Brantz Elliot exclaimed, turning round. "Well, I'll take it, and thank you too!"

"You are welcome to it."

"And I'll skin him," Daddy Welles said, with a smile.

The hunters grouped themselves around the dead panther, looking at him with much satisfaction, and Mr. Cary was attracted like the rest. He was a remarkably large animal, and it was a remarkably fine shot: the bullet had gone right to the vital spot. Mr. Cary looked round to say so, but Harry Vance had shouldered his rifle and walked away. Everybody had been so much absorbed that no one had noticed the fact but Frances Cary, who had made him a grateful bow, which he politely returned.

XXVII.

THE TRAMPS.

THE sitting-room at "Falling Water" —the name of Mr. Cary's house—was a very pleasant sight on this same evening. A slight blaze had been kindled on the old-fashioned brass andirons in the broad country fireplace, for the evenings were growing cool; and the Argand lamp, with a porcelain shade, upon the centre-table, covered with books, diffused a moonlight glimmer into every corner of the apartment. In the immediate circle around it the light was quite bright, and fell upon the figures of Mr. Cary and Frances seated in arm-chairs facing each other.

Colonel Edmund Cary, or Mr. Cary, as he preferred being called, retained, as he always seemed to do, his expression of mildness and composure. It was the air of a man who has seen so much and such singular things in life that he is no longer surprised by anything. You could see that he was essentially a man of books; it was strange that destiny had ever made a soldier of him, and he could not have loved the career very much. No doubt his view had been that when a man's native soil is invaded there is but one thing for the man to do—to shoulder a musket or buckle on a sword. There was enough of pride in his face to make it plain that nothing could have induced him to remain inactive at such a time. Beyond this the pride did not seem to be an obtrusive or aggressive sentiment. It was there, but he had little further use for it now; and having lived in the past a life of action, wished now to live tranquilly, indulging his affections and his literary tastes, unmoved by harsh emotions or by ambition. As he was alone in the world, except for Frances, she was his idol. You could see that from the expression of his eyes when he looked at her. Some human beings find their fullest delight in applause, celebrity, the glittering gewgaw of a name. This one plainly found it in his home and the face of his daughter.

It was a very sweet face as the girl sat sewing opposite her father, who was reading. There was in it an indefinable something which suggested the freshness of the first spring days, when the buttercups bloom. She was rather tall and quite slender, with brown hair, and blue eyes which had a confiding expression; and the lips were very red, in strong contrast to her fair complexion. She smiled habitually, from a natural tendency, it seemed, to mirth, but this sometimes gave way to another expression—that on the lips of the cabinet picture over the mantel-piece, which she exactly resembled. This was an expression of virginal modesty. Looking into her face, you could see that her being had been shaped in an atmosphere of purity, and that she no more affected modesty than the dawn affects freshness. She wore one of those ugly "pull-back" dresses which confine the knees unpleasantly, but she had arranged the scanty skirt in such a manner as to conceal, not display, her person. Her arms, from which the sleeves fell back, were slender, which is another word for beautiful. Some female arms are Amazonian, and produce the impression that they are ready to strike—this pair seemed intended to clasp the neck of some one whom their mistress loved.

"It is really like a novel!" the slim beauty said, laughing. "I was 'rescued' —that is the proper word—just like Lucy Ashton, in the 'Bride of Lammermoor.' And then he was a 'stalwart youth'— doesn't Mr. G. P. R. James call them that? —a romantic young woodman, perhaps a Locksley, Earl of Huntingdon, in disguise!"

"How your tongue runs, France!" said Mr. Cary, with a smile. "I believe you rattle on to make me laugh, my child."

"Well, why shouldn't I?" she said.

"It is a hard task. I have nearly lost the art. There's no help for it."

All the smiles disappeared from the girl's face, and a quick expression of sadness came to her lips.

"No, no! papa, do not talk so," she said; "please do not. It distresses me so—indeed it does."

Her eyes swam as she looked at him, and her lips trembled a little.

"Don't think of that," she said, in a faltering voice; "please don't."

"Well, I'll be more cheerful, dear. Look at me—I am smiling."

"It is a very sorrowful smile. Come, be bright, papa. My business is to make you cheerful and happy. We ought to be as happy as we can, and laugh as much as possible—don't you think so?"

"Certainly."

"I have been laughing to myself ever since Mr. Elliot's and Nelly's visit. He is certainly in love with her, and I mean to make the match. They might marry and live at Crow's Nest: the house could be fitted up for them. That would be delightful."

"They would be pleasant neighbors, but it would require a good deal of money to fit up Crow's Nest. It is a tumble-down old place, you know, and so far off in the hills that I really have not even thought of it for a long time."

"But it could be repaired, and Mr. Elliot could move in at once, as there is no one living in it, is there?"

The door opened, and an old servant said,

"Mr. Gibbs, sir!"

"Ask him to walk in," said Mr. Cary, and this was followed by the appearance of Mr. Gibbs, a weather-beaten personage in drab clothes, who had long managed Mr. Cary's property.

"Take a seat, Mr. Gibbs," Mr. Cary said, with his air of mild courtesy.

"I thank you, sir; it's not worth while," said Mr. Gibbs, remaining erect from respect, whereupon Mr. Cary rose too. "I came to say the people I told you about are at Crow's Nest yet—I can't do anything with 'em."

Mr. Cary, standing in front of the mantel-piece, reflected for a moment.

"You say they are tramps. Have they trespassed—I mean done any damage?"

"None to speak of, sir, unless it's burnin' brush and dead wood. But they're nuisances."

"Have you seen them again?"

"Yes, sir. There's an oldish fellow, who seems a little out of his head, and a younger man, and a little girl. The worst of the party, though, is the big man with the black beard. He did the talking."

"Well, what did he say?"

"He 'lowed they were doin' no harm, and didn't mean to; but the winter's comin', and then you'll miss something—maybe a lamb or a pig. They ought to be made to clear out."

"There is an old man, you say, who seems out of his head?"

"Yes, sir."

"And a little girl?"

"The littlest mite of a thing."

"And the winter is coming, as you say. I would not like to turn them out."

"It'll be the worse," said Mr. Gibbs. "The big fellow with the black beard looks like a hard subject. His fist would knock down a bull. I've made up my mind to take my pistol along on my next visit."

"That would be useless, probably. You informed them that the house was my property?"

"Yes, sir; and notified 'em to quit."

"And they refused?"

"The big man did. There was nobody there but him and the mite of a child when I give him the notice; and he doubles up his big fist, and looks black, and says, says he, 'What harm are we adoin' to anybody?'"

Mr. Cary nodded, and said,

"Well, I'll ride over myself in the morning, Mr. Gibbs. You need not give yourself any further trouble."

"I'll go with you, sir."

"That will not be necessary."

"But the big man's dang'rous, sir."

"I have had a great deal to do with danger in my life, Mr. Gibbs. It is the sort of thing which shrinks before a man when he faces it, and cares nothing for it. Not that I think there is the least here, or that your big friend is apt to make himself disagreeable to me. I am not thinking of him. I am thinking of the little mite of a child. I should not like to turn *her* out, when the winter, as you say, is coming."

Mr. Gibbs having made a renewed proffer of his company, which was again declined, thereupon retired, and Mr. Cary resumed his seat, and quietly went back to his reading.

"Poor little thing!" said Frances; "'the littlest mite of a thing,' he said, papa."

"That is the trouble," Mr. Cary said. "It is very easy to order a party of rough tramps to go, but not so easy to be unkind to a child. Well, we will see. I'll ride over to-morrow."

"Do pray take care, papa, and don't have trouble. There might be some risk."

"There is none, my dear. Would you try to frighten an old soldier? There will be no trouble; let me read you this page. There really are an enormous number of clever writers now; this is one of the youngest of them."

An hour afterward Mr. Cary read family prayers, kissed his daughter on the forehead, and said that he would himself retire after writing a letter. He wrote the letter, sealed and directed it, and then placed it behind a vase on the mantelpiece for the mail. This brought him in front of the cabinet picture. The lips seemed to smile upon him, the glad light in the eyes to caress him. He looked at the picture for some moments calmly, and then, putting out the lamp, took a smaller one from a side-table, and retired.

On the next morning Mr. Cary was occupied for about an hour after breakfast; he then ordered his horse, and set out for Crow's Nest. He had purchased this house, with a tract of land upon which it stood, many years before, in order to round off his own small estate, but chiefly for the fine timber on it: that at Falling Water was growing scant. As there was a very good overseer's house at Falling Water, Crow's Nest had been shut up; and he had almost forgotten its existence when his attention was suddenly called to it. It was not more than a mile and a half distant. The road which led to it was nearly unused, except as a short cut by the mountain people. It wound through a dense growth of pines along the slope of the range in rear of Falling Water, and here and there crossed a mountain rivulet, which had worn a channel deep into the slope, and gurgled over rocks, between abrupt banks, densely covered with evergreens. It was sometimes difficult to descend into and emerge from these ravines, but Mr. Cary seemed to be an experienced horseman, and pushed on, scarcely noticing the ground over which he passed. The whole tract was wild and solitary. From time to time the drumming of a pheasant was heard in the thickets, or the low croak of a wild turkey; and hares, with their white tails erect, leaped up and scudded off. The intrusion of the horseman on their domain seemed to astonish them.

Lost in reverie, and with a shadow upon his face, Mr. Cary went on at a walk, with his bridle on his horse's neck and his eyes fixed upon the ground. From time to time he raised his head and looked around him. Did the sight of the objects near him remind him of the time when he looked at them in company with another person? It was probable. When, after a long lapse of time, we return to scenes associated with brighter years, and faces that are gone, the past times and faces strike dolorously on the heart.

He came in sight of Crow's Nest at last. It was an old tumble-down house of weather-board, which once might have been bright with cheerful faces, but now was loneliest of the lonely, and the picture of neglect. The fences once enclos-

ing the yard were down, the window-panes were broken, and the path up the hill, once broad and beaten, was nearly effaced by the growth of grass. Behind the house, which stood upon a knoll, stretched the interminable thicket. There was no glimmer of light through the windows—no human being was seen. The door was closed: it was difficult to believe that the foot of man had been placed within the enclosure for a score of years.

Mr. Cary dismounted, threw his bridle over a bough, and went up the path. No one had yet appeared, and he walked up to the small porch, whose floor was rotting, and knocked with his riding-whip. As the sound died away the door opened, and the Lefthander, with his shaggy black eyebrows making the straight line across his face, confronted the visitor.

"What do you want?" he said.

Mr. Cary looked at him with some curiosity.

"There will be time enough to tell you that, friend, when you do not block up the door-way, and allow me to come in."

"I do not know you. I asked you who you were?" said the Lefthander, in his phlegmatic voice.

"I am the owner of this property," Mr. Cary said, looking still with interest on the remarkable face and figure of the Lefthander; "and I have a better right to ask who you are than you have to ask that question of me."

"So this is Colonel Cary—the proprietor," said the Lefthander, in a sinister tone. "You have come at last to order us away from this poor shelter."

The eyes of the speaker were not pleasant. The Lefthander's nature was a ponderous one, that rarely lost its balance from anger; but he was growing angry on this morning. The interview with manager Gibbs had been unpleasant. That personage had left him on the day before with the announcement that he meant to have "him and all his gang turned out neck and heels;" and there had risen before the Lefthander's eyes the picture of his little Mouse limping along on the highway, hungry and weary, which had begun now to excite what was latent in this man — a certain species of ferocity.

"So you are the proprietor—the master," he said, in his deep voice. "You are a well-to-do gentleman, with your carriages and horses, your servants and every luxury, while we are only a poor company of tramps you look down on, and intend to treat like dogs."

"I have never felt such a sentiment toward any human being," Mr. Cary said, in his composed voice.

"Why have you come, then? You come to drive us away, and my child will not have a roof over her head! What have we done to injure you? Are we thieves? You have a child, perhaps—so have I, and I love my child as much as you love yours. Do you think I will have you turn her out on the highway? There'll be trouble before that."

Mr. Cary had not ceased looking curiously at the Lefthander. The man seemed to interest him as a study. His eyes were fixed upon the broad face, with the black brows shut down over the eyes—he did not seem to be aware of the fact that the heavy hand hanging at his companion's side had closed with a covert threat.

"Come, come!" he said at last, "unbend your black brows, friend, and let us talk like reasonable people, not like children. I am not a child, to be frightened by your frowns. Who is here besides yourself?"

Harry Vance came forward and held out his hand. Mr. Cary, who had advanced toward the Lefthander with the intention of entering, stopped, looking with great surprise at the young man.

"You!" he said—"Mr. Vance?"

"Myself, Colonel Cary!"

"You are one of the—"

"The tramps — yes. But not a very dangerous one, I hope. You have the right to come into your own house. I told you we were neighbors."

The young fellow laughed, and said, "Father, this is Colonel Cary."

And Gentleman Joe, coming out, made Mr. Cary a bow full of earnestness and real dignity.

"I know you very well by reputation, sir," he said, "and am sorry we have trespassed on your property—but we are very poor."

"You do not trespass at all," Mr. Cary said, going into the room, which contained only a table and some old chairs, and mattresses rolled up in a corner. "Is this your little mite of a child? You are a mite, indeed, little one. What is your name?"

"Mouse, sir."

"Well, I have not come here to turn out the mouse."

Mr. Cary then sat down before the blaze in the large fireplace, and, turning to the Lefthander, said,

"Come, get back your good-humor, and stop scowling, friend, and let us talk. Anger is nearly always an absurd thing. You call me a well-to-do gentleman—I am a very poor one. It is the same; I am a man, and you are men like myself. One of you I know well;" he turned to Harry Vance and said, "I invited you to come and see me; as you did not, I have come to pay you the first visit, which you are entitled to."

Mr. Cary stayed at Crow's Nest for nearly an hour. He then got up, and said,

"Give yourself no further trouble—you are not trespassing here. You are very welcome to occupy this house. If I can assist you in any way, call on me, and I will do so gladly."

Mouse was standing near him, and he placed his hand paternally on her head.

"Poor little Mouse!" he said, "did you think I would turn you out of this poor place? No, indeed, my child, you are welcome to remain here with your friends as long as you choose, and to make yourself as happy as you can, poor little one! Your father was right—there is a right above the right of property, and I bear you no malice, friend," he said to the Lefthander. "On the contrary, I respect you."

He shook hands with each in turn, and

then went down the hill and rode away. As he was passing the overseer's, he said to Mr. Gibbs,

"Allow the people at Crow's Nest to remain — there will be no trouble, Mr. Gibbs."

When he reached home he said to Frances,

"The tramps are very honest people, my dear, and the little mite of a child is quite charming."

XXVIII.

THE HOME OF THE HOMELESS.

CROW'S NEST had become the place of refuge of Gentleman Joe, the Lefthander, Harry, and Mouse in a very simple and natural manner.

When the Lefthander left the home of Mr. Grantham before daylight, carrying Mouse in his arms, he went out of the town toward the mountain, the place of rendezvous which he had agreed upon with his two friends. This was a secluded spot about half-way up the slope of the Blue Ridge, on a little plateau, and not far from the stage-road, where a small stone chapel, as it was called, stood—a very ancient building, erected and used by the first settlers in the region. Service was still occasionally held in it by Mr. Grantham, who had it under his charge; but it was chiefly used as a burial-place for the older families, generation after generation of whom had gone to sleep in the grassy enclosure, surrounded by a low stone wall, with a willow drooping over the mossy slabs.

Just without the enclosure was a very fine spring, which gushed up from beneath the gnarled roots of an oak; and here, beside a cheerful fire, stood Gentleman Joe and Harry, the latter holding in his hand a rifle, which he had always carried about with him to hunt when the circus stopped in the rural districts to recuperate, as it often did.

"Here you are, Lefthander!" Harry exclaimed.

"And Mouse, too — but about breakfast?" said the Lefthander.

"You see, we t!
Gentleman Joe, poi
a coffee-pot was b
frying in a pan.

"We came here
fire and camped ou
the pot and frying-
some coffee and sug
so that you, and M
not go without you

The Lefthander
on the roll of blan
which Harry and hi

"Well, that's like
he said; "you're a
than all of us. Bu
What are you after

"I am after my
who was limping
superintending the
house-keeper—whic
derstand, and not ir

The Lefthander
at the child, as she
pleased smile on l
to have quite forgo
with one hand deftl
from the coals, too
and arranged them
bread and some tin
which were near by

"Well, whoever
Lefthander said, wit
your little mother a
the troupe."

"And we're a tr
selves!" said Mous
hand-organ, and t
feather in his cap,
the flowers and th
the hat around, as
Harry!"

"It really looks
laughing; "and I
Mouse."

"What is that, s
"That you're goi
commander-in-chief

They sat down a
ening their repast w
The air of the fre
fill their pulses wit

The sunrise bathed them in its golden beams, the birds were singing, the bivouac fire crackling; the wanderers, without a shelter, had found something like a home in this secluded nook, and enjoyed the present moment, without thinking what might befall them in the future.

Breakfast finished, that future demanded consideration. Where should they go, and what means of support could they have recourse to? Mouse's plan of organizing themselves into a troupe, with a hand-organ, a monkey, a tent, and wagon, was excellent; but, unfortunately, at the moment it was quite impracticable. With the exception of the Lefthander, who had a portion of his last week's salary yet unspent in bar-rooms, the little party were without money. It was, therefore, necessary to defer the troupe scheme, and cast about them for some means of immediate support. First of all, they must look out for shelter somewhere; then they would have time to think. So, having finished breakfast, they made a package of the blankets, cooking utensils, and the rest of the provisions—Harry took them on his back—the Lefthander lifted Mouse in his arms, though she declared that she could walk, and they set out up the mountain road leading through the Gap.

All at once the Lefthander stopped, and said,

"Where is your travelling-bag, Mignon?"

"My travelling-bag, poppa! Haven't you got it?"

"I have left it behind, fool that I am!" exclaimed the Lefthander.

"It must be at the fire."

"No, it was not left at the fire," Harry said; "neither you nor Mouse had the bag when you joined us, Lefthander."

"Then I've left it at the priest's—I mean the parson's," the Lefthander said, knitting his brows; "and I must go back for it."

He uttered these words with an excitement extremely unusual in him. It was plain that for some reason he attached the utmost importance to the travelling-satchel.

"Wait for me, I will not be long," he said.

He deposited Mouse on her feet, pointed to a grassy bank, which afforded her a good place to rest, and set out for Piedmont. In an hour he returned, with an expression of decided gloom upon his features.

"Did you find it, poppa?" Mouse said, quietly.

"No, Mignon. It was not left there. I must have dropped it. That will be unfortunate, if—"

He stopped, knitting his brows.

"The parson was not at home. A sick person had sent for him, but I saw his old servant, who attends to the rooms and beds, and she was in the room you slept in after we went, and saw nothing. It is lost. I looked all along the road, but could see nothing of it. It will be unfortunate. I will make another search when we have found a place of shelter."

After saying this, the Lefthander relapsed into silence, and, taking Mouse in his arms, carried her up the mountain and through the Gap. Having reached the western embouchure, they saw a country road leading to the left, struck into it at hap-hazard, and followed it for a mile or two along Falling Water, until they reached a spot where the stream fell over a ledge of rocks, from which it derived its name. Just beyond this was a ford, and, on the opposite hill, what seemed to be a deserted house. The Lefthander pointed to it and said,

"There is the place. From the look of things no one lives in that house, and we can go there and stay for the night, at least."

He shaded his eyes with his hand and added,

"It's forlorn enough looking, and there's no one there; we will not be disturbed unless there are ghosts."

"Ghosts, ghosts!" said Gentleman Joe, dreamily; "yes, there are ghosts. They are all around us—don't you believe that, Lefthander?"

The Lefthander looked at his companion. Gentleman Joe was falling into one of his strange moods.

"I have been here before," murmured Gentleman Joe, putting his hand to his forehead; "when was it? But it was a dream only, I suppose."

A piteous expression came to his face, but he said nothing more, and his companions, apparently accustomed to his vagaries, paid no attention to his words. The Lefthander led the way through the ford, which only came to his knees, carrying Mouse in his arms, and, following a path on the other side of the stream, they ascended the hill and reached the deserted house. It was dreariest of the dreary, and the rotting porch gave way under the Lefthander's tread; but in the bare room within there was a broad fireplace, and Harry had soon collected some dry limbs lying around, and kindled a cheerful fire. Then, as their long tramp had made them hungry, Mouse set about preparing dinner, which consisted of coffee and fried beef and bread — after which they made an examination of their new domicile.

It had probably been a very comfortable establishment once on a time, but now everything was going to decay. The creaking door had flown open under the Lefthander's ponderous pressure—it was only secured by a rusty latch—and the staircase leading to the rooms above trembled under their feet. The lower story was completely bare, but in an upper room they found a small pine table, and two or three old chairs without backs, which they brought down and arranged in front of the fire. Then Harry and the Lefthander went out and collected another supply of wood, and by that time the sun began to decline. When night came they made a bed for Mouse of the blankets, and stretching themselves upon the floor fell asleep. Such was the first day spent by the wanderers at Crow's Nest.

On the next morning a council of war was held, and they unanimously resolved to remain where they were for the present. They had provisions for some days, and another supply could be purchased and brought from Piedmont: there was an excellent spring fifty yards from the house, which they had made the coffee from on the preceding evening; and, if Mouse could only be made comfortable, it really was a very good place to live in, this deserted house. What they wanted was another supply of food and beds, and Harry said that he would go and buy them.

"Just buy some cotton, Harry, and I'll stitch up the beds," said Mouse; "that is, if you'll buy me some needles and a spool of thread — all was lost with that travelling-bag."

The Lefthander produced all his money and gave it to Harry.

"And don't fail to go to the parson's, and ask if they are certain about that bag —that it was not left."

Harry nodded, set out at a long, springy gait, and disappeared. He did not return until late in the day, but he had thought of everything. He brought a supply of sugar, coffee, flour, bread, salt, some beef, a ham, and the cotton, with the needles and thread.

"I went to the parson's, but he was away from home again," he said. "You must have dropped your travelling-bag in the circus tent, Lefthander."

"I could swear I did not!—it is possible. If so it will be safe, and I'll get it back. Clare de Lune will see to that."

As he uttered the name of Clare de Lune the Lefthander fell into a fit of musing. His thoughts had evidently gone back to the scenes at the circus.

"Some day I'll see her again, perhaps," he said; "she is a good girl."

Mouse had meanwhile set about stitching up the beds, which she did with a business air which was impressive. But she really was extremely expert with her needle. On the next day she had finished them all, and then they were filled with the pine tags from the thicket in rear of the house; and that night, after an excellent supper, the whole little troupe slept in perfect comfort.

Thus their life at Crow's Nest began

in earnest; and finding themselves un-molested, they remained.

Nearly a month passed in this manner. Mouse had completely recovered from her sprain, and the wanderers passed their time in rambling through the beautiful September woods, in talking to each other, and in resolving that they would in some manner organize the troupe with the monkey and the hand-organ without delay. But nothing was really done to-ward it, and day after day passed by, and their supplies dwindled. Then came the irruption of Mr. Gibbs, indignant at the presence of trespassers, with the subse-quent visit from Mr. Cary. The result, so far, was satisfactory: they would not be forced to leave, at least. But there re-mained the paramount question how they were to live in future.

The wanderers were face to face with want.

XXIX.

BY A FIRE IN THE MOUNTAIN.

On the night succeeding Mr. Cary's visit, after Mouse had gone to sleep in her warm corner, the Lefthander and Harry, seated before the fire, held a consultation on the subject of their fut-ure ways and means. It was a chill night, and the muffled sigh of the wind in the pines, waving to and fro in the moonlight without, gave notice that win-ter was approaching. The very rattle of the sashes in the windows told them that, and the prospect before them seem-ed gloomy. Gentleman Joe, seated in the corner opposite Mouse, took no part in the conversation. For some time—indeed, from the moment of their arrival at the Crow's Nest house—he had been serious and absent-minded. He rarely indulged now in his fits of fantastic laughter; something seemed to weigh upon him and oppress him. At times a singular expression came to his face; his mind appeared to be busy with some problem which he was quite unable to solve. While Harry and the Lefthander conversed on this evening, he was looking into the fire with a dreamy glance, and any one could see that he was utterly un-conscious of their presence.

The Lefthander was smoking his short pipe, and leaning one ponderous arm upon his knee. They had been discuss-ing the melancholy fact that they had almost nothing left to eat, and even Har-ry's powder was exhausted, and they had no money to buy more.

"The main thing is Mouse," said the Lefthander. He looked at the child, who was sound asleep, and his face softened, as it always did at such moments.

"One of us must stay with her," he said. "You and me, Harry, might find work by going off somewhere, but what would become of Mouse and Gentleman Joe?"

Harry shook his head.

"It would never do to leave them. Mouse is a child, and my poor father—"

He stopped, and touched his forehead sadly.

"He seems worse than ever of late. He wanders around in a strange, absent-minded way, looking at everything, and muttering to himself in a manner I don't understand. Only yesterday I heard him say to himself, 'Why, I remember all this!'"

"Strange enough," the Lefthander said, "I noticed the same thing, and asked him if he had ever been here before; but he made me no reply. I know he heard what I said, for he turned round and looked me in the face with a cunning look, as if he meant to keep his own counsel."

Harry listened to these words with a deeper impression of gloom upon his face than before.

"I never could understand father," he said; "and he always manages to turn aside any questions I ask him. But about the bread and meat, Lefthander—we must see about that. We must find work."

"Work!" said Gentleman Joe, sudden-ly arousing himself and turning round; it was plain that he had not heard what had been said before. "Work, did you say? Yes, we must work for Mouse."

"Well, that's the trouble, Gentleman Joe," the Lefthander said; "we're at the end of the rope. The provisions are about out—hardly enough for to-morrow. We might go and work, as I told Harry just now, but how about Mouse? I don't mean Mouse shall want anything."

He knit his brows.

"I won't steal, but it's come to this that somebody will suffer before Mouse does! You see, I don't mind myself. I've given up drink, and am willing to work; but if I can't—"

"Set traps," said Gentleman Joe, quietly.

"Why," exclaimed Harry, "we never thought of that, Lefthander! The mountains are full of game, and nothing is easier, if we only knew how."

"I know," Gentleman Joe said; and monopolizing with sudden ardor the whole conversation, Gentleman Joe entered upon the subject of constructing traps for game in a manner which showed that he was a master of the art. Harry and the Lefthander listened with admiration, and did not interrupt him.

"I'll make the traps to-morrow," said Gentleman Joe. And it was agreed that they should rise early and set about the work at once, in order to have the traps ready by the ensuing evening.

All then lay down in front of the fire, wrapped in their blankets, and were soon asleep—all but Gentleman Joe. He had closed his eyes, but in about half an hour opened them again and looked intently into the fire. Then he turned round and surveyed every portion of the room with a vague, dreamy glance.

"The same," he said, in a low voice, pressing his hand to his forehead. "This is Crow's Nest—where have I been all this time?"

His mind seemed to be struggling with some memory which came to him vaguely in dim outlines, like a landscape looked at through haze.

"I must not tell them—they must not know—but what have I to tell?"

He sighed deeply, and turned his head away from the fire, muttering,

"I must have dreamed all that! I seem to remember—but I must have dreamed it."

Another sigh followed these words, and muttering something further to himself he at last fell asleep.

Early on the next morning they set to work making the traps. In this work Gentleman Joe was the manager and director. With the assistance of bits of plank, some nails collected here and there, and strong twine string, made by untwisting an old rope discovered in an out-house, they succeeded in constructing the traps; and by evening they were done. It was then agreed that Harry should remain with Mouse, while Gentleman Joe and the Lefthander crossed to the mountain opposite and set the traps; and the Lefthander, taking the whole load upon his back, set out with his companion.

They descended the hill, crossed the stream at a narrow spot upon a log, and entered the woods clothing the slope beyond. The vicinity was wild and uninhabited. Here and there ravines penetrated the mountain, nearly concealed by overhanging trees which threw deep shadows, growing deeper as the sun sunk. Making their way into the silent depths the trappers set their traps, which were already baited, and then attempted to retrace their steps toward the crossing of the stream.

This proved far less easy than they had supposed it would be. Night had fully come now, and scarcely a ray penetrated the shadowy gorge into which they had advanced for a considerable distance. The moon had not risen, and a haze hid the stars—in addition to which they had lost the points of the compass. There were no paths to guide them, the steep sides of the gorge affording no foothold even for the mountain cattle; and, after wandering around for some time, the Lefthander and Gentleman Joe came to the depressing conclusion that they were lost in the mountain.

"Well, here's your Babes in the Wood!" said the Lefthander, with a low laugh; "we're lost, Gentleman Joe."

"Wait for moonrise," said Gentleman Joe. "I know where we are."

"You know! How?"

"Well, I know. That is the Hogback yonder."

"That ridge? Well, that's something. So we are near a place called the *Hogback?* You're no stranger here, then?—What does all this mean, Gentleman Joe?"

They were pushing through the thick fringe of pines at the moment — all at once a light shone in front of them.

"Some one is hunting," said the Lefthander; "they can tell us the way."

He advanced in front of Gentleman Joe, and they steadily approached the light, which they now saw was that of a fire burning in a concealed nook between two ledges of rock, and hidden from any one approaching in all directions except from the difficult spot to which the trappers had wandered in the darkness. There was something wild and weird about this light and its surroundings. The masses of rock rose above it to the right and left in rugged ledges, with cedar bushes and trailing vines starting from every crevice. On these the red light of the fire threw fantastic shadows, and as it soared aloft from time to time, the glare fell on the boughs of a mountain-ash reaching far over the ledge, and nearly drooping to the ground. What more than all astonished the Lefthander and his companion was an object only a few feet beyond the fire. Could his eyes deceive him? This something was a door in the side of the mountain; there was no doubt of that. It was nearly covered by the drooping foliage—but there it was.

The Lefthander stopped, and laid his hand on the arm of Gentleman Joe.

"These people are not hunters," he said, in a low tone; "look at them."

Shadows were moving to and fro in front of the fire, and dark figures, in rough dresses, were dimly visible as the trappers cautiously drew nearer.

"If I was in the Bohmerwald Mountain, I should say they were the wrong sort of people to go near," said the Lefthander, in a low voice.

The figures at the fire probably heard his voice, for one of them, with a gun in his hand, left the group and came in the direction of the sound.

"Who goes there?" said the figure.

The Lefthander continued to advance, whereupon the figure raised his gun to his shoulder, and ordered—

"Halt!"

The Lefthander was within twenty paces. He stopped.

"Well," he said, in his phlegmatic voice, "I have halted to oblige you. Who are you?"

"Plain people. Who are you?—What is your business here?"

"Setting traps," said the Lefthander; "and you'll do me a favor, friend, if you'll tell me how to get out of this devilish place."

The figure came nearer, and bending down peered into the Lefthander's face; as his back was to the fire, his own was concealed.

"You are the big man living at the Crow's Nest house," said the figure.

"Yes," said the Lefthander.

"Who is with you?"

"One of my friends."

"You are tramps?"

"You may call us that, if you fancy."

"Wait a little."

The figure went back to the fire and held a brief colloquy with the men there. He then returned to the Lefthander, and said,

"Come on, friends—both."

The Lefthander and Gentleman Joe approached the fire, around which Barney Jones and two or three others were standing. The person who had held the colloquy with them was Daddy Welles.

XXX.

DADDY WELLES RECONNOITRES.

ONE morning Brantz Elliot received a letter from a friend in New York, informing him that the Coaching Club was just about to be organized, and that, if he wished to have his name enrolled for all time among the "great founders" of that mighty enterprise, it would be essential to return at once, and take part in the deliberations.

To this note Elliot replied immediately, announcing his early return. He then decided not to return, but to remain in the little mountain-house beside Nelly Welles, who now in the October days had begun to be all the world to him.

It had come at last to that. The incident on the stream had nearly opened his eyes, and now they were quite open at last. He loved the girl with all the ardor of first love. He had forgotten her linsey dress, her poor origin, the social inequality between them, and could see now nothing but the glimmer of her eyes, and hear nothing but the voice which made sweeter music in his ears than all else in the world. True, he did not come to realize and accept this state of things without a struggle, or contemplate the idea of marrying Daddy Welles and his old dame, together with Nelly, without something like a shudder. The dear desire was balanced against the unpleasant condition—but love conquered pride. Having firmly resolved to tear himself away violently from the temptation, and return to New York, and after writing to his friend announcing his speedy return, he quietly determined to remain, and drift as before upon the stream.

Daddy Welles seemed quite unaware that anything but a love of hunting retained Brantz Elliot in the mountains. He never made sly jests, as old people will, about Nelly and the young man; indeed, he seemed much too busy, this excellent Daddy Welles, to bestow his attention on the affairs of other people. The mysterious going and coming of uncouth personages to and from the mountain-house, at almost any hour of the day or night, continued; and the absences of Daddy Welles grew more frequent. New faces had appeared in the vicinity—those of a big, black-browed individual, and a fantastic old gentleman, who laughed and sighed by turns. These faces had begun to make their appearance, Elliot remem-

bered, soon after a certain absence of Daddy Welles for a whole night, or rather until just before daylight, when the young man heard him come in cautiously, place his rifle, which he had taken with him, on its pegs, and retire to his room. The big man went by the name of the Lefthander, and seemed to be looked to and consulted by Daddy Welles as a co-adjutor of the first importance in some secret business. As to the fantastic old man, who bore the equally curious name of Gentleman Joe, he seemed to have no concern with any business whatever; looked around him in a dreamy manner when he visited the house; thrummed on his chair; fell into reveries, and woke from them with a smile or a sigh, scarcely conscious, one would have said, where he was, or what faces were around him.

He and Nelly had become the best friends imaginable. Gentleman Joe had joined Elliot and herself one day, as they were walking out in the evening, and politely informing them that he resided with some friends of his in the neighborhood, had bestowed his society upon them, smiling gently, and looking at Nelly with so much affection that Elliot did not have it in his heart to resent the unwelcome intrusion. As to Nelly, she was very far from discouraging the poor old fellow. A smile full of pleasure and relief always greeted him on such occasions; and Brantz Elliot, seeing that smile, was lost in a maze of perplexity, and far from pleased at what seemed to indicate a desire on the girl's part not to be alone with him.

What could it mean? If he had known, he would not have been so much displeased, and his love would have grown even stronger. That longing for the presence of a third person, on the part of Nelly, was susceptible of a very simple explanation if Brantz Elliot could have read her heart. He had come to be as dear to her as she was to him. All the pent-up feeling and romance of youth in the heart of the poor mountain-girl had broken the barriers and flowed toward him—or nearly broken them; for Nelly had not yielded to her heart. The very strength of her love gave her force to resist it. If she were to marry Brantz Elliot, she would darken his whole career. She was far beneath him, socially, and after awhile he would bitterly regret the step he had taken in a moment of impulse. Then the result would be misery for both of them—for him, from the consciousness that he was yoked to a wife unsuited to his station in society and his educated tastes; for her, from the conviction which would be daily forced upon her that he regretted having ever met her. This thought haunted Nelly day and night: it would not have haunted a mercenary person, or one without pride; but Nelly was proud, and so far from being mercenary that, if she had been an heiress and he a poor boy, she would have held out her arms to him and gladly given him herself, as she had given him her heart. As the fact was the reverse, and that terrible future of her imagination more and more possessed her, the poor girl, with a sinking heart, came to a fixed resolution —to discourage the attentions of Brantz Elliot, which were growing more and more ardent, and make him understand that their union was impossible.

This had led to the sweet smiles which she bestowed on Gentleman Joe when he joined them in their walks. And she had really grown extremely fond of him, and called him "Gentleman Joe," as he called her "Nelly," in the most natural manner. As to the poor old fellow, the time came at last when he seemed to be quite wrapped up in Nelly, and to fix his melancholy eyes upon her face with a longing tenderness which went to her heart. He would come across the stream almost every day, and wander through the woods looking for her; and if he did not find her, he would go up the path to the mountainhouse, and bow to Mrs. Welles, and ask if Nelly was at home. If she was, she came at once and sat and talked with him. If she was absent, he went away with a melancholy shake of the head. When one morning he made his appearance thus at the house, and heard that Daddy Welles and Nelly had gone to Piedmont in the little spring-wagon, he uttered a sigh which would have done credit to a lover.

The visit of Daddy Welles had for its object the purchase of groceries. With an eye to business in the way of a trade, the Daddy took with him in his springwagon a number of sheepskins, a large roll of fresh butter, a bag of dried apples, a haunch of venison, and a mighty pile of dried sumach, for which he knew he would receive one and a quarter cents a pound. With this and the proceeds from the rest of his load, he proposed to lay in a stock of sugar, coffee, and other "store" supplies, and purchase winter clothing for his wife and daughter.

As the spring-wagon, drawn by its ancient mare, drove into Piedmont, its occupants became aware that something was going on. As Daddy Welles looked around him, with a smile of more than ordinary sweetness, it may be that he was not as much surprised at the general excitement as might have been supposed—even that he had had some intimation of the state of things, and had come to see for himself. There was a large crowd in front of the tavern, and through this crowd passed from time to time figures which were evidently those of strangers—probably the owners of the long string of horses tethered in the stable-yard in rear of the tavern.

Daddy Welles did not proceed as far up the main street as the tavern; he stopped before the door of an establishment which seemed to deal in groceries and other articles of nearly every description, and he and Nelly got out and went in. After awhile the Daddy emerged from the store and bore in the articles which he had brought; after which, leaving Nelly apparently to make her selection of goods, he strolled in a leisurely manner toward the blacksmith's. That grimy-armed individual was holding the leg of a horse between his knees, and fitting a hissing shoe to the hoof which he had just pared.

"Well, neighbor," Daddy Welles said,

sweetly smiling, "something seems to be agoin' on in town to-day."

The blacksmith looked up and laughed.

"I believe you, Daddy. It's the revenue collectors. Look out for yourself."

"I'm agoin' to; but you don't mean they'd come after a poor man like me?"

"Well, I ruther think they will. Rich and poor are all the same when they're after *the taxes.*"

The blacksmith emphasized the last words, and seemed to enjoy them, for some reason best known to himself. His smile expanded into a grin, and he and Daddy Welles exchanged glances.

"How many of 'em?" the latter asked, in a tone of mild interest.

"About a dozen; and they say they've got troops coming on."

"Troops! Well, that will be something new. Haven't seen the blue-coats sense the year '65. It'll be quite like old times — quite like old times," repeated Daddy Welles, smiling, as in fond remembrance of past joys.

"Well, they won't be strangers to you, Daddy Welles. If people tell the truth you had a hand more than once in bushwhacking Sheridan's troopers, and were worse on 'em than a hornet. I wouldn't be surprised, now, if you had at home the same musket — or perhaps it's a rifle — that you used to go after 'em with!"

"Oh, you musn't believe these old tales, neighbor: we are peaceful people up in the mounting!—Why, here's Barney Jones on his old sorrel."

In fact Mr. Barney Jones, in a suit of worn homespun, a weather-beaten felt hat, and heavy boots, drawn up by his short stirrup-leathers, at this moment made his appearance coming out of town, and halted to speak to his friends. He and Daddy Welles saluted each other, and the latter went out into the street.

"Well?" the Daddy said, in a low tone.

"They're comin' to-night, blast 'em!" said Mr. Jones, expectorating tobacco juice as he spoke.

"Are you certain?"

"Sure of it, Daddy! Drat 'em!— They'll set out, I hear, before sundown."

Daddy Welles mused, his countenance illumined by an expression of sweet satisfaction.

"Well, they're not apt to find much, I ruther suppose, Barney," he said.

"They'll find a rifle-bullet if they git too near *me,* Daddy," said Mr. Jones, viciously.

"No, no! that's onreasonable, Barney. Go on and tell the boys to lay low and keep quiet. Why, who's that yonder, walkin' about and talkin' to 'em like he was one of 'em—young Mr. Lascelles?"

"The same, Daddy."

"Is he takin' a hand in this business? What! I thought he was a neighbor."

"He mout be or he mout not," replied Mr. Barney Jones. "He's lived half his life in forin' parts, I'm told, but they say he's not agin us. You see old Gineral Lascelles, he's a magistrate, and he had to give 'em sarch warrants, and young Lascelles is goin' along, they say, to see that nobody's meddled with that oughtn't to be."

"Well, well! I'm glad of that. I wouldn't like to think old Gineral Lascelles was onfriendly. He's a friend to the poor man. I'll go and hear a little of their talk."

"Better not, Daddy."

"You think I'd better not, eh, Barney?"

"I see the list, and your name's on it, Daddy," said Mr. Barney Jones, with a grin.

"Well, I s'pose I'd better not," returned Daddy Welles, with resignation; "and I reckon it's time for me and Nelly to be goin' back to the mounting. She's about through by this time."

And saluting his friend the Daddy returned to the grocery store, from which he soon afterward reappeared laden with bundles which he deposited in his wagon. He then assisted Nelly to her seat, and was about to get up himself, but seemed to change his mind.

"Hold the reins, Nelly, and mind the old mare," he said; "I'll be back directly."

He then strolled up to the tavern and

greeted his acquaintances in a friendly manner. At sight of him a general smile expanded upon all visages, and one of his friends whispered,

"Take care, Daddy!—they're on your track!"

"You don't say!" said the Daddy, tranquilly.

"They'll be at your house by night. There's nigh a dozen, and they're armed."

"Well, well; seems to me the war's beginnin' over again. And troops!—there's *troops* not far off, if wanted."

"They say they will be here to-morrow."

"Well, well, well! who would 'a thought it? Is there goin' to be another Confed'rate business, neighbor? Hard times! hard times!"

And, apparently overcome by forebodings of future suffering for his country, Daddy Welles shook his head sadly and returned to his wagon. Before he could whip up his old mare a person in undress official costume approached him quietly, and said,

"Your name is Welles?"

"Did anybody tell you that, friend?" said the Daddy.

"No matter who told me. Come with me to the tavern."

"Come to the tavern!—what fur, friend?"

"That's my business. Come along."

"Have you got a warrant for my arrest, friend? If so, I'm a peaceful citizen and regard the laws."

"No matter about a warrant. No, I've got no warrant, but you're to come with me."

Daddy Welles shook his head with a peaceful smile.

"Can't spare the time now, friend. My old 'oman's at home by herself, and it's nigh sundown."

And quietly touching his mare with the whip Daddy Welles departed, apparently taking his leisure, to the great disgust and wrath of the official, who did not venture to stop him. The wagon slowly followed the road through the Gap. Daddy Welles was smiling.

"What did he mean by wanting you to go back with him, father?" said Nelly.

"Well, only some of their contraptions, Nelly—a little matter of business. But I hadn't time to-day.—Did you git that cloth for your cloak, Nelly? Why, it's beautiful!"

And, displaying her purchases, the daughter of Eve forgot all about the incident.

XXXI.

MOONSHINERS.

As the sun was sinking a party of about a dozen horsemen rode out of Piedmont, and proceeded westward at a round pace through the Gap in the Blue Ridge.

These horsemen were internal revenue employés, going to break up illicit distilleries of spirit in the mountain and arrest the malefactors. At their head rode a portly gentleman, the marshal of the district, and beside him was Mr. Douglas Lascelles, whose presence had been accurately accounted for by Mr. Barney Jones. General Lascelles having been applied to as a justice of the peace for search warrants had granted them, but requested his son to accompany the party and see that unoffending persons were subjected to no improper annoyance.

The marshal was in a very bad humor. He had made more than one foray on the "moonshiners," as the illicit distillers were called, but always without result. Intimations had thereupon reached him from head-quarters that he was regarded as wanting in efficiency. Hence indignation, and a fixed resolution to break up the illegal establishments if they could be discovered. But this, unfortunately, was the trouble. The stills were known to be in the recesses of the mountain, but it was not probable that they would easily be discovered, unless there was treachery. Of that, however, there was small hope. The moonshiners were popular. They supplied spirits to their neighbors at half the cost of the taxed article. They were often men of good character, and otherwise observers of the law; and the manufacture of "moonshine whiskey" was generally laughed at, and regarded as only the harmless evasion of an oppressive Federal excise. The plausible view was taken that these honest people were only making "a little something" for their families in a quiet way, without injury to anybody. They were good ex-Confederates, impoverished by the war. What harm was there in privately distilling their own grain? They ate and sold it in the form of bread; why not allow them to drink and sell it in the form of whiskey? Betray them to the Federal officials? It was absurd!

"A disagreeable business, Mr. Lascelles!" said the marshal, in great ill-humor. "These fellows are worse than foxes, and are real desperadoes, I hear, ready to resist, arms in hand. Luckily, my men are armed, and if there is resistance it will be at the peril of the miscreants."

"They are said to be peaceful people," said Mr. Lascelles, indifferently.

"Peaceful! You deceive yourself, sir. They are a desperate set. Did you read the account in the papers the other day of the troubles in East Tennessee and West Virginia? The collectors were fired on from the crags of the mountains, and one of them killed. A murder, sir! and the men who commit murder are murderers."

The marshal grew red in the face as he thus denounced the moonshiners.

"They are just as bad here, I have not the least doubt," he added; "and I see well enough that they are supported by popular sentiment. The war antagonism has not died out. The Federal officials are looked upon as Federal soldiers coming back in citizens' dress to open war anew on the 'good old Confederates!' It is deplorable, sir! The law must be obeyed—but how enforce it?"

"That seems to be the problem," said Mr. Lascelles, with the same indifferent air. In fact, he was scarcely listening to the marshal. He had accompanied the party in accordance with the request of General Lascelles, but cared little or nothing, apparently, for the result.

"A perfect wild-goose chase, sir!" the marshal exclaimed. "How are we to discover these illicit distilleries? No one will inform on the law-breakers. They are all in league together. Not a man, woman, or child will open their lips. Ask them questions, and you have a laugh for your pains, Mr. Lascelles! They are banded together in one great conspiracy against the law, and it was only with the greatest difficulty that I obtained the names of some who are suspected."

"You have the names?"

"Yes. Here is a list. You can look at it."

Mr. Lascelles took the paper and ran his eye over it.

"Well," he said, returning it with a careless air.

"And the names are all. There's not a particle of evidence against them. This name at the head is that of the leader of them, I hear—a certain Daddy Welles, as he is called—and the Barney Jones mentioned is said to be his head man."

"Well, I know nothing of them. These names are all?"

"All, with the exception of a gang of tramps, who are said to have established their head-quarters on the farm of a Mr. Cary—who, for that matter, may be in alliance with the moonshiners. Their presence on his land is suspicious."

"I know Colonel Cary, and think it improbable that he has anything to do with the moonshine people."

"Well, to be frank with you, I suspect everybody, and will form my own opinion from what I see. I am a stranger in this region, and have had the greatest trouble in obtaining directions where to find the homes of these people. We must be near the first I propose to visit—that of the man Welles. That is the house yonder, probably."

The marshal pointed to what was, in fact, the residence of Daddy Welles, and turned into the mountain-road leading up to it. The *cortege* followed him, and side by side he and Mr. Lascelles rode up to the gate in the fence, where they dismounted.

The sun had just sunk behind the fringe of woods on the summit of the opposite range, and dusk was drawing on. There was no moonlight yet, but the stars were beginning to twinkle in the blue sky to the east, mellowing into purple and orange as it extended westward toward the rosy flush above the pines. The marshal opened the small gate, walked up to the porch, followed by Mr. Lascelles, and knocked at the door.

Daddy Welles promptly appeared, and greeted his visitors with an amiable smile.

"Is your name Welles?" said the marshal, referring to the paper which he held in his hand—"Daddy Welles?"

"They do call me that sometimes, friend," said the Daddy, mildly. "Won't you come in?"

"I wish to see you, sir," the marshal said, in a curt voice. "I am informed that you are connected with the illicit distillation of whiskey in this mountain."

"Why, what could have put such an idee in your head, friend? But come in, come in; the nights are gittin' cold, and I've got a tech of the rheumatiz—come in, friend."

With which Daddy Welles led the way into the sitting-room on the right, where Elliot and Nelly were conversing by a small fire, and Mrs. Welles knitting opposite.

"Set down, set down," said the Daddy, cheerfully; and addressing Elliot, he added, in dulcet tones, "Jest to think—these gentlemen are after moonshine whiskey men, and think I'm one of 'em. What a queer idee!"

Thereat the Daddy laughed, and the whole mystery flashed on Elliot. The word "queer" sent his mind back to the talk with the stage-driver, who had used the very term, and here at last was the explanation—Daddy Welles was a "moonshiner!"

The marshal declined the proffered seat.

"It is my disagreeable duty to arrest you, Mr. Welles," he said, in his curt official voice, "and to search your house for evidence of your complicity in these illegal proceedings."

"To be sure," the Daddy responded, cheerfully. "P'r'aps you've got a sarch warrant?"

"Here it is."

Daddy Welles spelled it over carefully, and returned it.

"That's accordin' to law, friend. Better begin at the cellar."

With this business-like observation he took one of the candles from the table and preceded the marshal, who followed him. The cellar was first inspected, and then all the rooms in succession, after which the Daddy suggested that there was the stable and the cow-house. It was perfectly plain, however, that, whether innocent or guilty, Daddy Welles was prepared for the enemy, and the marshal declined to search farther.

"This is all a farce!" he growled; "you are warned. Well, get your horse and go with me."

"To be sure," said the Daddy, cheerfully; "it's agin law to arrest a peaceful citizen in the bosom of his fam'ly; but, bless you, I don't mind that."

The Daddy then retired, and soon reappeared wrapped in an old overcoat, stating that he was ready, and a few minutes afterward the party were again on their way, leaving Brantz Elliot in a state of bewilderment at the whole scene.

A ride of half a mile brought them to the small residence of Mr. Barney Jones, who, hearing the clatter of hoofs, made his appearance armed with a gun, which he directed toward the group, demanding who they were, and expressing his intention to blow their heads off unless the question was speedily answered.

"Put up your shootin' iron, Barney," Daddy Welles called out; "it's only a few friends come to see you."

Thereupon Mr. Jones lowered his weapon, cheerfully observing, as they dismounted and approached, that he had come mighty nigh blowin' their heads off, as tramps were prowlin' round. Learning their business, he gave a dramatic start of astonishment, and manifested a strong desire, judging from the expression of his face, to perform the blowing-off ceremony on general principles; but, having been reduced to a peaceful state of mind by Daddy Welles, he expressed entire willingness, nay, the utmost anxiety, to have his premises searched, assisted in every manner, and professed himself rather pleased than otherwise at being arrested.

So Mr. Barney Jones swelled the *cortege* when it departed, and accompanied the party on its rounds to the residences of other suspected persons, whose premises were searched with an equally unsuccessful result. No more arrests were made. It was plain that the marshal was weary of what he had styled his "wild-goose chase." The night was chill, and he probably had visions of a warm fireside at the Piedmont tavern, with something hot to promote his circulation, and would not have inquired too curiously whether it had paid the revenue tax or not.

"Well, Mr. Lascelles," he said at length, "I think I'll go back. This is all moonshine and no moonshiners. There is one other place—only the house occupied by the tramps on Mr. Cary's estate. We will return by that route, if Mr. Welles will direct us."

"To be sure," said Daddy Welles, "we're most in sight of it now. It's called Crow's Nest, and yonder I see a light burnin' — or p'r'aps it's the firelight. That's the house."

They had forded the stream, and were returning over the farm-road leading by Crow's Nest and "Falling Water" to the bridge over the stream on the road to the Gap. In five minutes they were at the foot of the hill; and, dismounting, the marshal, accompanied by Daddy Welles, Mr. Jones, and Mr. Lascelles, made his way up the path to the door.

XXXII.

MR. LASCELLES MEETS AN OLD ACQUAINTANCE.

THE marshal went up to the door of the house and bestowed a thundering knock upon it with the butt of his riding-whip.

"Who is there?" said a voice from within.

"Open—in the name of the law!" said the marshal, with impatience.

Deliberate steps were heard approaching the door, a bolt was drawn, the door opened, and the burly figure of the Lefthander appeared upon the threshold. His powerful frame was lit up by the firelight from the broad chimney, around which were grouped the other members of the little family.

The marshal looked keenly at the Lefthander. He was evidently struck by his gladiatorial proportions, and the fixed gaze of the dark eyes under the shaggy brows: but as the marshal was a business man, and had come on business, he proceeded to it without delay.

"I have a warrant to search this house for illicit spirit," he said, "and to arrest its occupants, if I see reason to connect them with a violation of the revenue laws."

The Lefthander did not reply. He was looking at Mr. Lascelles, who was standing behind the marshal. It was a somewhat singular look; not one of surprise in the least, or indicative indeed of any clearly defined sentiment whatever. Nevertheless there was a covert fire in the dark eyes, which betrayed some latent emotion which the owner of the eyes, by a strong effort of his will, suppressed. As to Mr. Lascelles, he looked at the Lefthander with utter astonishment. He had changed color slightly, and his eyelids had suddenly risen, as though he had seen a ghost. Mr. Lascelles was a gentleman of so much self-possession, and commanded his feelings so thoroughly on ordinary occasions that this distended expression of the pupils of his eyes, and the change of color were circumstances of the most surprising character.

"Ottendorfer!"

The word escaped from his lips unconsciously, without an effort of the will.

"Make way!" exclaimed the marshal, in great ill-humor. "I have no time to waste in all these parleys."

And he pushed into the apartment, leaving Mr. Lascelles and the Lefthander face to face.

"Then it was you, after all—at the circus," said Mr. Lascelles, in a low voice. "I thought I was mistaken."

"Yes, it was me," said the Lefthander, with his eyes still fixed upon his companion, and speaking in his phlegmatic voice.

"And not your ghost!" Mr. Lascelles said, trying to laugh, but completely failing.

"No, not my ghost in the least—myself."

"You are not with that circus company now?"

"I have left it.

"Your object?"

"It is my business."

"And you are living in this house?"

"Yes."

Mr. Lascelles attempted a careless performance with his riding-whip upon his boot, but failed in it. He had grown a little pale. He stood for some moments without uttering a word. He then said, making a strong effort to speak coolly,

"I should like to ask you some questions. You, no doubt, understand why I wish to ask them."

"Yes," said the Lefthander, "I can understand that."

"They will overhear us here, and the marshal will go back in ten minutes. Meet me to-morrow, say at sunset, at the bridge on the stage-road. Will you do so?"

"Yes," said the Lefthander.

This was all that passed between them. They went into the house, where the marshal, in a worse and worse humor at his fruitless search for moonshiners and moonshine whiskey, was interrogating Gentleman Joe.

He had advanced toward the group in front of the fire, and said, curtly,

"You are tramps, and, as such, suspicious characters. Your names, or designation, at least, are on my list, as members of a gang engaged in illicit distilling. I am here to search this house and arrest your whole party. Light me in my search."

"With pleasure, sir," Gentleman Joe responded; "there are only the bare walls —we are new residents, and the house is not yet furnished."

As Gentleman Joe smiled while uttering these words, the marshal considered that he was being trifled with.

"Light me!" he said, with asperity.

"We have no candles, sir," Gentleman Joe politely replied, "but a brand will perhaps answer. Be good enough to follow me."

The marshal looked with curiosity at the tramp who addressed him in such terms. Gentleman Joe, however, did not notice the look. Stooping down he took a flaming pine-knot from the fire, and went before the marshal, lighting up the deserted rooms one after another.

"There is nothing here, you observe, sir," said Gentleman Joe, entering one of the rooms on the second story; "nothing but what I can see."

"What *you* can see? What do you mean?"

Gentleman Joe shook his head with sudden sadness.

"I see many things here which other people do not," he said. "There was a cradle yonder once."

"A cradle!"

"Under the window. It had a little baby in it. I can see the cradle now, and the baby, too."

As he spoke, his voice trembled and his eyes filled with tears. He was looking with a vague glance at the spot which he had indicated as that where the cradle formerly stood.

"Yes, it was there," he murmured, "and she was leaning over the baby singing. The chair she used to sit in stood there by the side of the fireplace—why, there she is sitting in it now!"

The marshal suddenly retreated in the

direction of the door-way. The deserted house, the darkness lit up only by the flaming torch, and the weird figure of his companion, produced a disagreeable effect upon his nerves. He measured the distance to the ground through the paneless windows. He had little doubt that his companion was a lunatic, and he might prove dangerous — lunatics were often seized with the idea of clutching their fancied foes, and leaping with them to destruction on such occasions. The worthy marshal therefore exclaimed hastily,

"Yes, yes — I understand. Farther search is useless."

With which he beat a hasty retreat down the creaking stairs to the room below, where Daddy Welles was standing with his back to the fire warming himself, and conversing in a low tone with Mr. Barney Jones and Harry. On the reappearance of the official he greeted him with a cheerful smile, and said,

"Did you find any of the moonshine article, friend?"

"None at all — I might have known that — you are all in collusion with each other," the marshal replied, in great ill-humor.

"What an idee!" responded the Daddy, smiling.

"I'm tired of the whole business and am going home. Who are these people? Tramps? What right have they to be trespassing here?"

"Squire Cary lets 'em stay, I'm told, friend. But that's none o' my business."

"Nor of mine. Come on; I'm going back. What am I to do with these people? I can't arrest lunatics and children, and these men have no horses."

"To say nothin' of havin' nothin' aginst 'em, friend."

"Mr. Welles," said the marshal, sardonically, "I begin to think you are a lawyer by profession. You are right. I have no warrant to arrest even these tramps on such slight suspicion."

"But Daddy Welles and poor Barney —oh yes! they're the onlucky ones, friend! You can arrest them, and drag 'em off from the bosom o' ther fam'lies— but no matter! no matter! we'll be bac to dinner to-morrow."

"You seem certain of that, sir."

"Oh, yes, I'm sartain. You see we' sue out a have-his-carcass by daylight— or it mout be on in the day—it's all th same: we can stay in jail for a week The jailor's a friend of ourn, and we'll b well keered for."

The marshal knit his brows. Th Daddy's remarks impressed him unplea antly. He designed leaving Piedmot after breakfast on the next morning, bt a writ of habeas corpus—evidently mean by the phrase "have-his-carcass"—woul necessitate an unpleasant delay.

"It's a fine thing, a very fine thing that have-his-carcass," said Dadd Welles, regarding the ceiling of th room with an air of contemplation "and then there's no evidence agin: us—no evidence at all."

"That's true!" muttered the marsha irritably; "the old rascal is a bett lawyer than all of us!"

"But I s'pose there's no law the hard times—no law at all!" mused th Daddy, sotto voce. "We poor people ole Virginny ain't got no rights wut speakin' of. The law's made for th l'yal people, not for us poor rebs—we' out in the cold."

The marshal knit his brows. He w a thorough respecter of the laws, and ha come to see them enforced; but here w the charge brought that the law was pa tial and oppressive, since it operated u equally and unfairly on different classes.

"Well," Daddy Welles said, cheerfull "there's the have-his-carcass, after al I reckon it won't take more'n a week, maybe a fortnight, to git a poor body ot of jail and let him see his friends an fam'ly agin."

The marshal succumbed, and, in spit of his ill-humor, felt a disposition t laugh.

"Friend Welles," he said, "would yo like me to say an honest word to you that expresses exactly how I feel towar you?"

"To be sure, friend."

" Well, I am tired of you, and of ev-erything connected with you. There's a hing called a wild-goose errand, and I've come upon it. And, as I am speaking of myself in terms not very complimentary, 'll take the liberty of comparing you to a fox. We are fox and goose, you see, and the fox has the best of it. Get on your horse—you and your friend Barney Jones, confound him!—and go home and go to bed, and go to sleep. I mean to do the same."

He turned his back on the group and went out of the house, followed by Mr. Lascelles, who exchanged a look with the Lefthander, apparently to remind him of his engagement. Daddy Welles, follow-ing them to the bottom of the hill, took an affectionate leave of them.

"Good-night, friend, good-night!" the Daddy said, bestowing all the treasures of his guileless smile upon the marshal. 'I'm glad to git back to my ole 'oman—he must be oneasy. It's jest as well to be at home and asleep in bed—though, after all, it wouldn't 'a made much differ-nce, on account o' the have-his-carcass."

"Curse the have - his - carcass, and the whole concern of you!" exclaimed the irate marshal.

"Oh no!" the Daddy retorted, shaking his head in pious reproof; "don't curse, riend! it's agin the Good Book, and never loes a body any good. Well, well, you must come agin—we poor mounting peo-ple like to meet with strangers—it sort o' tirs us up and puts us in good spirits. f I hear anything of them moonshiners might drop you word—the business 's unlawful."

"Go to the devil, you old fox!" roared he marshal, in huge wrath, as he mount-d his horse.

"Oh no! I wouldn't like to go there," aid the Daddy, shaking his head sadly; 'there's no have-his-carcass there. Come in, Barney. Good - night, friend. If I vas in your place, I'd git back to Pied-nont before the night grows late. They lo say the moonshiners shoot at people ometimes when they wear a han'sum uni-form like yours. But maybe that's on-true. Good-night—good-night!"

Daddy Welles and Barney Jones then rode away toward the ford, and the mar-shal, with Mr. Lascelles and his retinue, to-ward the stage road leading to Piedmont.

XXXIII.

MR. LASCELLES KEEPS HIS APPOINTMENT.

When Mr. Lascelles reached Wye the family had all retired, and he went to his chamber, where he divested himself of his riding-coat and boots, and put on a flow-ered dressing-gown and a handsome pair of slippers. He then stretched himself in an easy-chair in front of the fire, and fell into reflection.

These reflections were evidently un-pleasant. In fact, Mr. Lascelles had not regained the color which he had lost in his brief interview with the Lefthander. It might even be said that he grew a lit-tle paler now as he mused. This was un-usual with him. He rarely gave way to emotion. To move him so much some-thing singular was required—and this was probably the unexpected meeting at Crow's Nest.

Now and then he muttered disconnect-ed words, as people will when they are alone and occupied by absorbing thoughts. From these *disjecta membra* of speech it was possible to follow with tolerable ac-curacy his train of thought. He had been doubly deceived as to the Lefthand-er. Seeing him at the circus performance he had doubted if it was himself; but even if it were, he would probably disappear with the company and be seen no more. He had, therefore, dismissed the whole subject from his mind, as the soldier forgets the cannon-shot which rushes by him without striking him; now when the shot, having disappeared, returned upon its course, and seemed to be coming point-blank at him, he shuddered a little. It was no fancy at all. There was the man whom he evidently feared in his near vicinity—big, powerful, cool—the individual, above all others, whom no rational person would choose for an adversary.

Were they adversaries, and if so, what was the explanation of their hostility? Mr. Lascelles did not betray this in his disconnected utterances. One thing however was plain—that as he leaned back in his chair on this night, with no desire whatever to retire to bed, he was taking down from a private shelf of his memory certain recollections long consigned to oblivion, and covered with dust, and doing so far from willingly. Very plainly certain passages in his life were recalled to him by his meeting with the Left-hander, and he could not shake off the unpleasant impression on his mind. This was a most unwonted circumstance. Mr. Lascelles was very much of a philosopher. He had an excellent stomach, and an exceedingly tough and serviceable moral epidermis, which generally exempted him from much trouble in the way of reflection. He had the fixed habit never to brood over the past, and to regard it as a matter with which he really had nothing to do, in a practical point of view. Why worry about it? It was the past. He frankly acknowledged to himself that it would have been much better if he had conducted himself differently on certain occasions. His judgment disapproved of the course he had pursued, and he would now act in a different manner—probably. But then there was much to say on the other side. Young men were young men —they were led by impulse often to do what it would have been better for them not to do ; human nature was weak—even preachers and the best people were not faultless. On the whole, it was best not to take things *au grand sérieux*, and let the dead past bury its dead, if it had any to bury.

Unfortunately this convenient philosophy did not avail him at the present moment. It was plain, from the expression of his face, that Mr. Lascelles was confronted with a real peril, which was different from a mere uneasiness of the conscience. The one was theoretical, the other practical. Here, rooted in his im-mediate neighborhood, was a man whose eyes, as they looked at him, sent a sligh chill through him. Cool and brave as he was—and he was both—Mr. Lascelles had not been able to control his emotion a this meeting.

It really was painful to observe what moody and vicious knitting together o the brows ensued when Mr. Lascelles had come to this point in his muttering. A mingled expression of wrath and appre hension quite changed his handsome countenance, and made it ugly, and re pulsive. He rose suddenly from his seat with his right hand closed, as if he were grasping a weapon, and said aloud,

"Curse him! why didn't he break hi neck when he fell from the ropes? wish he had!"

He then went to bed muttering, "I wil know more to-morrow," and after awhile fell asleep.

On the next morning he came down and joined the cheerful group around the family breakfast-table without a cloud upon his face. He had excellent nerves.

"Well, how did your ride turn out Douglas?" said the general, who wa sipping his coffee and reading his morn ing paper. "Did you find any of the moonshiners?"

"None at all, sir—or, at least, none o the stills."

"I thought so. I told the marsha he would have his trouble for his pains Was no one arrested?"

"No one, sir. The marshal did take old Welles and a man named Jones along with him, but released them."

The general smiled and said,

"I was pretty certain that would b the result. Daddy Welles is a cunning old fox. Not a bad man at all; I know him very well from having electioneered in Bohemia, and he is quite an honest man. With all his simplicity, he is mor than a match for the marshal."

"I think he was, and his friend Barney Jones, too, who seemed desirous of put ting a bullet through somebody."

"Yes. I know Barney Jones, too. He is what is called a hard subject, and should prefer not prowling around his house in the night. Were these two all? I was applied to and granted a search-warrant against a gang of tramps on Colonel Cary's estate."

"We went there but found nothing. They are mere vagabonds, and will soon disappear, no doubt."

"Where did you find them?"

"In the Crow's Nest house."

"Ah! in the Crow's Nest house?"

The general had raised his cup to his lips, but set it down. His face, which had worn a smile of amused interest, became all at once thoughtful.

"In the Crow's Nest house?" he repeated.

"It is deserted, you know, sir, and they took up their residence there—no doubt without permission from Colonel Cary, who must be aware of the danger of harboring such vagabonds."

General Lascelles did not reply. His newspaper was lying in his lap and his eyes were fixed upon the table. Then he woke, as it were, from his reverie, finished his coffee, and rising from his seat went slowly to the library. Mr. Lascelles also rose, took a cigar from his case, lit it, and walked out to the portico.

He remained at home all day, smoking steadily. At dinner, which was about four o'clock, he had a very moderate appetite, and when he rose resumed his cigar. Then about an hour before sunset he ordered his horse, and rode slowly in the direction of the Gap.

He went along with his head bent down and his brows knit. There really seemed to be something the matter with Mr. Lascelles. For many years now his brows had not knit themselves together in that manner.

He reached the western opening of the Gap and descended, following the stage-road toward the bridge. As he did so he quietly put his hand behind him, apparently to assure himself that he had not forgotten something in a rear pocket. The something was there: it was a Derringer pistol, which Mr. Lascelles generally carried, in case of accidents.

He came in sight of the little wooden bridge over the Falling Water just as the sun was about to disappear on the summit of the range above. In fact, it had sunk so low that the dead limb of an enormous pine, extending horizontally, divided the red disk. Long shadows ran down the slope, reaching far into the valley of Bohemia.

Mr. Lascelles came on at a walk, with his eyes still fixed upon the ground. He seemed not to be aware how near he was to the bridge or to see the shadows. All at once the hoofs of his horse clattered on the timbers, and he raised his head. A long shadow ran toward him. This shadow was that of the Lefthander, who was standing on the bridge waiting for him.

XXXIV.

AT TRIANON.

Two days afterward Mr. Lascelles mounted his horse and set out for Trianon.

He had become a regular visitor, and the excellent Mrs. Armstrong's plan of bringing about a match between the young people seemed to be in a fair way of fulfilment. Mr. Lascelles was unquestionably smitten—otherwise so reserved a person would not have paid such frequent visits. It was true that there was nothing in the demeanor of Miss Juliet to produce the impression that she desired to become Mrs. Douglas Lascelles; but then Mr. Douglas Lascelles probably found that *piquante*, since his visits were regular and prolonged in spite of it.

Now and then Mrs. Armstrong ventured to remonstrate with the young lady—she did not venture very far. She intimated, in an incidental manner, that at twenty-three a maiden was in her freshest bloom, but that in two or three years thereafter the rose began to change color a little, and a slight diminution of the freshness followed, when the flower was not so acceptable to people as before. If the rose was meant for a bouquet in a golden holder, it was best to allow itself to be plucked in its fresh stage. . After awhile no one would care to pluck it, since it would be faded.

This was plain, and Miss Juliet probably understood it; but she paid no attention to it. She received Mr. Lascelles with perfect politeness, but with nothing more. Still, there were the visits of the gentleman, which he would never continue if he did not hope the fair statue would melt, and Mrs. Armstrong, who had a knack of hoping, hoped for the best.

She was a very sanguine, high-spirited, and aspiring lady, the mistress of Trianon. She held her head exceedingly high, and never lost sight of the fact that the Armstrongs belonged to the very best people. When she visited Piedmont with Juliet in her handsome family carriage, she and her daughter were both superbly dressed, and she treated the shop-keepers with the kindest condescension. She turned over the goods in the dry-goods stores with her little kid-gloved hands with the air of a duchess, and it was evident that she regarded the persons of the establishment as moving in quite a different sphere from herself. She was scrupulously polite to them, but then it was to be distinctly understood that she was Mrs. Armstrong of Trianon, and any dealings between them must be confined to the subject of the price of dry-goods.

Indeed, Mrs. Armstrong of Trianon was bent on higher things than conciliating popularity with the Piedmontese. What she aimed at was to spend her summers in travel, and her winters in Paris, with Mr. and Mrs. Douglas Lascelles. Her handsome family coach, which outraged the feelings of the Piedmont gossips, was a very modest equipage, indeed, in her own eyes, compared with those of her imagination. She looked down with superb disdain on her handsome wardrobe, her rich silks and plumes, and other personal adornments; they were old-fashioned and shabby in the opinion of a lady whose aspirations soared to the serene empyrean ruled over by Mr. Worth. Paris — dear, delightful Paris! That was her dream, the heaven of her ambition, and Mr. Douglas Lascelles

possessed the golden key which would open the golden door of her Elysium.

Now, when human beings are possessed by any ardent desire, and are not entirely certain that their desire will be accomplished, the result is apt to be an abnormal tension of the nervous system. Mrs. Armstrong was not exactly a nervous person, and had not the least tendency toward hysteria, but she had a good healthy excitability of temper in private, the indulgence of which afforded a safety valve to her pent-up anxiety. She kept this temper as a private luxury, never cheapening it by a public exhibition; but as an object is necessary to the enjoyment of quarrelling, Mrs. Armstrong sought for it in her own household. She found it there, but not in the person of Juliet. She never quarrelled with that young lady under any circumstances—it is doubtful whether she did not stand a little in awe of the maiden. From her earliest years Juliet had developed a quiet independence of character which was proof against every assault. It was not an unamiable trait, or in any manner disagreeable. Juliet was very sweet-tempered, never uttered ill-humored speeches under any circumstances, was exceedingly quiet in her manner, and quite devoted to her mother; but beyond a certain point Mrs. Armstrong had found by long experience that it was useless to argue with her or attempt to persuade her. Did this arise from a sensitive delicacy of conscience? It did not arise from obstinacy, for Juliet was not obstinate. She was very sweet and complying on ordinary occasions, and even if her mother had been tempted to vent her ill-humor upon the girl, her maternal tenderness, which was extreme, would have prevented her.

Fortunately there was another person at Trianon who afforded Mrs. Armstrong an opportunity to relieve her feelings— Miss Bassick, her "companion," who had or had not listened at the door on the evening of Mr. Lascelles's first visit. Miss Bassick was a young lady of about twenty-five, and of very striking appearance. She had a finely developed figure, a superb suit of hair, seductive eyes, which she had a habit of veiling with the long, silken lashes modestly, and a pair of ripe, pouting lips, which habitually smiled and seemed to beg people to be friendly to their mistress. In fact, Miss Bassick needed friends, for, as she said, she was alone in the world. She had been consigned to Mrs. Armstrong from an orphan asylum during her girlhood, and had ever since remained with her in the character of companion and housekeeper. She never dreamed of going into society with Mrs. Armstrong. She accepted her subordinate position with perfect resignation and submission, and never, under any circumstances, lost her temper, or was anything but a model.

Mrs. Armstrong, to repeat, was uncertain of temper, and though she never boxed Miss Bassick, or used personal violence, she had a stinging weapon, which cut deep—her tongue. Of this the lady was a complete mistress. Long practice had sharpened it to the keenest edge, and its management had been reduced to a science. The performance generally began in the morning, when Mrs. Armstrong rose and placed her feet on the handsome carpet of her chamber. On these occasions Miss Bassick, who was nominally a companion, but also a lady's maid, was promptly summoned by a small bell. She would come at once, leaving everything else, and assist the lady in her toilet. Now, in the morning, before breakfast, people are often a little nervous and ill-tempered. Misunderstandings took place at such times between Mrs. Armstrong and Miss Bassick. Sometimes the latter did not come at once — then the storm descended, and wrathful lightnings flashed from Mrs. Armstrong's eyes. What was the meaning of the delay? Where were her stockings? Miss Bassick had certainly hidden them—where were they? Then Miss Bassick would glide quietly to the arm-chair upon which the lady had deposited her garments, search under the female *débris*, return with them in her hand, and proceed to assist the lady in her toilet. At each moment during the ceremony of dressing there was a misunderstanding. Miss Bassick was implored by the unfortunate victim of her awkwardness, for heaven's sake, not to lace her corsets so tight. She was not assuming a strait-jacket, as she believed she was not precisely out of her mind; though if Miss Bassick persevered in lacing her until she could not breathe, she was not certain that the result would not be the wreck of her physical system, and the probable overthrow of her reason.

When the ceremony of dressing had proceeded to the detail of hair-arrangement, Mrs. Armstrong generally read a novel in her velvet arm-chair while Miss Bassick combed out her locks. This was a critical moment. The lady's skin was tender. If the comb encountered a tangle, and a tug ensued, Mrs. Armstrong dropped her novel, and, figuratively, boiled over. Good heavens! was she to have her hair torn out by the roots? Did Miss Bassick aim at making her *bald?* What did she mean? Give her the comb — that was enough! She could endure a great deal, but this was really *too* much! Miss Bassick would perhaps kindly consent to go down-stairs and see that she was not kept waiting for her breakfast. She had never learned to wait, and could not be expected to begin now at her time of life. Miss Bassick would please understand that breakfast must be on the table *at the moment she came down*—not a minute sooner or later. She could go.

Juliet took no part whatever in the torture of this innocent creature. She never, under any circumstances, called on Miss Bassick to assist her in dressing, and never, on any occasion, spoke to her with discourtesy. It is true that she was not familiar with her. Whether this arose from a sentiment of pride, or from personal disinclination to such an intimacy, Juliet never told any one. But then she was a very reserved young person in the expression of her feelings, and it was difficult to understand her. The young lady's sentiments toward Miss Bassick were as little known to her mamma as her feelings toward Mr. Lascelles. These Mrs. Armstrong, however, hoped would be all that she could wish in time; and when Mr. Lascelles made his appearance on this afternoon she said to Juliet, as the gentleman rode in at the gate,

"There is Mr. Lascelles, my dear! Do go up-stairs and put on your new dress which came yesterday—and the blue necktie, dear—Mr. Lascelles is fond of blue!"

Juliet was seated at her piano in the drawing-room, where she had been singing an air from one of her beloved operas. Her tall figure looked superb in her ugly "pull-back" dress, which defined every outline, and her dark hair, worn in a crown above the serene white forehead, made the beautiful head look queen-like. Her mother gazed at her with fond admiration, and exclaimed,

"You really are a perfect Diana, Juliet!"

"And you are enough to spoil an angel, mamma," Miss Juliet said, quietly.

"No, indeed—it is the truth. But do go and put on something fit to be seen, my love!"

Miss Juliet did not move.

"Why should I, mamma?" she said. "This is a very nice dress, and I cannot bear to be worrying at my toilet all day long, and changing my dress for every visitor."

"But think, my dear! Mr. Lascelles, you know, is very critical."

The argument seemed to make no impression whatever on Miss Juliet. She did not move.

"I really am too tired, mamma," she said, touching her piano.

"Well, my dear, you will do as you please, and if you are tired I will. not insist."

She approached her daughter, and arranged the ribbon confining her hair.

"You must sing, my dear," she said, "for Mr. Lascelles. He is fond of music, is he not?"

"He says so, and I suppose he is. I cannot fancy any one being indifferent to it."

The steps of Mr. Lascelles were heard on the porch, and Mrs. Armstrong ran her fingers over the keys of the piano, in the midst of which performance Mr. Lascelles appeared at the door. Mrs. Armstrong turned her head.

"Mr. Douglas! Why, you quite startled me!" she exclaimed.

Mr. Lascelles came in and bowed low over the fair hand held out to him, and then to Miss Juliet. At his appearance that young lady had quietly abandoned the piano-stool, where her dress had been drawn so tightly around her person as to make her resemble, in some degree, the heathen goddess to whom her mother had compared her. She now inclined her head to Mr. Lascelles, and sat down in an arm-chair near the centre-table, arranging her skirts as she did so, and leaning back in her habitual attitude of tranquillity.

"All are well at Wye, I hope:—what exquisite weather," said Mrs. Armstrong.

"Quite charming, madam. I always enjoy the autumn. Were you playing? I am afraid I have interrupted you."

"Oh, not at all. I have quite forgotten my music."

And sinking gracefully into a chair, Mrs. Armstrong conversed with Mr. Lascelles for about five minutes. She then smiled sweetly, rose, took a bijou of a key-basket from the table—deposited there by Miss Bassick, who had attended to the house-keeping—and glided from the room. This model mamma and head of the establishment was evidently intent on household duties, and disappeared in the room opposite, the door of which she closed behind her.

Mr. Lascelles remained at Trianon until nearly sunset. His demeanor toward the young lady was ambiguous, and the keenest observer would have found it difficult to penetrate his real sentiments. It was plain that he admired her beauty, and his manner was assiduous and devoted; but the conversation never trenched on delicate ground. During a considerable portion of the time Juliet played and sung for him; for Mr. Lascelles was very fond of music—it was one of his sensualities. Like other men of his class he liked to gratify all his senses, and music afforded him a distinctly physical enjoyment. This is not uncommon, and has little to do with the moral organization of the person. Nero had music in his soul, and so had Mr. Lascelles.

His visits to Trianon were thus always pleasant to him. Juliet gratified his musical taste as it had seldom been gratified. Her *repertoire* of airs ranged from Bellini to Offenbach, but she did not like the latter, and only sung the *Sabre de mon père*, and other music of a similar character, when she was urged to do so. She then sung "Bonny Jean," and other simple ballads, with a tenderness which showed how deeply she entered into and felt the words and music, and rising from the piano went back to her seat—a model of serene composure, as before.

The conversation between Mr. Lascelles and Miss Juliet need not be recorded. And, after all, is there not something rather indiscreet in listening to the confidential utterances of young people who say what they think and feel, since no one overhears them? It is true that Mr. Lascelles and Juliet were overheard on this occasion; but then it was quite indefensible in Miss Bassick to steal silently through the passage, and lean forward just outside the door and listen. Candor compels the statement that she did so, and heard all that was said—or nearly all. After listening for about half an hour, she retraced her steps with the same caution, and opening the venetian door in rear of the passage, closed it without noise behind her. Ten minutes afterward she emerged from the rear of the house with a little chip hat upon her head, and a small basket on her arm, and went toward a grove at some distance, apparently intent on gathering something in her basket. Mrs. Armstrong, who was looking at her from an upper window, saw her collect some bunches of red berries, such as are used for decorations; then she wandered on in the direction of the town and entered a belt of woods; and Mrs. Armstrong, watching her, not without suspicion, lost sight of her.

The movements of Miss Bassick then became eccentric. She threw a rapid glance over her shoulder in the direction of the house—saw that the foliage concealed her—made a wide circuit, walking quickly, and at last came out, just at sunset, on the county road through the woods leading in the direction of Wye. The point where she stopped was not more than half a mile from Trianon. Seating herself upon a rock, which a screen of shrubbery concealed from the road, she waited.

XXXV.

MISS BASSICK.

As Miss Bassick half reclined—for she was a little tired from her walk—on the picturesque mass of rock, nearly covered with moss, in the grassy nook, she made a very pretty picture. The foliage afforded an excellent background for her face and figure, and both were exceedingly attractive. The figure was full and graceful, the face rosy and enticing. But the great charm about Miss Bassick was her eyes. They were very remarkable eyes. The submissive expression had quite disappeared from them, and the heavy lashes no longer half concealed them. They were clear, brilliant, and had a singular expression of irony and blandishment. As she sat, with her elbow on one knee and her head leaning on her hand, she looked toward the road and listened attentively; and nothing more subtle and seductive can be imagined than her expression. She was evidently waiting for somebody, and at last this somebody seemed to be approaching. Just as the sun sunk like a ball of fire behind the woods toward Wye, the sound of hoofs was heard in the direction of Trianon; and a few moments afterward Mr. Lascelles made his appearance around a bend in the road, coming on at a canter.

As he came in sight, Miss Bassick rose, came out of her place of concealment, turned her back upon the approaching horseman, and went across the road, with her little basket, nearly full of red berries, on her arm.

"Miss Bassick!"

Mr. Lascelles had suddenly drawn rein and stopped within ten yards of her. She turned her head quickly, and remained standing in the middle of the road, looking at him and smiling. Mr. Lascelles dismounted, threw his bridle over his arm, and came up to her. He was smiling, like the young lady.

"You are taking your evening ramble—you walk out every evening, do you not?—how glad I am to meet you!"

Mr. Lascelles took the hand of Miss Bassick, and pressed it to his lips. She drew it away with an offended air, and seemed very much displeased; but this expression did not last—it gradually gave way to her seductive smile again. Holding up her basket, she said, in her low voice, which resembled the cooing of a dove,

"I walk out every evening, as you say, and have gathered these pretty red berries for the pictures at Trianon—Mrs. Armstrong likes them."

"And you are fond of doing what will give Mrs. Armstrong pleasure?"

The question was asked in a tone of covert irony, for during his numerous visits to Trianon the quick eyes of the young gentleman had descried many things, and he had come to understand perfectly the relations between Miss Bassick and the lady of the manor.

"It is one of the pleasures of your life, is it not," he said, "to administer to the pleasure of that charming person?"

Miss Bassick looked attentively at him. Her head slowly drooped, and the long lashes half concealed her eyes.

"I try to do so," she murmured. Mr. Lascelles uttered a hearty laugh.

"Well let me be frank with you and tell you that you must be an angel. I know that I am very unceremonious to be talking to you thus. But come—let us be honest. Do you really enjoy the life you lead? I have seen what it is."

Miss Bassick turned away her head, apparently much embarrassed, and seemed looking for something in the road.

"Have you lost anything?" said Mr. Lascelles.

"My glove; I must have dropped it," she replied, in a confused voice, "and yet I had it a moment ago."

"I will walk back with you and help you to look for it."

"I am afraid it will give you trouble."

"None at all."

Whereupon Mr. Lascelles went back with Miss Bassick, who led the way to the little nook behind the screen of foliage, where her companion threw his bridle over a bough, and assisted her in her search.

"Here it is," he said, spying the small thread glove lying beside the rock where Miss Bassick had rested. He stooped to pick it up; and as the young lady did so at the same moment, a very simple and natural accident occurred. Their heads came together, and the face of Mr. Lascelles touched the rosy cheek and warm curls of Miss Bassick.

Miss Bassick drew back instantly with a deep color in her cheeks, and an expression of extreme dissatisfaction.

"I really must beg your pardon for my awkwardness," he said, "and hope you will give me an opportunity to make my peace before I go. You must be tired—there is an excellent seat."

He pointed to the rock covered with moss, and, after a moment's hesitation, the young lady sat down, and Mr. Lascelles took his seat beside her. The color in her cheeks had not quite disappeared yet, and her eyes were cast down.

"Yes, I feel very tired; but I ought not to stay long," she said; "Mrs. Armstrong will require me."

Again Mr. Lascelles smiled.

"You say require. Are you Mrs. Armstrong's servant, then? It is absurd."

"I am scarcely more," said Miss Bassick, sadly. As she spoke her bosom heaved, and she caught her breath as though to suppress a sob. Her eyes were still hidden by the long silken lashes and fixed upon the ground. She was playing with a pebble, which she rolled to and fro under the point of her small slipper; and Mr. Lascelles, who was a connoisseur in female beauty, looked with unconcealed admiration at his companion, taking in every detail of her face and figure, from the small foot peeping from her skirt to the short curls resting on her white neck, which bent forward with a pathetic grace, as she continued to gaze with half-closed eyes on the moss beside her.

"Things were very different once," she murmured, "but I am alone in the world now. My father and mother are both dead, and I have no relatives to give me a home. I am little better than a servant. I would not speak so plainly of myself, but you have seen and understood how I am treated. Let me go now: I am afraid I will burst out crying if I say any more, and that, you know, would make you laugh at me."

Miss Bassick put her hand into a side-pocket, and took out a small white handkerchief, which she pressed to her eyes. Her voice, as she uttered the last words had sunk to a murmur, and she uttered a slight sob.

"Do not mind me — I can't help it," she said, raising her beautiful eyes, which were swimming in tears, "but it is very hard to bear. My childhood was surrounded by every luxury—I never knew what it was to have an unkind word addressed to me—and now—"

She stopped, and turned away her head, letting one of her hands fall hopelessly at her side. Mr. Lascelles took it in his own and kissed it.

"You have one friend left, at least!" he said.

And Mr. Lascelles was quite in earnest. The very strongest trait in his character was his admiration for female beauty. Women had always exerted a powerful influence over him, and often as his judgment had combated his weakness he had never yet succeeded in resisting them; not that he cared at all for their tears and pathetic speeches—those uttered by Miss Bassick had had very little effect upon him. It was the subtle seduction of the female eye and lip which swayed him; and the absence of these physical attractions in the serene Juliet probably repelled him. In Miss Bassick, on the contrary, he found what he wished. Her story about her childhood and past luxuries, might be true or false—her pathetic complaint of her ill-treatment might or might not be exaggerated—but what was certain was that here was a magnificent young animal, with a pair of eyes which had some magnetic property about them—a face, figure, carriage of the person which thrilled him with a vague admiration.

It was not by any means their first meeting. They had frequently met in the same purely accidental manner, and with every meeting the subtle charm of her eyes and lips had grown more enthralling. She was perfectly formal, and had drawn away her hand, as she did now when he took it in his own; but there were the wonderful, seductive eyes, and the pouting lips, which smiled upon him a moment afterward.

They smiled now, as she rose and held out her hand to him. The sun had set, and the rosy flush on the woods was fading.

"I must go now," said Miss Bassick, with a timid but caressing glance; "what would Mrs. Armstrong say if she saw me talking to you here?"

"Let her say what she fancies—don't go yet!" exclaimed Mr. Lascelles. "If you only knew how often I have thought of you since that night when you opened the door!"

"Of me?"

She shook her head.

"You must not think of me—remember what I am. Think how people would laugh—"

"What do I care for that?" he said. "I remember only one thing—shall I tell you what it is?"

She turned her head over her shoulder, and looked at him with an expression which made his pulses throb.

"What is it?"

It was a low murmur. The red lips scarcely moved.

"That you are the most beautiful woman I have ever seen!" he said.

Miss Bassick laughed.

"What would Juliet say if she heard you, Mr. Lascelles?"

"I don't know or care," he said, knitting his brows.

"I shall take care not to tell her," the young lady said. "And now you must really let me go. Think how late it is!"

She held out her hand.

"Good-bye!" she said. "Will you think me too forward if I tell you something—that I am so very glad I met you. It is like a gleam of sunshine."

For a moment he held her small, warm hand, and looked at her in silence. Her eyes met his own, and they exchanged a long glance.

"Shall I see you again? I cannot see you yonder," he said, pointing toward Trianon.

"Perhaps," she said, laughing.

"What do you mean by that?"

"I mean that it is pleasant to walk in the woods here for wild-flowers and fern."

The light in the beautiful eyes of Miss Bassick deepened. She looked straight at Mr. Lascelles, and the golden smile made her face a picture.

"Are you often near this spot about sunset?"

"Yes."

It was a whisper, almost, but Mr. Lascelles heard it quite plainly, and it was evidently all that he desired.

"I shall probably come—to see Miss Juliet—again the day after to-morrow," he said, "and as I like to be at Wye before night these chill evenings, I shall pass this place on my return about sunset. Shall I see any one, do you think?"

"Perhaps," repeated Miss Bassick.

The smile was brighter, and the long look caressed him once more. With a little nod Miss Bassick then walked off toward Trianon. Mr. Lascelles stood looking at her until her figure disappeared. He then mounted his horse and set out for Wye; as he did so he muttered,

"That girl is a witch! I really believe I am going to fall in love with her."

XXXVI.

A STRUGGLE.

"NELLY, I am going back home."

"Going home!"

"Are you very much surprised? It is time to go back, if I am ever going. I have been here since early in September, and it is nearly winter now."

"It is—very—soon," poor Nelly faltered.

"It is very late," said Brantz Elliot, moodily. "I ought to have gone home long ago. Well, the bright days always end—if they could only stay, Nelly!"

They were talking under a huge pine crowning a shoulder of the mountain, with the valley of Bohemia at their feet. A fresh wind made the leaves dance and flutter down. The sky was blue, and slightly veiled by a translucent haze. The far headlands of the Blue Ridge swam in rose-tinted mist, and from time to time the wind ceased, and a breath of warmth pervaded the atmosphere of the mountains.

Brantz Elliot had gone out with his gun, but had wandered on aimlessly, quite forgetful of game, and thinking of Nelly. The struggle between his love and pride had long ended. The inequality of a union with the poor mountain maid had quite ceased to occupy him. He had long banished from his mind the smiles hidden behind fans in the hands of his lady acquaintances—the sudden change in the conversation when he entered his club—all the social astonishments and silent protests against so curious a *mésalliance*. This moved him no more, and rarely even entered his mind. He was thinking of a far more serious matter—Nelly's reserve, which plainly indicated that there was a more serious obstacle—her own unwillingness.

It was plain that it would be useless to ask her, and yet he intended to do so. He could not go without telling her, at least, how much he loved her; and he had been looking for an opportunity, day after day, until on this morning chance befriended him, and they were alone together. Nelly, thinking that he was far away in the mountain hunting, had strolled out to the knoll, which was not far from the house, and on his return Brantz Elliot had seen her, and approached her. She was sitting on the brown carpet of pine tags, with one shoulder against the pine, and seemed to have been musing, for she started as he came up behind her.

"If they could only stay, Nelly!" he repeated, mournfully—"I mean the bright days; but they always go. The winter is coming. Look at the trees. My autumn's over, and I must go back home. Yes, I must go, Nelly—"

He stopped and looked at her, and exclaimed, taking her hand,

"I must go back, Nelly; but how am I ever to get along without you?"

The words were spoken at last, and seating himself beside the blushing girl, Brantz Elliot pressed the hand he held to his lips.

"I know it is no use to talk so, Nelly; but then I had to tell you this before I went—for I am going. I am not much in the way of romance, and all that. I can't make love to you as I've seen it made on the stage, but I can tell you what I have told you, and tell you again, that I don't see how I can go on living without you."

"You will do very well without me," poor Nelly faltered out, with a beating heart.

Brantz Elliot shook his head and said,

"You do not know how much I have come to love you. I think of nothing else. I am a plain sort of fellow, and not up to fancy talk; but if you only knew how I am wrapped up in you, Nelly! If you will marry me, I will love you, and be good to you to the last day of your life!"

This was not a romantic speech, and did not deal in raptures, neither did the speaker fall upon his knees, or exclaim "Oh!" or "My own darling!" or anything of the sort. But his meaning was plain, whether he rolled his eyes or not. He asked Nelly to marry him, telling her

that he would be good to her—and no lover can make a more rational statement to his sweetheart.

"This is foolish enough, I'm afraid, Nelly," he went on. "You've not looked at me lately in a way that made me think you cared much for me. But what am I to do? I can't go without telling you this. I love you more every hour, and have been loving you since that day when I kissed you at the stream. Do you remember that day?—perhaps you have forgotten it; but I have not. I meant to save you or die with you."

"How can I ever forget it?—and—and —I did not mean to—look at you as you say I did—as if I cared nothing for you!" sobbed Nelly.

The young man's face suddenly flushed.

"Then say yes, Nelly!" he exclaimed; "if you care for me, that settles everything. Say you will marry me, Nelly!"

"Oh no, no — I ought not to! indeed I ought not to!" the girl exclaimed. "You would not be happy, and—I should be miserable if you were unhappy! I am a poor ignorant girl—you would be sorry you had ever seen me—I could not bear to have people laugh at you for marrying a poor thing like me. I could not bear that."

Brantz Elliot raised his head with a sort of disdain, and said,

"Laugh at me! what do I care for that? Am I to choose my wife to please a parcel of foolish women—all for fear of their gabble? You needn't mind about that. You need never see them. I'll come and live in the mountain here, unless you fancy going to Europe. Only say you will have me, Nelly! I love you so dearly! Tell me I need not go, Nelly. Only tell me that!"

He held both the girl's hands and drew her toward him. Her face was covered with blushes and her eyes swam in tears. It was a very hard struggle—for Nelly loved Brantz Elliot just as dearly as he loved her. If she had followed the impulse of her heart she would have leaned her head upon his breast and cried, and said yes; but, even with this sore temptation before her, she thought of the consequences to the man she loved. If she married him he would soon grow ashamed of her; his family would look down upon her; he would regret his union with her —and for him to do so, she felt, would break her heart.

"Indeed I cannot!—do not ask me!" was all she could say.

"But I will ask you, Nelly! Don't tell me to go. You are the only wife I want, Nelly!"

He put his arms around her neck and drew her close to him as he spoke, and Nelly, worn out by the long struggle, seemed about to yield, when a startling and unexpected incident ended their interview. Something resembling a wild-cat bounded from behind the pine, and fell on his shoulders. He felt the claws of the animal and his hot breath on his cheek, and with the instinct of the hunter his hand went to the knife in his belt. But as suddenly the hand fell at his side, and, in spite of himself, he burst out laughing. The wild-cat of his fancy was Dash, the favorite deer-hound of Daddy Welles, who, recognizing his intimate friend Mr. Brantz Elliot, had leaped on his shoulders to caress him. Dash now gambolled about in a manner indicative of extreme pleasure at the *rencontre*, and then bounded to meet his master, Daddy Welles, who at that moment came in sight, gun on shoulder.

Brantz Elliot was fond of Daddy Welles, but it is doubtful if he felt much disposition to greet him warmly upon the present occasion. The Daddy, however, displayed an amount of cheerfulness, as he joined the party, which sufficed for everybody.

"Well, here you are, Nelly, you and Mr. Elliot, and I thought you were a-hunting deer!" said the Daddy. "Well, well, it's human natur', I s'pose. Young men will be young men, and gals will be gals. I was no better'n the rest of you once on a time. The sight of a petticoat put everything else clean out of my head."

Having thus unbosomed himself of his views on the propensities of young persons, Daddy Welles proceeded to observe that he was going into the mountain t see if he could not pick up a wild-turkey and invited Brantz Elliot to accompan him. The latter looked at Nelly with faint hope that she would retain him, i only by a look, but this hope was prompt ly dispelled. Nelly said she must g home, as her mother would need her and turning away her head, in order t hide her blushes from Daddy Welles, sh left them and went slowly back in the di rection of home.

"A good girl, Nelly—there's few lik her," was the fatherly comment of Dadd Welles as he looked after her. "But it' time to git on. The turkeys mostly sta in the hills across the stream yonder; an I hope we'll have better luck than som friends of ourn had that night they hunt ed the moonshiners!"

Daddy Welles smiled sweetly at th recollection of his ride that night, and h and Brantz Elliot soon disappeared in th pine thicket.

XXXVII.

THE BOHEMIANS.

On this evening the little family o wanderers were grouped around a chee ful fire at Crow's Nest — all but Harry He had gone out in the afternoon to fish and as a storm was evidently coming, the were looking for him anxiously: fo some days he had been laboring under very severe cold, and every moment Mous went to the door to see if he was coming

The table was set with plates and ti cups, and knives and forks; the coffe was boiling; the meat was broiling; an over all Mouse presided with a busines air which was impressive. The little on was house - keeper and general manage and her rule was autocratic. She di not tolerate interference, or permit an breach of the rules of good-breeding. A her request Harry had purchased at Pied mont a small bell, which Mouse proudl placed upon the mantel-piece, as an orn ment to and evidence of the respectabilit of the *ménage*. Until this bell sounde no one presumed to take his seat at th table. All waited, however hungry, watching the small autocrat at her work, with submission. Then when her viands were ready, Mouse dished them up and placed them upon the table; still there was no movement. Lastly, Mouse reached upon tiptoe to the high mantel-piece and possessed herself of the bell, rang it cheerfully with a prolonged tingle, as though to summon numerous members of the family from remote apartments of the establishment, and then observed, with a serious air, "Sit down, gentlemen, we cannot wait for the lazy people up-stairs. The things are getting cold." Whereupon all would take their seats, and Mouse would preside at the head of the table, putting the brown sugar into the tin cups with a pewter spoon, and pouring out the coffee with an air which evidently filled the Lefthander with extreme enjoyment.

Mouse, in fact, humanized and ameliorated all her surroundings. She infused the feminine element which households are the better for when it does not turn sour. As to Mouse, the idea that she could possibly become sour seemed absurd. She was sunshine incarnate, and lit up everybody. She took charge of them with a motherly air, and reprimanded and then petted them. They called her "Old Lady," and she called them her "Big Babies;" and as she was expert at her needle, and did all the mending, it really did seem as if they were young people who required looking after.

As night came on, a huge mass of clouds, as black as ebony, drifted up from the west, and the red glare of the sinking sun lit the valley, turning everything crimson. A faint mutter of thunder rolled through the gorges like the angry growl of a wild animal, and from time to time vivid flashes of lightning revealed every feature of the wild landscape slowly disappearing in the darkness.

Mouse went to the door and looked out, again.

"I wish Harry would come," she said, in a low tone. "There is going to be a storm. How black it looks!"

Then she suddenly recoiled. A flash of lightning, so dazzling that it blinded her, lit up the whole valley and the Blue Ridge opposite, and a crash of thunder followed. Then the storm descended, and a torrent of rain, driven by a fierce wind, lashed the mountains.

"Oh, why don't Harry come?" Mouse exclaimed, looking and listening.

As she spoke a step was heard on the porch, and Harry came in, completely drenched. Mouse rushed to him.

"You have got yourself wet, you bad, disgraceful boy!" she exclaimed. "You promised me you wouldn't."

"I didn't mean to break my promise; I couldn't help it, Mouse."

"You always have excuses," said the autocrat. "There, you are coughing — your cold is worse. Sit down here at once and let me dry you."

Mouse drew off his coat, which she hung close to the fire, and taking a blanket from her pallet wrapped it around his shoulders. She then directed him to take the seat which she drew up; he sat down submissively, and Mouse proceeded to scold.

"Well, let him off this time," said the Lefthander; "he sha'n't do so any more. Why, you have a bad cough, sure enough," he added to Harry.

"Bad enough."

The words were followed by a long, hoarse fit of coughing, at the end of which Harry shivered a little, although his face seemed to indicate fever. In a moment, however, he seemed at his ease again, and the bell having been formally rung by Mouse, they sat down and ate their supper. Thereafter the Lefthander lit his pipe and smoked contemplatively, gazing with much satisfaction at Mouse, who, having cleared away the table, was seated opposite, mending one of Gentleman Joe's two or three shirts.

It was a cheerful group. These poor Bohemians, mere waifs of humanity without a resting-place, had made something like a home here in the lonely house in the hills. There was little beyond the bare walls, and the panes rattled in the gusts dashing the rain against them; without, all was darkness and chill uproar, but within the fire burned cheerily, and was reflected from the faces of the wanderers. It was their home, this poor shelter—all they had in the world. The waves of fate had cast them ashore here, and, like shipwrecked mariners, they hailed their good fortune, looking on that side of things, not on the darker side. Others had elegant houses, and rich carpets, and warm curtains, and soft beds. They had only this deserted shell, with the bare floors and the broken panes, and hard mattresses, but they were content. And was it not enough? Is there not, after all, something attractive in such remoteness—in exemption from the demands of "society" and the world—the *great world*, as it is called, perhaps because it is so little? No wearying claims of artificial life, no mask on the features that the lurking glance that watches may not read the thought of the mind, the emotion of the heart;—life under the sky, and in the free sunshine, with something seen, in the tranquil days, beyond the sky and the sunshine!

Harry had drawn up to the fire and warmed himself, and the little family made a cheerful semicircle in front of the blaze, which roared up the chimney in triumph, though the storm was roaring louder still without.

"Winter's coming," said the Lefthander, after musing for some moments, "and we'll have to look out for a better place than this."

"Yes, this is sad, very sad," said Gentleman Joe, dreamily; "but what are we to do?"

"The troupe," said Mouse.

The Lefthander uttered a grunt, and said,

"I thought you had given up that idea, Mignon."

"Given it up!" cried Mouse, pinning her work to her knee. "You are very much mistaken. I dream about that monkey, and I've arranged everything. You're to be the clown, Gentleman Joe, and make people laugh, and Harry and

you, poppa, will perform the tricks, and maybe I'll dance the rope, as well as carry round the tambourine."

"No, I don't mean you shall dance any more, Mouse," said the Lefthander "there's been enough of that. You teased me till I let you do it once; but you're too little; that's come to an end.'

"Little!" said Mouse. "Yes, I'm little, more's the pity, but I'm not so little that I can't do my part."

"You do a great deal—far more than your part, Mignon; and I really think we are having a better time here than we had with the circus. It was easier living with eight hundred dollars a month for swinging on the trapeze and lifting—but then there were the bar-rooms. As long as I was there I couldn't keep away from the bar-rooms, and that was bad, Mignon Now I never go near them, or drink any thing at all. I've cut loose from the Unrivalled Combination, and so have you You'll not dance any more. If you bother we'll get up the little troupe and leave you behind!"

"Leave *me* behind!" Mouse exclaimed in immense derision; "and what do you think would become of *you*, if I was not with you to take care of you?"

The Lefthander grunted. As he looked at the child, his rugged features grew soft. A quiet smile just moved his huge mustache, and he said,

"Well, that's true—I really never thought of that. I suppose, after all, we'll have to take you along."

"I should think you would!" Mouse said, with a lofty air. "It's as much as I can do to keep you all straight now If you wandered off, there's no telling what would happen to you without me."

"That's true, Lefthander," said Gentleman Joe. "We can't leave Mouse. I'd lose my good spirits if I didn't see Mouse every day."

"You seem to have lost them any way,' was the rejoinder. "You've been moping lately. Come, laugh a little for us, Gentleman Joe! I like to hear you laugh."

At this Gentleman Joe shook his head sadly.

"I see too many things that make me sorrowful," he said. "The pines talk to me, too, and seem to bend to me and whisper sometimes, as if they had something to tell me."

The Lefthander exchanged a glance with Harry, who looked much depressed.

"Then the mice in the walls seem to know me and talk to me," said Gentleman Joe, looking dreamily into the fire. "'Squeak! squeak!' they go, just as they did when I used to listen to them."

"Do you mean *here*, Gentleman Joe?"

"Here or somewhere—I don't know exactly where; my memory is weak. Yes, here—or somewhere. 'Squeak! squeak!' And then the pines—they are never done whispering to me, day and night."

Gentleman Joe was often in these moods now, and would remain in them for days at a time, during which he scarcely spoke to anybody, but went wandering about the vicinity with the air of a person looking for something. Then, at some chance speech or jest recalling his life with the circus, and some odd incident, he would suddenly brighten up, utter a hearty laugh, and fall to grimacing after his old fashion. These mirthful outbursts were growing, however, more and more unusual, and his friends endeavored in vain to ascertain the cause of his depression. He either could not or would not explain. His replies were either evasive or indicative of inability to account for his moods. He had the cunning of half-witted persons, and might be concealing something, but it was just as probable that his apparent recollection of events and persons associated with the Crow's Nest house were vague fancies—mere imaginations of a mind clouded with the mists of unreason.

"Well, well," the Lefthander said, in reply to Gentleman Joe's last words, "let the mice squeak, and the wind blow in the pine-trees—they do nobody any harm. If they are not agreeable, you can always go away and pay somebody a visit. There's Daddy Welles and little Nelly—they'll keep you in good spirits."

"Nelly? Oh yes, Nelly!"

Gentleman Joe's face lit up with a smile.

"Nelly's like the sun shining," he said. "I don't mind the mice squeaking when I'm thinking about Nelly."

"You certainly are good friends, and it is easy to see how fond of you she is."

"I'm glad of that," the old fellow said, with a bright smile on his face; "and Daddy Welles, too—he is an estimable man, though perhaps he hunts too much by *moonshine*."

To these words the Lefthander made no reply. He had never told Mouse of his connection with the moonshiners, resulting from that night meeting with them in the mountain. A very few words from Daddy Welles had induced him to join them. The little family was coming to want, and the Lefthander did not hesitate. And the worthy moonshiners looked upon him now as a most important acquisition. Resolute, powerful, a man to "count on," as a glance at his face showed, he had become a sort of leader with them, and infused new energy into their illegal occupation. And it must be said he enjoyed his new pursuits. He was tired of idleness. The profits, too, were very considerable, for the illicit spirit was sent in all directions, and disposed of readily, and the Lefthander's pockets, growing painfully empty when he went to set his traps that night, were now full of bank-notes.

Both Gentleman Joe and Harry were in the secret, but not Mouse. Why had he concealed it from the child? It was difficult to say. The Lefthander acted largely from a sort of instinct. The moonshine business was illegal—it was not regarded by strict moralists as very creditable. Mouse, therefore, should have nothing to do with it, and not even know of his connection with the moonshiners. The star lighting up the little company of wanderers was to stay where it belonged—in the pure upper air. Rugged natures often have these finer instincts.

The Lefthander had been enabled thus to provide for the Crow's Nest household; but the time was near when this resource would probably fail. With winter the manufacture of the whiskey would be discontinued; and then reports were rife that the government officers were coming back — when there would be trouble. The report had reached Piedmont that a company of mounted regulars would harry the mountain, and then something very unpleasant would no doubt ensue. Arrests would take place, perhaps, and among the persons arrested there might be a certain individual called the Lefthander. The rest would follow—imprisonment, trial, and a term of years in prison, perhaps. Then what would become of Mouse?

"I wouldn't like that," the Lefthander muttered, after a pause: he had fallen into a reverie and thought of all this now. "After all, I like a wandering life, and Mouse is right. The troupe is the right thing."

As he spoke a knock came at the door, and a voice without cried,

"Can you give a poor man shelter, friends?"

XXXVIII.

FLOTSAM.

The Lefthander rose, and went and opened the door. The rain, driven by the wind, dashed in his face and nearly blinded him; but through the cloud he could see a man in rags, with a bundle on his back hanging from a stout stick.

"Who are you?" said the Lefthander.

"A poor man nigh starved and wet to the skin, and lookin' for a shelter," said the man.

The Lefthander opened the door wide. "Come in," he said; "this is the place."

The man came in and drew near the fire, ducking his head to the company. He was a wiry-looking fellow of middle age, with a rough beard and mustache, sharp eyes, and the expression of the houseless vagabond. His dress had reached the last stages of dilapidation, and seemed to be held together by some innate principle of cohesion. One of the skirts of his shabby old coat had disa peared, and his knees were covered wit patches. His bony wrists ended in clay like hands, and his naked toes protrude through his worn boots. His hat was rag: he seemed to have no shirt. I was a vagabond, and a thoroughly drenc ed one.

"Sit down and warm yourself," tl Lefthander said; "then we'll give yo some supper."

Mouse placed meat, bread, and the r mainder of the coffee on the table, ar the tramp ate ravenously, grinning as l did so. When he had finished his me he drew a long breath of satisfaction, ar coming closer to the fire, said,

"That's the sort o' thing that sets feller up."

"Where are you from?" said the Lef hander, looking fixedly at him.

"Well, I'm from Philadelfy, and n name is Rooney Ruggles," he said, gri ning. "I'm what they call a tramp, guess."

"What brought you south?"

"Want o' work."

"The old cry," said the Lefthander.

The tramp grinned again, and warm his hands at the blaze.

"That's so," he said, "and there'll l trouble about it. If a honest man got to starve, him and his famuly, he jest as leave fight. Things 'll have change, or we'll change 'em—and do pretty quick."

As the Lefthander continued to smol with a meditative air, the visitor was e dently encouraged to further unboso himself, and said,

"What right have the rich swells ride over poor people? They sit in th fine houses and drink their wine, and ri in their carriages, and take life eas while better men 'n they are don't have bone to pick, or a kennel to lay down at night! I say, down with 'em! I yer boy. I'm up to anything, from sett fire to a wheat-stack to burnin' a fact' Let 'em look out! Jest take a good lo at me, mate. I've been a-starvin' a a-sleepin' in barns all along the road!"

He had set the remainder of his coffee y the fire to warm. He now raised it) his lips, and said, grinning,

"Here's down with the swells! Cuss m, let 'em look out!"

As the Lefthander continued to smoke, 1e vagabond went on, gazing around him ; he spoke.

"You're tramps, too, to judge from the look o' things. We're the right sort o' eople. We don't wear fine clothes and look down on a honest man. Things ught to be divided—sheer and sheer alike. lake it a law a man sha'n't own mor'n a atch o' land. Make the big-bugs stand out and take off ther coats and go to ork. They've got to do it, or the amps 'll know the reason—what do you y, mate?"

"I say you are talking bosh," said the efthander, coolly, "and that men like ou are making trouble. I heard you trough, and if it was worth while I ould tell you, you talk like a fool! You te the rich people, and mean to rob em if you can, because you are the rongest. What has that got to do with ? I can pick you up and toss you trough that window—I am stronger an you are. What right have I to do at?"

The tramp's countenance fell. He had 'idently blundered; and a glance at the onderous frame of the Lefthander was 'idently not reassuring.

"You talk of burning wheat-stacks and ctories," said the Lefthander; "why on't you go and work in the wheat-field : the factory instead? The ground is onder in the West, and labor is needed. istead of working, you tramps sit on the nce, and sneak and beg."

The tramp did not reply. His elo- ience had all disappeared.

"A man's money is his own," the Left- ander added; "he either made it, or some- ody made it for him. If you take it way from him you are a thief, and a neak too. Don't be that, if you must eal. Go on the road and put a five- looter to the rich man's head, and take is purse—it's more respectable."

Suddenly the tramp's face expanded into a grin, and he exclaimed,

"Well, you're right, mate, and I was only jokin'. Burn a wheat-stack! You didn't really think I was in earnest? Rooney Ruggles ain't the man to be doin' that, and as to five-shooters and stoppin' people, that's out o' my line entirely."

"Yes, I think it is," said the Lefthand- er, somewhat disgusted with his visitor; "if I was one of the rich people you stopped on the road it wouldn't take me long to do for you."

This remark was open to criticism, per- haps, as being more frank than polite; but the Lefthander was plainly tired of the vulgarity of his guest. His eyebrows shut down a little, and the tramp saw that ominous sign. He renewed his dec- laration that he was only joking, and then asked whether he could lie down. The Lefthander pointed to one of the mattresses, and the tramp went and brought it. Then the rest were spread, as the hour was late, and soon afterward the whole party were stretched upon them and asleep.

For about an hour there was a pro- found silence in the house, and nothing was heard but the plashing of the rain without. Then the tramp raised his head slowly and looked cautiously around him. The whole party were plainly asleep— their long breathing indicated that—and rising on his elbow, then on his knees, the tramp dragged himself cautiously toward the Lefthander, and looked at him. He was in a dead slumber, and with rapid and skilful hands the vagabond searched all his pockets. This was done in a very few moments, and the result was an ex- pression on the tramp's countenance of the greatest disappointment. He had found nothing but a knife, and a pocket- book with some money in it, which he re- stored untouched—and from this it seem- ed that Mr. Rooney Ruggles was more honest than he professed to be.

After his stealthy search for something which he expected to find, apparently, but did not find, on the person of the Left- hander, the tramp dragged himself back to his mattress, looking around him as he did so. The result seemed discouraging. The apartment was perfectly bare—there was absolutely no place whatever to conceal anything. He then lay down on his mattress, closed his eyes, and after awhile fell asleep.

On the next morning, which was quite bright, Mr. Rooney Ruggles rose much refreshed, partook of breakfast, and stated his intention of applying for work in the neighborhood. Did anybody really think that he was in earnest about the wheatstacks? He would scorn it, and meant to live by the sweat of his brow.

"It is better," said the Lefthander, sententiously.

"I mean to do it, mate, for I'm a honest man," said Mr. Ruggles.

And having swung his stick with the bundle over his shoulder, Mr. Ruggles grinned amicably, and took his departure.

Three days after this scene, Harry tried to raise his head from the pillow one morning and could not do so. He was a vigorous youth, but there are enemies which spare no class. One of these enemies is pleuro-pneumonia.

XXXIX.

SHINGLES.

OWING, apparently, to admiration for the scenery of the mountains, and no doubt inspired by an ambition to earn his living honestly, Mr. Rooney Ruggles, after leaving Crow's Nest, stopped at the first house he saw to ask for work. This happened to be the residence of Mr. Gibbs, the manager of the Falling Water estate; and chancing to find Mr. Gibbs in an uncommonly good humor, he preferred his request under favorable circumstances.

Looking at his rags, Mr. Gibbs at first hesitated, whereupon Mr. Ruggles grew painfully modest and submissive. This conciliated Mr. Gibbs, and Mr. Ruggles then made a plausible speech. He was poor but honest—he was a lover of law

and order. His clothes were poor enough, but they were good enough to work in. All he wanted was a job, and he would give satisfaction or leave at once.

This was straightforward talk, and Mr. Gibbs invited him in to dinner. Beef and turnips having further ameliorated the sentiments of Mr. Gibbs, he asked what his guest was good for? He was mainly good for shingles, Mr. Ruggles responded; that was his trade where he came from. But he was willing to do anything. As to pay, he would not expect much. All he wanted was to make an honest living, and have enough to eat, and any sort of farm work—   .

But Mr. Gibbs reconducted the conversation to shingles. He required a large number to reshingle his barn, and concluded an agreement; and on that very day Mr. Ruggles went to work.

Mr. Ruggles evidently understood his trade. Having been provided with an axe, a drawing-knife, a crosscut-saw, and an assistant in the shape of a youthful African, he repaired to the woods, constructed a work-bench, and proceeded to fell the timber and saw it into proper lengths. This effected, he informed Mr. Gibbs that he required no further assistance; and splitting up his blocks, he was soon surrounded with piles of shavings and shingles, which the manager in his rounds surveyed with much satisfaction. On these occasions Mr. Ruggles was always found extremely busy, and was even unaware, from absorption in his work, of Mr. Gibbs's approach until he was close behind him and accosted him. This assiduity produced a good impression. Here was a treasure; and Mr. Gibbs continued his rounds with a high opinion of his employé's industry.

As soon, however, as Mr. Gibbs was out of sight, Mr. Ruggles would yield to reverie. His drawing-knife would cease to produce shavings, and sometimes he would rise and wander away, looking at the trees with the air of an expert deciding upon the adaptation of certain giants of the wood to the purpose of shingles. These tours of inspection would generally lead him toward Crow's Nest. Here he would sometimes find Gentleman Joe and the Lefthander—sometimes only one of them — at other times neither of them. Finding them at home, the visitor would enter into friendly conversation, and mention with honest pride that he had just finished a lot of five thousand superior shingles for Mr. Gibbs's barn, and liked the neighborhood so well that he thought he would take up his permanent residence in it. Finding his hosts absent, he did not at once retire, and seemed, indeed, to think that the next best thing to seeing them was to see how they were getting along.

There was a lock on the door, of which either the Lefthander or Gentleman Joe always kept the key; but Mr. Ruggles regarded the fact as unimportant. The back window afforded a perfectly convenient means of entrance; and, availing himself of it, he reached the interior without the least difficulty. On such occasions his proceedings were curious. He seemed to be inspecting the establishment with the view of renting it. He surveyed every object around him with great interest — the blankets, the walls, and the floor. Neither of the latter seemed to meet wholly with his approval. Where there was a hole in the plaster of the room he examined it, inserting his claw-like fingers into the cavity; but for the absurdity of the idea, one might have supposed that Mr. Ruggles was looking for something. Where the planks of the floor were in like manner defective, and an orifice appeared, Mr. Ruggles repeated his examination, as though speculating upon the expense of improving the premises, previous to which he apparently considered it desirable to remove any rubbish beneath, which he proceeded to do by inserting his arm up to the shoulder, and feeling about under the flooring.

The result of these inspections had not appeared satisfactory, and he had ascended to the upper rooms, where he displayed redoubled interest in every object. A dark closet full of dust and broken bottles aroused his attention, but ended in becoming a subject of indifference. He then sounded the plastering, to ascertain, probably, if the house was well-built—the conclusion being, to judge from the dissatisfaction on his countenance, that it was not. After three visits of this description, during which every part of the premises, including the out-houses, were subjected to an exhaustive examination, Mr. Rooney Ruggles ceased to enter through the back window, or in any other manner, and had evidently made up his mind not to rent the establishment as a residence for himself and his family.

Occasional cessation of the work of shingle-making seemed, however, to be necessary to the well-being of Mr. Ruggles, who evidently liked variety, and a little recreation now and then. This craving induced him to absent himself at intervals, with the concurrence of Mr. Gibbs, and visit Piedmont for the purpose of lounging on the tavern porch there. He was not regarded as a vagrant by the landlord. He had reconstructed his habiliments until they approached the limits of respectability, and patronized the bar in a creditable manner. He never exceeded or was boisterous. He took his drink like a gentleman, the landlord declared, and was a genial sort o' feller, who never liked to drink by himself. He was, indeed, remarkably jovial and friendly on such occasions, and anybody could see that he was an honest, open-hearted person, of social tastes and generous disposition.

He asked a great many questions, and seemed to take interest in everything and everybody. He himself was a stranger— he had come from the West, he said. He liked the Virginians; they were a healthy, hearty sort of people. There was one man he had seen in the town who was worth looking at—a big man with black eyebrows and a heavy beard: did anybody know him?

Thence information, communicated by one of the tavern-loungers. The big man had been a circus man. He lived somewhere up in Bohemia. He had quarrelled with old Brownson, of Brownson's Unrivalled Combination, and he and a child of his had left the company, and he, the lounger, had met them. The big man asked where he could find a night's lodging without going to the tavern; had been informed that Parson Grantham never turned anybody away; and he supposed they had spent the night at the parson's. On the next morning they had gone away, as nobody saw them again—the big man might have got into trouble for striking old Brownson—and that was all that he knew about him.

Mr. Ruggles listened with a careless air, said he supposed that *was* the reason the big man had gone off; and strolling idly away, reached the suburbs where Mr. Grantham's house was situated. He had been directed to it by a citizen whom he met, and was about to open the small gate when he seemed to change his mind. Perhaps the subject of shingles suddenly occurred to him, and, with the natural solicitude of an honest man, he felt that he ought to return to the hills, and add to the pile already standing neatly arranged in rectangular fashion in the woods. Something certainly did cause him great preoccupation of mind, and this apparently led to his taking the wrong path. Having left the town, he did not proceed in the direction of the Gap, but toward Wye, the vicinity of which he reached in the afternoon just as the sun was sinking. He ascertained the exact time by looking at a handsome gold watch which he drew from a private pocket, and the time of his arrival seemed to afford him satisfaction. He was in a glade in the woods between two rows of large oaks within sight of the house when he looked at his watch, and stood there for some moments, apparently admiring the large establishment.

As he was thus engaged, Mr. Douglas Lascelles, who had been accidentally looking from an upper window in this precise direction, at this precise hour, issued from the front door of the mansion, cane in hand, and carelessly strolled through the grounds until he reached the glade in which Mr. Rooney Ruggles was standing. The appearance of the tramp trespassing upon the Wye grounds did not seem to excite as much indignation in Mr. Lascelles as might have been expected. Indeed, the expression of the gentleman's countenance was rather one of animation and inquiry. He even made a sign of intelligence to Mr. Rooney Ruggles, and they retired together into the depths of the woods, conversing guardedly as they went.

XL.

A SLIGHT SILHOUETTE OF MISS GRUNDY.

As Mr. Ruggles left Piedmont, the Trianon carriage drove past him, and entered the main street. It contained Mrs. Armstrong and Juliet, and they had come to shop, in which delightful occupation they were soon engaged. Drawing up in front of Messrs. Smith & Jones's, they entered, and subjected the fall goods to a careful examination. Nearly the whole stock was assiduously displayed upon the counter, and an hour was spent in rearranging them after the ladies' departure. But then Mrs. Armstrong purchased two spools of sewing-silk, and was bowed out to her carriage with distinguished consideration.

She then proceeded in a sort of triumphal progress through the town, stopped at numerous shops, where she made small and discreet purchases, and ended by visiting her milliner, whose new hats she tried on, but did not purchase one.

All this consumed an hour or two, and the sun was now declining; so the lady and her daughter re-entered the carriage to return to Trianon. They had just taken their seats, and the carriage was about to move off, when a girlish voice near them exclaimed,

"You really must not go before I speak to you, dear Mrs. Armstrong."

The lady turned her head, and uttered a profound sigh, which was followed by a radiant smile.

"Miss Grundy!" she exclaimed, "I am really charmed to see you."

Whereupon the person addressed came up and pressed the hand, extended through the window.

Miss Grundy was a maiden of perhaps thirty-five summers, which, robbing her cheeks somewhat of their youthful bloom, had restored it to the point of her nose. But any one could see that the perennial girlhood of her disposition defied the passing years, and that her feelings were infantile in their sweetness and freshness. She was dressed in the height of the fashion, and could scarcely walk, she was pulled back so tightly. A little chip-hat, such as is worn by school-girls, rested upon her curls—they were from the milliner's, but then they were just the color to match. Her gait was gentle and timid, her smile full of a caressing ardor; as she spoke to Mrs. Armstrong and Juliet, she seemed ready to clasp them in her arms from pure girlish impulse.

"Dear Mrs. Armstrong!" said Miss Grundy, "you and Miss Juliet really look charming. I never saw such roses!"

"How you do flatter people, dear Miss Grundy," said Mrs. Armstrong, with her sweetest smile.

"You must not say that—I never flatter; what a lovely day—"

"Quite charming. We came to town to look at the new goods. But what is the use of doing so? The times are so fearfully hard. Our few small investments scarcely bring in anything. Poor Juliet has not even a winter hat; and as to myself, I am positively in rags, Miss Grundy!"

Mrs. Armstrong smoothed down her rich silk, which was loaded with lace, passing her hand as she did so over a pocket-book in her side-pocket, which had a very considerable number of bank-notes in it.

"Yes, positively in rags; and how we are to live I don't know!—You seem so prosperous in Piedmont! What a lovely scarf you have on! But you always dress in such exquisite taste, Miss Grundy! Do come and see us—we are so lonely at Trianon! Drive on, William, or we shall not be home in time for tea. Do come and see us, dear Miss Grundy; we shall enjoy it *so* much; we have so little society: be sure and come! *Good-bye!*"

And the carriage bore the lady away. As soon as there was a considerable interval between herself and Miss Grundy, Mrs. Armstrong drew a long, deep breath, apparently of relief. Then a heavenly smile expanded upon her countenance, and she said,

"What a horrid old thing! Just think of her girlish airs. She's forty if she's a day, and such a fearful old chatterbox! She would have stood there for hours and talked me to death, but I did not allow her to say a word! I saw her catch her breath—she was ready to burst—I really did not feel safe until the carriage moved."

And Mrs. Armstrong positively laughed aloud at the success of her diplomacy. She then assumed a tragic expression, and said,

"To think *you* might grow like Miss Grundy, my love! and have a pinched old nose, and a dreadful scarf like that on your bony old shoulders, and pass your time in tittle-tattle and picking people to pieces!—For heaven's sake, just think of it, and *do* not run the risk. You know what I mean, dearest! When I die you cannot live by yourself at Trianon, and may be compelled to come and live at Piedmont. Would you like that?"

"No, I should not like it in the least, mamma," said Juliet.

"Then you really ought to take steps to avoid it, dear. Don't you think it would be better to spend your winters in Paris, and your summers—shall I go on?"

"Yes, mamma."

"And your summers at *Wye?*"

Miss Juliet looked out of the window, and did not reply. This was a habit with her, and her mamma did not further allude to her darling scheme. Experience had told her that it was useless to attempt to *worry* her Juliet into anything, and she wisely changed the subject by exclaiming, with a smile which showed her still beautiful teeth,

" Was there ever such a fright as that old Miss Grundy, with her red nose and her fearful scarf, and that simper on her face?—she gives me a chill! Just as sure as we are sitting here she has gone back home, and is tearing our characters to pieces, Juliet."

Harsh as these views in reference to Miss Grundy may appear, we regret to say they were fully justified by the young lady; for Miss Grundy's life was absorbed in attention to the affairs of her neighbors. She had been a blooming girl once, with a pretty face, and a zest for something better than tittle-tattle; but gradually the bloom disappeared, her visitors fell off, her suitors—she had had them—cooled, and she was quite deserted. This arose from a want of skill on Miss Grundy's part; she unfortunately allowed some traits of her character, which she thought were concealed, to reveal themselves. It is difficult to define the traits in question without using harsh expressions; let us call one of them *indirectness*. She liked to act—to smile upon people and caress them, and then go away and blacken their characters. She dearly loved a dish of scandal, and concocted it from the slenderest materials. When facts were wanting, she took refuge in her imagination. Her curiosity was morbid, and her suspicion immense; and if there was anything to be known, she would know it by some means; and what she could not discover or accomplish by direct means she accomplished indirectly. She had a taste for indirectness, and was sly by nature. *Finesse* was her life—a canker eating into her whole character. She liked to be roundabout and secret in her movements—that fooled people. Unluckily she ended by completely fooling herself. People crossed the street to avoid meeting and conversing with the smiling Miss Grundy. Her nose was red and pinched. Her pretty figure had grown bony. She was very, very girlish still, but people laughed. In a philosophic point of view Miss Grundy's life had been a failure.

After leaving Mrs. Armstrong, or rather being left by her, Miss Grundy raised the train of her pull-back dress with a girlish air, and proceeded to the store of Messrs. Smith & Jones, where she made minute inquiries of a young clerk, whom she occasionally invited to tea, as to Mrs. Armstrong's purchases. Having been informed by the smirking youth that Mrs. A. had bought two spools of sewing-silk, Miss Grundy smiled, and called upon Mrs. Wilkes, the milliner, where she found that Mrs. Armstrong had not purchased a winter hat; and then, having ascertained what she wished to know, she went back to her small home in the suburbs, where she found a friend who had dropped in to tea—a young lady with tastes similar to her own.

Warm kisses and embraces were exchanged between the maidens, and Miss Grundy said, as they sat down to tea,

" That old thing, Mrs. Armstrong, was in town to-day. I never saw such airs and graces, and such overdressing—and in the worst taste, my dear—the very worst taste you can imagine!"

Miss Grundy was accustomed to proceed steadily when she talked, without much regard to pauses, and to catch her breath at intervals, apparently to avoid being interrupted.

" I really have no patience with these people—they are nothing but sham—and just as mercenary—oh! it really is awful —they are doing all they can to catch that horrid Douglas Lascelles — though the way I hear that girl goes on ought to open his eyes, and I don't believe he has the least idea of marrying her."

Miss Grundy drew a deep breath; and finding that her friend was about to reply, exclaimed,

" Just think, that old thing turned over all the goods at Smith & Jones's, and then bought only two spools of sewing-silk, they told me—and nothing at all at Mrs. Wilkes's — there was nothing good enough for her, I suppose—for she really thinks she is above us, and looks down on us poor people in Piedmont as if we were dirt beneath her feet—I assure you she does."

The maiden visitor slowly shook her head, and as she was sitting near the tea-pot she poured out, in an absent and pre-occupied manner, a third cup of tea for herself, and said that she never had had much opinion of Mrs. Armstrong.

"Opinion of her!" exclaimed Miss Grundy, "who can have any, dear?—her shameful treatment of that sweet Miss Bassick would be enough if there was nothing else—it really is disgusting!—'Cinda—she's the maid, you know, and used to live with us—came and told me everything, and anything more shocking than the way she goes on with that sweet young thing could not be imagined—I assure you, on my word, my dear, it could not be imagined. Just to think! she beats her—positively beats her, and then locks her up on bread-and-water in the garret till the poor dear thing is nearly starved! And then to come, after such disgraceful conduct, sailing into town with her silks and satins, and her daughter dressed up like a peacock, with her smirks and sim-pers, and her airs and graces, while that poor Miss Bassick is locked up in the garret!"

The maiden friend shook her head with deep solemnity, and as her cup was empty she casually refilled it—it was her fourth. "Is it possible, my dear?" she said. "Oh, it can't be possible!"

"But 'Cinda told me all about it, and you know that she would never have said so if it was not true—yes, poor Miss Bas-sick! I pity her, and no one but a tyrant would be cruel to a helpless, inoffensive girl — the best and sweetest creature in the world, as you can see from her face, and—"

"People say she's sly," said a thin, piping voice with a shake in it—which voice came from the chimney-corner, where the half-palsied old aunt was nod-ding over her knitting.

Miss Grundy's face suddenly flushed with displeasure. As she, Miss Grundy, was the owner of the house, and her aunt lived with her, this ill-bred intrusion and virtual contradiction very naturally excited her indignation.

"Miss Bassick *sly!*" she exclaimed. "I really would be glad to know what you mean."

"She's a sly one, they do say," piped the thin voice in reply. "I've heard it said she's a sly, designing creatur'."

At this Miss Grundy's indignation over-flowed, and she frankly stated her opinion of those people who regarded nothing as sacred, and wantonly repeated every idle and ill-natured word, every vulgar scan-dal, tending to the injury of others. If such a thing were tolerated, no one was safe. To call Miss Bassick *sly!* with that heavenly face! It really was too bad! Would the aged lady kindly con-tinue her knitting, and not interpose with such ill-natured snarls? which—she was sorry to have to use the word—were quite disgusting.

Miss Grundy, to be brief, fell into a good, wholesome fit of anger.

"Miss Bassick is an angel, and her life is made a burden to her — 'Cinda says so!" she exclaimed; "and I shouldn't wonder if that frumpy old creature has gone back, and is storming at the sweet dear thing at this very moment."

Now it really was singular that some-thing of that sort was occurring at Tria-non. Mrs. Armstrong had told Juliet that Miss Grundy would go off and pick her character to pieces; and Miss Grundy now intimated the possibility of a slight misunderstanding between Mrs. Armstrong and Miss Bassick. The two ladies seem-ed to appreciate each other.

XLI.

MISS BASSICK'S PRIVATE POST.

As the Trianon carriage drove into the grounds, on its return from Piedmont, the two ladies observed that a horse was standing at the rack, and this they recog-nized as belonging to Mr. Lascelles.

The carriage rolled up to the door, and as it did so the keen eyes of Mrs. Arm-strong saw a shadow pass across the win-dows of the drawing-room; the lamps were not lit, but a fire was burning in the apartment; and as the front-door was open, this shadow was seen to disappear silently up the staircase, taking as it did so the graceful shape of Miss Bassick. A moment afterward Mr. Douglas Lascelles came out of the drawing-room, and assisted the ladies to descend from their carriage.

Mrs. Armstrong rustled in, expressing warmly her pleasure at the gentleman's visit — she was *so* glad he had waited; would he excuse her while she went upstairs to take off her wrappings?—Juliet would stay and entertain him — what a charming evening! And then, beaming outwardly, but internally raging, Mrs. Armstrong went up-stairs. She did not go to her own apartment but to Miss Bassick's, and there she found the young lady seated by her little table industriously sewing, and looking innocent.

Mrs. Armstrong, having entered the room, stood looking silently at Miss Bassick. She gasped a little — her feelings seemed to overcome her. She had plainly seen Miss Bassick flit by the drawing-room windows and up the staircase, and she was naturally outraged by this sudden fit of industry.

"Miss Bassick!" she said.

"Yes, ma'am," said Miss Bassick, meekly.

"Will you be good enough to inform me why you were in the drawing-room just now?"

"In the drawing-room, ma'am!" exclaimed Miss Bassick, with an air of heavenly innocence.

"Yes, miss! I will make my meaning plainer, if you desire it. What were you doing in the drawing-room? Replacing Juliet and myself with Mr. Lascelles?"

"Replacing you with Mr. Lascelles, ma'am!"

"You dare to deny it?"

"Oh, Mrs. Armstrong!"

Miss Bassick drew forth her handkerchief and wiped her eyes. Her innocence was touching. She seemed to be overwhelmed with sorrow and surprise at such an accusation, and cooed in her low, sweet voice,

"I should never think of doing such a thing, Mrs. Armstrong!"

Thereat the elder lady quite lost her temper.

"I saw you!" she exclaimed; "I saw you as you ran out of the room and up the staircase, you designing thing! You *were* in the drawing-room—sitting there with Mr. Lascelles! Two of the chairs were drawn up close to each other!—do you hear what I say, miss?—*nearly touching* each other; and you occupied one of them!"

At this very rude and unfeeling insinuation Miss Bassick sniffed, and exhibited an intention to dissolve into tears.

"How could you think of such a thing, ma'am?" sobbed Miss Bassick, wiping her eyes.

"Persons are not obliged to *think*, or exercise their imaginations as to *your* proceedings, miss!" said Mrs. Armstrong. "You were there in that drawing-room! you were seated in one of those two chairs, and Mr. Lascelles was seated in the other close to you—heaven knows how close! You presumed to occupy my drawing-room and do the honors of my establishment in my absence! Deny it, and I will ascertain the fact from Mr. Lascelles!"

Now, as Miss Bassick *had* been seated in the drawing-room, in one of the chairs close beside Mr. Lascelles, and as she had unfortunately been detected in her hasty retreat, which she made at once when she heard the carriage coming, it really seemed a very difficult matter, indeed, to conceal or deny the fact any longer. Finding this impracticable, Miss Bassick had recourse to the next best thing—a plausible explanation. She did not mean to say, she faltered, in her low cooing voice, that she *had not been in the drawing-room.* She *had* exchanged a few words —they were very few — with Mr. Lascelles. She was in the room arranging the fire when he came, as she knew Mrs. Armstrong liked a cheerful blaze when she returned in the evening; and Mr. Lascelles had bowed to her, and engaged her in conversation—and—and—she had not intended—" Here Miss Bassick wept and sunk to silence.

Now, long and intimate acquaintance with Miss Bassick had not tended to impress Mrs. Armstrong with the conviction that her word was to be relied on. The statement may seem ungallant, but such was the fact. The handsome face was wet with tears, and the graceful figure shook; but then it was barely possible that what the aged aunt of Miss Grundy had said was true—that Miss Bassick was a "sly one."

Mrs. Armstrong stood looking at her for some moments. Then she said,

"Very well, miss! You are very good at explaining away what you cannot *deny* —that is one of your traits. You *were* in the drawing-room, then, with Mr. Lascelles. If the circumstance occurred so naturally as you say it did, why did you steal off in that secret way? No, don't answer me. You are ready, no doubt, with another plausible explanation — I am tired of them. I have only one thing more to say, miss, and that is that you will either keep your place in this house or you will leave it!"

"Oh! ma'am, if you will only overlook it this time—"

"I will overlook it if you give me your promise that you will claim no further acquaintance with Mr. Lascelles, retire to your room when he visits Trianon, and never exchange another word with him."

"I promise you I will not, ma'am," Miss Bassick said, in her sad, sweet voice.

"We understand each other, then. If what occurred this evening occurs again, you will please find another home, Miss Bassick."

Mrs. Armstrong turned her back and swept out of the room, banging the door behind her. As she disappeared Miss Bassick's handsome arched eyebrows suddenly came together, and rising to her feet, she looked after Mrs. Armstrong with her red lips slightly opened. Under them her teeth were set together.

"The old hag! how I hate her! I could have sprung upon her and choked her! I'll do it some day!" she said.

And it really did seem from the expression of Miss Bassick's face that she would be equal to the performance of this tragic act. Her cheeks were flushed, her bosom was heaving, and her face and figure had the powerless and yet menacing look of a woman in a rage.

The paroxysm did not last very long. The flush disappeared gradually from her cheeks, and her handsome eyebrows resumed the arch. She went to her mirror, carefully brushed and arranged her hair by the light of her small lamp, and, looking at herself, began to smile. As she continued to look into the mirror the smile grew brighter, the red, pouting lips showed the white teeth under them, which were parted now; and with a coquettish toss of the head Miss Bassick said, in a confidential tone,

"I think you will do, miss. He ought to see me now, instead of that stupid Juliet."

As she had set the tea-table, and was not required down-stairs, Miss Bassick opened her desk and began to write a letter. She wrote rapidly and in a beautiful hand, filling two sheets of note-paper in a very brief time. She then folded them, placed them in a dainty envelope, and, cautiously opening her door, listened. The ladies and Mr. Lascelles were at tea, and descending silently the back staircase, Miss Bassick stole through the grounds, emerged from them through a small gate used for pedestrians going to Piedmont, and then, making a circuit, came out near the larger gate in front. She then hastened along, walking very rapidly, until she reached a spot completely concealed from the house, where a ledge of rock, nearly covered with cedar-bushes, extended along one side of the road.

It was now quite dark, but Miss Bassick did not seem to mind that. She went on with the air of a person perfectly acquainted with the ground, and passing behind the ledge, which dipped toward the east, put her hand into a crevice and drew out a letter. This she put in her pocket, and replaced with the letter which she had just written in her chamber.

It was the private post-office of Miss Bassick and Mr. Lascelles.

Having transacted the business connected with her private mail, Miss Bassick retraced her steps, and regained her chamber unseen. She had not been absent more than a quarter of an hour, and during that time, at least, she calculated, the ladies would be at tea. They had not returned with Mr. Lascelles to the drawing-room yet; but they did so in a few moments; and then Miss Bassick descended to her own modest meal, which, when company came, she took after the rest.

She heard the murmur of voices in the drawing-room, and would have liked to listen, perhaps; but a maid was in the room, and that was impossible. At last she rose, and, as it was not against orders, she went up the front staircase toward her chamber. The drawing-room door was open, and Mr. Lascelles was sitting nearly facing it as Miss Bassick came out.

As she passed over the few feet between the door and the staircase, Miss Bassick found time to do three things: the first was to assume an exquisitely coquettish attitude; the second was to fix her seductive eyes on Mr. Lascelles and smile; and the last was to make a significant gesture toward the wood, where she had deposited her letter. She then flitted up the staircase and went to her chamber. Not the least indication had appeared on the face of Mr. Lascelles that he had seen Miss Bassick as she passed.

XLII.

NAILS.

MR. LASCELLES returned to Wye at about nine o'clock, and after indulging in a meditative cigar in the library, retired to his chamber.

He had found Miss Bassick's letter in the private post-office. It was a very witty and brilliant composition, on pink note-paper, and described the interview with Mrs. Armstrong in a delightful manner. The style was gay and *riant*, for the most part, but the note ended with pathetic sighs. Her poor life was wasting away under this terrible tyranny — she tried to laugh, as he could see, but it was by no means real laughter. She had made up her mind at last. She must leave Trianon !

Coming to the end of the note, Mr. Lascelles pondered. Was Miss Bassick in earnest ? Would she really go away ? It was doubtful. Women were curious creatures, and did not tell the truth always. You could divide them into two classes — the weak and the wicked. If they were intellectual, they made up for that by being bad. If they were good, they were apt to be feeble-minded. Those who were personally attractive were generally wicked, and he preferred that class — but they must be really attractive. Was Miss Bassick wicked ? She was certainly fascinating. If she went away he would miss her. To see her had become a sort of necessity. He would go on the very next day and have a confidential conversation with her on the subject.

Mr. Lascelles then proceeded to meditate upon another and, apparently, less agreeable subject. He passed in review a series of incidents following each other in rapid sequence. The first of these was a ride which he had taken some weeks before to the nearest railway station. On this occasion Mr. Lascelles had evidently expected some one by the night train, and this some one seemed to have duly arrived. He was a respectable looking person, with a travelling-valise, and got out quietly. When Mr. Lascelles as quietly nodded to him and rode off, the new-comer slowly followed him. Having reached a body of woods near the station, Mr. Lascelles had stopped—the traveller had joined him—and they had remained in conversation for nearly an hour, after which Mr. Lascelles had ridden back home. As to the man with the valise, whose appearance at the station had excited a mild amount of speculation in the

ﬁnd of the agent there, he was not seen
again, and passed into oblivion.

It is true that there was a remarkable
likeness between the respectable night-
traveller and Mr. Rooney Ruggles, but
then resemblances not unfrequently occur—and it was quite absurd to regard it
as anything more than a chance likeness.
There could be no possibility that the respectable personage *was* Mr. Ruggles, unless he carried a tramp outﬁt in his valise,
which was preposterous. Such things
are read of in novels, but never happen in
real life, which, being a real thing, is necessarily commonplace, and never violates
probabilities. Therefore the night-trav-
eller had disappeared, and Mr. Ruggles
had made his appearance upon the scene.
That was all. The former was highly respectable, as anybody could see from his
black suit, while Mr. Ruggles was a tramp,
as both his costume and his accent plainly showed; but he was not on that account unworthy of respect. We must
discriminate. The man who scorns to
burn a wheat-stack, and means to live by
honest work, is not a tramp, however
homeless he may be. Now Mr. Rooney
Ruggles was living by honest toil; he
had a contract for making shingles; this
supplied him with daily bread. But, then,
the winter was approaching, and Mr. Gibbs
might have no further need for his services: under these circumstances it was
not unnatural that he should look for
work elsewhere, which may have led to
his accidental interview with Mr. Lascelles
in the grounds of Wye. It was not a
pleasant interview altogether, and soon
terminated. Mr. Lascelles was now thinking of it, and of another interview—that
with the Lefthander at Crow's Nest, and
also of the conversation with him on the
next day on the bridge.

Mr. Lascelles looked extremely dissatis-
ﬁed. He was smoking a cigar as he re-
ﬂected, and emitted short, hot puffs instead of languid smoke-wreaths—a sign of
mental disturbance. He was obviously
very much disturbed, indeed, and a moral
lecturer might have set him up on a platform as an illustration. Here was a
young gentleman surrounded by every
comfort and luxury. He had no cares
connected with the low subject of
money. He was in excellent health,
and occupied a high social position.
Here, assuredly, was one of the fortunate
ones of the world—but appearances are
often deceptive. A nail seemed to be
hidden in his shoe somewhere, and it
fretted him. He had probably driven
the nail himself, and was, no doubt, very
sorry that he had done so; but there it
was. And nails of that description are very
diﬃcult to extract. They have a fashion
of clinching themselves on the other side,
and no matter how you tug at them they
will not come out.

Why had Mr. Douglas Lascelles ever
hammered in that nail in the sole of the
handsome slipper he was wearing? And
the obstinate thing had a way of shifting
about. When he came down in the
morning to the bright breakfast-table in
his low-quartered shoes, there was the
nail in the low-quartered shoes. When
he drew on his elegant riding-boots to
take a ride, there was the same nail in
the boots. And at night, when he put
on his worked slippers, and leaned back
in his arm-chair, a sharp prick seemed to
say, "Here I am waiting; let us talk a
little." Why had Mr. Lascelles ever had
anything to do with nails? Oh, why
had he been so thoughtless and injudicious as to insert this one? The inser-
tion of nails shows a want of good sense.
They always prick you. Is not honesty
the best policy, even in a worldly point
of view, and the pleasure of hammering
in nails an inadequate recompense for the
festering sores which they occasion?

He was still holding Miss Bassick's
note in his hand, and, as his cigar had
gone, out he twisted it and made use of
it as a lighter.

"What a little devil she is!" he muttered; "she's setting her cap at me!"

He uttered a short laugh, and threw
away his cigar.

"I am not fool enough to marry a
head-servant!" he muttered. He then
went to bed.

XLIII.

THE DANGER OF DELIRIUM.

HARRY VANCE had a hard time of it. For a week or two he was burnt up by a raging fever, and his mind constantly wandered, as his vague muttering indicated.

An old physician of the neighborhood had been promptly sent for, and visited him thereafter regularly, doing all that was possible for him. One other visitor made his appearance as regularly — Mr. Cary.

He had hastened to the bedside of the poor boy at once, and at first was urgent that he should be removed to Falling Water. It was obviously impossible to move him, however; and Mr. Cary contented himself with watching over him, and riding every day to Crow's Nest.

On one of these occasions Frances begged permission to accompany him—the young man had saved her life, she said, on the day of the panther hunt—and her father agreed to her wishes.

The consequence was that Mouse and Frances became acquainted, and on other visits which duly followed they became intimate. The spectacle of the minute house-keeper "in command" seemed to amuse and touch the young girl. One day she stooped down and kissed Mouse, and said,

"I think I am beginning to love you very much."

They were alone at the moment, and Harry was lying asleep on his poor couch. Mr. Cary had ridden a little farther to see some one on business, promising soon to return; and as both Gentleman Joe and the Lefthander were temporarily absent, the three persons were the sole occupants of Crow's Nest.

"Of course *I* love *you* very much indeed, Miss Frances," said Mouse. "I am sure you are good, from your face, and it's a comfort to have you. Will you please be still, sir, and go to sleep?" she added to Harry, who was muttering something. "Your gruel's not ready, sir."

There was a wistful affectation of hu-
mor in the address. The poor boy w feverish, and wandering in his mi Frances turned her head and looked the pale face.

"Poor fellow!" she said.

"Take care, Lefthander!" mutter the young man; "that weight's t heavy! You will hurt yourself, Le hander!"

He then turned his head faintly, wi his eyes still closed, and said,

"It's a shame, father! You ought n to make fun for such rabble! You are gentleman—come, go away with me, : ther. Don't make faces any more. will work for you; what better can yo boy do than take care of you? You to care of me when I was a little one; n it's my turn, father."

"He is kind," murmured France "what a pity! Oh, what a pity!"

Her eyes filled as she looked at hi but a quick blush followed, burning l cheeks. Harry had begun again, and tl is what he muttered:

"Take care, Mouse! you'll fall. Do dance without chalk on your feet. Y frighten me. I have been frighten once before to-day. Did you notice tl carriage in the street which ran agait the car? There was a girl in it—she w so beautiful! Oh, so very beautiful! She was near losing her life under t hoofs of the horses, and I caught her my arms, and held her close to my her a moment! Only a second! — close me—her heart against mine! I can c now, remembering that!"

Frances stole a quick look at him; h face was glowing. She knew now w: had saved her that day.

"I never saw her again but once," t sick man went on muttering, "it was o day when her horse ran off—there w some danger from a panther. She w more beautiful than before; is it wro: to say that? I am nothing — but t star can shine on the clod of earth. shall not see her again; is it wrong to : member her—and—love her?"

A burning blush reddened the chee of Frances Cary, and she attempted smile; but her eyes filled. Then this poor boy had twice saved her life; he had told no one; but he had saved her!

"My own poor Harry!" said Mouse, piteously, "what is he saying?"

"His good, brave heart is speaking!" said Frances, with a little sob. Then the smile came; it was delicious to the woman's heart to have inspired this love.

"He is still now," she whispered. "Oh, if he were to—not to get well! He seems to love—his father so!"

"The doctor says he will get well now," sobbed Mouse, "and I think he will. He is *such* a good boy! We could not live without him."

"You love him very much, I can see that, and I trust he will not leave you, Mouse. I know your little heart would break if he were to."

"Y-e-s," sobbed Mouse, "we'd never hold up any of our heads after it, and never think of getting up the troupe any more."

"Getting up the troupe? What do you mean, dear?"

"I mean the troupe with the monkey," replied Mouse, sobbing, and wiping her eyes. "We are going to have a troupe and go on our travels again. You know we can't stay here always."

"Why can't you stay?"

"This house is not ours."

"Yes, indeed, it is!"

Mouse shook her head.

"People must not be idle in this world, neither must they be dependent."

Mouse uttered this noble sentiment with the air of a Roman matron, but the less heroic Frances put her arms around her and said,

"You dear, good, kind little Mouse! Did you ever hear of the flowers in May? Well, you are as welcome here as they are."

As though to intimate that other persons were included in this welcome, Frances looked at Harry, and, nodding toward him, said,

"Is he related to you, Mouse?"

"No, not exactly related," said the small nurse, with a meditative air; "but

it's pretty much the same, as Gentleman Joe is like a father to me. My real father is the Lefthander."

"What curious names!" said Frances, smiling. "Where did they ever get them?"

"Well," Mouse replied, with a serious look, "of course they are not their real names, as Gentleman Joe's name is Mr. Vance, and poppa's is Ottendorfer."

"But why not keep their real names?"

Mouse shook her head.

"You never belonged to a circus—they give everybody a nickname. There was Mr. Melville—*he* was 'Long Tom,' and Mr. Robinson, he was 'Old Jimmy.' Gentleman Joe was so polite that they gave him that name in the circus, and poppa was called the 'Lefthander' because he is left-handed."

"He is very strong, is he not?"

"Strong!" cried Mouse. "He is so strong that I believe he could lift up a horse or a cow and carry it on his shoulders—I really believe he could!"

"And is he good to you?"

"Good to me?—Poppa? Why, of course he is good to me! He is good to everybody—he wouldn't hurt a mouse."

"Well," said Frances, smiling as she looked at the fresh little face, "that accounts for his not hurting you, you dear little Mouse! Who in the world ever gave you such a name?"

"I think it was Long Tom. He was very fond of giving people nicknames."

"And he gave you yours because he thought you were so little?"

"Yes, I suppose that was the reason. There's not much of me, you know."

"What is your real name?"

"Do you mean my *real*, real name? My real name is Mademoiselle Celestine Delavan—that's on the bills—but my *real*, real name is Mignon Ottendorfer."

"Mignon! That is very pretty. So you are Miss Mouse Celestine Delavan Mignon Ottendorfer? Mercy! what a tremendous name! It is more than you are entitled to."

"I haven't much use for all of it. Mouse is sufficient for the Big Babies."

9

"What Big Babies do you mean?"

"Gentleman Joe and Harry and poppa," said Mouse. "I call them my Big Babies because they require so much looking after, and are always on my mind. You really have no idea of the trouble they give me. Sometimes I can't manage them at all—they're *so* contrary. They'll tramp about and catch cold, and do all sorts of things they ought not to do—oh! men are so contrary that there's hardly any way to get the better of them. The Babies treat me sometimes just as if I was not responsible. Oh me! they're a hard set—and yet they're very respectable people. Sometimes I feel almost like giving up—and Harry's sick because he wouldn't mind me. I told him not to go night-fishing, but he would, and got wet; and now see what's come of it—oh me! what's come of it!"

"You dear little mamma, don't be depressed; he's sure to get well. What a venerable head of an establishment! You odd little Mouse, you make me laugh so sometimes that it ends in my crying—you dear little mamma, with your responsibilities and your Big Babies!"

Thereupon Frances kissed Mouse, and smoothed her curls back from her face.

"Do you know one thing, Mouse?" she said, "you are not the least bit like a tramp's daughter."

"That's what Harry says," responded Mouse; "but he's always trying to get around me, and blind me, so as to make me let him do as he chooses. That's the way with all of them. But I don't mean to let 'em fool me."

"So he's good to you, like the rest? Is he amiable and considerate? Does he behave himself?"

"Not always. I haven't much to complain of except that he tries to get around me by petting me."

"That's not such a terrible proceeding. What's *his* nickname, Mouse?"

"He hasn't got any except Harry. That's his real name."

"And he's the youngest of your Babies?"

"Yes; he's nothing but a boy, and yet he is just as hard to manage as the rest. He's harder. Oh, he's an obstinate one, I can tell you! It is all I can do to— Go to sleep again this minute, sir! What do you mean by opening your eyes and staring at me so?"

And as Mr. Cary returned at this moment for Frances, the young lady's interview with Mouse terminated.

She rode home by her father's side in silence: she was thinking. At last she said,

"Papa, did you see who saved me that day in Piedmont?"

"When we had the accident to the carriage? It was one of the circus men, I think."

"It was this poor sick boy here at Crow's Nest. I found it out from his muttering. And then he saved me again from the panther—how brave he must be!"

XLIV.

THE CLOD AND THE STAR.

HARRY VANCE grew better. It is good to have a close-knit constitution. It is better than huge muscle which excels in lifting; but the slender race-horse limbs are made for endurance.

Mouse was by the young fellow's side all the time as before, and one day they were speaking of his delirium during the fever. Mouse told him that he had spoken of the accident at Piedmont, and of holding Frances Cary in his arms, while she was listening by his bedside; whereupon Harry Vance blushed crimson, and demanded just what had escaped him. Mouse had no difficulty in repeating his words, and the blush grew deeper. He had said that he *loved her.*

"That was unfortunate," he said, in a low voice.

Mouse looked at him with an inquiring glance.

"To have told her—that—"

He stopped.

"That you *loved her?* That's what

you said, you foolish Harry, and I'd like to know why you shouldn't say it if you wanted to."

"I was crazy—out of my head—or I never would have said so."

"You *were* out of your head," said Mouse, philosophically; "but that's not the point, sir. I don't see why, if you were *in* your head, you haven't a right to love people, and have people love you, too!"

Harry looked with wide eyes at Mouse, and said, in a low voice,

"You can't mean—"

"Yes, I do," said Mouse, manfully; "I mean you are good enough for any lady in this land."

Harry Vance knit his brows; then he said, mournfully,

"My poor, dear little Mouse! it is good to be as young and ignorant as you are. You love me—you love everybody, for that matter, your heart is so big; but you forget who and what I am."

"You are my own dear Harry," she said, putting her arms around his neck, and pressing her lips to his pale face.

"Yes, you love me, I say, and your love is precious to me. But *you* are not others. To them I am a poor vagabond, neither more nor less. Did you ever hear of what is called a zero, Mignon? It is a thing which stands for nothing. I am a zero."

"You are our Harry, sir; and any one might be proud to love you—even dear, sweet Frances Cary!"

Harry Vance shrugged his shoulders, blushing. For the first time the latent spirit of bitterness, and revolt at his low fortunes, betrayed itself in the manner of the poor boy.

"You might as well expect the star to stoop to the clod," he said. "The star shines on the clod, but does not stoop to it; and if the clod is wise it will keep its place."

"Oh, Harry!" protested Mouse, "don't think of yourself so."

"I think of myself as I am, dear," he said, losing his bitterness, and speaking softly and gently. "We are poor and humble, but that does not matter much. The sun shines for us, and the sky is as blue as it is for others; only your talking in this wild way makes it not so blue to me. That is enough now, dear—it is rather sad to talk of such things."

He put both arms around her.

"At least *you* love me," he said.

Whether it was that Harry Vance had risen from bed sooner than he ought to have done, or that this scene with Mouse acted unfortunately upon his nervous system, it is certain that on the very same evening he had a return of fever; and this led to an incident of an unexpected character.

The young man had lain down on his couch, telling no one that he felt the fever back in his pulses; and as he had covered his head, they supposed that he had fallen asleep. The rest, therefore, retired, and in an hour the long breathing of one and all indicated that they were asleep.

Then Harry Vance rose quietly, left Crow's Nest, and went out into the night. He was hot with fever, and his steps were uncertain. Did he even know where he was going? It seemed so, since he went straight on, through the night, toward Falling Water.

Frances Cary was in the library finishing a letter; it was about ten at night, and Mr. Cary had gone to his chamber only a few moments before — Frances promising to retire, in her turn, when she had filled her sheet of note-paper.

All at once she raised her head. Steps crossed the porch, the front-door opened, then the door of the library; and Harry Vance came in, his head bare, his face flushed, his eyes full of a vague pain.

"I did not mean to," he said, in a faint, trembling voice; "you heard me—I did not wish you to hear me—it was my fever—and I did not know you were at my bedside."

He drew a long breath, trembling and looking at her. His eyes betrayed the secret of the poor boy's heart—an unutterable tenderness transfigured his whole face.

"I am nothing," he went on, in a broken and faint voice. "I would not dare

—not because you are a young lady; because you are—what you are. I did not mean to say that I had held you in my arms. You will not think of it any more —since I tell you I am sorry. I was very sick and weak—I am well now, you see, and have come to ask you to forgive me."

"Oh no!" exclaimed Frances, blushing, and with tears in her eyes, "there is nothing to forgive. You saved me—I should have been killed."

"I never meant you to know," he murmured. "I thought it might make you feel ashamed. I had to lift you from your carriage. I could not do that without putting my arms around you. I did not mean to tell any one."

His eyes half closed, and his body, which he seemed to have held erect by a strong effort of the will, moved a little as a tree does in the wind.

"I only came to tell you this—I could not live without telling you. You will forgive my raving, as it was only raving. You will never see me any more—"

He stood for an instant looking at her and trembling. She had half risen. He came one step toward her.

"I shall never see you again. Goodbye!" he said, looking at her as if his heart were breaking, and holding out his hand. Frances held out her own, and he tried to take it. The effort was too much for him. He tottered, fell upon one knee beside her chair, and, if she had not put her arm around him, would have fainted and fallen.

When Mr. Cary, in his dressing-gown, hastened to the library, where he heard voices, the young man was on his knee thus by the young lady's chair, with his face resting on the hand he held, and her arm supporting his head. She ran and got a glass of water and moistened his forehead. At the touch of her fingers he opened his eyes and rose to his feet, looking vaguely around him. Ten minutes afterward, in spite of every effort which Mr. Cary made to persuade him to remain, he went away.

The clod and the star had made each other's acquaintance!

XLV.

A FEMALE MANŒUVRER.

"Nelly, you certainly are the greatest goose I have ever known in my life! It is *such* a luxury to know any one well enough to speak one's real sentiments. Mercy! not marry him when he loves you so much? You deserve to die an old maid, which you certainly will, if you go on so—and your last days will be embittered by remorse, too, you unreasonable thing."

It was Frances Cary who made these few remarks to Nelly Welles. Finding that it was a superb morning, and a little tired of confinement, she had proceeded to tease her papa into allowing her to ride, and see Nelly, without escort; had duly overcome him—for she was a spoiled child, and naturally argued that what she wished was from the nature of things perfectly proper—and mounting the small riding-horse kept for her special use, had soon reached the house in the mountains.

Having beamed on the whole household, with whom she was by this time well acquainted, for she and Nelly had exchanged numerous visits, and had become desperately intimate, Miss Frances inquired with interest after Mr. Elliot— had he gone? Receiving from the guileless Daddy Welles, who was in the room at the moment, the assurance that Mr. Elliot had not yet been able to tear himself away from the deer, and was that morning in pursuit of these wild animals, Miss Frances smiled significantly, and, turning to Nelly, proposed—ferns.

"You know you dote on ferns, Nelly, as much as I do, and papa is just as fond of them. Think of an old soldier like papa being as fond of flowers as he is! He loves his zinnias and petunias, I do believe, as much as he loves me. I prefer ferns and grasses, don't you?"

Nelly responding that she did, Frances proceeded to observe that there were no ferns worth speaking of in the vicinity of her own home, but superb varieties among the rocks near Daddy Welles's, and it was decided that they should take a ramble in the woods and look for them. Nelly put on her hat, and Frances Cary having skilfully pinned up her skirt, to leave her movements free, they set out on their ramble.

Ferns are an innocent passion of the female sex, and have this advantage—that looking for them admits of conversation. So, as they rambled about, Nelly and Frances talked.

"What's become of Mr. Brantz Elliot —why isn't he at home making himself agreeable, Nelly? I don't pretend to compare myself with the lordly sex, but if I were a young man—which Heaven knows I'm glad I am not—and lived in the house with you, I'd find something better to do than hunt."

"Dear Frances!" Nelly said, with a faint color in her cheeks, "how you do run on."

"Hunting deer! He'd show his taste by hunting another sort of deer, spelled with an a."

Having made which brilliant witticism Miss Frances laughed approvingly. Nelly did not reply. She was looking with deep interest into a crevice in the rocks, where some ferns were growing, and this seemed to render it necessary for her to turn away her head. Her face was thus hidden from her companion, but her neck was not, and there came such a flush upon it that Frances suddenly cried,

"You are blushing, Nelly. Your very neck is crimson. Mercy! is there anything you've not told me, you mean thing? There *is* something! He's courted you—you know he has—or he is going to!"

Nelly was quite overcome by this abrupt charge. It brought to mind every detail of the scene between herself and Brantz Elliot. There had been no repetition of that scene. Nelly had not given her lover the least opportunity. She avoided private interviews with the skill of her sex, and Brantz Elliot had not found a single opportunity to renew his suit. He no doubt intended to do so— if not, why did he not go? He still lingered in the mountain, putting off his

departure from day to day; and it was evident that he did not regard his suit as entirely hopeless. In spite of all, however, Nelly had adhered to her resolution. It was hard, and nearly broke her heart; but she was more determined than ever not to yield, and become the wife of the man she loved, who loved her too, but would regret their union afterward. Self-sacrifice ennobles and endues us with a mysterious strength. Nelly had resolved to sacrifice her own happiness to Brantz Elliot's.

"You know he's courting you? Don't deny it, miss. Don't attempt to conceal anything from me—tell me about it, Nelly. Oh, it's delightful! So romantic! Just like a novel! Mercy!"

Having concluded with this supreme expression of delighted astonishment, Frances put her arms around Nelly, and taking that young lady by the chin, turned her face to her.

"What a blush!" she cried. "That's enough. Good gracious! Have you said yes, Nelly?"

Poor Nelly! She could not resist her friend's inquiry. She was so unhappy that it had become almost a necessity to confide her unhappiness to some one; and as she and Frances were bosom friends by this time, she told her everything.

"It was so hard, Frances," she said, with a little sob, after which she turned away her head, and put one of her hands to her eyes.

This was pathetic, but Miss Frances preferred a more cheerful view of the subject; also, the occasion admitted of the luxury of scolding; she therefore burst forth into the tirade recorded in the beginning of this chapter, to the effect that her friend was a goose for refusing Brantz Elliot, and would linger out a life of ancient maidenhood and remorse in consequence.

"Yes, you certainly are the most unreasonable thing that ever lived," she added. "A judgment will come of it! Just to think of your refusing such a fine fellow because he's rich and you are poor."

"I wish it was just the opposite," Nelly Welles said, with a huge sigh.

"And have *him* getting proud and refusing to marry Miss Welles because *she* was richer than he was. That's very fine reasoning, miss! How would you like him to do that?"

Having never contemplated the subject in this light, Nelly only sighed.

"You are *such* a goose, Nelly, I feel as if I could pinch you. Go and tell Mr. Elliot you'll marry him this moment."

"That would be wedding in haste, and we'd repent at leisure, I suppose," said Nelly, with a rueful smile.

"You know what I mean, miss. *Tell him* this moment, I mean — that is, just as soon as you have an opportunity. Have you seen him again?"

"Of course I've seen him, Frances. I see him at every meal."

"There you are with your evasions again, miss. Seeing people at meals is not seeing them. Have you had any delightful romantic scenes, I mean? — by moonlight, for example — lover seated and gazing upward into responsive eyes, low voices, expressions such as 'my own!' 'my dear one!' Has there been any of *that?*"

"No," murmured Nelly, laughing and blushing.

"Then you're a monster! We're told to love our enemies, and you don't even care for the happiness of those who are devoted to you."

"Oh, I wish I could make him happy, but I cannot, Frances! Indeed, I ought not to marry Mr. Elliot. Such marriages never come to good. He would become ashamed of me, and then stop caring for me."

"The idea! You must despise him!"

"It would be only natural."

"It would be contemptible, Nelly! Gracious! what can one think of a man who's ashamed of his wife? He can't be a gentleman. He may marry a poor girl when he is poor himself, and afterward grow famous and be courted by everybody; but if he is ashamed of her he is not really a gentleman, Nelly. I don't

know how you feel, but if I was a man I'd marry for love, and cherish my wife more than everything in the world besides — as I know *he* would."

As this "he" evidently referred to Mr. Brantz Elliot, Nelly uttered another sigh.

"So it's all arranged, isn't it, Nelly?"

"No, it is by no means arranged, Frances."

"Do you mean to say you will go on saying no to the end of time?"

"I can't say yes."

"You can, you obstinate thing. You know you want to, and — goodness! yonder is Mr. Elliot, wandering disconsolately down the stream. He's found no deer. I'm certain he's been sitting down somewhere sighing, and not seen a single object around him."

"Come, we must go home, Frances," exclaimed Nelly, in sudden alarm at the prospect of being joined by Mr. Brantz Elliot.

"We will do nothing of the sort, miss," returned Frances, in high delight at the idea of bringing about an interview between the lovers.

"Oh, Frances, don't keep me!"

"I am not keeping you, miss; but common politeness requires that we should not run away when a gentleman approaches us: and look, he has seen us, and is coming up the mountain. What a fine-looking fellow he is. If you won't have him I am determined to set my cap at him! Why, he walks as if he was 'shod like a mountaineer,' which reminds one of the song, miss,

"'With music to fill up the pauses,
And nobody over-near!'

I shall discreetly retire. Common propriety requires that I should do so."

This proposal evidently produced extreme alarm in Miss Nelly Welles, which she proceeded to give evidence of by exclaiming,

"Oh no, don't, Frances!"

"Good-morning, Mr. Elliot! — have you been hunting? What a beautiful day! Nelly and I were just gathering some of these exquisite ferns."

"They certainly are pretty, Miss Cary," said Brantz Elliot, who had joined them by this time.

"Are they not? Could you get me some grasses to go with them? I dearly love grasses. Such ferns! and what a load we've got! I really must go and beg Daddy Welles to lend me a basket. No, you must not go for me; you must be so tired from your hunting. I'll be back in a moment!"

With which innocent words Miss Frances Cary shot a glance of triumph at Nelly, and turned to go back to the house. Suddenly she screamed. They had all been standing facing the rocks in which the ferns were growing, and had not heard the steps of a person who approached them. This person was now close to them, and indeed Miss Frances, as she turned round, suddenly found herself face to face with him. It was Gentleman Joe.

"Mercy!" exclaimed the young lady; "I thought it was a bear!"

Thereupon Gentleman Joe burst into boyish ecstasies at the success of his ruse to surprise them. He seemed quite convulsed, and executed his most astonishing grimaces, winding up by contorting his system from a sense of deep enjoyment.

Nelly plainly hailed his appearance with satisfaction, and gave him her sweetest smile.

"How you frighten people, Gentleman Joe!" she said, for she and the ex-clown had become perfectly intimate with each other; "you might have thrown us all into hysterics!"

"I wouldn't like to do. that, Nelly—I love you too much, my dear," said Gentleman Joe, gradually recovering his equanimity.

"Then you must go back, as a punishment, and get Miss Cary a basket; she wants it for her ferns."

"Oh no!" Miss Frances exclaimed; "I will go myself—he will never know where to find it; but he may carry it. Come, Mr. Vance!"

A wicked smile accompanied the words, indicating to Nelly her friend's intention to thus leave her alone with Brantz Elliot. She blushed to the very roots of her hair, and seemed not to know what she should do, when Elliot came to her assistance. The young huntsman had or had not comprehended the scene—if he had understood it, he had resolved not to inflict himself upon Nelly if she did not wish it. He therefore said to Frances,

"Let me go with you and carry the basket, Miss Cary. I have nothing in the world to do. Don't trouble yourself, Gentleman Joe; we'll be back soon. I am ready, Miss Cary."

Thus came to an abrupt end the whole series of wiles resorted to by Miss Frances Cary. She was obliged to accept Mr. Brantz Elliot's proposal, and, without a single smile of triumph, went with that gentleman in the direction of the house, leaving Nelly to enjoy the charms of the society of Gentleman Joe.

XLVI.

GENTLEMAN JOE AND HIS GHOSTS.

As Brantz Elliot and Frances Cary walked away, Nelly said to Gentleman Joe, with an affectionate smile,

"I am glad you came over to see us to-day, Gentleman Joe, for I am sure you wanted to see *me*— It has been nearly two weeks since you were here."

"Oh, yes, I wanted to see you, Nelly," replied Gentleman Joe. "I always want to see you, and when I am not with you I am thinking about you, my dear."

There was no trace of his recent grotesquerie in the speaker's voice or face—he was quite sedate and earnest, and looked at the girl with an expression of great affection.

"Harry's been very ill, and I could not leave him," he added; "we thought he was going to die, but he is nearly well now."

"I am so glad of that. He has been very kind and sweet to me whenever he came to see us—almost as kind and sweet as you have been, Gentleman Joe, and that is saying a great deal."

"Have I really been kind and sweet to

you, Nelly?" Gentleman Joe said, looking wistfully at the girl.

"Yes, indeed, you have."

"I am very glad to hear it. But I don't see how anybody could help loving you, my dear. You see I am an old man, and old men can tell little blossoms like you that they love blossoms. People have various tastes in this world, you know—I like the south wind."

"The south wind?"

Gentleman Joe smiled.

"I mean people who are like it. I think of people in that way, and *feel* about them instead of making up an opinion of them. One person chills me like a north-wester, and cuts me to the very bone. It's no use telling me that it's a fine, healthy wind, and clears up the air, and is altogether the right sort of wind—it makes me shiver!"

"Yes, I know what you mean."

"And there is the south wind when the spring comes. People may abuse it, and say it's a weak, poor sort of thing, and makes you lazy, and is not a high *moral* wind; but I like it. I seem to open like a flower when it blows softly over the flowers and the green grass under the blue sky. You are my south wind."

Gentleman Joe might be a lunatic, but there was evidently a method in his madness. Not being familiar with Shakspeare, Nelly did not say that to herself in the identical words, but had the very same idea in her mind, which was a proof that Mr. William Shakspeare was a man of ability, and had observed human nature.

"Well, I'm glad enough to be anybody's south wind," she said, with the rather sad smile which had become her habit of late.

"You are mine!—you warm me," returned Gentleman Joe, "like the sunshine. The sunshine is a great thing, and I like people that carry it about with them. Some people bring a cloud along when they come—a black cloud, and the chill wind that cuts. You bring the south wind and the sunlight, Nelly, and a poor old body like me requires that."

"You are a very good, kind body, if you *are* a poor old one," Nelly said, with an affectionate smile; "and I must be just like you in my character, for every word you say just expresses what I feel, and it seems as if I had known you for years."

"Yes," Gentleman Joe said, lost in reflection, "perhaps we have met somewhere. I have been in many places, and played the clown before a world of people. If you were in the crowd I am certain I saw you."

"In such a crowd?"

"No matter about the crowd. I always see the faces I like to see. Often, when I've been turning and tumbling in the ring, I've fixed my eyes on some child's face in the audience, and seen nothing else from that minute. I was playing for the little one, you see, and had nothing to do with the rest. If I could only make my little friend laugh and please her, I was satisfied, Nelly."

This was said in such a simple, wistful way that Nelly looked at Gentleman Joe with eyes full of affection. There was a hidden poetry in the feelings of the old ex-clown which touched a chord in her own breast, and was in unison with her habitual mood now—rather a sad sort of poetry, but then poetry is generally tinged with sadness.

"What a strange life you must have led," she said, musing.

"A very strange life; but you know life is always strange."

"And very sorrowful."

"Well, I don't know," said Gentleman Joe, cheering up—"not when we have our south wind; we depend mostly on that. Are you going to marry the young deer-hunter, Nelly? I ask, you know, because if you do you will go away, and some north-wester will come along and chill me for want of my sunshine."

Nelly colored, and a slight movement of her corsage indicated the impression made by Gentleman Joe's question.

"No, I am not going to marry anybody," she said, in a low tone.

"I am very glad. I would not like

you to get married. I don't think I could do without you, my dear."

They were nearly the very same words used by Brantz Elliot, and produced a dolorous feeling in Nelly.

"Well, I'm not going away anywhere," she said; "and as you are going to stay in the mountain, there will be no trouble about seeing each other."

Gentleman Joe, having reflected for a moment, proceeded to shake his head and reply,

"I don't know about that. We shall probably make up a troupe and go about the country again. We were thinking about that when Harry was taken sick; and as he is nearly well now, there will be nothing to keep us here."

"Why don't you stay?—are you tired of Crow's Nest? I'm sure Mr. Cary would not care if you stayed."

"No, he would not care—he says we may. But I am not sure I like Crow's Nest. The mice go 'squeak, squeak!' all night—they are talking in the wall, you know—and then the pine-trees, how they do whisper!"

Nelly looked at Gentleman Joe; he was evidently lapsing into one of the reveries, in which his mind seemed to wander a little.

"I don't mind the mice," he went on, "though I wish they would not squeak in that unpleasant way at night, when I am lying awake listening to them. But then the pines! That is not so agreeable. They say a quantity of things to me; which is, perhaps, natural, as we used to be well acquainted. Then there is the water yonder. That talks to me, too, and sometimes it laughs; or when there's a freshet it booms along so sullenly that it seems to be in a bad humor. I often think it wants to quarrel."

"What a curious idea! You must not give way to these fancies, Gentleman Joe."

"Bless you, my dear, I never give way to fancies. I am a plain old fellow, and much too matter-of-fact for that. But any one can hear the water laughing and the trees whispering, just as you can easi-ly see castles and people in the fire, and what the cloud-shadows are."

"The cloud-shadows?"

"Yes, Nelly—the shadows that gallop along the mountain in August, when the white clouds are piled up like so much wool, and the wind is blowing. How they gallop! faster than a hawk can fly: and I've seen his shadow too, but that's not much. The other shadows are wild horses running before the wind; but it can't catch them. They trample on, with manes and tails flying back, and the curious thing—I can't account for that—is that they make no noise at all as they pass you."

"Why, they're only shadows, Gentleman Joe."

"I don't know that. They may be ghosts for what we know; there are so many ghosts around us. I believe the mice, and the pines, and the shadows are all ghosts."

Nelly saw that Gentleman Joe was falling into one of his fantastic moods, and, as she had often done before, strove to divert him from them.

"Well, don't mind them," she said; "they won't do anybody any harm. If nobody will keep them from hurting you, Gentleman Joe, I will."

Thereat Gentleman Joe brightened up and smiled.

"*You* can make them behave, Nelly—you are the only one that can!" he said; "and, bless you, I don't mind them in the least. I often say to them, 'I'm not afraid of you—you and I are old friends, and often played here together before; but go away, I've no time to think about you to-day!' I often tell them that. Then, if they *will* go on whispering and laughing, I say 'I'm going to see Nelly now; she's waiting for me in the mountain.' And then I tell them another thing that is the most important thing of all."

"What is that?" said Nelly, kindly, humoring the old fellow.

"That you are the image of some one it breaks old Gentleman Joe's heart to remember."

As he spoke Frances Cary and Brantz Elliot made their appearance with the basket, and Gentleman Joe said no more.

XLVII.

MR. RUGGLES REAPPEARS AT CROW'S NEST.

THE Lefthander was obviously in a depressed mood of mind. What was the origin of this depression? Not the illness of Harry Vance, for that scene at Falling Water seemed to have lifted a load from his heart, and he was regaining his strength day by day.

Was it the report that the revenue-officers were coming with troops to look after the moonshiners? There was such a report in the village. The long-suffering Government had decreed the extermination of the malefactors, people said. The department was certainly growing indignant, if any faith was to be placed in the public journals. The Secretary of Finance was badgered by his political opponents. These moonshiners were tapping a hole in the national strong-box, and depleting the same in an irregular and unauthorized manner. The moonlight trade must come to an end: if it did not cease peacefully, it must be made to cease. If the civil officers were unable to enforce the law—then troops. A good troop of cavalry, with sabres and repeating carbines, would prove a much better argument than mere proclamations.

Perhaps the Lefthander was a little out of spirits at hearing this. As the mountain would be harried probably for moonshiners, he might be arrested—and so might Harry and Gentleman Joe. Then what would become of Mouse?

But something else troubled him; the fact was evident from certain words which he muttered now and then. Whenever he found himself doing so, he stopped suddenly and looked round him. He had the air of a man who is fearful that some one has overheard him. In fact, a gloomy discussion seemed to be going on in the Lefthander's breast. There was something to be done, or not to be done.

At such moments his eyebrows made the straight black line across his face, and that meant trouble.

He was seated on the fence at the bottom of the hill at Crow's Nest one morning, smoking his pipe and reflecting. All at once a shadow ran toward him; he raised his head—there was Mr. Ruggles.

He was clad much more respectably than on the occasion of their first meeting, and had a jaunty air. There was the consciousness that his improved wardrobe had elevated him socially, which is a valuable hint to slovens. He had a stick in his hand; there was no bundle on it, however, he was walking with it.

"The top o' the mornin' to you," said Mr. Ruggles, in a friendly way. "I was jest passin', and thought I'd drop in and see you. Family well? I'm gittin' along—ain't burnt no wheat-stacks yit! Honest work's the thing for Ruggles, and I'm right on the money question."

"Well, that's a very good question to be right on," said the Lefthander, indifferently.

"You can bet your life on it!" said Mr. Ruggles, cheerfully; "and if I can't git more work there's always one thing to do."

"What's that?"

"Jine the moonshiners."

"You mean the whiskey men?" said the Lefthander, looking intently at him.

"Jest so—the only trouble is the thing's so risky; they might ketch a feller and take his loose change; but they wouldn't git mine—I bury it."

"Bury your money?"

"In a holler log, at a place I know in the woods. That's to keep it out of the bar-rooms. I mostly spend every red cent I take along with me on sich occasions."

"Well, that's not a bad idea," said the Lefthander, indifferently.

"No extra charge for telling of it to a friend like you, mate. You might have some greenbacks to put away, too—not as bein' a moonshiner, which it is not my meaning. Greenbacks or papers—I put all them things away, and as the Scripture says, 'Go thou and do like unto it.'"

Now, as Mouse had read aloud this precept from her Bible in different terms, the Lefthander recognized the fact that Mr. Ruggles quoted incorrectly. He did not set him right, however, but only said, "I always carry what money and papers I have about me."

He uttered the words in a matter-of-fact and indifferent tone, but they produced a striking effect. Mr. Ruggles shot a piercing glance at him.

"Well, you're right, mate," he said. "You don't drink, p'r'aps, as I do; or maybe you do. Take a mouthful?"

Mr. Ruggles had produced a black bottle, and smiled in a cordial manner.

"You're welcome!—it's a good ar-*tikle.*"

The Lefthander hesitated. Was his old fondness for drink unextinguished, and the temptation too great? It really seemed so; for, after looking quietly at Mr. Ruggles, he took the bottle and swallowed a deep draught of the whiskey.

"You are right; it's a very good article indeed," he said.

"My turn next," said Mr. Ruggles, with a cheerful and friendly air; and he held the bottle to his lips for a protracted period, swallowed repeatedly, and—drank nothing at all.

He then said he must be going, and solicited the Lefthander's company for a part of the way. Finding this request reasonable, the Lefthander walked on at his side, and they entered the woods, and were soon near the steep banks of the Falling Water above the ford. Here Mr. Ruggles, professing himself weary, sat down upon a ledge of rock, and the Lefthander took his seat beside him.

"Take a little somethin', mate," Mr. Ruggles said, producing his bottle. The Lefthander responded with avidity. It was a melancholy sight to see the bad old habit again returning. His tongue began to grow thick, and he stammered slightly; then Mr. Ruggles, after an interval, proposed another little something, and another, when the Lefthander closed his eyes, and leaned back against the ledge of rock behind him.

Mr. Ruggles, who had raised the bottle to his mouth repeatedly, watched his companion with a perfectly sober glance. The Lefthander was falling asleep under the effect of his potations. There could be no doubt at all, at last, that he was sound asleep, and Mr. Ruggles proceeded rapidly to search his pockets. They contained nothing but his pipe and tobacco, and a few bank-notes, which the honest Mr. Ruggles replaced. He seemed bitterly disappointed, and even muttered an oath.

"Curse the whole cursed affair!" he said, turning to walk away.

All at once something grasped Mr. Ruggles by the collar of his coat. He shrunk back with a cry. The something was the heavy hand of the Lefthander.

XLVIII.

MR. RUGGLES FINDS HIS SITUATION RATHER UNPLEASANT.

"Sit down, friend," said the Lefthander, who exhibited neither in face nor voice any traces of his recent potations; "don't be in a hurry. I want to talk a little."

The astonishment of Mr. Ruggles was overpowering. His eyes were full of terror, and seemed to project from their orbits. All the color had faded out of his face, and, though his lips moved, his tongue refused its office.

"You seem to be a little dumb," said the Lefthander, phlegmatically. "I'll doctor your case—nothing brings a man to like cold water."

The spot where they had held their conversation was on the slope of a declivity sinking to the banks of the stream. From this a sort of shoulder projected, terminating in a pile of rock which hung over the water. These rocks go by the name of "Lovers' Leaps," and are common on the Shenandoah, the Opequon, and other streams of the Virginia valley. They are generally crowned with pines, and paths lead to them, made by wild animals, possibly. There was such a path leading to this one, and the Lefthander went down the path, which was covered with pine tassels, half leading and half dragging Mr. Ruggles with him, his hand still grasping his coat-collar.

It was not far to the summit of the rock, which might have been called without the least exaggeration by the name of precipice, and they soon reached it. There was a sheer descent of about fifty feet, and glancing at the water foaming over the rocks below, Mr. Ruggles perceptibly shuddered. In fact, it is not precisely calculated to soothe the nervous system to be suspended in the grasp of a Hercules over an abyss. Mr. Ruggles was evidently unnerved, and made wild gestures; he had become very pale. As the Lefthander continued to grasp his throat, a gurgling sound issued from his lips.

"Are you going to talk?" his enemy said, in his deep voice. "We are losing time. Do you mean to make a clean breast of it, or do you mean to be dropped over this rock?"

The terror of Mr. Ruggles was so great that he was unable to speak. They were on the very brink of the precipice, and he hung in mid-air.

"Do you mean to talk, I say?" the Lefthander repeated; "I am a little tired of this. What do you mean to do?"

"I will—tell you everything," Mr. Ruggles managed to gasp out.

The Lefthander looked at him attentively, and saw that he meant what he said. He therefore dragged him back, and released his hold on his collar.

"That's the very best thing you can do," he said. "You may as well talk in a straightforward manner. I'm not in the humor to be trifled with—it is better to tell you that. You came here to make me drunk and rob me: I know all about you now. If you look at things in the right way, you will see that I am sparing your life. Who sent you?"

Mr. Ruggles drew a long breath of relief. It was plain that he realized what an imminent peril he had just escaped. Would the peril return? was the question which he probably asked himself. A glance at the cold face of the Lefthander was not reassuring.

"Well, there's no use trying to hide anything, and I don't mean to try it," he said. "I mean what I say, and I'll tell you everything."

The Lefthander sat down, filled his pipe, and began to smoke.

"It will be well to remember, friend, that we are by ourselves here," he said.

"I understand."

"Who sent you?"

"Young Lascelles," said Mr. Ruggles.

"I thought so. Then you belong to the detective police?"

"Exactly."

"I've thought so for some time. You overdid the tramp business. You detectives often make that mistake."

"I rather think you're right."

"Well?" said the Lefthander, and as this was evidently a comprehensive interrogatory, Mr. Ruggles said,

"Mr. Lascelles wrote or telegraphed to the New York Chief of Police to send a good man, with a tramp's get-up in his valise, to the station not far from here, where he would be met and receive instructions — there would be no trouble about the money, which would go up to four figures."

"Just so," said the Lefthander.

"Well, I was sent, and found Mr. Lascelles waiting when I arrived, and he explained what he wanted."

The Lefthander at these words turned his head round slowly, and looked fixedly into the face of Mr. Ruggles from beneath his straight, shaggy eyebrows.

"It would be better for you and me to understand each other," he said, phlegmatically; "I have no time to waste in listening to a made-up story. What I want to know is everything. I know a good deal already. You had best lose sight of being a detective, and remember that we are by ourselves here, as I said, and talking in a friendly way."

The Lefthander looked straight into the eyes of Mr. Ruggles, and then, turning his head in the same deliberate fashion, glanced toward the summit of the rock a few steps distant.

"I understand," said Mr. Ruggles, who had gradually regained his equanimity; 'a nod's as good as a wink to a blind horse.' I mean to tell you the truth. For that matter it's not so hard—I don't like this young Lascelles with his high-headed ways; he's a little too much of the swell for my use, and I rather think if he had been in your place he'd have dropped me over there."

"I think he would," said the Lefthander, candidly.

"I mean to tell you the plain truth."

"It would be better."

"I found him waiting at the station, and we went off into the woods and had a long talk. What he wanted was to get possession of some papers he thought you had, and he offered one thousand dollars for the papers—to run up to half as much again if the business was dangerous."

The Lefthander nodded.

"There was no more to say, after I heard where I could find you. I had my tramp get-up with me, and came and asked you for a night's lodging; and when you were asleep I searched your pockets and the whole room for the papers."

"I thought you must have done that," said the Lefthander.

"Well, I found no papers on you, or anywhere about—either then or afterward. I got the shingle job to be in the neighborhood, and was often in the house when you were away; but there was nothing there, unless you hid it where I could not find it."

"As you say, there was nothing there. After that?"

"Well, I tried then to track you up after your fight with the circus manager. I learned you had gone that night to the house of a Mr. Grantham, in the town, where you slept. This amounted to nothing; and though I started to go and see Mr. Grantham, and pump him, I gave up the idea as not worth the trouble. He could only tell me what I knew—that you had slept there, and gone away in the morning; and as to *his* having your pa-

pers for safe-keeping, that was too unlikely to make it worth my while to inquire, even if I had made up a story to account for asking him the question."

The Lefthander again nodded.

"So you went to Mr. Lascelles, and told him you were thrown off the scent?"

"Yes; and was snubbed by the gentleman. He made no bones of telling me that I was a new hand at the detective business; and I agreed to try you again with a bottle, thinking you might say something."

"Yes."

"Or search your pockets again—you might have the papers on you. But you didn't talk on business matters, and you got drunk too quick."

Mr. Ruggles smiled, and evidently accepted the situation like an old hand and a philosopher. He was not at all a green hand at his business, as Mr. Lascelles supposed, and had only failed on the present occasion from the difficult material on which he had been obliged to work. He had repeatedly tried in private interviews to pump Harry and Gentleman Joe, but they knew nothing whatever of the existence of the papers—which for the rest Mr. Ruggles did not venture too plainly to allude to, for obvious reasons. As to Mouse, he had never been able to see her by herself, and thus the Lefthander was the knotty obstacle against which he had struck. All attempts to penetrate so hard a rind had failed, and all failed with it. Lastly came the present unsatisfactory state of things: he and the Lefthander were together in a most unpleasant locality. But Mr. Ruggles, being a philosopher, made the best of things, and uttered his harmless jest.

The Lefthander passed some moments in reflection; then he said, slowly,

"This is a poor trade of yours, friend. I would rather plough. When a man takes up the business of hunting other men, and running 'em down, he grows tricky and lives by lies. Besides, he gets his neck twisted sometimes—which is not a good thing to get twisted—to say nothing of dropping from the tops of rocks! When I brought you here I thought I would drop you over there and do for you. I'm not a bad sort of fellow, but a man loses his temper sometimes. I thought I'd stretch out my arm and strangle you when you were feeling in my pockets. I could have done that; it wouldn't have been much. And as to dropping you over there—I'm too strong a man for you to trifle with."

Here, by way of illustration, the Lefthander extended his arm and caught Mr. Ruggles by the breast, just at the upper button of his waistcoat. He then rose, drew Mr. Ruggles up with him, stiffened his ponderous arm, and lifted him into the air.

It was an impressive spectacle. Mr. Ruggles, with his legs and arms hanging down and gesticulating, his face expressive of horror, and his voice issuing forth in a gurgle, was helpless in the grasp of the giant.

"It would be easy," said the Lefthander, looking toward the rock.

He set Mr. Ruggles on his feet, and pointed up the path.

"Go away," he said, "and don't come back. It will be dangerous."

Mr. Ruggles availed himself of this permission with alacrity. Picking up his stick, he hastened up the path and was soon lost to view. After some moments the Lefthander followed him, talking to himself in a contemplative way.

"So he's after the papers: I might have known he would be. And this detective is sent for. Well, I don't drink now, but it is just as well I did to-day. It's a good thing to know what cards you are playing against, and the rock yonder made my friend show his hand."

He then went back to Crow's Nest. The detective had disappeared.

XLIX.

IN THE BÖHMERWALD.

ONE morning, a few days after the incident just related, the Lefthander and Mouse were alone together at Crow's Nest. It was just after breakfast, and Gentleman Joe had gone to pay a visit to his dear Nelly, and Harry had wandered away into the pine thicket in rear of the house, to look after some traps with which he amused his convalescence. The Lefthander was smoking, and leaning forward in a meditative attitude, with one of his hands resting on his knee; Mouse was busily putting away the tin cups and plates on a shelf in the corner. Having at last arranged everything to her satisfaction, she came and sat down by the Lefthander, and opened a small Bible, which she took from her pocket, and began to read to him.

This was her daily habit, and the reading was one of the Lefthander's greatest enjoyments. What was the explanation of that? Was there lying latent in this rugged organization that religious sentiment which, denied often to the scientist, fills the heart of the ignorant and humble? Possibly; or the Lefthander might have liked to hear the earnest voice of the child, and to feel that her character was taking shape under purifying influences. He always put out his pipe at once as a mark of respect, and listened with deep attention, asking a question now and then as to what Mouse thought a particular passage meant. Receiving from the child a statement of her views on the subject, he generally nodded with an air of conviction, and said he supposed that *was* what it meant. He then composed himself to listen again, and, when Mouse finished her reading, said "Amen." On this morning he remained silent for some minutes after the child closed her book; then he said,

"After all, that is the only Bible—which is strange."

"What do you mean, poppa?" said Mouse.

"I mean, Mignon, that there's not a different Bible for different people. This is the only one—for lords and ladies and tramps and beggars. And the strange thing is it suits every one of them, wherever they are and whatever they are."

He mused a little, and added,

"But I wish *you* were one of the ladies, not the poor little one you are."

"A lady? I'm just as good a lady as I want to be, sir," said Mouse, with a grand air.

"Yes; I really believe you are—in your character. But I was thinking of the easy time the real ladies have. I wish you were one of them for that reason—not such a little chit, only the child of your poor mother."

Did the Lefthander utter these words accidentally or with intention? The latter seemed to be the case. He glanced quickly at Mouse and then back to the fire. If his object was to excite her curiosity, and induce her to question him, his ruse succeeded.

"You never told me anything about mother, poppa," said the child. "You always said I was too young, and you'd tell me some day. Won't you tell me now? I'm old enough. Can't you tell me, poppa?"

"Yes, Mignon—there's no sort of trouble about that. You are right. You are growing up to be a little woman now, and ought to know about things. I met your mother in the Bohemian country—I belonged to a circus—I ran away from my father and joined it when I was a boy."

"Ran away, poppa?"

"Yes; I ought not to have run away; but my father was a very stern man. He was a peasant, and very poor, and made me work hard from daylight to dark, so I joined a circus that was passing, and never saw him again."

The Lefthander spoke rather sadly.

"My father died soon afterward, and I was very heavy-hearted," he said. "It would be much better if people avoided doing what makes them heavy-hearted when they think of it."

"But if they did not really mean to do wrong?" said charitable Mouse.

"I ought not to have done as I did. I am very sorry. Well, I went off with the circus, and grew up to be a young man, and found I was strong, and became an athlete. At last the company travel-led into Bohemia, and I met with your mother. It was an accident."

Mouse rose and came to the Lefthander, and, sitting in his lap, put one arm around his neck.

"What do you mean by saying it was an accident, poppa?" she said.

"I will tell you about it. There was a performance at a place called Prague, in the Bohemian country. I had taken by that time to the trapeze business as well as lifting, and one night I had a fall and hurt myself. It laid me up for the time, and when the company left Prague I thought I would have to remain behind; but they put me into one of the wagons on a mattress, and we went west toward the Bohmerwald."

"What is that, poppa?"

"A high mountain on the boundary of Bohemia. It was a tedious matter crossing it, and as to myself, I did not cross it at all; I was in so much pain that they had to take me out of the wagon and leave me at a house we passed, where an old hunter of the mountains lived. Your mother was his daughter."

The Lefthander drew a long breath.

"She was very beautiful, your poor mother, Mignon," he went on, "and nursed me till I was well of my hurt. So I came to love her, and loved her more and more every day, and she loved me, and it was not so surprising, therefore, that she should be willing to go away with me at last as my wife. I was a gay young fellow then, though I am often so quiet and sorrowful now — her death made me so. She died in less than one year after her marriage, but she left me you. I should have gone crazy without my little Mignon when my other Mignon left me. At first I could not even cry; I was thinking of her, and breaking my heart about her, day and night. But one day I was holding you in my arms, and you put yours round my neck—they were rosy little arms—and you babbled 'Poppa! poppa!' and then I began to cry at last."

"Poor, dear poppa!" sobbed Mouse, holding him close.

"Well, she was dead, you see," continued the Lefthander, "your poor little mother, far off in the Bohemian country, which you don't remember, for I brought you away with me when you were a baby. Your mother's name was Mignon, and sometimes I say the name to myself quietly : she is gone, but then I have my small Mignon—I couldn't get along without *her*. What would the big oak do without the bird that sings on the top branch? It would be a tiresome business to the tree not to hear the bird singing, and not much matter how soon it would be cut down."

"But the bird is not going away," Mouse cried, clinging to him, and smiling through her tears. "Go away, poppa? Where would I go, and how could I live without *you*?"

"The tree may go, Mignon—I mean it might be cut down: something might happen to me. I was thinking of that just now—I think of it very often—and that is why I said that I wished you were a lady. What I meant was this: If you were a lady you would have a family and friends to take care of you. If I were to die, what would become of you? That is on my mind all the time, Mignon."

"Oh, poppa, don't talk of dying! I should die, too, if you were to."

The Lefthander shook his head sadly. "Young people think that," he said, "but they are mistaken. People forget in this world — that comes after awhile, and it is best. Or if they don't exactly forget, they manage to live on somehow, just as a man shot through the body, and as good as done for, hangs on and don't die for years afterward."

"But you are not shot through the body, poppa, and you're not to think of dying, if you please, or of my being able to get along without you."

The Lefthander drew the small head down to his broad chest, and smoothed the child's hair. "My good little Mignon," he said, with the look of trouble still on his face; "I don't believe any father ever loved his child as much as I love you; and it's pitiful to be so poor, and not be able to make life easier to you."

"Easier! Why, what do I want more than I have? I have *you*."

"You might have a good deal more if we were not such mere vagabonds! It's pitiful! Here you are in rags, nearly, a poor little one, doing everything. How you ever learned to read, even, I can't understand. You learned yourself at odd times, and read better than I can. Ten years old, and here in this old shanty, without a mother or sister, or almost a bed to sleep on!"

"You will do for mother and sister, and my bed is as warm as toast."

Mouse laughed, and tightened the small arm around the Lefthander's shoulder.

"But think," he said, "if you were a lady—you see I come back to that—you would have ladies to associate with, and servants to do the work for you, and easy chairs, and a mahogany bedstead, with a white counterpane, and no end of pleasant things. You would have silk dresses, and little boots that button up with black buttons, and a little hat with a feather in it, maybe, and a carriage to ride in, and life would be easy for you."

Mouse reflected, and did not dissent from this. She evidently would have liked what the Lefthander spoke of.

"That would be pleasant," he said.

"Yes, it would be."

"And you'd enjoy it?"

"I think I would."

"I thought so," said the Lefthander, sorrowfully.

"But not without you, poppa. Of course it's natural to like pretty things, and I should certainly like it all — but how could I get along without *you*?"

The Lefthander's rugged face seemed to melt at the words. There was an indescribable tenderness in the very manner in which he caressed the child's hair.

"You would soon get used to it," he said.

"I don't think I would," Mouse replied, shaking her head slightly; "I know I would not. I don't see how nice things and easy living can make us forget the people we love. I am sure if I lived that fine life, and you were not with me, I would lie awake in the bed with the pretty counterpane and think of you and cry — and then, you know, that would spoil all the fine things, and the boots with the black buttons would pinch me."

The Lefthander was overcome by the mixed pathos and gayety of the child. He held her close to his heart, and his lips moved as if he were praying for her.

"Well, well," he said, "you mustn't mind my talk, Mignon—I'm a little down to-day. It is natural that a father should be thinking about what might happen to his child if he were to die. It would be better if you were a little lady, as I said—but then I would not see you any more; and if I were not to see you I think I should die, Mignon!"

His breast heaved and a tremor passed through his frame.

"I must go and see about Harry," he said, rising suddenly; "he is not well yet."

Was this to conceal his emotion? It seemed so; Mouse had never seen him so much agitated. He took his hat and went out, turning his head as if to conceal his face from the child. A few moments afterward she saw him disappear in the thicket.

L.

MOUSE'S VISITOR.

MOUSE sat down after the departure of the Lefthander, and fell into deep thought. She was thinking of her mother. Her vivid imagination filled up the picture of the scenes in the Bohmerwald—her father lying sick in the home of the old hunter, her mother nursing him, no doubt, their love and marriage, and her death in less than one year afterward. That was very, very sad. She understood now why her father was so quiet and sorrowful often. He had been gay once, he said—now he was no longer gay, and that was natural, since he had lost the person he loved best upon earth.

Mouse sobbed, and remained for some time quite absorbed in thoughts of her poor mamma; but then that would not do, she reflected. She had a shirt of Harry's to mend; so she went and got the shirt and her work-basket, and sat down to mend the garment. As there was no back to her chair, she placed her feet on the round in front, and pinning the shirt to her knee began to sew.

She was thus engaged when she heard a step approaching, and a long shadow ran over the porch. Mouse looked up suddenly. There stood an elegantly-dressed gentleman, with a riding-whip in his hand. He was the same who had accompanied the United States marshal on his search for the moonshiners that night. In fact, the visitor was no other than Mr. Douglas Lascelles.

He stood looking at the child and her surroundings with apparent interest, although his face continued to wear the expression of coolness and nonchalance which was habitual with him.

"Good-morning, miss," he said, bowing carelessly, for Mr. Lascelles was too well-bred ever to omit any of the forms of politeness.

"Good-morning, sir," said Mouse, who had been a little startled by his appearance and wished Harry would return.

She had risen quickly, and, as the visitor now came toward her, instinctively retreated a step.

"You seem to be all by yourself," said Mr. Lascelles.

"Yes, sir—poppa and all are away."

"Who is your father?"

"His name is Ottendorfer."

"And he is absent this morning?"

"Yes, sir."

Mr. Lascelles slightly knit his brows, apparently from a sentiment of disappointment. His face, as he stood looking at her, evidently did not produce a very agreeable impression upon Mouse, who lowered her eyes. As the shirt was still pinned to her dress, and she held it in her hand, her skirt was raised, showing the slender limbs in cotton stockings; and Mr. Lascelles, looking at them, wondered a little at the delicacy of the small feet, and, indeed, at the same trait in Mouse's features, framed in the light hair.

"You are young to be left in such a lonely place as this by yourself," he said, indifferently; "are you never afraid?"

"N-o, sir," responded Mouse, with a strong conviction that she was not speaking the exact truth; "that is—not when nobody comes—"

"Well, *I* have come—and you are evidently afraid of *me*, which is absurd."

This did not seem to altogether reassure Mouse. The face of Mr. Lascelles was plainly not at all to her taste.

"Where is your father—Ottendorfer? You said he was your father."

"He has gone away, sir—for a little while," added Mouse, by way of indicating that she was in reach of assistance; "he will soon be back."

"Then I will wait—for a short time, at least."

He sat down on one of the broken-backed chairs, in evident ill-humor.

"What a kennel you live in!" he said, looking around him with covert disgust. Mouse felt that it was necessary to say something, so she replied, in a voice which did not indicate either the recovery of her self-possession or an improved opinion of Mr. Lascelles,

"It's not very nice, sir. There's not much furniture; but it's all we've got."

"Not much furniture: not an oppressive amount, and rather old-fashioned. This chair is enough to break one's back. I'd like to break it's own, except that it has none!"

Mr. Lascelles was not in an amiable state of mind, plainly. He was not generally ill-humored; but people will fret sometimes when they have wound themselves up to go through an interview of an unpleasant character, are anxious to have it over, and find that it must be deferred.

As Mouse, less and less pleased with her visitor, whose face exhibited mingled dissatisfaction and distaste for all around him, did not make any reply to this attack upon her furniture, Mr. Lascelles, glancing indifferently at her and cutting his boot with his riding-whip, said,

"Ottendorfer is your father, you say. Where is your mother?"

"She is dead, sir," replied Mouse.

"One of the circus women, probably. You belonged to that company, too, I remember now. I saw you dancing on the rope. What was the cause of your leaving the company?—what made your father drag you off here to this cabin, when your life yonder was so easy?"

"Oh, it was very hard—not easy at all, sir! I like living here so much better."

"Rather a queer taste," said Mr. Lascelles, indifferently. After this careless comment he stretched his handsome riding-boot, and looked out of the window.

"When will your father be back?" he said.

"I hope he'll be back very soon."

The tone of the words seemed to attract Mr. Lascelles's attention.

"Perhaps your meaning is, miss, that his return will terminate an interview which is not particularly pleasant. You do not seem precisely at your ease with me."

Mouse looked down, a little confused, and at a loss for a reply.

"One would say you were afraid of me."

Mouse did unquestionably look a little fearful, and only murmured some vague words.

"It is unnecessary, and absurd, too, as I said before. I am not a bear, or a Giant Blunderbore, to devour children. Your father may be; he is certainly a Blunderbore in appearance at least. Why did he leave the circus?"

"There was a fight with—with Mr. Brownson," Mouse said, not having regained her nerves.

"What was it about?"

"About me, sir, I think. I fell off the rope, and Mr. Brownson was angry."

"Oh yes, when you sprained your ankle, or something. And you went away that night?"

"Yes, sir."

"Where did you sleep?"

"In the town—my foot hurt me, and poppa was carrying me."

Mr. Lascelles fell into reflection. After awhile he looked intently at the child, and seemed to have conceived some project. This was apparent from the sudden disappearance of his air of indifference.

"Well, miss," he said, "it was fortunate that your father was not arrested. He had assaulted a peaceful person, and left the circus company without a moment's warning. Ill-natured persons might have said that he did so to prevent being searched."

"Searched, sir!" exclaimed Mouse.

"I am sorry to shock you, miss, but people sometimes leave a place suddenly to avoid that. There is such a thing as carrying away what is not one's property."

Mouse was so much shocked at this imputation that she flushed, and looked almost defiantly at Mr. Lascelles.

"Poppa does not steal things!" she said, with the air of an outraged princess.

"Not to your knowledge, doubtless; but that is no proof. How could you know what he had in his baggage?"

"He had no baggage at all—nothing but my old travelling-bag," Mouse replied, so much offended that she seemed to forget her uneasiness.

"Your travelling-bag, eh?"

"And there was nothing in it but a few clothes of mine and some old papers."

"What old papers?"

Mr. Lascelles asked the question with an abruptness which showed how much the words of Mouse affected him. There was the indefinable change, too, in his whole manner that is seen in the fox or deer-hound, when, after circling around, he at last comes on the scent of the game.

"Old papers—what old papers?" he said.

"I don't know what they were, but poppa had kept them for a long time."

"Where are they now?—I mean, you brought your bag with you to this house, I suppose."

"No, sir, I lost it. Poppa thinks it must have been dropped, but *I* think it was left at a good man's house where we slept that night."

"What good man?"

"His name was Mr. Grantham, I heard."

"Mr. Grantham!—Parson Grantham?"

"That was his name."

Mr. Lascelles lost a little of the color in his face.

"Why have you never gone back for it?"

"Poppa did go, but the good man was away."

Mr. Lascelles fixed his eyes on the floor, and was quite silent for some moments. His expression of face was extremely gloomy and uneasy.

"How do you think you came to leave it there?" he said, in a low voice.

"I think it was left on the bed where I slept," Mouse replied.

"Well," Mr. Lascelles said, after a moment, "I suppose that was all your fancy. The good man, as you call him, would have looked for you, to restore the bag if he had found it."

"It was not worth thinking of, sir."

"Why not? The papers may have been valuable. How did they ever come to be in the bag?"

"Poppa put them there; his own old trunk had a broken lock, but my bag had a very good one, only I think it was unlocked that night."

Mr. Lascelles knit his brows; then he grew suddenly savage. Perhaps the child had been drilled to tell the whole story.

"You are deceiving me!" he growled.

"Oh no, I am not, sir."

"Where are those papers?"

"I have told you all I know about them," said Mouse, retreating before his fiery eyes.

Mr. Lascelles rose and advanced toward her, whereupon Mouse hastily retreated.

"If I thought you were trifling with me—"

Mr. Lascelles, without intending to do so—from the mere force of habit, probably—raised his riding-whip as though he meant to strike the child with it. Thereupon a great change suddenly took place in Mouse. She stopped and stood erect, with a deep flush in her cheeks, looking straight at him. It was really wonderful to see how her whole expression had changed in an instant.

"Don't strike me!" she exclaimed, her voice trembling, but with a covert defiance in its tones. "Harry will be here soon, and he will not let you strike me."

For a moment they stood facing each other. The threat, or apparent threat, to inflict a degrading punishment on the poor child seemed to have changed her whole character in an instant: she defied and threatened him.

"Strike you! Who spoke of striking you?" he exclaimed, moodily. "Who is the Harry you speak of?"

"He is one of the family, and will be here soon," Mouse said, still defiant.

Now, to meet "one of the family," other than the Lefthander, was not contemplated by Mr. Lascelles when he came, nor was it now. There were reasons prompting him to hold a private interview with the Lefthander. As that gentleman was absent indefinitely, and another member of the family was about to make his appearance, Mr. Lascelles seemed to abandon his project, for he turned toward the door.

"Well, I have no further time to waste on you and your *family*, miss," he said, almost roughly. "Your surroundings are not very inviting, and your own manners not particularly engaging. The sight of my riding-whip seems unpleasant to you; but if your father used a switch occasionally it might teach you a little better how to behave yourself."

With these words Mr. Lascelles tapped his boot with his whip, walked out of the house, and, going down the hill, mounted his horse and rode back toward Piedmont.

<hr>

LI.

IN THE WYE WOODS.

MR. LASCELLES gained the Gap and rode on in the direction of Wye, lost in moody reflection.

His visit to Crow's Nest had been the result of a resolution which he had come to on the preceding night. As Mr. Rug-gles, to his great disgust, had completely failed to obtain possession of the coveted papers, and seemed unable to devise any means of attaining that object, Mr. Lascelles had determined to bring the whole affair to a point by a direct negotiation on the subject with the Lefthander. He had no reason to believe that the Lefthander, in his depressed financial condition, would prove deaf to golden arguments. Men were always for sale, he reflected; the only difference was that some cost more than others. It was possible that the Lefthander might cost a good deal. He might take an unmanly advantage of the state of things and mulct him, Mr. Lascelles, heavily. But such misfortunes must be put up with. To attain our ends in this world we must make sacrifices. Mr. Lascelles was ready to make them, and proposed to purchase what he could not otherwise lay his hands on, and in order to effect this had visited Crow's Nest.

Not finding the Lefthander at home he had failed in his negotiation; but the visit had not been by any means thrown away. He had made a very important discovery, indeed: the papers had been in the child's travelling-bag—this had not probably been dropped, as something would have been heard of it in that event; it was, therefore, no doubt in possession of Mr. Grantham. At this thought Mr. Lascelles slightly shuddered. Had Mr. Grantham opened the bag and examined the papers? If so—but it was improbable. As before, something would have been heard of it in that case, and nothing *had* been heard of it. It was just as likely that Mr. Grantham had *not* examined them: at all events it was necessary to prevent his doing so, if they were still in his possession.

How could he ascertain the fact and lay his hands on the papers? It was a difficult affair to manage. There really did seem to be no means of doing so in a straightforward manner. Why were people thus compelled, Mr. Lascelles reflected, to adopt "crooked" means? He would have much preferred the simpler course, but that was impossible. He certainly could not go to Mr. Grantham and say, "A travelling-bag was left with you, containing papers which you will be good enough to deliver to me." Explanations would be asked, and he would be obliged to state that the papers were of right his property. But then the explanation would require an explanation, and that second explanation Mr. Lascelles was not apparently prepared to make.

On the whole, it would be much better to quietly resume possession of his property without raising a scandal. There would be no moral transgression in so doing. Mere forms were not of vital importance where there was no real violation of the laws of *meum* and *tuum*. Molière had claimed the right to take his own wherever he found it, and why should not he? If by taking it quietly he avoided strife and contention, was it not all the better?

The trouble was to devise the means, and he naturally thought of Mr. Ruggles. At first he hesitated to have recourse to the assistance of that gentleman, of whom he was growing a little weary. His views as to the efficiency of "detectives" had undergone a shock. The perusal of modern novels had elevated the detective police very high in his estimation. He was very much surprised now to have his eyes opened, and to find that they were the merest pretenders. There might be some efficient ones, but Mr. Ruggles was evidently an ignoramus or a new hand; else why had he failed? It was really absurd. The papers were in existence, and there was the money ready. Why were they not forthcoming? The result — contempt for Mr. Ruggles, and ill-suppressed *hauteur* of bearing in that gentleman's company. Not even the narrative of Mr. Ruggles's ruse with the black bottle, and of what followed, had moved him. He was evidently no match for the Lefthander, and the struggle was over — but he might be for Mr. Grantham. He might suggest something, at least, and if it was found necessary to determine on the hazardous proceeding of—

Mr. Lascelles took out his watch. It was nearly half-past three in the afternoon. Four o'clock was the hour when he was accustomed to meet Mr. Ruggles, and there was just time to reach the rendezvous. He put spurs to his horse, and went on at full gallop. This soon brought him to the Wye woods, and turning a bend in the road he saw Mr. Ruggles seated on a root awaiting him.

"I was looking for you," said Mr. Lascelles, rather curtly.

"Well, here I am," returned Mr. Ruggles, retaining his seat on the root of the tree, and speaking in a careless tone.

Mr. Lascelles was already in a bad humor, and by no means relished his companion's tone.

"You appear to be rather indifferent whether you see me or not," he said.

Mr. Ruggles had been picking his teeth with a straw. This ceremony he still proceeded with.

"Well, to tell you the fact, Mr. Lascelles, I'm a little tired of this business," he said.

"Indeed!" Mr. Lascelles returned, ironically.

Mr. Ruggles nodded.

"I've done all I could, and I can't find your papers. Are they really to be found anywhere? They have been destroyed, maybe."

"They are *not* destroyed," said Mr. Lascelles, knitting his brows but restraining himself.

"Are you certain?"

"Yes. Perhaps your not finding them is due to another circumstance."

"What circumstance is that?"

"That you are a new hand at your business."

This observation evidently offended Mr. Ruggles considerably; his face assumed a sullen expression.

"Been twenty years in the force, and think I know a thing or two!" he responded, not without covert defiance.

"No one would think so," replied Mr. Lascelles, unable to suppress the retort. "This business is simple enough. I want something — a part of my property—

which another person has in his hands. I employ you to get possession of it and you fail to do so. I don't tell you you are inefficient, exactly — but I say you must be new at your business."

"Been nearly twenty years in the force!" reiterated Mr. Ruggles, with a rather morose glance.

"Well, I have not, and yet I've found out more in half an hour than you have done in a month."

"Found out what?"

The tone of voice employed by Mr. Ruggles was open to the criticism of being rather unceremonious, and Mr. Lascelles lost his temper slightly.

"Mr. Ruggles!" he said.

"Well, sir?"

"It would be better, probably, if you were a little more friendly—or polite, at least — in your manner of speaking. I mention it as a thing apt to cause bad feeling."

"I'm polite to everybody!" said Mr. Ruggles.

"You are devilish short to me!" replied Mr. Lascelles, with a dangerous look. "But all this talk is folly. The papers are in the town, at a Mr. Grantham's. They were left there in a travelling-bag containing a child's clothes. Can you, or can you not, get hold of them?"

His professional character being thus in question, Mr. Ruggles replied that he had no doubt he could get hold of them. "It's a serious matter," he said, "something like burglary — it will cost you money."

"Burglary! Who speaks of burglary? I might go and demand my property, but that would cause talk. It is mine—why not go and take it, if it can be found, without making a scandal?"

"A scandal! Yes, that's disagreeable," said Mr. Ruggles, looking significantly at Mr. Lascelles.

"It would be infernally disagreeable— I make no concealment on that point— but that is all. As to the business, there is no wrong done anybody; it is my private affair. The papers are of no value to any one but myself. They are kept from me by that obstinate rascal, who has some bad end in view. They are probably lying about somewhere yonder; what is to prevent you from quietly picking them up and bringing them to me? Your check is ready."

This latter observation seemed to have far more effect upon Mr. Ruggles than the whole preceding train of argument.

"Well, I'll try," he said. "The matter's simple enough. If they are lying about I can easily get hold of them."

"Well, the sooner the better. I have been to the house in the mountain and had a talk, and by this time Ottendorfer *knows that I know.* There is time to try to-night."

Mr. Lascelles looked at his watch.

"You might get there toward dark, and that would be better. If you say so, I will meet you here at ten to-night to hear what has happened."

Mr. Ruggles reflected, hesitated, and then nodded.

"I'll try to-night, then. My cape will hide the bag if I get hold of it, and I won't be seen coming back."

He rose and buttoned up his coarse brown cape.

"At ten, then," said Mr. Lascelles.

"At ten," said Mr. Ruggles.

They then parted, Mr. Lascelles riding on toward Wye.

LII.

THE TRAVELLING-BAG.

Mr. Grantham had just finished his early cup of tea, and had returned to his study, in which his two candles were burning. The half-written MS. of his next sermon lay upon the table, but, while taking his solitary meal, he had been thinking of Ellis, and the impulse to write to him was uncontrollable.

He had a great deal to say to him, as he had not written for nearly a week. Then, on that morning he had stopped at Wye, on his ride to visit his poor people, and Mrs. Lascelles had spoken of Ellis in a way which warmed his heart. Anna

Gray had also alluded to the young man, asking when he would return, in a tone of voice which seemed to indicate a stronger feeling than friendship; and Mr. Grantham suddenly began to suspect that closer relations existed between the young people than he had supposed. Was this really the case? Were Ellis and Anna Gray more than friends? That demanded thought. It would be an altogether excellent arrangement; for the young lady was a most exemplary person. But could it be so? He would write and ask Ellis. They had never had any secrets from each other.

So, turning his back for the moment on his sermon, and losing sight completely of his "History of Ritualism," which had reached its most denunciatory chapter, Mr. Grantham took a sheet of paper, and began, "My beloved Ellis—"

As he wrote the words a knock was heard at the outer door, and he rose and went out. At the door stood a plainly-dressed man, with a coarse brown cape on his shoulders.

"Do you wish to see me, my friend?" said Mr. Grantham. "Come in; it is growing cool."

The visitor entered, and, by way of explaining his visit, presented a soiled paper, which Mr. Grantham took and read. This paper recited the fact that the bearer was a respectable resident in the mountain, who had been "burnt out" some days before, and was an object of charity, owing to a large family who were homeless and destitute in consequence of their misfortune. Under these circumstances contributions in money or provisions would be thankfully received.

Mr. Grantham's first impulse was to put his hand in his pocket. He found the least possible amount of currency therein; but this he at once handed to the unfortunate man. It was received with thanks, but the visitor did not depart.

"Oh yes," said Mr. Grantham, "I quite lost sight of the last part of your paper. You wish for provisions, and I am glad of that. I am poor in money, but Heaven has blessed me with plenty of food."

He went out to obtain the provisions, saying that he would return in a moment, whereupon the movements of the visitor became eccentric. He looked quickly around him, saw a small travelling-bag hidden away under the old secretary in the corner, and went straight and pounced upon it. A quick trial of the lock showed him that it was open, and he hastily examined its contents. The animated expression of his face showed that this examination was thoroughly satisfactory. The travelling-bag contained a child's under-clothing, and at the bottom was a package of papers. These Mr. Grantham's eccentric visitor just glanced at and thrust back. He then closed the travelling-bag, and, concealing it under his cape, returned toward the door, just as the footsteps of Mr. Grantham came along the passage from the rear of the house.

The worthy pastor carried in his hand a plate containing an ample supply of bread, meat, sugar, and coffee. This he presented with a friendly smile to his visitor, who wrapped it in an old newspaper and gratefully thanked him. He then took his departure, and Mr. Grantham closed the front-door behind him and returned to his study. It was not until the next morning that he discovered a singular fact. His eccentric visitor had left money and bread and meat on the bench of the small porch. As Mr. Ruggles afterward said, in relating the incident, he really could not take the articles away with him—it looked *too* mean to be imposing on a man like *that;* he positively could not do it.

With swift and joyous steps Mr. Ruggles hurried out of the town in the direction of Wye. He was astounded at his good fortune. He had not expected to secure his prize in so simple and easy a manner. It was almost too good to be true; but there it was under his cape, held tightly beneath his left arm; and as he went along, and emerged safely from the town, unfollowed, he hugged it rapturously, and a smile expanded upon his features. Under the effect of his rare good fortune, Mr. Ruggles's whole soul, indeed, expanded. His ill-humor had disappeared, and he was at peace with all the world. A part of his recent sullenness had arisen from a sense of humiliation. He had failed in all his efforts hitherto—now he had fully succeeded. His happiness was unalloyed. He had nothing to reproach himself with, even in connection with the Lefthander. Toward that gentleman his sentiments had undergone a great change since their interview on the rock above the stream. Mr. Ruggles was really touched by having had his life spared. His new feeling of regard for the Lefthander was perfectly sincere, and he had even half resolved not to take part in any future machinations against him. But his present proceedings scarcely involved that. The papers only concerned Mr. Lascelles. Securing them was in no manner personally prejudicial to the Lefthander. It was all in the way of business, and he was only carrying out his agreement with Mr. Lascelles — at least there they were! And Mr. Ruggles bestowed another hug upon them, breaking forth into confidential laughter.

"It's a real Saratoga trunk to carry under a man's arm!" said Mr. Ruggles, humorously; "couldn't be handled, one would say, by less than four baggage-smashers, at the very least! But I don't mind the weight. A cool thousand dollars in gold never felt so light before."

He reached the rendezvous in the Wye woods a little before the hour agreed upon. It was quite dark, and he had had some difficulty in finding his way. He generally carried a dark-lantern and matches about him, but was accidentally unprovided with them on this occasion. But they were unnecessary. A few stars were shining, and afforded quite sufficient light for his interview with Mr. Lascelles. Mr. Ruggles, therefore, sat down on his favorite root, and while waiting fell into reflection as to the manner in which he would dispose of his thousand dollars. His thousand dollars? His fifteen hundred, at the very least! He was to have that amount in case his services were attended with *danger*. And had they not been? To be suspended over a precipice was rather dangerous, one would say. And then the commission of petty larceny —that also was rather hazardous. There were such persons as constables, and such places as State-prisons. Decidedly, there could be no question about it. It was absurd to say that danger had not been an element of the affair—and danger meant at least fifteen hundred dollars, if not two thousand.

This sum Mr. Ruggles contemplated with great satisfaction. He was not a bad fellow, and had an old mother whom he cared a good deal for. He meant to give her one-half the amount, and treat his friends and himself with the rest.

He was thinking of this when he heard steps, and a moment afterward a figure came toward him. He rose quickly and waited. The figure came nearer. It was Mr. Lascelles.

"Well!" he exclaimed, ardently.

"I've got it," responded Mr. Ruggles in the same tone.

"Give it to me! You are lucky! I take back all I said about you."

"Perhaps you've got the two thousand about you, Mr. Lascelles?"

"Two thousand? One thousand was the agreement."

"Yes, if there was no danger. Now there was danger enough, I think. Hanging in the air a hundred feet above rocks and water is dangerous."

"It amounted to nothing. It was only done to frighten you."

"Well, it did frighten me — rather," said Mr. Ruggles, sullenly; "and larceny does too—stealing your papers, I mean."

It was quite obvious that Mr. Ruggles meant to insist on his point, and with a suppressed growl Mr. Lascelles said,

"Well, say fifteen hundred."

"Two thousand."

"No!"

"Well, split on eighteen hundred— that's the lowest figure I swear I'll go at."

Mr. Lascelles felt a strong desire to strangle Mr. Ruggles, but controlled himself.

"Well—let it go at that! Give me the bag. Are you certain it is all right?"

"Certain of it—papers and all. Have you got a match?"

Mr. Lascelles produced his match-case, and illuminated a small wax cigar taper. He then hastily took the bag, opened it, and saw that it contained a child's under-clothing.

His face glowed, and, thrusting the articles aside, he plunged his hand into the bottom of the bag and drew out a package of papers. He had handed the taper to Mr. Ruggles, who held it between them, and the dim light lit up the two ardent faces, producing a decidedly Rembrandt-ish effect.

Mr. Lascelles opened the package of papers, which were in a brown wrapping secured by an ordinary cotton string. It contained a number of Sunday-school tracts. With eyes wide open Mr. Lascelles unfolded a letter accompanying the package, and read by the light of the taper:

"DEAR MR. GRANTHAM,—I send the clothes I promised you for 'your poor,' and some tracts. I made the clothes up myself. Your affectionate

"FRANCES CARY."

On the next morning Mr. Grantham prepared to ride out and visit his poor. To his great surprise he missed his travelling-bag with the children's clothes in it, which he had placed beneath the secretary in his study; strangely enough it had disappeared.

LIII.

IN THE LIBRARY.

WHEN Mr. Lascelles returned to Wye, after his interview with Mr. Ruggles, it was not quite eleven. A light was burning in the library, which indicated that every one had not retired.

As Mr. Lascelles had left the house by the back-door, he now re-entered in the same manner, intending to go to his chamber. Perhaps it occurred to him that his face might prove an index of strange matters. He was very bitterly disappointed, and his expression was sullen. The best of us are mortal, and cannot smile always. The first glimpse of the clothing and papers in the travelling-bag had brought a thrill of triumph to the heart of Mr. Lascelles. When he discovered the real character of the articles he fell into a rage, and used shocking expressions reflecting personally on Mr. Ruggles. A long conversation with that gentleman had thereupon ensued, during which Mr. Lascelles gradually grew more composed. The sea was going down after the storm now, but it was not by any means tranquil yet—so Mr. Lascelles thought he had better go to his room quietly.

Unluckily he found that he would be unable to do so. Just as he was passing under the old cut-glass lamp, with its red octagonal sides, in the hall, a voice from the library said,

"Is that you, Douglas?"

It was the voice of the general, and Mr. Lascelles went at once to the library, where he found his father leaning back in his easy-chair. For a wonder he was not reading his newspaper, but smoking a cigar. This was unusual with him. He used snuff, like most gentlemen of the old school, but rarely smoked. When he did so he resorted to a mild cigar, and used it as an aid to reflection.

"Come in, Douglas," he said.

Mr. Lascelles did so, and took his seat in an arm-chair at the corner of the fire-place, facing his father. The general tranquilly smoked for about a minute, and then, moving his portly form slightly, crossed one leg, ending in a neat slipper, over the other. He had evidently something to say, and Mr. Lascelles quietly waited.

"Do you know you are nearly thirty-five, Douglas?" the general said.

"You have a good memory, sir."

"A father remembers the age of his children. You will be thirty-five on the twentieth of next month."

"Yes, sir," said Mr. Lascelles, wondering a little what was coming.

"And I think it is time you were married, if you propose to marry."

Mr. Lascelles smiled slightly.

"I am very well satisfied with my present life, sir. Marriage is something of a lottery, if we are to believe the trite maxim, and I confess I should not like to draw a blank."

"But you have your responsibility as the head of the family after my death, Douglas. You are my only son, and a son of yours should succeed you. Then you have travelled and enjoyed yourself —or had the means of doing so, as I think I could show you by my check-book, during your absence in Europe. You spent a great deal of money. I do not complain of it; on the contrary, it was exactly in accordance with my wishes that you should do so. A young man who keeps good company has no taste for bad company, and to go into good society requires a certain expenditure."

"That is very true, sir: and remember the rank and character of my father. You were very well known as a states-man in London and Paris, and I bore your name."

This was not displeasing to General Lascelles. The reference to ourselves as persons of "rank and character" rarely is.

"Well, well, I am glad you enjoyed yourself. But to come back to the point. It is time you were thinking of taking a wife. Unless you do so, and have a boy to succeed you, the property will go to Judge Warrington as the next male kin, you know."

"To Judge Warrington!" exclaimed Mr. Lascelles.

"Certainly."

"What is to prevent you — or me — from leaving the property to others?"

"The *Salic law* of the Lascelles family," said General Lascelles, tranquilly smoking. "Have you forgotten it? A woman cannot represent the family. The next male kin takes the estate. Our ancestor, the Sieur Lascelles, brought the custom over the ocean with him, and it has been respected for nearly two centu-ries—I must respect it in my turn, and so must you."

"And leave the estate of Wyc to Judge Warrington?"

"The house and a sufficient amount of land to keep it up, at least; the rest would go to my daughters, either by my will or yours, since you succeed me."

"Judge Warrington!"

"I understand your feelings, my dear Douglas, but there's no help for it. I confess I do not like Judge Warrington, or fancy his ever being the master here. But he may be. He would be obliged to add *Lascelles* to his own name, but there is little doubt that he would do so."

"Very little."

Mr. Lascelles reflected for some moments after uttering these words. He then added,

"I have no objection to marrying, sir; but I really have not thought seriously of it. There ought to be some sentiment in an affair so delicate—"

"Oh, certainly; but then there should not be too much. Mere romantic feeling is not necessary."

Mr. Lascelles smiled slightly.

"I heard of a gentleman," he said, "who was going to his wedding in a light carriage, and came to a stream so swollen that fording it was extremely dangerous. There was a bridge only half a mile distant, but he would not go back. He lashed his horses, and went through with the water washing over their backs. The gentleman was yourself, sir."

"Well, well, well!" the general said, with a smile.

"And when my mother fainted one day, you seized a glass which chanced to have no bottom, and poured water through it from a pitcher, exclaiming 'Marie! Marie!' You really must have had some of the romantic sentiment you denounce, sir."

"Well, well," said the general, in a mild voice, and with an expression in his eyes which seemed to show that memory had carried him back to his golden years, "all that was a long time ago. My marage has been happy, and I find no fault with real feeling; but do not let it blind you in selecting a wife. Good birth and sweetness of temper are better than curls and roses."

"I fully agree with you," said Mr. Lascelles, though it was exceedingly doubtful whether he did.

"Good blood is of course essential," the general said; "as to money, that is extremely desirable, but it is not everything. You had better live in comparative poverty with a wife whose tastes and habits suit your own, than in splendor with a different sort of person."

"But where shall I find the young lady, sir?" said Mr. Lascelles, smiling.

"There is my goddaughter, Frances Cary. She is really a little beauty."

"Miss Cary! Yes — she is certainly pretty."

"Such a match would be most acceptable to me. I am extremely fond of Colonel Cary, and would like to see more of him than I now do."

"I am afraid Miss Cary is not my style, sir—excuse the slang of the day. There's no accounting for one's tastes, you know."

"I am aware of that. Well, what do you say to Miss Armstrong?"

The general touched the ash on his cigar with his little finger, knocking it off. As he did so he glanced at Mr. Lascelles and smiled.

"Miss Armstrong? She is very handsome."

"Very handsome indeed," said the general. "And the Armstrongs belong to the best people, and were once quite wealthy."

"Mrs. Armstrong still lives in great comfort."

"Well, what do you think of requesting the pretty Miss Juliet to become Mrs. Douglas Lascelles? If rumor is true—and even an old fellow like myself hears them sometimes—you have been considering that question."

"Rumor has always a great deal to say of people's affairs," said Mr. Lascelles; "but we have wholly neglected another very important point in the discussion—whether any one of these young ladies would be desirous of becoming Mrs. Lascelles."

"That is uncertain, I confess—where women are concerned everything is uncertain. But then there are the probabilities. You are in your prime, a gentleman in manners and character, and Wye is a handsome property."

"Very handsome, indeed."

"I do not mean that the sort of person I wish you to marry would be apt to attach undue importance to the property. Girls are not so mercenary as they are represented to be — the good ones. Of course there are plenty who are silly and worldly, and would marry you for your acres, if *you* were silly enough to permit them to do so. Women are either good or bad—the line is drawn more distinctly than with men. The good ones are angelic; as to the other class, I wish I could never see any more of them, they degrade their sex so, in my estimation. Choose one of our little beauties in the Piedmont neighborhood. They are charming girls—and there is nothing in your character to object to. Your great merit is that you have passed through every temptation, and have returned to your family without vices of any description."

"I am gratified at your good opinion, sir."

"It is doing you simple justice. I hoped, of course, that in visiting Europe you would avoid what was discreditable —but long observation has shown me that it is impossible to be certain of anything in this world. We cannot count on human nature. When it is tempted it generally gives way, and is apt to puzzle us more and more as we go on in life. I am not a pessimist, but I am not often astonished. People disappoint all your theories. If you told me that the Rev. Mr. Grantham had robbed me of a fat mutton last night, or had broken into a hen-roost, and stolen the eggs and chickens, I should say I did not believe it, but I should not say he did not. That is merely an illustration—perhaps an extravagant one. What I mean is that human nature is a very curious compound. It is the unexpected that almost always happens, and what people do is often precisely what you would never have expected them to do."

"True enough, sir."

"Life and circumstances try men and women. You often find the best of them conducting themselves in a manner equally astonishing and discreditable."

As Mr. Lascelles inclined his head, by way of assent to these philosophic maxims, the general proceeded to add,

"I am glad I can say that I have never been disappointed in any such way in your case. You have passed through many scenes calculated to try a young man's *morale*, I am glad to say, without soil on your character."

Mr. Lascelles looked modest.

"Your good opinion is certainly a source of the highest satisfaction to me, sir," he said.

"You deserve it. I should have been equally candid in expressing my dissatisfaction. It is due to you to say that your career in Europe was highly honorable; and you have returned home to pursue the occupations of a country gentleman without a regret or a remorse. To say that of a man of thirty-five is to say that he is a respectable person, and would make a good husband, and I assure you that intelligent young ladies consider these points as much as their parents."

Mr. Lascelles made a movement of modest and respectful assent. True, there was something in the expression of his eyes which it was rather difficult to understand, but then his face was generally inscrutable.

"I will give the whole subject mature reflection, sir," he said. "I need not say that the expression of your wishes has always great weight with me."

"That is gratifying. There really need be no trouble about it. No neighborhood in Virginia has more charming young persons than our little Piedmont circle. Marry at home, where you are certain whom you marry—that is the important point; for, let me repeat, it is essenti that a gentleman should not go out c his own sphere, or marry a person h knows nothing about. If he does, th chances are that he will marry an adven uress."

"You are right, sir."

"You had much better put your han in the fire than offer it to such a persoı But I think I need not caution you o that point. You are not an inflammabl boy, to be caught by the stereotyped wile of such creatures. Look in your ow sphere of society, my dear Douglas, fc the future Mrs. Lascelles; and now, as have preached long enough, I think will retire."

When Mr. Lascelles reached his chan ber he put on his dressing-gown, and fe into a fit of musing; he was probabl thinking of the conversation with his fa ther, as an ironical expression slowly stol over his face. After awhile he got u and unlocked a drawer in his table. Froi this he took a small oval case, covere with blue velvet, and, touching a sprinȝ opened it. The case contained a colore photograph of Miss Bassick, very fir.el executed. The young lady had evidentl dressed herself with great care to have taken, though perhaps the term "dressed is not strictly appropriate. The neck an shoulders were bare, and emerged from cloud. They were very handsome shou ders, and the eyes and lips of the pictui had the seductive expression of the orij inal. The full suit of hair was elaborat ly dressed. The portrait had been takɛ a year before, in one of the Atlantic citie when Mrs. Armstrong was accompanie by Miss Bassick in the character c lady's maid and general travelling coı venience.

Mr. Lascelles sat down again and lool ed at the picture, which seemed to loo back at him. The seductive eyes brougl a slight color to his face—it might hav been called a sudden glow. It was quit an unusual expression with the cool M Douglas Lascelles. Something was th matter with him; and if there had bee any doubt of that, what followed woul have demonstrated it. He pressed the picture to his lips.

"The little devil! she has made a complete fool of me!" he muttered; "but 'll soon be her master."

This confidential remark of Mr. Lascelles is easily explained. He was engaged to be married to Miss Bassick.

LIV.

THE MORNING PAPER.

MR. LASCELLES made his appearance at the breakfast-table with such an air of nonchalance that it was obvious he had not a care in the world. As he was undergoing at the moment, as will soon be seen, a very considerable amount of anxiety and suspense, this self-control was all the more creditable; and it is only justice to Mr. Lascelles to say that his coolness and force of character were remarkable. He sauntered in and took his seat with an easy and cheerful air, and the pleasant family breakfast proceeded on its way.

Anna Gray, who relieved her aunt of much of the house-keeping, sat behind the tray, at the head of the table, and Mrs. Lascelles at the side next to the fire. At he bottom of the table the general was, as usual, sipping his coffee and reading his newspaper, with his old body-servant, James, standing motionless with his silver waiter behind him. This old body-servant was quite a character. He and General Lascelles, in their callow youth, had aided and abetted each other in robbing birds'-nests, and other objectionable proceedings; and when the future head of the house of Lascelles became a young man, it was James who groomed his riding-horse, and waited upon him as his body-servant. When young legislator Lascelles represented his county at Richmond, James went with him, and afterward accompanied his master to Washington, when he became a member of Congress. All this had elevated the views of James, and impressed him greatly. He was very proud of "the family," and looked down with unspeakable scorn on "poor white people." His other names for them were "common man" and "trash." As to instituting any comparison between such persons and the Lascelles family, he would have regarded the idea as an evidence of lunacy. He never discussed the subject, if any one seemed disposed to introduce it. He simply nodded in a lordly way, as the proud Duke of Somerset might have done if a parvenu had compared their respective pedigrees, and a gesture of the hand indicated his desire to drop the subject.

James had never for a single instant thought of leaving his master during or after the war. Emancipation Proclamations were plainly only so much waste paper in his eyes. There were certain new-comers in the county, who remonstrated with him upon this unmanly subservience. Was he not equal to his master now? He was a free American citizen, and just as good as General Lascelles, and if he had a proper respect for himself he would vote the Republican ticket—and perhaps he wouldn't mind taking a drink? But James was obdurate. He was much obliged, but knew his own business, and did not want any advice. His political sentiments coincided with those of General Lascelles. He seldom drank—when he did, his master always had a plenty, and of the best.

The strangest part of all was that James would receive no wages—which was his supreme protest against the new order of things. He had never wanted for money, he said, in past times, when his young master had any, and did not mean now, when his old master was often pressed, to take anything from him. If presents of money were made him he would take them, of course—it was the place of a servant to accept presents from a gentleman. There was no change in him; he and his master maintained their former positions: General Lascelles remained General Lascelles, and old James remained old James. The one sat at the table, and the other stood behind him. The one handed the decanter on his silver waiter, and the other sipped the wine. One brushed the other's clothes, and the other wore them. Both heads were gray now, but the feeling toward each other under the gray hairs was the same as when they went bird-nesting together half a century before.

The breakfast-room at Wye was a very pleasant apartment in rear of the library: it was papered in fawn color, with bronze figures, and comfortably carpeted, and on the old-fashioned brass andirons blazed a pile of hickory logs. The table-service was of blue India china and the old family silver. On the hearth a tea-kettle was simmering cheerfully. It was a scene of domestic peace and happiness, and the faces of the little group were as cheerful as their surroundings. Mrs. Lascelles, in her black bombazine and frilled cap, was talking with Anna Gray, whose appearance was remarkable for its neatness and absence of pretension. This was her appearance uniformly, for never was there a person more delightfully neat and lady-like. It was impossible to associate her with the idea of undress; and to have seen her hair in disorder, or the little white collar around her neck in the least degree soiled, would have filled her friends with apprehensions that something had happened.

The general was reading his newspaper, and interrupted himself in this performance to say good-morning to his son, as he came in and took his seat.

"I am afraid there is going to be trouble for our friends in the mountain," said the general, addressing his observation to no one in particular.

Mrs. Lascelles looked at him with her placid smile, and said,

"What did you say, my dear?"

This old couple thus addressed each other, and the words seemed really to express their feelings.

"I mean for the 'moonshine' people. I see that troops are to be sent to arrest them."

"It is a great pity that these poor people will continue their unlawful business," said the lady.

"Yes, my dear; a great pity. I hav repeatedly advised them to discontinu it."

"It is sad to think what the conse quences may be to them, and then mak ing whiskey is so sinful," said Mrs. Las celles, who was a strong advocate of tem perance; "it would be so much better i no more was ever made."

"Well, perhaps you are right, my dea but that is not what the revenue official wish. Of course the business is illegal but after all there is no real harm don They are poor people, and must live, ur less you reply to that argument in th words of the French wit, 'I do not se the necessity.'"

The general smiled, but the lady shoo her head, as unconvinced.

"I saw a picture the other day," sh said, "of a fox holding a hen in hi mouth, and under it, 'An honest fox mu live.'"

"Well, my dear, the moonshiners a not that bad, I hope. I must really g and advise them—"

"Not to break the laws, do you mea my dear?"

"To be more prudent, at least."

The general smiled at his retort, an raising his paper, said, "Here is a deligh ful paragraph:

"'It is reported that the moonshine are giving great trouble in Virginia, e pecially in the Blue Ridge, near the tow of Piedmont, where repeated raids hav been made upon them, but no arrests e fected. The illicit manufacture of whi key has assumed frightful proportions i Virginia, and is estimated at fifty millio gallons per annum. The whole of th is consumed in the State, and a simpl calculation will exhibit the enormou quantity to each inhabitant. The eight Census shows that Virginia contains population of twenty-two millions; an thus the amount of spirit consumed b every man, woman, and child in the con monwealth is nearly two hundred an fifty gallons per annum — that is rath more than three gallons a day. This really appalling. Is it to be wondered hat a population sunk in such wretched ibits should have contracted another bad ibit — that of never paying the public reditors? There is absolutely no future r a society so abandoned to all sense of iame. Any appeal to the sense of pro-riety of such people is a farce. They penly defy the government in this moon-iine business, and the only course to ursue with them is to resolutely enforce ie laws. There is little doubt that this ill be done at once. Troops will be nt without delay to support the revenue ollectors. The Secretary of the Treasury as issued his orders, and troops will be nt to enforce them. If the moonshiners sist, they will be dealt with as they de-rve.'

"Poor people," said the general, laugh-g; "but why not deal with the whole opulation of the commonwealth, and ut the bayonet upon them? They are wretched set, it seems, and ought to be nade an example. But here is something iore agreeable, which will interest you dies:

"'*Proceedings at the Theological Sem-iary.* — The annual commencement at iis Institution took place on Thursday ist. The sermon was preached by the ev. Dr. Andrews, and the candidates ere then examined. The following ere admitted to the order of deacons: Illis Grantham, and'—a number of oth-rs"—said the general. "That will please ou, my dear, as Ellis is such a favorite ith you—"

"And with my Cousin Anna," said Mr. Douglas Lascelles, rather satirically.

Thereat Anna Gray flushed up, and aised her head with the air of an offend-d duchess. There was something in the one of voice of Mr. Lascelles which seem-d disagreeable to her.

"I shall be very glad to see him, if hat is what you mean," she said.

"I have no doubt of it!"

Having made this satirical response, Mr. Lascelles rose and sauntered out to enjoy his cigar, after which, as the fore-noon advanced, he ordered his horse and ode toward Trianon.

LV

MRS. ARMSTRONG BITES HER NAILS.

On the same morning Mrs. Armstrong was seated in her chamber biting her nails. It was a very bright and attract-ive room, with a low rosewood bedstead, elaborately carved, in one corner, a very elegant carpet, an oval mirror surmount-ing a toilet-table with a white marble top, and easy-chairs were seen in every direc-tion. On the toilet-table were the im-plements and accessaries of the lady's toi-let—inlaid brushes, cut-glass flasks of es-sences, hair-oils— But ladies of middle-age, who like to appear young, have con-fidences with their toilets, and further reference to the subject might be indis-creet.

Every object in Mrs. Armstrong's bou-doir was indicative of the lady's taste for "pretty things," and even the doors of her wardrobe were heavy mirrors. A bright fire was burning, with a highly-polished brass fender in front of it, and near it stood a pair of elegant morocco boots side by side, as if their owner were standing in them, and had put her foot down. She had replaced them with worked slippers at the moment, and was reclining in an arm-chair. It was nearly noon, and the day was beautiful. Mrs. Armstrong's face was the only object in the apartment that jarred.

She was biting her nails—a fact above stated—and when a lady bites her nails in that manner trouble is brewing. You could see that Mrs. Armstrong was in a very bad humor. In fact, she had re-ceived a piece of intelligence which both startled and enraged her in the highest degree. She was thinking of it at this moment, and hence that performance so dangerous to the rounded proportions of her pink finger-nails.

Her darling project, connected with Paris, seemed about to fail. It was very doubtful, indeed, if she would spend her winters there with Mr. and Mrs. Douglas Lascelles. She had ardently desired the marriage, and not selfishly at all. She was thinking a great deal more of Juliet than of herself, for this worldly woman loved her daughter with all her heart. She knew that Juliet was not much pleased with life at Trianon, while fine toilets, equipages, and excitement would afford her enjoyment—and it was to have Juliet make her appearance in this splendid world that her mother had planned and almost intrigued, thinking first of her Juliet, and only of her own incidental pleasure in the second place.

It had really seemed for some weeks as if Mr. Lascelles had become a hopeless captive. He came to Trianon regularly; he occasionally remained late *tête-à-tête* in the drawing-room, from which Mrs. Armstrong persisted in retiring in spite of Juliet's protest. All this appeared to indicate that Mr. Lascelles was enslaved. He had not stated the fact, but there seemed to be no doubt of it. Romantic devotion, and extravagance and absurdity in general were not to be expected. He was not an impulsive boy with his heart in his hand, begging somebody to take it. He was thirty-five, and at that age men were apt to conduct themselves in a more rational manner. They might feel deeply, but not consider it necessary to act in such a way as to make the world laugh at them. Looks and tones of the voice were sufficient to express their sentiments, and no doubt Mr. Lascelles resorted to these in his interviews with Juliet, if he said nothing. Mrs. Armstrong was persuaded that she had occasionally intercepted such glances, and was satisfied that nothing but time was necessary, when all at once the atmosphere began to grow chill.

It was a very slight chill at first—frosts approach almost imperceptibly. Things are not nipped in the bud with cruel abruptness: a slight glimmer of silver on the grass appears, but the sunshine dissipates it in an instant. At times the quite perceptible chill in the manner of Mr. Lascelles seemed to melt under the sunshine of Miss Juliet's eyes; but the day at last came when it did not melt. It was not an obtrusive and killing frost; but it was so plain that there was no pos-

sibility of mistaking it. The weath had grown cool, and it was very doubtf indeed if it would ever again recover th lost caloric.

What did it mean? Mrs. Armstron received intelligence which enabled h to understand, or to think that she di There was a dusky maiden of the estal lishment whose name, Lucinda, had bee abbreviated to Cinda. She was maid all work, and had been at Trianon for considerable time, in spite of Mrs. Arm strong's little peculiarities. She "na ged" Cinda very much, and Cinda woul have taken wing, but remained from pu fondness for Juliet. This grew fro slight circumstances. Juliet was und monstrative but exceedingly amiable, an so generous that she bestowed upon Ci da almost any article of wearing appar which she coveted, thereby enabling tl maiden to produce a sensation at color assemblages. Then Juliet was not exac ing, and gave very little trouble. Cinda herself acknowledged, 'Miss Juli was a angel, and never quarrelled n nothing when she was lacing her corsi-lg in the morning.' So the *entente cordia* was thoroughly established between mi tress and maid; and finding it necessa to abuse people, Cinda relieved her min by abusing Miss Bassick, who never pr sented her with anything. This is crime in the African eyes, and Miss Ba sick, therefore, came to be cordially d spised by the disinterested Cinda. As necessary consequence, she resolved to i jure her if it was ever in her power do so.

The Cindas, as a class, are dangerou foes. Their sharp eyes see a great dea and their tongues are as sharp as the eye What they do not see, they say they ha seen; and such is the vigor of their fanc that they make a very good narrative, i deed, out of very slender materials, whic foretells a great race of black female no elists.

Cinda, watching and listening, ha conceived suspicions in reference to tl proceedings of her dear enemy, Miss Ba sick. She thought that on one occasio

itered the hall, and
to be passing, that a
ibling a salute had
iter. Then Cinda
ble ambition of dis-
nd warning her dear
t Mr. Lascelles com-
ick, when he made
to see Miss Ju-
ime! She, Cinda,
!—and she did see

ceding this morning
was biting her nails,
appearance in the
tle after dark, and,
, had made disclos-
to look for mush-
be some yet, when,
rough the woods in
bout dusk, she had
and Miss Bassick
Mrs. Armstrong was
, with a hair-pin be-
this announcement
y bit the hair-pin in
sping slightly. Be-
tely and exhaustive-
It was Mr. Lascelles
d they kissed each
iying good-bye, for
Miss Bassick walked
t was *them*, and she
tell about it.
ated this incident
s Cinda retired, and
ed her lips in a fu-
be possible? Yes,
at interview in the
had almost forgot-
attach the least im-
here was something
ig!—the vile young
as aiming to secure
ilf—to become Mrs.
Wye. Again Mrs.
It really was too
greatly overcome to
Miss Bassick that
next morning they
iew, and come to a
ç.

LVI.

AN INTERESTING INTERVIEW.

HAVING bitten her nails nearly to the
quick, and scowled at the inoffensive fire
in a manner apparently indicative of bitter hostility, Mrs. Armstrong rung a small
bell on a table beside her, and in a few
moments Cinda answered it.

"Tell Miss Bassick I wish to see her,"
the lady said.

"Yes'm," Cinda responded, retiring
with an effulgence of joy on her face, and
a few moments afterward Miss Bassick
came into the room.

"Did you send for me, ma'am?" said
the young lady, quietly.

"Yes. Be good enough to sit down."
Miss Bassick glanced at Mrs. Armstrong.
It was easy to see that the lady was struggling to suppress a fit of anger, for, cool
as her voice was, her face was flushed
and her eyes sparkled. A storm was
plainly brewing, and Miss Bassick wondered what occasioned it. She braced
her nerves to meet it, and took a chair
opposite Mrs. Armstrong. Her air was
respectful, and her eyes modestly cast
down.

"Miss Bassick," said Mrs. Armstrong,
"when did you meet Mr. Douglas Lascelles last, and where?"

"Mr. Lascelles, ma'am!" exclaimed Miss
Bassick, with an air of the profoundest
astonishment.

"Mr. Lascelles! I will repeat my
question if necessary. When and where
did your last interview with Mr. Douglas
Lascelles take place?"

"I have not had any interviews with
Mr. Lascelles, ma'am," said Miss Bassick.
"I cannot think what should have in-
duced you to suppose such a thing."

"That is a falsehood!"

"Oh, Mrs. Armstrong!"

Miss Bassick exhibited an intention of
sniffing, but the lady cut short that ceremony.

"Perhaps you will be good enough,
miss, to omit your usual performances on
such occasions, and not attempt to impose
upon me by acting the part of an injured

person. I assure you that you are putting yourself to unnecessary trouble. It is quite thrown away. I ask again, when did you see Mr. Lascelles last?—in the woods after dusk yesterday?"

Miss Bassick could not suppress a slight movement of surprise, but she exclaimed, "In the woods, ma'am—after dusk—with Mr. Lascelles! Who could have told you such a thing, Mrs. Armstrong?"

"It is quite immaterial where I procured my information, miss. It is enough that I know of your proceedings, and that you were seen."

"*Seen* after dusk, ma'am?"

"Yes, *seen*—in a gentleman's company—not talking to a bush!"

Miss Bassick sniffed.

"I can only say it is not true. I can't think who could have told you such a thing. I did walk out, as I generally do, in the evening, and went beyond the grounds—but I met nobody, Mrs. Armstrong; and even if I had met some friend — or a servant — and stopped a moment to talk with them, no one could have known them, as it was nearly dark."

"Your friend was seen, miss," exclaimed Mrs. Armstrong, with slumbering wrath.

"*Seen*, ma'am? Why, I met no one. If some busybody was passing, and thought they saw me talking with a gentleman, they must have taken a bush, as you say, for a man, in the darkness."

Miss Bassick spoke with an accent of truthfulness. Her denial was certainly flat—there were no ambiguities whatever about it. She was evidently telling a fearful fib, or was injured innocence in person.

"That is a fine story, miss! A bush—a bush mistaken for a man!"

"I only mentioned it, as they really are like the figures of people sometimes in the dark, and it was quite dark yesterday evening when I was coming home from my walk."

Mrs. Armstrong was the victim of suppressed wrath; but even in this condition of mind Miss Bassick's reply had a certain effect upon her; not that she regarded the question as in any degree decided by any statement made by the young lady. Long experience had told her that Miss Bassick was not exactly reliable, and by no means above little occasional wanderings from the straight path of truth in her statements. But there were the natural probabilities. She might be telling the truth. Bushes did resemble human beings after dusk, for she herself in her walks had mistaken the one for the other. It was, therefore, possible — even if barely possible — that Cinda's eyes, sharpened by malice and the delight of discovering things, had seen a little more than there was really to see—in a word, confused mankind with inanimate objects.

Having thus begun to doubt, and argue with herself that Miss Bassick might *not* possibly have met Mr. Lascelles after all, Mrs. Armstrong naturally proceeded to reiterate her charge.

"I know you are telling me an untruth; I am perfectly certain of it. I am aware, as you probably know, that you are not above such things. You *did* meet Mr. Lascelles — last night, as on former occasions!"

"On former occasions, ma'am?"

"At the same time and place—as surely as you were with him that evening when Juliet and myself returned from Piedmont, and found you together in the drawing-room—that is, would have found you together, if you had not started up and stolen away as we came in."

Mrs. Armstrong had begun to speak through her teeth slightly. This was a bad sign—it signified exasperation. Miss Bassick encountered it with a look of injured innocence and a prolonged sniff.

"I explained that, ma'am; I thought you understood," she said. "I was stirring the fire when Mr. Lascelles came, and I only stayed a little—and—and talked a little—"

Mrs. Armstrong interrupted her in a tone of great disgust.

"I am tired of this trifling, miss—you are always ready to explain away what you cannot deny. It is one of your very charming traits."

"I never denied it. I didn't say I was not in the drawing-room."

Mrs. Armstrong greeted this observation with a histrionic curl of the lip. She was fond of stage expressions.

"You *would* have denied it," she said, "if I had not seen you with my own eyes. But I do not wish to discuss this further. Did you not meet Mr. Lascelles in the woods?"

"No, ma'am."

"Is that the truth?"

"Yes, ma'am. I can only say that I have not met Mr. Lascelles."

Nothing more ought surely to have been necessary beyond this distinct disavowal. But Mrs. Armstrong was in a rage, and was not at all convinced.

"Perhaps you will deny next that you are even personally acquainted with him," she said, with much sarcasm, looking at Miss Bassick. The look was unfortunate, as Miss Bassick had never appeared so handsome, and Mrs. Armstrong exclaimed,

"You are deceiving me! There is an understanding between you. You have had secret meetings. You are acting a part—with your hateful cooing, and way of looking at gentlemen. I wonder that any one calling herself a modest girl could look so. It is sickening!"

This was unpleasant. Miss Bassick had great self-control, but was growing angry; she took refuge, therefore, in a sob, to conceal her sentiments.

"There you are, sniffing again! You may save yourself the trouble," said Mrs. Armstrong. "I ask you again—what do you mean by conducting yourself in this manner?"

"You must have a very poor opinion of me, ma'am."

"I have—a very poor opinion, indeed," said the lady, with candor. "What do you suppose people will think when they hear of your goings on, and your base ingratitude? I took you as a homeless orphan, and this is the return you make for all my kindness. You know perfectly well that Mr. Lascelles comes to see Juliet, and in the face of that you presume to thrust yourself upon his notice. You have meetings—in the drawing-room—in the woods; and yet you deny it!—you tell falsehood upon falsehood to hide your goings on! You really sicken me, you shameless, designing thing!"

It is not pleasant to be called "shameless," and a "designing thing." It was not pleasant to Miss Bassick. She had an almost irresistible inclination to get up, go to Mrs. Armstrong, and slap her in the face. As she was a high-tempered young person, under all her submissive meekness, she at first thought she would do so—give the lady about three good slaps, and defy her. But Miss Bassick was much too politic to venture upon that. They would necessarily part from each other after such a scene, and it did not suit Miss Bassick's views to leave Trianon just yet. She therefore said, submissively,

"I am afraid we will have to part, ma'am. You do not like me, and I ought not to stay. I do not know how I will explain my going; but it will be better to go. I have a l-little money, and will f-find friends somewhere. There is a room to let, I see, at my f-friend, Miss Gr-Grundy's."

Miss Bassick ceased, and, covering her face with her hands, looked covertly at Mrs. Armstrong between her fingers. If this look was one of curiosity and expectation it was rewarded. Her last words had plainly made a very strong impression. In fact, they were truly terrifying. It was disagreeable enough to think of the meetings which would ensue between Miss Bassick and Mr. Lascelles if the young lady left Trianon; of the efforts she would make to completely divert the gentleman's attentions from Juliet; but far more unpleasant, nay, frightful, was the idea of Miss Bassick seeking a retreat for her wounded feelings with Miss Grundy! That was paralyzing! Mrs. Armstrong knew Miss Grundy's peculiarities. She shuddered at the thought of having herself and all connected with Trianon photographed for Miss Grundy's entertainment; and seemed to see, in bodily presence, the aforesaid Miss Grundy, wrapped in her shawl, and hurrying from house to house to hold confidential interviews with other members of the Grundy family. The thought was really too much for her. No, Miss Bassick should not go on any account. She should stay at Trianon, where she was under her own eye. She could watch her there — and she would! Having come to this resolution, Mrs. Armstrong slowly grew calmer. The interview gradually toned down; slight explanations ensued; promises were made — in fact, when two persons wish the same thing it is easy to come to an agreement. It suited Miss Bassick, for private reasons, to remain at Trianon for the present, and it suited Mrs. Armstrong that she should not go away; so that half an hour afterward the interview terminated without an open quarrel, or any further mention of a separation.

Mrs. Armstrong cautioned the young lady that she should expect her in future to be extremely careful in her conduct. To this Miss Bassick readily assented, and, gliding from the apartment, went quietly to her own room.

There was a canary bird in a cage there, of which she was very fond. She proceeded to pet the bird, and call it fond names, and held up her red lips for it to kiss, whereupon the canary pecked at them once or twice, and began to sing for pleasure. Miss Bassick stood looking at him with delight, and then sat down at her table and wrote a long letter to Mr. Lascelles, describing her interview with Mrs. Armstrong in pathetic terms—to be delivered on the first opportunity.

While engaged in writing, she occasionally stopped to lean back in her chair, thrust out her handsome foot, and yawn—after which she laughed. She was a very fine-looking young female animal—a little like a handsome cat. There was no evidence about her, however, of the possession of claws. She was apparently in a very good humor, and now and then tossed a kiss to the canary, laughing, and calling him pet names. After these intermissions she proceeded

with her pathetic epistle, the composition of which appeared to amuse her. She only made one confidential observation aloud while writing. This was:

"I am glad I did not slap the old thing; it would have been a great mistake. I know a much better way to slap her than that!"

———◆———

LVII.

JULIET.

AFTER the departure of Miss Bassick, Mrs. Armstrong continued to reflect, in a perturbed state of mind, on the very unpleasant condition of affairs around her. The result of her reflection was more and more depressing. She did not believe Miss Bassick. There *was* an understanding between herself and Mr. Lascelles; and if that were the case, there was an end to all her plans looking to a union between her daughter and the gentleman. What should she do? The question was perplexing, and irritating beyond words. Turn Miss Bassick out of the house with opprobrious epithets, and thus be rid of her? Impossible. The hateful thing would go straight to Miss Grundy, with whom she had formed an intimacy, and regularly visited when she went to Piedmont; and, there, Mr. Lascelles would be able to visit her without trouble or espionage. The idea of such a state of things quite chilled Mrs. Armstrong. Her vivid imagination painted Mr. Lascelles *tête-à-tête* with the H. T. (hateful thing) during long hours of the morning, and no doubt many hours of the night, discussing their little arrangements, and laughing at herself and Juliet; and what was equally present to her excited fancy was the delighted face of Miss Grundy, as she smiled, giggled a little, and poured into the attentive ears of the Grundy family of Piedmont every detail relating to Trianon, and her own little peculiarities, derived from her unfortunate young friend, Miss Bassick.

Sincere terror filled Mrs. Armstrong at

the very idea of such a thing, and she at once made up her mind that nothing should separate herself and her young friend. But how could things continue as they were? She felt ruefully that Miss Bassick was more than her match. Looking back over the years of their personal association, she could see that, humble as Miss Bassick was, she had almost always attained her ends. What she could not effect directly she effected in other ways. She never "asserted herself," much less insisted on anything, but quietly manœuvred until she accomplished her object. She would certainly manœuvre now, and meet Mr. Lascelles somewhere, in some manner. Mrs. Armstrong was really at her wits' end, and the very same longing possessed her which had possessed the young lady: she would have liked of all things to have slapped Miss Bassick.

Mrs. Armstrong passed about an hour in these gloomy reflections; she then went down to the drawing-room, where Juliet was playing upon the piano. It was a very cheerful scene, and the fire blazed merrily, as if in defiance of the wind without. Juliet wore a morning wrapper, and had a little plain white collar around her neck. She looked very pretty, indeed, as she turned to welcome her mother—the curves of her figure and the pose of her fine head were striking. Mrs. Armstrong came in, and said, half aloud,

"And he prefers that creature to such a beauty!"

"What did you say, mamma?" Miss Juliet asked, in her tranquil voice.

"Come here, my dear," said her mother; "I have something to tell you which will, no doubt, surprise you."

"Surprise me?" said Miss Juliet, quietly, rising from the piano as she spoke, and coming to the fireplace.

"Sit down, my dear, and listen to me."

The voice was not precisely the same which had said to Miss Bassick, "Be good enough to sit down, miss." The words were nearly the same, but were now uttered as caressingly as they had before been uttered briefly and harshly. Juliet quietly sat down, arranging her hair with one hand, and looking at her mother somewhat curiously.

"Are you aware that Mr. Lascelles does not come to Trianon to visit *you?*" said Mrs. Armstrong.

Miss Juliet looked a little surprised.

"I suppose his visits are to the family—to you and myself, mamma," she said.

"You are mistaken!"

"Mistaken?" said Juliet, with the same slight air of surprise.

"Very greatly mistaken! Mr. Lascelles does not come to this house to see either you or myself; he comes to see that designing creature, Miss Bassick."

Juliet did not reply for some moments. She sat looking into the fire, with a slight color in her cheeks, and was evidently very much struck by her mother's statement.

"Very well, mamma," she said, at length, in her quiet voice; "that is a little surprise to me. I have seen nothing to induce me to think so."

"You observe *nothing*—nothing whatever!" said the lady, with a little irritation. "You really are too absent-minded, my dear."

"I believe I am rather unobservant," said Juliet.

"Unobservant? You would not know it if two people made love to each other under your very nose! You never suspect anything or anybody. I believe Mr. Lascelles might put his arms around Miss Bassick in your presence, and if you saw them you would think that they were simply shaking hands."

"His arms around Miss Bassick, mamma?" Juliet said, smiling slightly, with the color still in her cheek; "but I understand—you are speaking figuratively."

"Indeed I am not," exclaimed Mrs. Armstrong. "There is no figure of speech at all, my dear, in the matter. As you are blind to everything that is going on around you, and never can be brought to think ill of any one, I will inform you that Mr. Lascelles and this shameless creature have a thorough understanding with each other, and that the embracing ceremony is no fancy at all. They were seen—kissing each other—by Cinda."

"Mr. Lascelles!—*kissing* Miss Bassick?"

"Yes, at dusk, in the woods. There is no doubt at all that it has taken place."

"Indeed, you surprise me, mamma!"

The color in the young lady's face had disappeared, and she had resumed her air of tranquillity.

"You seem to receive the information very indifferently, my dear," exclaimed Mrs. Armstrong.

"How would you have me receive it, mamma? I do not care much."

Mrs. Armstrong looked shocked, and said,

"Do not care! Good heavens, my own Juliet! What *are* you made of? Are you a marble statue instead of a young girl of flesh and blood? Have you no pride?"

"I have a good deal."

"If you have you keep it all to yourself, my dear. Just to think of it! Here is a young gentleman who comes to visit you, and pays you every attention, month after month—his visits are known to every one, and your names are in everybody's mouth in the whole neighborhood—and this goes on and on, and people are waiting to hear what day has been fixed for the wedding, when suddenly everybody begins to laugh, and giggle, and whisper, 'That *poor* Miss Armstrong!—Mr. Lascelles was only amusing himself with her—all the time he was making love to another person directly under her nose—a mere servant!' If *that* does not touch your pride, I do not know what can, Juliet."

Juliet slowly raised her hand and arranged her back hair, subsequently patting it.

"Miss Bassick is not a servant, mamma," she said.

"There is no difference!—a mere hired person."

"It is no disgrace to be hired. That is what you call a 'business matter,' and Miss Bassick seems to perform the duties for which you employ her."

"She is no better than a common servant! And here she is scheming, and making eyes at *your* visitors, and coo-cooing in her hateful way, and meeting them in the woods, and having everybody laugh at you—to say nothing of the insult offered you by that person, Mr. Lascelles!"

"I do not feel very much insulted."

"Then nothing can insult you, Juliet. You really put me out of patience! You know very well, my dear, that it is a gross insult—such as no *gentleman* would offer a lady—and that this is the end, as far as anybody can see, of all my exertions to secure a future of ease and comfort for you."

"It does seem so, mamma."

"And you take it all as indifferently, my dear, as if it did not concern you in the least. Are you so much enamored of Trianon as to shrink from ever leaving it?"

"I like it well enough, but it is not particularly amusing."

"Are you contented to spend your life here in this dull round of every-day occupations?—with nothing of interest to attract—no change from the humdrum routine but to drive out and talk commonplaces with commonplace people, or go to that stupid Piedmont and cheapen dry goods with those smirking tradesmen, and meet the Miss Grundys, and hear them tattle and giggle, and come home and yawn, and eat, and go to sleep? Are you satisfied with such a life?"

"I must say I am not," said Miss Juliet, candidly.

"One would think you certainly were."

"It is not very agreeable. I should not like to spend the rest of my life in such a way. I like Trianon—it is natural to like one's own home—and I have you, mamma; but then it is natural, too, to like more novelty than we can hope for here."

"It certainly is, if anything is natural!"

Juliet looked into the fire and said, thoughtfully,

"I think I should not be satisfied if I was certain I should never go anywhere, or see anything. Hardship and discomfort would be much better than no change or incident at all. I would rather be Mrs. Robinson Crusoe on a desert island, and live in the midst of privation, if something new happened every day, than live in luxury where one twenty-four hours was just like another. You see, my definition of happiness, mamma, is 'When the days follow and do not resemble each other.'"

Miss Juliet aimed apparently at a full statement of her views upon the subject of spending the remainder of her existence in the tranquil shades of Trianon, which she evidently contemplated with very little pleasure.

"Well, if that is your feeling," said Mrs. Armstrong, "why are you so indifferent? Mrs. Robinson Crusoe!—that is not your sphere. You are a lady, and entitled to surroundings suitable to a person of your birth and bringing up. A *hard* life would never suit you in the least."

"I really do not know, as I've never tried it."

"You would grow unhappy in a week. What you require — what is absolutely necessary to your comfort, my dear, is a sufficiency of everything—I mean, to live the life of a *lady*."

"I confess I should prefer that. I am fond of nice dresses, and a good cup of tea, and playing my piano, and I suppose I would not have time for these if I was a drudge."

"My daughter a drudge!—your *father's* daughter, who was not satisfied to walk across the room for a book if a servant was within call, and unhappy if his wine was not iced enough or too much. *You* a drudge!"

"I should certainly not like to be."

"Very well. We understand each other then, my dear. All my plans were to avoid ever seeing you want anything—servants or carriages, or an elegant wardrobe, or other luxuries suited to your tastes. You would be singled out in a queen's drawing-room, I have always felt, for your beauty and distinction — and

what is more absurd than to have you spend your life in this poky place, where no one will ever see you, and you will slowly become a dried-up old maid like Miss Grundy!"

Juliet did not reply, and certainly seemed to have no desire to combat the views expressed in these latter words of her mother.

"I have therefore done all in my power," continued Mrs. Armstrong, "to place you in the station of life which it is no irreverence to say heaven meant you to occupy. There is a great deal of nonsense—absolute foolishness—talked about 'match-making mammas.' Why should not mothers be match-makers, as the matches made by their daughters decide the whole future of their lives? If an ineligible person presents himself, why have I no right to dissuade my daughter from accepting his attentions? And if the proper person makes his appearance, why not urge you not to repulse his addresses?"

"I do not see why any one should think you were wrong in either case, mamma."

"Very well, apply what I say to the present occasion. Mr. Lascelles is an eligible person, holding a high position. Why should I not wish you to marry him?"

"It really seems that he does not intend to ask me," said Miss Juliet, with some humor.

Mrs. Armstrong gasped.

"I am afraid no one will have me, and I shall die an old maid at Trianon."

Miss Juliet uttered these words with simplicity and a slight smile. Her mother knit her brows and her face flushed.

"And you are ready to retire and leave the field to this shameless hussy!—to submit to her insolence, and see your suitor carried off beneath your very eyes!—to have everybody pitying you, and jesting at your expense—this creature, more than all, laughing in your very face, and sweeping by you in her rustling silks, the triumphant Mrs. Douglas Lascelles!"

Juliet quietly smoothed the small collar around her neck, in which there was a slight wrinkle.

"I really do not see what I am to do, mamma," she said. "If Mr. Lascelles prefers marrying Miss Bassick, I suppose he will do so if Miss Bassick consents. How can I prevent it ?"

"Good heavens, Juliet! Will nothing arouse a feeling of the commonest pride in you?"

Juliet rose and strolled toward the piano, and seating herself sidewise on the stool, touched one of the keys, which rung out in the silence.

"I have a good deal, I believe, mamma, which probably serves me better than you think. Pride is a resource."

She ran her fingers over the keys of the piano and a gay trill followed — it sounded like a sudden burst of laughter. So gay, indeed, was it that it quite puzzled Miss Bassick. It was difficult to associate the idea of a tragic interview, full of wrath, mortification, and indignation, with that merry outburst of the piano; and Miss Bassick would have given a good deal to have heard what was said, if she could have done so from her position on the landing of the staircase.

LVIII.

A TERRIBLE INCIDENT.

HAVING heard Mrs. Armstrong go down-stairs, Miss Bassick had promptly discontinued the composition of her letter to Mr. Lascelles, and carefully locking it up in the drawer of her small table, had emerged from her apartment and cautiously followed. She did not proceed down the staircase — the drawing-room door was open, and it really was too dangerous. The relations between Mrs. Armstrong and herself were in an unsettled condition, and rendered a state of suspicion on the part of the elder lady highly probable. She might be listening; the slightest footfall, even the fall of the silent feet of Miss Bassick on the carpet of the staircase, might attract her attention; and then there was the odious Cinda, whom

Miss Bassick now saw in her true light — Cinda might pop upon the scene by opening a door at any instant, and that would be disastrous in the extreme. In fact, anything might happen ; and as Miss Bassick did not wish anything to happen, she observed precautions.

She did not venture to proceed far down the staircase, and, indeed, stopped at the landing, from which she could make her retreat at once, if a low suspicion induced Mrs. Armstrong to dart out and reconnoitre. From this station she thrust her handsome head over the baluster, and bent every faculty to the task of hearing what was said. It really was a pity; she could only hear a word here and there ; it was impossible to catch so much as a single connected sentence. This left her in a state of painful doubt and curiosity, and more than once she resolved to risk discovery and steal down the staircase. She even took a step or two, but then returned to her position. It really was too great a risk ; and, with a keen sense of being wronged, Miss Bassick continued to crane her head downward, and strive to catch at least the purport of what was said by the two ladies. She could only suppose, from the sudden laughter of the piano, that there was nothing very stern and gloomy in the interview—a fact which she could not understand. She might go a little nearer, perhaps—presently, that is ; meanwhile she would wait.

Having replied to her mother's charge that she had no pride of character, Miss Juliet, after running her fingers over the keys of the piano, added,

"I have plenty of pride, mamma, and I do not relish being laughed at or pitied in the least. But I really cannot see, as I said before, how I am to prevent Mr. Lascelles from marrying Miss Bassick if he wishes to do so, and she does not object. You say I am a young lady, which I am glad to think I am. Well, mamma, a young lady cannot go to a gentleman and say, ' Won't you please marry me?—I thought you were going to. I have all my wedding things ready, and will fix any day for the wedding that is most convenient to you—the earlier the better —as my chief happiness consists in looking forward to the moment when I shall belong to you, and be all your own!' A young lady cannot very well say *that* to a gentleman, mamma."

"Juliet!—for heaven's sake! you will drive me to distraction!"

"You must not become so much excited, mamma. I have no desire to distract you. But we should look at everything in the true light. You say I have no pride, because I am not furious at being treated as you describe. But what good will it do to grow angry? I cannot possibly say to Mr. Lascelles, 'I am mortified to death at your preference for Miss Bassick. Won't you please marry *me* instead of her? I am pining away for you, and ready to sink into your arms if you will only permit me!' I cannot say that—or even look it. I have quite enough of pride to remain silent."

"And so you mean to submit, and let this hateful, designing, immodest thing carry off your suitor?"

"I suppose the carrying off will be done by Mr. Lascelles—it generally is in the story-books. If Mr. Lascelles wishes to marry Miss Bassick, I ought not to have any objection to his doing so."

"No objection!—after all that has passed between you?"

"Very little has passed between us."

"He has been here every evening nearly, and stayed very late."

"That is true—much later than I liked. I wish you had not gone up-stairs so early. It was frequently as much as I could do to avoid yawning in Mr. Lascelles's face. I do grow *so* sleepy."

"I went because I thought your relations amounted to an engagement," exclaimed Mrs. Armstrong, in tones of outraged propriety.

"Well, I am not blaming you in the least, mamma," returned Juliet; "I only meant that you have often left me to entertain Mr. Lascelles by myself, when I would much rather have been curled up snugly in bed."

"The designing creature!" exclaimed Mrs. Armstrong, apparently shifting her pet name for Miss Bassick to Mr. Lascelles. "To use such low, ungentlemanly arts."

"Perhaps you think too harshly of him," said the young lady, quietly. "You know he is very fond of music."

"A mere pretence."

"I think he is. During his visits I was playing and singing for him the greater part of the time."

"And he was hanging around you with his smirking, lackadaisical smiles, I suppose."

"He was generally talking as other gentlemen talk in morning or evening visits."

"Then he did not—make love to you at all?"

"No; I don't think I can say he ever did—that is—exactly, I mean. That was very natural. No doubt he came to see Miss Bassick."

Mrs. Armstrong uttered a sound composed of a groan, a gasp, and a sniff.

"So you mean to give him up?" she said.

"What else can I do?"

"To look on and see him kissing this shameless creature in your very presence!"

"I suppose they will retire before they begin, mamma. As they are probably engaged, they will follow the habits of such persons and seek privacy in their interviews."

"Good heavens! and that is all you have to say in the matter, Juliet!"

"I do not see what else I am to say, mamma. I have tried to express my meaning. Mr. Lascelles, I suppose, came here to see *me* at first, but he met with Miss Bassick—I remember I introduced them—and, instead of choosing Miss Armstrong, he chose the other young lady. He surely had the right to do so. You wish me to find fault with him, but I think that would be very unreasonable. He thinks Miss Bassick's face and society are more attractive than mine, and he ought not to think of me if he prefers another person. Don't be so indignant, mamma, and make allowances. Why not shut your eyes, and let them do as they please? You certainly don't mean that *I* ought to go to Mr. Lascelles and protest! No, I thank you, mamma; I should not be able to speak to him for laughing."

Miss Juliet touched the piano with her white fingers, and they laughed out again.

"No, I thank you, mamma," she repeated, smiling.

"And so," said Mrs. Armstrong, with quiet desperation, "we are to sit here calmly, with our hands in our laps, and accept our fate?"

"That would be the most dignified proceeding, would it not?"

"Dignified! — we are to submit in humble resignation to everything?"

"At least that would be cultivating a Christian state of feeling."

"For patience' sake, my dear Juliet, do not speak in that way! One would really say you were amused rather than outraged by this creature's conduct."

"I believe I am a little."

"And all the while she is laughing at the thought of humbling you. It is intolerable!"

"I do not feel humbler than usual, or as if any one were humbling me, mamma."

"My *dear* Juliet, *have* you no pride — no spirit?"

"I have plenty of both — a great deal too much to permit myself to be *humbled* by Miss Bassick or any one. I suppose people follow their characters: I have always done so. If any one wishes to affront me — to cut my acquaintance publicly, for example — they are quite at liberty to do so; it would not irritate me much. That is the good of being proud. And as to Miss Bassick, it would not be possible for her to insult or wound me."

"I do trust not — the vile, shameless creature!"

"I should be wounded by unkindness or injustice from a person I loved. As to Miss Bassick it is quite different: I have never liked her much."

Mrs. Armstrong suddenly held up her finger, and Juliet stopped. To her great surprise her mother then hastened to the door of the drawing-room and looked around her, in the hall and up the staircase.

"What is the matter, mamma?" said the young lady.

"I was certain I heard steps," said Mrs. Armstrong, returning to her seat. "I could have sworn it."

"Steps?"

"That creature's!" said Mrs. Armstrong.

Juliet laughed quietly, and said, "*Dear* mamma, you really have Miss Bassick on the brain! Did you think she was listening?"

"I was perfectly certain of it when I went to the door."

"What an idea!"

"She is not too good for it. I have reason to believe that it is a common habit with her."

"Very well; but you see it was all your fancy just now. She was not there."

"Unless she heard me rise and ran upstairs. I will close the door."

"Please don't. The room is so warm. There is no possibility of any one listening."

"I am not at all sure of that, but I suppose it *was* my fancy. Good heavens!"—the lady clasped her hands and knit her brows—"to live in the house with such a *serpent!*"

"It is not very pleasant," said Miss Juliet, tranquilly. "To be frank, mamma, it has been a very long time indeed since I enjoyed Miss Bassick's society. She was a very attractive person at first, and I quite mistook her character. I am sorry to say I soon saw she was quite a different person. She is very insincere. I could not conceal my opinion of her, I suppose, and perhaps that is why she dislikes me: I think she does."

"And for that reason she will enjoy her triumph over you all the more!" exclaimed Mrs. Armstrong, piteously.

"She is entirely at liberty to do so. She is quite welcome to Mr. Lascelles, if she wishes to marry him. You see I am frank; and to be entirely so, I must tell you—as the time seems to have come for it—that I really have no desire whatever to become Mrs. Lascelles."

"So that is the end of the whole matter!" groaned the elder lady, preparing to shed tears by pulling out her handkerchief.

"Don't cry, mamma," said Juliet, quietly; "you must have more pride. If you cry I shall have to pet you, and that will make me forget what I had to say."

"What you had to say?" Mrs. Armstrong sniffed.

"I was speaking of Mr. Lascelles, and wished to say something more. You know I do not talk much about people; so you ought to listen when I do—as it is such a novelty."

"Ah me!" came with a long breath from the lady.

"I must say that Mr. Lascelles is not at all to my taste," said Juliet, in a tone of great frankness. "I received his attentions because you desired me to do so —for no other reason. I form my opinion of people very much by a sort of instinct, and generally like or dislike them at once. I never liked Mr. Lascelles: he is by no means a candid or sincere person, and there is a peculiar expression of his face which I do not at all like—he seems to be watching. His manners are very good, but he wants frankness. I do not like that sort of person, and could not have married him unless my feelings had entirely changed. I did not tell you this before, as I was afraid of causing you disappointment and pain, mamma; but it is useless now to conceal anything, as Mr. Lascelles won't have *me*. You will see now why I am not so much distressed, and quite willing that Miss Bassick shall monopolize him."

This by no means pleased Miss Bassick, who had descended the stairs far enough to hear every word that was said.

"And as to Miss Bassick herself," continued Miss Juliet, who seemed to be in an unusually communicative mood, "I may have been a little too harsh in my estimate of her character. Her position

should be remembered. She's an orphan, with no home or family, and naturally wishes to secure one. The Lascelles are very nice people, and Wye is a very attractive place, and Miss Bassick sets her cap for the heir; that is her own affair. I can only say that I could never do so unless the attraction were the gentleman himself. I cannot find a word for such a thing, and if Miss Bassick has done so I am sincerely sorry. I hope she is not capable of disgracing her sex so much. I have not a very good opinion of her, I fear, especially as she has been so very cruel to me"—here Miss Juliet's voice laughed quietly—"but I should not like to lose every particle of respect for her."

Listening, and inwardly aware of her real sentiment for Mr. Lascelles, which was sincere indifference, Miss Bassick felt gall and wormwood—to express the idea succinctly. She had a good deal of a certain sort of pride, and an extremely favorable opinion of herself; and Juliet's indifference exasperated her. This sentiment was much increased by Juliet's careless touch on the piano and her next words:

"And now, mamma, I really think we have said enough. There, don't cry; why should you? There never was a single moment when I *could* have married Mr. Lascelles. Miss Bassick is perfectly welcome to him. She may suppose that she is triumphing over me, to use your own phrase, and be pleased at the thought that she will pay me back for my coldness to her, which I was really unable to conceal. You see I shall not be as much hurt as she thinks. If she were present I could tell her with perfect sincerity that all her acting and concealments were quite unnecessary, and that I, at least, should make no sort of objection if she came into the drawing-room and received Mr. Lascelles as a lady should do. But as she is not present, and we are abusing her behind her back," Miss Juliet said, touching her piano, and uttering her frank laugh, "we ought not to—"

"She *is* present!" cried Mrs. Armstrong, rushing to the door.

Thereupon a terrible incident occurred —the writer almost shrinks from attempting to paint it. Such occurrences are much better understood and appreciated from scenic representation than from mere descriptions through the agency of pen and ink. Miss Bassick's position upon the staircase just without the door of the drawing-room has been alluded to. She had ventured to steal down the softly carpeted staircase until she had reached this position, trusting to her "shoes of silence" not to be discovered. But staircases will creak in the best regulated houses, and however carefully the skirts of dresses are held up they will rustle a little. Twice thus Miss Bassick had advanced carefully, and managed to listen. What she heard did not put her in a very good humor; but clinching her pretty fist, she leaned forward endeavoring to catch every word, when she heard a noise at the back-door of the passage and rapidly ran up-stairs.

It was this sound which had induced Mrs. Armstrong to exclaim "She *is* present!" and to dart toward the door and into the passage. This resulted in the terrible incident referred to above. She was precipitated into the fragrant arms of Cinda, and their faces came into collision. Cinda, in fact, had occasioned the noise which Miss Bassick had heard. Having discovered that the young lady was not in her room, the colored maiden had hastened delightedly down the back staircase to report the fact—to be mysterious, and express with a giggling accompaniment her private opinion that a secret interview was in progress; and entering the passage, had reached the door of the drawing-room, in which she heard voices, just in time to be rushed into by Mrs. Armstrong.

Cinda staggered, and threw out her arms wildly, clasping the lady to her bosom. As the maiden was somewhat slovenly, not to say dirty, this embrace was rather ardent than pure. In the midst of "silvery laughter" from the direction of the piano, Mrs. Armstrong violently extricated herself from the embrace of Cinda; and that fair one, with hasty explanations, and in a state of discomfiture, vanished. As to Miss Bassick, she was nowhere to be seen.

The interview between mother and daughter soon terminated. Being appealed to as to what should be done, Miss Juliet very quietly replied, "Nothing, mamma." It would be extremely unkind, she said, to turn Miss Bassick away, as she had no home: it would be better to give her time, at least, to seek for one—and as the fearful Miss Grundy rose before the eyes of the elder lady, she consented. She had recourse to her handkerchief, and sniffed in a painful manner, clasped Miss Juliet to her breast, and bemoaned the presence of shameless creatures, when the gate of the grounds was heard to open, and looking through the window she saw Mr. Douglas Lascelles riding in.

"There he is!" she exclaimed.—"I can't trust myself to speak to him."

"I would not, then," said Juliet, quietly.

"And you ought not to, Juliet. Come, my dear; I will send word that you are engaged."

"I am not at all engaged, mamma; I am uncommonly idle."

"You do not mean to see him, Juliet?"

"Why not?"

"After our conversation?"

"Certainly, mamma. That makes no difference. My opinion of Mr. Lascelles has not altered, and I have nothing in the world to complain of."

With these tranquil words the young lady went and sat down in one of the arm-chairs in front of the fire, just as Mr. Lascelles approached the house.

As to Mrs. Armstrong, she tossed her head and walked up-stairs to her chamber, slamming the door behind her.

LIX.

THE FOE OF RITUALISM.

It was about half-past eleven o'clock at night. Mr. Grantham was seated in his study at the parsonage, engaged on his "History of Ritualism," upon which he had been writing assiduously since his early tea.

It was the general subject of High Churchism, under the form of Ritualism, that Mr. Grantham attacked in his history; the English movement first, then its extension into the United States. Dr. Pusey and Dr. Newman had a very hard time of it. Mr. Grantham did not wish anybody to be burnt at the stake, and Servetus would never have suffered the least personal inconvenience at his hands; but he stood up for the faith, and smote its foes with all his might. He denounced opinions so vigorously that those who held them received a full share of his blows. That was their fault —they got in the way. He was equally unceremonious with his American brethren. He figuratively took the leaders of the Ritualistic movement in the United States by the beard, and haled them to and fro, chastising them with their chasubles, and suffocating them with the incense of their censers. In doing so, of course, he was doing his duty. He had the kindest feeling, personally, toward the High - Church magnates. He was a very mild man, and would have invited the Pope of Rome into his study, and given him his best cup of tea, and laughed and talked with him in a friendly way. But then he was Antichrist, and polemically was to be overthrown and exterminated. So with Ritualism.

Midnight was near now, and Mr. Grantham was still at work. He had forgotten everything else—even Ellis and his beloved poor. Toil absorbs. The writer goes into another world when he writes. He is not living here and now, but elsewhere, and a long time ago, perhaps. Thus he forgets, and toil brings him that blessing. Blessed toil! After all it is the grand comforter. Company does not replace it. The empty rattle of tongues offends the man who seeks silence and himself — the hubbub jars on the tired ear and the tired heart, which goes away from it to remember. And books?—travel? They are not much,

after all. Blessed toil! you take the heavy - hearted in your soft arms and soothe him. You touch his eyelids, and he no longer looks backward groaning. You wave your wand, and all the past goes into oblivion. Blessed toil of the lonely writer! There is something better for the unhappy than pleasure, or ambition, or the glitter of life's tinsel. It is the toil that absorbs, and takes the toiler away into another world, where the memory of his woe cannot reach him.

At last midnight struck, and Mr. Grantham decided that he would retire. He was not weary of his work, but as his health was not robust, he was physically somewhat fatigued. He therefore arranged the written sheets of the "History" just composed—they were quite a pile—and put them aside. He then rose and stood in front of his fire, reflecting. You would not have supposed that he had been engaged in bitter denunciation of anybody. His expression was sad. In fact, he was thinking about his poor people, and that they would probably suffer on so chill a night. The weather had blown up cold, and the gusty wind was whistling around the gables of the house. That is not generally an uncomfortable sound: one thinks how pleasant it is to be housed, and enjoying the warmth of a cheerful fire. It was, however, unpleasant to Mr. Grantham. He was thinking that perhaps his poor folks might be without fuel, which was saddening.

From this subject he passed to Ellis. He had not finished the letter begun just before the visit from the poor man who had been "burnt out" in the mountain —that strange personage, who, perhaps by way of contempt for the humble offering made him, had left the whole lying upon the bench of the porch that night. This fact had aroused surprise and speculation, but Mr. Grantham had now quite forgotten it. He was thinking about his dear Ellis, who was coming home at once, a young deacon. The face of the father glowed at that thought. He would soon see Ellis now, and enjoy long hours and days of talk with him—if the young man was not too much at Wye. The worthy pastor had given much reflection to the subject of Ellis and Miss Anna Gray, and had pretty nearly convinced himself that something was going on in that quarter. Ellis and Anna had been brought up together. She was precisely the person calculated to make an impression upon his son. She was not only very attractive in the beauty which perishes, but had the sweetest possible disposition, and was devotedly pious. It was thus very natural that Ellis should have become fond of her—she would exactly suit a young minister. As to whether the young lady's sentiments responded to the young man's, there could be very little doubt of *that*, Mr. Grantham inwardly decided. Who would not be glad to marry his Ellis?

This train of thought led to another. Ellis married, and soon to be regularly ordained as a minister, would no doubt be stationed in some small country parish for his year of trial. Then he would be transferred to some more extended sphere—perhaps to Piedmont, as his own assistant and successor. Mr. Grantham did not want an assistant. Bishop Meade, his dear friend, had often urged him to devolve on some young associate his onerous labors for the poor, at least. But this did not suit Mr. Grantham, and he had always refused. It was his place, he said, to spend and be spent in his Master's service. He was quite strong enough to labor still, and did not need an assistant. When old age came, and his strength was worn out, he would retire, when his Master would take care of him. As to having, therefore, an ordinary assistant to divide his labor, Mr. Grantham was intractable. But to have Ellis as his assistant meant not so much to have an assistant as to have Ellis. They would be together, and life would be sweet. Grandchildren would grow up around him in the quiet parsonage—for they would, of course, live with each other. Mrs. Anna would sit at the head of the table, Ellis at the foot, and he at the side. The

children, in lofty chairs, would flourish their spoons and request to be helped first. There would be a delightful hubbub, and a great deal of laughter and love. When he went back to his study and his "History of Ritualism" he would shut all this out, it was true, before paying his respects to Dr. Pusey; but then he would have the delightful consciousness, from the patter of small feet overhead, that his dear ones were there near him, and might burst in—which would be charming.

Lastly, there was the successorship. The assistant would one day become the principal, perhaps. Everybody loved and admired Ellis—in fact, the whole parish were entirely devoted to him. Why not look forward to the day when a younger Rev. Mr. Grantham would officiate in the mountain parish? The years were passing steadily, and more and more rapidly. There was a day hidden somewhere in the future when the burial-service would be read in the village graveyard, and it would not be Mr. Grantham, Sr., who would read it. In fact, that would be impossible. This particular Mr. Grantham would not only not read it, but would not even hear it read. His ears would be quite deaf, and he would not see the crowd of weeping friends around the grave, since it would be his own grave. But that would not matter much. His poor would have a friend still in the Rev. Mr. Grantham, Jr., the new incumbent of the Piedmont parish, who would grow old there with his dear Anna, following the same routine of quiet duty which another one of the same name had followed before him.

This thought was quite delightful to Mr. Grantham. He gazed placidly at his old secretary, as that happened to be the object which his eyes rested upon at the moment, but did not see it, owing to the fact that he was looking at Ellis, and holding out his arms to his grandchildren. Nevertheless, the fact of the existence of the secretary slowly dawned upon his mind, and the old piece of furniture connected itself with the subject of his reflections. He always kept Ellis's letters in a drawer of this secretary, and had a special bundle there containing those written during the young man's boyhood from school—in fact, his very first he had even preserved. He thought now that he would take a look at these; so he went and opened the drawer containing them, with a key which he drew from his pocket, and took out the bundle and untied the red tape around it. A cheerful perusal of several of the letters followed. They were written in a very juvenile, not to say illiterate, manner, but the reader did not observe that fact, or notice any fault in the grammar. This was natural. Ellis had written the letters. Having refreshed himself with this fatherly occupation, Mr. Grantham then tied the letters up again, replaced them in the drawer, closed it, and returned quickly to the fire to extinguish a coal which had popped out upon the old worn carpet. From this resulted a simple circumstance. He quite forgot that he had left the key of the drawer in the lock. He then thought he would go to bed—and this he proceeded to do, first covering up the fire with ashes, which was his regular routine.

With his candlestick in his hand, Mr. Grantham went slowly up-stairs and reached his chamber, in which there was a glimmering fire. Then succeeded a ceremony which was based on principle with this worthy man. He put out his candle. It is true the candle was not more than an inch long, but then an inch of candle was an inch of candle. It would be valuable to many a poor person; and in any event it ought not to be burnt unnecessarily. The firelight was quite sufficient to retire by. Therefore, Mr. Grantham put out his candle, and knelt to perform his private devotions. These were not especially protracted, as the good man did not believe in much speaking, and uniformly omitted all adjurations involving the phrase "Thou hast," as being unnecessary, since He whom he addressed did not need to be informed in what manner He had blessed or afflicted his children. He prayed for those in authority,

but only that they might be endued with heavenly grace, after which he left the details unmentioned. As to the North or South, or this party or that, he had nothing to say on the subject. He prayed for his enemies, and forgave them in his heart as he did so. He always ended with "Lord keep me from uncharity."

After rising from his knees, Mr. Grantham took off his voluminous white cravat and hung it over the back of a chair. He then remained standing in front of the fire without further disrobing. In fact, his ardor in the composition of his History had excited his nerves. He was not at all sleepy—and then there was Ellis to think about. He would be home in a few days now. That broken pane in his chamber must be attended to the very first thing in the morning. The wind whistling around the gables admonished him that broken panes were not desirable as December approached. He must not fail to think of it. All at once a low sound mingled with the shrill song of the wind. This sound came from below—apparently from his study—and resembled stealthy steps.

LX.

THE BURGLAR.

Mr. Grantham was not at all nervous, or given to hearing strange sounds; and yet the idea occurred to him that he must really have overworked himself during the evening. Now, overwork produces tension of the nervous organization. Mr. Grantham was aware of the fact, and informed himself that he had been imprudent.

This view of the case, in fact, seemed supported by circumstances. The noise had ceased at once, which was a proof that it was due to his imagination. Where there was nothing to hear nothing could have been heard. It was a mere illusion of his overtaxed senses that steps had moved about in his study. That was impossible. The house was locked, and he had not been up-stairs for more than half an hour—at all events, not an hour. All was secure—his old servant had long been asleep—it was physically impossible that a person could have entered the house, even if it were conceivable that any human being could have reasons for doing so. Enter a *parsonage* between the hours of midnight and one in the morning? With what object? There was nothing to steal in a parsonage, unless the thief were theological in his tastes and coveted works on Divinity.

This idea caused Mr. Grantham to smile. He was the impecunious *viator*, he reflected, who need not be afraid of robbers. And as to murdering him, what living creature had any reason to thirst for his blood? Mr. Grantham's smile grew more cheerful, and he reflected that he must have overworked his nervous system very much indeed, to have it play him such vagaries. Then suddenly he heard the stealthy steps a second time.

At this Mr. Grantham moved his head quickly, and remained perfectly still and motionless, listening. He did not hear the steps again, but what he did hear was a low, grating sound, which resembled that produced by the opening or closing of a drawer which is a little swollen and does not readily slide forward or backward. This satisfied him that he had not overworked his nerves, after all. He had really heard what he thought he had heard. Some one was in his study!

Mr. Grantham was a very sweet-tempered and peaceful man in his disposition, but a very cool and resolute one. A great deal of force of character lay under his gentle smile. He lit his candle at the fire, went to his door, opened it quietly, and went out into the little passage leading to the staircase. Here he stopped and listened. For some moments all was quite silent, and he began to think that after all he had really heard nothing. Then an indistinct sound again came from the study.

This decided Mr. Grantham, and he walked quietly down the narrow staircase. As he wore slippers—his habit in the evening—his steps made no noise whatever. He reached the bottom of the stairs, went along the passage, and opened the door of the study.

As the door opened, a man, who was kneeling in front of the old secretary from which Mr. Grantham had taken Ellis's letters, rose suddenly to his feet. The fire had been stirred up, and lit the apartment—a light which was not needed, however, as Mr. Grantham had his candle. He came into the room and stood facing the man, who was coarsely dressed, and had hastily drawn a short black veil over his face, apparently sewed to the lining of his hat. This disguise had two holes for the eyes, and reached to his upper lip, which was bearded like his chin.

"Who are you, friend, and what is your object in entering my house?" said Mr. Grantham, mildly.

The intruder had put his hand into his pocket, apparently to draw some weapon, but at these words took it out again, as if convinced that it was unnecessary. He stood looking at the master of the house, but said nothing.

"What is your object in entering my poor house?" said Mr. Grantham. "I cannot imagine how you did so, or why. There is nothing here of any value, if theft is your aim. How can there be?"

To this second question the man made no more reply than to the first. He was apparently hesitating what course to pursue, or what to say. He had in his hand the very bundle of letters, tied with red tape, which Mr. Grantham had examined an hour before, and grasped it irresolutely. Mr. Grantham noticed that.

"Those letters you have in your hand," he said, mildly, "were written by my son when he was a child. They are valuable to me, but can be of no value at all to you. Why do you disturb them?"

"I don't want the letters," said the man, in a gruff voice, letting the bundle fall to the floor, and fixing his eyes upon Mr. Grantham.

"Why take them from my drawer, then, friend? And why do you stand like a robber in a stage-play, looking at me and scarcely speaking? You must have some object in putting yourself to so much trouble."

"I have an object," said the intruder, coolly: "it is not to rob you of your property. As you say, there is nothing here to tempt anybody. I was looking for some papers."

"Some papers? What papers?—and what possible value can any of my papers be to you?"

Feeling a little tired standing, Mr. Grantham sat down, and said to the burglar,

"Take a seat, friend. I always prefer to sit when I am talking, and perhaps you may prefer it, also."

The burglar obeyed this suggestion by sitting down in a hesitating manner—his eyes fixed upon Mr. Grantham, who was, however, quite unable to see their expression.

"Now tell me all about it, friend," said Mr. Grantham, in the same mild voice. "You will acknowledge that this incident is a little out of the common path of every-day experience. It is unusual to find my house entered at dead of night, and my drawers searched for papers. Papers! What papers do you wish? I have only letters and sermons. You can scarcely wish the latter, friend — they would not suit your occupation precisely. Explain your object, and what papers in my possession could possibly be of any interest to you."

"Mr. Grantham," said the burglar.

"Well, my friend?"

"You are a brave man."

"Brave! It is true that was said of me when I was a young man—and, I am afraid, a very bad one. But I do not wish to be thought brave in all things. If you mean that I do not grow pale and tremble from fear of you, you are right."

"You are brave all the same," said the burglar. "What is to prevent my murdering you? I am armed and you are not. This is an ugly looking toy—what do you say to it?"

He put his hand into his breast, and drew from the inner pocket of his coat a bowie-knife.

"I am a stronger man than you," he said, "and one wipe with this would do for you."

Mr. Grantham looked at the knife quite calmly, and said,

"That *is* a murderous-looking weapon, friend. It is not possible that you could have the heart to use it against a fellow-being."

"A fellow-being might crowd a man a little too close—then a bowie is a good thing to have about you."

"If you are attacked, you mean, no doubt. But then it is not necessary to be attacked. I am nearly seventy, and I have never been in a brawl. Come, put up your knife, friend. I suppose you do not mean to use it to take my life. If it is meant to frighten me, you may as well put it up also. It does not frighten me."

"I said you were brave," was the burglar's reply; "and I'll be plain with you, and say I'm rather ashamed of this business—meddling with a man like you."

He put the knife back in his pocket, and said,

"You asked me just now what I came here for. I came to get some papers. Do you want a story to explain why I am after the papers? Here is the story."

"I should like to hear it," said Mr. Grantham. He had placed his candle on the table, and was leaning back in his chair, with his elbows resting upon the arms, and the tips of his fingers just touching—the palms of the hands open. In this attitude he presented the appearance of a person at ease in his elbow-chair, and listening to a friend conversing. Opposite sat the burglar, erect in a stiff-backed chair near the open drawer. As Mr. Grantham had closed the door behind him when he came in, they were alone together.

"Here is my story to account for my wanting the papers," said the burglar: "There was a friend of mine who got into trouble, and while people were after him he slept here one night. He was a big fellow with a little girl. He had papers about him which he wanted to keep from the officers. They were in a travelling-bag, and this was left at your house by accident. He was afraid to come and call for the papers, so I came to get hold of them—not to hurt or rob anybody."

"Your friend lives in the mountain, no doubt," said Mr. Grantham.

"Why in the mountain?"

"And you and your family were burnt out recently, were you not?"

"My family—"

"I mean, that it was you who came the other evening and asked alms for your family, who had just had the roof burnt over their heads. I recognize you now—and shall I tell you how I feel, friend? I feel ashamed for you."

The words seemed to produce some effect upon the burglar. He did not reply, but a movement of the disguise on his face was evidently produced by a contraction of his brow.

"Do you know that you were guilty of a very unbecoming action?" said Mr. Grantham. "It is painful. You came and appealed to me in *forma pauperis*, as we say, friend—to ask assistance for your poor family, and that family was only an imaginary one. Your object was to deceive me, and, in return for my kindness, carry off my property—or what was intrusted to me."

"I put the bread and meat and the money on the bench of the porch," the burglar said, in protest.

"Yes, that is true; but you robbed me of the clothes of my poor. That was the unbecoming act I referred to. I was afraid it was you."

The burglar pointed to the corner.

"There they are," he said.

And, in fact, there in the corner was the small travelling-bag, with the poor children's clothes, and Frances Cary's note and tracts.

Mr. Grantham was obviously gratified.

"I am truly glad to see that you have brought the clothes back. They are not mine; they belong to my poor."

"Well, there they are, Mr. Grantham.

It *was* a mean act, but not intentional. You see, I thought it was the other bag."

"And you have come for that to-night. How did you enter?"

"It was easy. I slipped the bolt of your back-door, which is not exactly a Chubb lock."

"Little precaution is taken against intrusion in a quiet place like this, friend. I had supposed that *I* needed no locks at all. A poor clergyman I thought was quite safe, at least, and it was some time before I could persuade myself that I really heard a noise in this room."

"Sorry you heard it. I tried not to disturb you," said the burglar, with a short laugh.

"I scarcely heard you, and thought at first it was only my fancy. I was up late, working, and then read my boy's letters. He is a very good boy. You have thrown the letters I value so much on the floor, I see."

The burglar stooped down quickly and picked them up.

"I am sorry—I didn't mean to throw the letters down. They fell out of my hand."

Mr. Grantham rose and took them from the man. In doing this their hands touched. It was as if they had shaken hands. The old pastor's hand did not retreat quickly, as if contaminated by that contact; on the contrary, the two hands remained touching each other for about a second. Mr. Grantham then went to the drawer, and, stooping down, placed the bundle of letters in one corner, taking care to do so neatly. During this ceremony his back was turned to the burglar, who was within two paces of him. He was also bending over, and nothing would have been easier than to strike him or master him. Of this, however, he seemed to have no thought whatever. He carefully arranged the letters in their place, and, returning to his arm-chair, resumed his former attitude, with his elbows resting on the arms and his finger-tips touching.

"It is easy to see you are not afraid," said the burglar. "I might have done for you just now, when your back was turned."

"I feel no apprehensions of your resorting to personal violence with me," said Mr. Grantham.

"Why not? I came for the papers, and I may as well tell you I must have them."

"The papers—"

"That were left in the travelling-bag. They belong to my friend—not to you. They are of no use to you. I forced your door, and am committing burglary, I know, but that hurts nobody. Where are the papers?"

The speaker had raised his voice. It had become somewhat threatening. Mr. Grantham did not move.

"Why did you not come and ask for them in open day, my friend?" he said, calmly. "It is bad to break in by the back-door of a house when you may enter by the open front-door."

"I have told you. How could I know that you would give up the papers, and not have me arrested?"

"So you resorted to burglary. Burglary is a great offence. Did you ever reflect why the law authorizes the killing of a burglar? It is because the supposition is that the person committing that crime is ready to commit a greater one rather than be taken in the act—I mean murder."

"I have no sort of intention of murdering you, Mr. Grantham, but I intend to have the papers."

"No intention of committing murder? Perhaps not. But you come armed with murderous weapons."

"I have not used any—yet."

"You come to a peaceful house—the home of a minister of the Gospel—and force the lock of his door, and search his drawers for his property, or property left in his charge; and when he makes his appearance to discover who it is that has entered his quiet home, you draw a knife from your breast and brandish it before him. That is a criminal act, friend. You are a man like myself—no worse, perhaps —in some things a better man, it may be.

Ask yourself if you have not committed a crime which you should be sorry for."

"I am not particularly sorry, as I am doing you no harm—now. I want the papers, Mr. Grantham. Where are they? I mean to have the whole lot before I go."

"Impossible," said Mr. Grantham.

"I say give me the papers. It will be unlucky for you if you stand out against me."

"It is impossible for me to deliver them to you, my friend."

"Where are they?" exclaimed the burglar, starting up; "what are they to *you*? You say it is not possible to give them up. Why not? You are not acting in bad faith: no fault can be found with you. They belong to my friend. Where are the papers?"

Mr. Grantham slowly shook his head.

"Do you mean, or do you not, to hand them over?" exclaimed the burglar, with violence. As he spoke he drew his knife and took a step toward the old pastor.

Mr. Grantham looked at him attentively, and said,

"It is sorrowful, very sorrowful, friend, to see a fellow-creature act so sinfully. This is a very bad errand. Do you know what such things result in?—the State-prison or the gallows. Is that reasonable —is it worth the risk? The sin is the main thing—the crime in the eyes of the law of man follows that. Come, friend, put up your knife. It is quite useless, and offends my eyes."

The burglar advanced straight upon him with the knife raised.

"The papers!" he exclaimed.

"I have said it is impossible for me to deliver the papers to you, my friend," said Mr. Grantham, quietly.

"Why is it?"

"I delivered them to their owner more than a month ago."

The burglar, who was close to Mr. Grantham, took a step backward, and the hand holding the knife fell at his side.

"To the owner—a month ago?"

"Somewhat more than a month, I believe," returned Mr. Grantham, tranquilly.

"To the owner?—the big man who brought the child to your house that night?"

"The same, friend. He left the travelling-bag by accident, it seems. My old servant informed me that he came for it, but I was absent. He came again, however, and of course I delivered it. I had not examined its contents."

The burglar remained standing, without uttering a word, for a full minute. He then fixed his eyes upon Mr. Grantham, as though aiming to read him through and through.

Mr. Grantham smiled a little, and said,

"Do you doubt my statement? If you do, I venture to say that you are the only person in this parish who would do so."

"No, I do not doubt what you say, at all," said the man, in a voice of very great disappointment. "The papers are gone, I see that. There's no use for further talking. Good-night, Mr. Grantham."

He went to the door and opened it. Mr. Grantham rose, and, taking up his light, followed him.

"A cold night, friend," he said, listening to the shrill whistle of the wind; "do you know what has just come into my mind? I ought not to turn you out in such a night. There is a bed at your service."

A gruff laugh indicated that the burglar appreciated the humor of his host's suggestion.

"No, I thank you, Mr. Grantham," he said. "I might not feel at my ease exactly at breakfast to-morrow morning."

"Oh, do not be alarmed at that. I am an easy sort of person, and bear no malice."

"Easy or not, you are a brave man," said the burglar, going toward the door in rear of the passage.

"No," said Mr. Grantham, laying his hand upon his arm.

The man turned round and looked at him with quick suspicion.

"I did not mean to arrest you," Mr. Grantham said, with a smile. "You see, I wish to forget our discussion, and only meant to do you a courtesy. I do not regard you as an ordinary burglar. You only came for a few papers—I have not asked you to explain how it is that the owner of them sent you, when he has them already. That is your business, not my own. Let it remain so, friend, and do not enter any more houses. Go home, and go to sleep, unless you will stay with me to-night—you are very welcome. When I touched you I meant to say, 'Do not go out by the back-door.' Here is the front-door."

Mr. Grantham opened it, and the burglar went out.

"Good-night, friend," said Mr. Grantham, in a friendly voice; "take care, or you will stumble; it is extremely dark."

"I will take care," said the burglar, turning round and looking into Mr. Grantham's face, lit up by the flaring candle, "and I mean to take care of another thing, too."

"Another thing, my friend?"

"I never mean, so help me Heaven!— you'll not find fault with that sort of swearing, Mr. Grantham—I never mean, I say, to break into a preacher's house again, if I live to be as old as Mathuselem."

"Methuselah, my friend," said the pastor, correcting him.

"It's all the same, Mr. Grantham, and you're a trump, or my name's not R—"

Fortunately catching himself, Mr. Ruggles sunk to silence and so departed.

LXI.

DOVES.

Mr. Lascelles spent about an hour with Miss Juliet in the drawing-room at Trianon. He then rose, took his leave, and went away in an extremely bad humor.

Nothing in the demeanor of the young lady had put him out of temper. She was not at all cold or *distrait* during their interview; on the contrary, she was charming. She laughed a great deal for a person of her quiet temperament, and was unusually gracious. Something seemed to have pleased her. This was so plain that Mr. Lascelles referred to the subject, and asked if some piece of good fortune had not occurred to her? "Perhaps," Miss Juliet had replied, with a silvery outburst: but then it was unnecessary to go so far for a reason. Autumn always charmed her and made her happy.

Juliet had actually followed Mr. Lascelles to the front-door—an evidence of unusual favor. She laughed more than ever as she held out her hand to tell him good-bye. Her face was so bright, and had such an expression of pleasure in it, that Mr. Lascelles thought in a vague way that she was extremely pretty, and wondered what had occurred to make her so gracious to him. She positively beamed upon him, and seemed to have the greatest difficulty in suppressing a tendency to laugh, and thank him for something. He wondered at this a little, but gave up the problem and went away.

There was thus nothing whatever in his reception by Miss Juliet that irritated Mr. Lascelles. Nor had any one else frowned upon him. Mrs. Armstrong had not made her appearance, but that was not unusual. She generally had something to occupy her attention up-stairs when he called to see Juliet. The source of the young gentleman's bad humor was the absence of Miss Bassick from their place of rendezvous in the woods. Affairs were now well arranged between them. When Mr. Lascelles called at Trianon, the hour of his intended visit was always known in advance, in some manner, to Miss Bassick. Just before he made his appearance she would be seized with a desire to go and look for ferns or wild flowers, or perhaps to collect cedars for the vases in the drawing-room — cedars were attractive as a background to chrysanthemums or their vagrant sisters of the woods and fields. On these occasions Miss Bassick generally went toward Piedmont, which was in a direction nearly opposite to Wye; but it happened almost uniformly that there were very few flowers or ferns in that quarter, which induced her to make a circuit, when out of sight of the house. This naturally brought her out on the road to Wye, about half a mile from Trianon; and, by a singular coincidence, she generally met Mr. Lascelles at a certain spot, on his return homeward.

This had occurred so frequently that no doubt Mr. Lascelles had contracted the habit of looking for the young lady. When our slippers are out of place we are aggrieved, and feel that we are the victims of wrong. Were they not in that corner yesterday, and the day before that, and the day before that? Why should they not be there to-day?

Miss Bassick was also in the habit of incidentally appearing in the passage at Trianon when Mr. Lascelles entered or retired, when, if not observed, they whispered a little. This was when circumstances prevented the young lady from prosecuting, at the moment, her search for wild flowers. These meetings were brief, but not unpleasant; they refreshed. There was even time, occasionally, for a chaste salute, and the employment of two pairs of arms. This, however, was infrequent, Mrs. Armstrong and the dangerous Cinda being not far off. The place of rendezvous was a spot of greater privacy, where rude and prying eyes did not intrude. If the interchange of sweet confidences did not occur in the passage casually it might occur at the rendezvous. Now, on this day it had taken place at neither one place nor the other.

Miss Bassick had not made her appearance, and was not at the trysting-place. Mr. Lascelles was not aware that this resulted from the scenes of the morning, and that Miss Bassick considered it imprudent to either show herself in the establishment or prosecute her explorations in search of wild flowers. He simply contemplated the naked fact, and felt angry. What did it mean? Was he to be trifled with in that manner? He would not be trifled with! He cared nothing for her absence any more than for her presence. After which confidential statement to himself he rode on with an expression of countenance which indicated that he cared a great deal.

In fact Mr. Douglas Lascelles was very

much in love indeed with Miss Bassick. She was precisely the person to captivate this gentleman. She was extremely handsome, in the first place, but this was unimportant in comparison with the expression of her eyes. It was Miss Bassick's eyes which had done the business for Mr. Lascelles. He had laughed at them at first, then had struggled against them, but had yielded at last. If he had not been so tough and unbirdlike a personage, one might have thought of the stories told of snakes charming birds. That, however, was too fanciful. Mr. Lascelles was not a young bird and Miss Bassick was not a serpent, although Mrs. Armstrong applied that term to her. She was simply a very seductive young creature, with an uncommonly fine pair of eyes, which had fascinated Mr. Lascelles.

As was said above, he was by this time very much in love with the owner of the eyes. She was bright, witty, and had a charming *malice*, as the French say, in her talk — not malice in the English meaning, but roguery. She mimicked Mrs. Armstrong so delightfully that Mr. Lascelles could not restrain his laughter — little as he was given to that. She also made fun of Juliet—imitating her erect carriage of person with humorous exaggeration. Her wit sparkled and cut, edged with laughter. She was a "perfect little devil," as Mr. Lascelles often told her: and he added that she had been intended for a vaudevilliste on the Parisian stage, not for a staid "companion" to a staid American lady. After which he laughed heartily.

Sometimes Miss Bassick was in quite a different mood—variety being one of her chief attractions. On such occasions she was deeply serious, and did the pathetic as well as she had done the humorous. There was no longer the brilliant smile on the ripe red lips, or any malicious gayety in the large, brilliant eyes. The R. R. lips grew mournful, and the L. B. eyes were half closed, weighed down apparently by scarcely suppressed tears. Miss Bassick then grew pathetic, and spoke of her wrongs and misfortunes. She was

alone in the world, the victim of a cruel woman, who treated her with the grossest insult. It had not been so once. Her family had been one of high social position, and she had enjoyed every luxury—her childhood had been cradled in the arms of a mother's love—her dear father had lavished upon her all the treasures of his affection. She had thus begun her life with the brightest skies bending above her, but the change had swiftly come. Her dear father and mother had died—the family estate had been sold in consequence of her father's generous endorsement for a friend — she had been thrown upon the hard world, a poor flower, to breast the current alone; and here she was, with her wounded heart, seeking some one to cling to who could feel for her and comfort her.

When she spoke of her lonely situation in this manner, Miss Bassick generally shed tears, and looked extremely handsome and interesting. As this adds to one's appreciation and sympathy, Mr. Lascelles felt moved to say that *he* would feel for and comfort her; and on such occasions her feelings would overcome Miss Bassick, and she would hide her blushing face and tearful eyes in the gentleman's waistcoat—a storm-tossed dove seeking its place of refuge.

This allusion to waistcoats may mislead. It must not be supposed that Miss Bassick was at all deficient in propriety. On the contrary, if there was any one trait more fully developed in her than the rest it was this latter. It was plain that Miss Bassick even objected to having her hand kissed, and this unpleasant state of things would not probably alter unless they became engaged to be married. Engaged to be married! Enamored as he was, Mr. Lascelles drew back suddenly. It was an immense enjoyment to look into the seductive eyes, to dream of fond words and caresses, but —to *marry* Miss Bassick! There was the rub. A more unsuitable match, in a worldly point of view, could not be imagined. She was penniless, an unknown person, and as to her family, and that "high social position," he had only her word for that, and he was not entirely convinced that Miss Bassick's word was sufficient. It might possibly be true. There were many ups and downs in the histories of families. What *was* certain, however, was that Miss Bassick occupied at present a very humble position indeed, and, socially speaking, was a nobody! People would laugh. It was impossible to think seriously of such a marriage, and he would not give it a thought again. After which he proceeded to think about it—and then to think about it again—and finally to think about it almost all the time.

The result of these reflections has been seen. After a long and uncommonly interesting interview, in which the shrinking modesty and maiden sense of what was proper had been more conspicuous than ever before in Miss Bassick, Mr. Lascelles, in the ardor of the moment, had been carried away, and had proposed. Miss Bassick exhibited wonder and suggested difficulties. The match was, indeed, not to be thought of for a single moment. What would his family and friends say? She was a poor companion—a mere upper servant; she had absolutely nothing, and might be turned out of Trianon without a roof over her head whenever Mrs. Armstrong chose. Then there was Juliet. She had evidently determined to marry him, Mr. Lascelles: what would Juliet say if he dared to think of her, Miss Bassick? Altogether it was quite impossible. He must not urge her. If she only consulted her own heart—she was p-poor and f-friendless, and his affection had touched her—deeply. She f-felt—as if she really could—return it—and be—be—his; but, no—she could not consent to t-t-take advantage of—

Here Miss Bassick broke down, sobbed, and looked so extremely fascinating that Mr. Lascelles burst into perfectly sincere protestations, and finally induced the young lady, whose head had sunk upon his shoulder, to promise to take the advantage of him alluded to—that is, to become Mrs. Douglas Lascelles.

It was only then that the waistcoat of Mr. Lascelles became Miss Bassick's habitual place of refuge.

As Mr. Lascelles rode past the trysting-place, on his way back to Wye, he glanced moodily in the direction of the spot. He was both angry and depressed, and eased his mind by uttering very improper expressions. He then set spurs to his horse and rode on rapidly, meditating upon a much more serious subject—the burglary. It was to take place that very night. What would be the result of such a daring and dangerous attempt? Why had he authorized Mr. Ruggles to undertake it? He must have been mad! It was frightful to think what might ensue.

He was passing near the Wye quarters at the moment, and saw a group of negroes in front of one of the cabins. A strapping freedman, who did not look at all "down-trodden," was leaning back on an old chair, with his bare feet emerging from his ragged pantaloons, and holding a banjo in his hand on which he was playing. The merry rattle of the banjo filled the crowd with delight, and some children, nearly naked, were dancing uproariously to the music.

"Haw! haw! darkeys,
Don't you go 'way!
Walk into my parlor—
Don't you hear de banjo play?"

The grinning musician shouted his ditty, and the crowd burst into laughter. Mr. Lascelles wheeled his horse, to avoid passing near these ignorant creatures; their empty and vulgar mirth was disagreeable to him.

LXII.

THE BANK-NOTES.

THE little family at Wye were assembled in the library on the same evening, after tea, and each pursued his or her favorite occupation. The general was reading the last magazine, Mrs. Lascelles sat opposite to him, knitting a stocking, and Anna Gray was absorbed in a letter which had just been brought in the mail-bag. Mr. Lascelles was smoking his cigar in an easy-chair, at one corner of the fire, and was the picture of tranquil enjoyment.

After some moments of silence Mrs. Lascelles said to Anna,

"Who is your letter from, my dear?"

"From Ellis, aunty," said the young lady, quietly.

"I hope he is well."

"Very well, and he says he will soon be back. He sends his love."

Miss Anna Gray then folded up her letter and put it in her pocket. Mrs. Lascelles continued to knit at her stocking, and said,

"I am very fond of Ellis; he is so very frank and sincere. I am afraid all young men are not. They do wrong, and then very naturally attempt to conceal what they have done, but seldom succeed in doing so."

Mr. Lascelles moved slightly in his chair, as if his position was cramped, and he wished to change it. The general, absorbed in his paper, said,

"The troops are really coming to look for the moonshine people. I am afraid there will be trouble."

"I do hope they will not fight, my dear."

"The moonshiners? I don't know. There are some very determined men among them, and many of them are old soldiers."

"You seem to know them."

"Oh yes; I know a great many of them. I used to electioneer in Bohemia when I ran for Congress, and they all know me very well. There are some new-comers, I am informed — a party of tramps—at the Crow's Nest house."

The general made a slight pause, and then added,

"The marshal told me about these people, after his visit to them. He was much struck with them. One of them is an old man, apparently weak in his mind, and another a big powerful fellow, of foreign appearance. How they drifted here it is difficult to say. I should like to visit them."

"Visit them, my dear?" said Mrs. Lascelles. "I hope you will not. That desperate class of people are often dangerous."

"Dangerous? Do you think they would see anything in a plain old gentleman like myself to excite their suspicion or ill-will?" said the general, with a smile. "A politician learns a great deal about human nature, my dear, and how to deal with it. If I were thrown with this big fellow, who is known as the Lefthander, I hear—no doubt a nickname—I am sure we should become good friends in half an hour."

"I hope you will not be."

"Well, I am not very sure that I should not like to see him. The marshal really excited my curiosity. I have often been interested in listening to stories of adventure from nondescript characters— they show you life on the rough side, which is different from the side seen by people of good society, as it is called. This Lefthander must have seen a good deal of life of all sorts. I think I'll go and visit my friends the moonshiners and talk with him, and induce him to tell me all about himself and his history."

Mr. Lascelles, leaning back in his chair, continued to smoke. The fire seemed to have flushed his face slightly—there was a red spot in each of his cheeks.

"You soon make friends with people if you take interest in them and their views and pursuits," added the philosophic general. "Did you observe, when Mr. Grantham was here this morning, that I touched on Ritualism and defended the poor Tractarians? That aroused and interested the worthy man, who became animated at once!"

Mrs. Lascelles smiled and shook her head.

"You must not amuse yourself, my dear, at that good man's expense," she said; "and I was quite shocked to hear you speak approvingly of Ritualism. But I am sure he saw that you were jesting, as he stopped arguing with you and laughed. What a singular loss that was of his black carpet-bag."

Mr. Lascelles turned his head a little and listened with attention.

"Who could have robbed a parsonage?" the lady continued. "And there was nothing in the bag, Mr. Grantham says, but a bundle of children's clothes, made by Frances Cary, and some tracts. How very strange it was that these were stolen in our honest little community."

"Possibly Mr. Grantham mislaid them—he is very absent-minded," said the general.

"I fear, from what he said, that some one stole them."

"Well, at all events, it is as well that Mr. Grantham was absent, my dear," said General Lascelles. "He is a very mild man, but as cool and resolute as any one I know. I should not like to be the thief or burglar who entered his house to commit a robbery."

Mr. Lascelles threw his cigar into the fire and unfolded a newspaper, in which he seemed soon to be absorbed. At last he yawned, rose, said that riding in the wind had made him sleepy, and went to his chamber. Having reached that place of refuge, he fell into reflection, and then, toward midnight, retired to bed.

During the whole of the next day Mr. Lascelles remained at home in an extremely moody condition of mind. In the evening he again retired at an early hour, and was in bed before ten. It was perhaps in consequence of this that he lay awake for a long time, as nothing less disposes to slumber than anticipating our habitual hour for retiring. Indeed, he did not go to sleep until nearly daybreak—he was thinking about things. Mr. Ruggles was probably at that moment exploring the recesses of Mr. Grantham's secretary.

Mr. Lascelles slept for about an hour only. He then awoke, and, getting out of bed, went and looked at his watch by the glimmer of the expiring fire. This examination seemed to be satisfactory. He lit his lamp, proceeded to dress, and having put on his riding-boots, went quietly down-stairs. In the hall, which was dimly illumined by the first light of day,

he put on his hat, and found his riding-whip, which he preferred to spurs. He then left the house by the door in rear of the passage, which he unlocked for the purpose. He took every precaution in doing so, but the bolt grated, and the sound rung out like a trumpet in his ears in the profound silence. He stopped and listened. The house was so still that he could hear his own breathing. It was apparent that its inmates were sound asleep, and Mr. Lascelles mentally laughed at himself for supposing that the sound, even if it had been heard, would have startled anybody. It would have been attributed at once to a servant opening the house.

He went out in the chill dusk of morning, with the glimmer of daybreak to light him, and proceeded to the stables. These were very large, and for the most part quite still; the horses were probably sleeping, as horses will toward daybreak. Here and there they were stamping their feet and rattling their halters, meaning that corn had occurred to them. Mr. Lascelles went to a stable detached from the rest, opened it with a key which he took from his pocket, and, going in, saddled his favorite horse himself and led him out. Having first looked around, he then mounted and rode quietly into a clump of woods adjoining the grounds. Once in the woods, he touched his horse with his whip and set out at a gallop.

The object of this early ride was to meet Mr. Ruggles at sunrise, at a spot agreed upon some miles from Wye. The nearer rendezvous was unsafe. They might be seen, and Mr. Lascelles particularly desired not to be seen on this special occasion.

As he went on at a rapid gallop he soon reached the spot—a highly desirable locality, as it was a little dell hemmed in by woods—and there, with the first rays of sunrise illuminating his figure, was Mr. Ruggles waiting for him.

Mr. Lascelles rode straight to him, and throwing himself from his horse, slipped the reins over the animal's head, and confronted Mr. Ruggles.

"You have the papers, I suppose?" he said.

"No, I've not got them," said Mr. Ruggles, in a business-like tone.

Mr. Lascelles shut his eyebrows down, and closed the hand holding the bridle-rein so tightly that the nails dug into the palm.

"Why? Explain it to me. Did you get into the house, or were you only boasting when you said you could do so without difficulty?"

"I don't remember any boasting, Mr. Lascelles," said Mr. Ruggles, in a cool tone.

"You boasted enough about it," said Mr. Lascelles, losing his temper and frowning, under the effect of his huge disappointment and early rising after a nearly sleepless night.

Now, nothing irritates people like seeing people who are irritated. Expressions of face are contagious. You smile back at the smiling face, and scowl at the scowler, or, at least, you feel disposed to do so. Thus the displeasure of Mr. Lascelles highly displeased Mr. Ruggles, who was himself greatly disappointed.

"Look here, Mr. Lascelles," said Mr. Ruggles, with dignity, "a man don't like to be talked to in that way."

"What you like or dislike is a matter of indifference to me," said Mr. Lascelles, "and I have no time or desire to be trifled with. What happened?"

"This is what happened," responded Mr. Ruggles, with severe brevity of utterance. "I got in the house — there was no trouble about that. I told you so—I didn't *boast* about it. I found the secretary and searched it. Nothing there."

"Searched it thoroughly?—every drawer?—everywhere?"

These questions came one by one, jerked, as it were, from Mr. Lascelles's lips.

"No."

"What do you mean?"

"I mean I would have searched through it, but I stopped to talk with the owner of the piece of furniture."

"With Mr. Grantham?"

"The same."

"Are you trifling with me? You stopped *to talk with Mr. Grantham?*"

"It looked like it. He came in and sat down, and I took a seat too. It might have been his ghost, but I rather think it was the man himself."

Mr. Ruggles was growing sarcastic.

"What the devil does all this mean?" exclaimed Mr. Lascelles, in great irritation and bewilderment. "Are you telling me a cock-and-bull story for your amusement?"

"Not as I'm aware of," said Mr. Ruggles, with indifference. Indeed, his coolness amounted decidedly to disrespect.

"Tell me in plain words what happened, and stop all this tomfoolery," observed Mr. Lascelles, growing quite angry, but speaking coolly. "You say you entered the house and searched the secretary, but not thoroughly, in consequence of being surprised by Mr. Grantham—do you mean to say that?"

"I do, em-phatically," said Mr. Ruggles. "I never was more surprised in my life."

As Mr. Lascelles seemed to be rendered speechless for the moment by the announcement, Mr. Ruggles availed himself of the fact, and related all that had happened.

"So you see the whole affair's at an end," he said, in conclusion. "The Left-hander has got your papers safely stowed away somewhere, and, as I'd rather not fool with him again, I may as well say I am going back to New York."

Mr. Lascelles, with his eyes fixed on the ground, was reflecting, with evident disgust and disappointment, upon all that he had heard.

"I can't see my way to serve you further in any way, Mr. Lascelles," said Mr. Ruggles; "and as I think I'll take the night train north, I'd be glad to arrange our little business matters."

"You mean your pay?" said Mr. Lascelles, suddenly raising his head.

"Exactly, Mr. Lascelles. There was no special bargain as to what I was to have if I couldn't lay my hands on your papers; but I've done my best, and nearly got my neck broken by that big fellow in the mountain — besides, I've committed burglary, which is risky—and all that is worth considerable."

"What do you suppose it is worth to me?"

"Well, not much, maybe — but I'm talking about myself. I think I've earned at least eight hundred of the thousand, to say the least."

"Eight hundred! You are crazy. Do you suppose I am made of money?"

"You offered a cool thousand, and maybe more, if you got your documents."

"Well, where are they? I am no nearer getting hold of them than the day you came. It was throwing away time to send for you. I thought you were a *detective.*"

This greatly enraged Mr. Ruggles, and he could not suppress a frown.

"Well, if you are going to insult me, and refuse to pay me, after sending for me, Mr. Lascelles, you can!" he replied, angrily.

"What do you mean?" said Mr. Lascelles, with an ominous shutting down of his eyebrows; "do you mean to hint that I am acting unfairly? Here's your money, and more than you deserve."

He took out his pocket-book and detached five one-hundred-dollar bank-notes from a bundle which it contained, and handed them to Mr. Ruggles, who took them, looked at them one by one, folded them up, and placed them in his waist-coat pocket.

"Well, when an honest man can't get his full pay," he said, evidently much dissatisfied, "the best thing is to take what he can get."

"What do you say?"

"I thought I was dealing with a gentleman—" Mr. Ruggles paused after the word for an instant—"who would not beat down a poor fellow in this way."

Mr. Lascelles had flushed suddenly. The pause after the word "gentleman" had produced a disagreeable effect. In fact, it had enraged him.

"If you mean that I promised you more, you lie," he said, looking straight at Mr. Ruggles. "I thought you knew your business, and could be counted on. You are a mere greenhorn, and have your lie ready—I doubt if you ever entered that house at all or made the search."

Mr. Ruggles could stand much in the way of business, but he could not stand the imputation on his professional character, and to have the term "lie" applied to his statements.

"You'd better not repeat that," he observed, with a flash of the eye.

"You are a liar!" responded Mr. Lascelles, promptly.

"And you're a fraud!" exclaimed Mr. Ruggles, yielding to rage.

As he uttered the words Mr. Lascelles struck him in the face with his small whip—a sharp, telling lash, which left a long red mark on his cheek. Thereat Mr. Ruggles, driven to fury, drew his bowie-knife, and was apparently about to do something dreadful, when he suddenly changed his mind. Mr. Lascelles had put his hand under his coat behind and produced a small but dangerous-looking pistol of the Derringer pattern, which he cocked with the rapidity of long practice and placed upon Mr. Ruggles's breast.

This was evidently unpleasant to Mr. Ruggles. He was in a rage, but not too much so to lose sight of his personal safety. He retreated, moving his body quickly to one side, to get out of range of the muzzle of the Derringer.

Mr. Lascelles looked at him for a few seconds in silence. He then quietly uncocked his pistol and restored it to his pocket.

"There's no fight in you," he said, coolly.

He took out his pocket-book, extracted an additional bank-note from it and tossed it toward Mr. Ruggles; after which he mounted his horse with great deliberation and rode off in the direction of Wye. He did not even turn his head. If he had done so he would have seen Mr. Ruggles restore the bowie-knife to his breast pocket and pick up the bank note. Whatever course Mr. Rooney Ruggles meant to pursue in consequence of this unpleasant scene, it was obvious that he considered that business was business, and hundred-dollar bank-notes were hundred-dollar bank-notes.

LXIII.

IN THE TRIANON WOODS.

It is a very imprudent thing to tread on people, however humble they may be, and very injudicious to strike them with riding-whips; they will probably strike back in some way, at some time or other. Mr. Ruggles intended to strike back if he could, and, reflecting maturely upon the subject, thought he would be able to do so. He and Mr. Lascelles were not done with each other, he said to himself, with a malignant expression of countenance; and conscious of the possession of bank-notes, and a few days of leisure, he resolved to gratify, if possible, his personal feelings before his return to New York.

He had been lodging at the cabin of a poor man in the vicinity of the railway station. He now moved to the Piedmont tavern, where he took a room, and on the next day set out in his neat citizen's dress to call on the Lefthander.

They had a long conversation, in which Mr. Ruggles, giving way unintentionally to anger, related all that had occurred between himself and Mr. Lascelles, and made no secret of his intention to "get even with him." The trouble, he said, was to discover the means of doing so. It was true that Mr. Lascelles gambled frightfully at the residence of one of his friends in the neighborhood, but very little could be made of that. There was something more promising in another direction, however—he was engaged to be married to a Miss Armstrong, who lived near Piedmont; and if there was any reason why such a marriage ought not to take place, it was the duty of honest people, who were aware of such reasons, to inform the young lady of them.

Mr. Ruggles looked at the Lefthander. He was smoking, and made no reply.

There might or might not be an obsta-cle to the gentleman's marriage, continued Mr. Ruggles. Such obstacles often existed, and were yet disregarded. You had only to read the newspapers to see what a queer world we live in. Men who bore irreproachable reputations often married when they had wives living, or had forged, or committed crimes which, if known, would utterly destroy their position in society, perhaps subject them to a criminal prosecution. Now, if such were the fact in the case of Mr. Lascelles, and if documentary evidence on the subject were in existence, it was the bounden duty of honest men to expose the whole affair, and not permit a young lady to marry a bigamist, a forger, or perhaps a murderer.

Mr. Ruggles then looked again at the Lefthander; but his face was as serene as before.

"You know what I mean," said Mr. Ruggles, coming to the point.

"Yes, I know what you mean."

"The papers in the travelling-bag."

The Lefthander made no reply.

"You think this is only another trick —this story about the quarrel and the cut with the whip"—exclaimed Mr. Ruggles. "and you are right to be on your guard; but I swear it's true."

"I rather think it is," the Lefthander said; "but I have nothing to say on the subject of the papers you mention—at present."

He spoke moodily, and seemed to be reflecting. Something evidently troubled him. Mr. Ruggles made another attempt to draw him out, but again failed; and as Gentleman Joe came in at the moment, the conversation ended, and he took his departure.

On the afternoon of the same day Mr. Ruggles walked out of Piedmont, and went in the direction of Trianon. The road which he followed intersected that leading from Wye to Trianon, about a mile from the latter place, and Mr. Ruggles had just reached the point of crossing when he observed a horseman approaching from the direction of Wye. A single glance showed him that the horseman was Mr. Lascelles, and as he had no desire to hold another interview with that gentleman, he concealed himself in some bushes.

Mr. Lascelles passed at a gallop. He had evidently not seen Mr. Ruggles. In a few moments he was out of sight, and Mr. Ruggles cautiously followed in the same direction.

The sun was sinking toward the summit of the woods when Mr. Lascelles rode into the grounds of Trianon. He dismounted, threw his bridle over the rack, and entered the house. As he did so a figure flitted up the staircase, making him a coquettish sign accompanied by a smile. This was Miss Bassick, who was lost to view a moment afterward.

Mr. Lascelles knocked and the sable Cinda appeared, with a polite grin on her features. Missus Armstrong was at home, but Miss Juliet, she had a headache: and Mrs. Armstrong, having made her appearance in the drawing-room in due time, confirmed this statement. Juliet had been suffering from a headache all day—would Mr. Lascelles excuse her? Then the conversation proceeded. It was not a very cordial interview. Mrs. Armstrong did not like scenes, but there was the blessed resource of *hauteur*. You can show people what you think of them, fortunately, without telling them, which is a comfort; and Mrs. Armstrong, without uttering a word on the subject which occupied the minds of both, quite froze her visitor.

Under such circumstances visits are not prolonged. Mr. Lascelles smiled sweetly, lamented Miss Juliet's headache, hoped it would soon disappear, and made a low bow, after which he took his departure and rode away. As he turned his back on the house, his expression suddenly changed.

"She has found out everything," he said, "and that headache has already left the sweet Juliet, probably. Who could have told her?—the devil!"

After this succinct but comprehensive expression of his surprise and dissatisfaction, Mr. Lascelles rode on rapidly, and about sunset reached the spot where he was accustomed to meet Miss Bassick.

He was sure he should find her there. As she flitted up the staircase she had made him a peculiar sign, which signified that she was going to disappear from Trianon by the back staircase, go in search of flowers, and in all probability would not be far distant when he passed on his way to Wye.

It said a great deal for Miss Bassick's punctuality and reliability that he was not disappointed. There she was at the trysting-place, with her little basket full of red berries, and her handsome face glowing with the roses of healthy exercise, and perhaps of anticipation. Can we blame her? Is it not natural that the innocent heart of a maiden should throb at the approach of her dear one? She was exceedingly handsome as she stood leaning against the trunk of an oak; and it is not to be wondered at that Mr. Lascelles, a few moments afterward, relieved the oak-tree of the trouble of sustaining her.

The conversation which ensued was not particularly interesting: such conversations rarely are. There were reproaches, explanations, blandishments, and so forth. It was a strictly private interview, and therefore ought not to be made public. The *denouement* alone is necessary to a comprehension of the narrative.

Mr. Lascelles was seated on a mossy rock with his arm around Miss Bassick, and her head leaning on his shoulder, when Miss Juliet Armstrong came out of the woods, from behind some evergreens, within about ten paces of them. This vexatious incident occurred in the simplest manner. The young lady had really been suffering from a headache all day, but toward sunset had come quietly down-stairs and set out to take a walk, without the knowledge of her mother or Miss Bassick. Finding the evening mild, she had gone wandering through the woods, and was now returning home, when, unfortunately, she stumbled upon the young people.

No sooner had Juliet caught sight of them than she attempted to retreat undiscovered; but that was impossible. They had both looked round, and their glances met. Miss Bassick was so much startled that she remained motionless with the arm of Mr. Lascelles still around her, and a deep flush upon her face; then she suddenly retreated from him.

As to Juliet, she was standing still, coloring a little and smiling. There was absolutely nothing to do but to accost them, and she said,

"I have been walking—what a pleasant evening, Mr. Lascelles."

"Very pleasant," stammered Mr. Lascelles, who had risen.

"And the woods are full of flowers, in spite of the lateness of the season. I have found a quantity of autumn primroses and this pretty little star of Bethlehem—have you ever noticed it?"

She came forward quietly and held up her nosegay with a smile on her lips.

"You admire flowers, Miss Bassick," she added, "and you will find every possible variety if you will look for them."

Miss Bassick, who had risen to her feet, looked extremely stiff and haughty. Mr. Lascelles, to judge from the expression of his countenance, would have preferred being in some other place.

"I regretted hearing that you had a headache, and am glad to find it has left you," he stammered.

"Yes, I am scarcely suffering at all now. I thought a walk would relieve it, and I suppose you were walking out also, Miss Bassick?"

"Yes," said Miss Bassick, curtly, and knitting her handsome brows. At the same moment Mr. Lascelles's horse neighed, and Juliet looked at him admiringly.

"What a beautiful horse!" she said. "I really envy you your ride. I hope all are well at Wye."

"Thank you—very well; and as I promised to return to tea, I will now take my leave, ladies."

Mr. Lascelles bowed low, and, mounting his horse, rode off: in all his life he had never felt a sensation of such relief.

Miss Bassick and Juliet stood facing each other—the face of the one a vivid crimson, the lips of the other smiling quietly.

"Shall we return, Miss Bassick?"

"Yes, I am ready to return!"

Was it the voice of Miss Bassick, or somebody else's? The coo-coo had quite disappeared—it was brief, abrupt, and metallic. They walked on together in silence for some moments. Then Miss Bassick said, in the same abrupt tone,

"So you think it honorable to steal up and surprise people?"

"To steal up!" said Juliet, composedly, though a slight color came to her face.

"As you did while I was conversing with Mr. Lascelles."

Juliet smiled. It seemed impossible for her to take any but the humorous view of what she had witnessed. Perhaps the term "conversing," employed by Miss Bassick, suggested the retort that she and Mr. Lascelles had been conversing in a very peculiar attitude.

"I did not steal up. I was going home, and came out of the woods by mere accident. If you knew me better than you do, Miss Bassick, you would not accuse me of stealing up on people."

"I know you well!" said Miss Bassick, yielding to anger; "and you need not attempt to deceive me, as you deceive other people!"

Juliet's smiles disappeared and her head rose haughtily. But this had no effect upon Miss Bassick, who felt, probably, that she had destroyed the bridges behind her.

"You followed me, to spy out my movements and listen!" she exclaimed. "You are jealous of the preference Mr. Lascelles has for me! You have been watching, and sending others to watch all my movements! You have never liked me, and take this means of wreaking your spite and dislike on me!"

Juliet listened with a sort of wonder. Did Miss Bassick really believe what she said? Could it be possible that, after their necessarily intimate association for years, she could honestly take any such view of her character? Then her surprise yielded to slight indignation. She was not exactly angry, but felt that her companion's words were an outrage. Still she remained calm, and replied,

"I have really no spite to wreak upon you, Miss Bassick. I am obliged to say —since you charge me with 'dislike'—that I do not particularly like you. I have tried to do so, but found it impossible, probably from a want of congeniality in our characters, which really do seem utterly unlike. Shall I tell you just what I mean? You state your opinion of me frankly—I will be frank with you also. I am afraid you are not a sincere person, and resort to indirect means to attain your ends. You seem very angry, but I cannot help that. It is better I should tell you all, as you say I am in the habit of deceiving people but cannot deceive you. I am not at all angry with you, and since you have lived with us have never uttered an unkind word to you; but I never could grow fond of you—I have told you why. It may be unfortunate, but I feel an actual aversion for insincere and indirect people."

"Very well!" cried Miss Bassick, in a good wholesome rage; "and now shall I tell *you* my opinion of *you?*"

"You may in a moment, if you fancy. I wish to say only one word on another subject. You accuse me of spying, and watching, and every dishonorable proceeding, from *jealousy* — jealousy of the preference of Mr. Lascelles for yourself!"

"Yes, I do accuse you of that, and of following me this evening! It was an outrage to—"

"Be present at your private interview with Mr. Lascelles?"

Juliet, suddenly recalling the peculiar attitude of the group, and their startled expression, could not suppress a smile.

"I am not at all jealous, Miss Bassick," she said. "I don't know whether you will believe me, but any preferences of Mr. Lascelles are a matter of indifference to me. I really have no desire to marry Mr. Lascelles, and you are quite at liberty to do so, if you wish; I see no objection. I might say that it would, perhaps, be better to receive his visits in the drawing-room than in this secret manner; but you will decide for yourself, of course. And now, Miss Bassick, I think we understand each other. It is better that we should, and I have, therefore, spoken plainly. *Do* marry Mr. Lascelles, if you wish, and he is anxious. I shall certainly not oppose it, and you must not think I am a policeman. If I had known that you and Mr. Lascelles were talking in that romantic spot this evening, I assure you I should have gone a mile out of the way to avoid interrupting you."

In spite of everything—of Miss Bassick's wrath, insults, imputations — Miss Juliet Armstrong was evidently unable to restrain her sense of humor. Suddenly she uttered a gay laugh, which enraged Miss Bassick to the last degree. As they had entered the grounds, however, the interview came to an end, and the maidens separated without further words.

Mr. Ruggles, lying concealed behind a thick clump of cedars on the side of the road opposite the trysting-place, had heard nothing that was said. But then he had witnessed everything, and his sharp glances left nothing in doubt. He had heard the report in Piedmont that Mr. Lascelles was engaged to be married to Miss Armstrong, and the attitude of the gentleman and his companion, as they sat upon the rocks, clearly showed that the report was correct. The minor circumstance that he mistook Miss Bassick for Miss Armstrong was natural, but not important. Mr. Ruggles gazed at the romantic couple and smiled; remained in his place of concealment until Mr. Lascelles and the ladies had disappeared, and then, emerging in the dusk, went back to Piedmont.

Having shut himself up in his room, he proceeded to write a note. This note was brief, but very much to the point. It contained these words:

"Miss Armstrong, — An unknown friend takes this means of putting you on your guard. Don't marry Mr. Douglas Lascelles, of Wye. He is a forger, and has one wife living!"

Having placed this communication in an envelope, and directed it to "Miss

Armstrong, Trianon, near Piedmont," he put on his hat and went and deposited it in the post-office; and half an hour afterward old William came and bore it off with the rest of Mrs. Armstrong's letters to Trianon—the mail having arrived in the stage a short time before. Mr. Ruggles was lounging at the post-office when Mrs. Armstrong's mail was asked for. He saw his letter handed to the old servant. Then he sauntered back, with a smile on his lips, to the tavern.

———◆———

LXIV.

THE OLD CHAPEL.

THE "Old Chapel" was a well-known edifice in the Piedmont neighborhood. It was the ancient stone church, on the slope of the mountain, near which Mouse and the Lefthander had met their friends on the morning after the scenes at the circus.

It was built of limestone, and had a venerable appearance. There were old-fashioned folding-doors on three of the sides, brushed by hanging boughs, a gallery at one end, ranges of straight-backed pews, a cylindrical stove in the middle aisle, and a lofty pulpit, with a sounding-board above it, flanked by two small square windows. The other windows were lofty, and closed by solid shutters. There was no paint about the building—if there ever had been, it had disappeared. The edifice dated back to the times of the earliest settlers in the region, and looked down from the little plateau on the side of the mountain—a venerable relic of the past. Once a year service was held in it by Mr. Grantham, to whose parish it belonged. He loved the spot very much, as his friend Bishop Meade had loved it, and it was equally dear to his parishioners. In the graveyard, enclosed by a stone wall and overshadowed by weeping-willows and sycamores, were buried the ancestors of half of the families of the neighborhood. You could trace out the familiar names—and some of them were famous—on the mossy slabs, half covered by the luxuriant growth of ivy and myrtle, instep deep. It was a sort of pious pilgrimage which the good people of the little parish made once a year to the Old Chapel. They were not willing to have it moulder away. A little attention would prevent that, for the stone-work was still solid and enduring. So service was still held there, and the parishioners made it a point of duty to attend: it was only once a year. If they went thither oftener it was in a long procession of carriages, with a black vehicle in front, moving slowly up the mountain road: some member of the little community, a gray-haired elder or little blossom, was going to sleep beside the dear ones already there.

One bright Sunday morning of early December the annual service was held at the Old Chapel. The "Indian summer" had come and the fall lingered still, and as it often does in Virginia until January. The mild air caressed and did not chill. A low whisper in the few dry leaves still clinging to the trees seemed the murmurous farewell of autumn as it departed.

The old house of worship was filled at an early hour. Ellis Grantham was going to preach his first sermon. He had reached home on the week before, a newly-made deacon, and this would be the first time he had risen to address a congregation; so the attendance from Piedmont, where the young man was a great favorite, was very large, and persons were also present from the whole neighborhood, including Bohemia. Mr. Cary and Frances were seated in the body of the church, not far from Brantz Elliot and Nelly and Daddy Welles. General Lascelles and his family occupied a pew near them, and Mrs. Armstrong and Juliet sat in front of them. In the gallery were Mouse, Harry, and the Lefthander; Gentleman Joe having remained at home to look after the establishment. Just in front of the preacher was seen the portly form of the United States marshal who had made the night descent on the moonshiners. He had reached the town on the day before, and was waiting for the arrival of a detachment of cavalry, it was reported. Meanwhile, like a respectable citizen, he attended public worship.

Ellis read the service clearly and distinctly, and preached a very good sermon. It was remarkable for the absence of ambitious rhetoric, and was conversational rather than declamatory. His gesture rose naturally from the feeling, and was an aid. His views were Low-Church, and were very far from implying that confession to a priest and absolution refilled the lamp of grace, a part of whose oil had been spilled by sinful stumbling. These fancies, and that other, that the priest must refill the lamp before death, or the bearer of it would be shut out, were very ridiculous, and very offensive to him, the preacher. It all arose from the absurdity of regarding the priest as more than a man. He was simply an ecclesiastical official with prescribed duties. To speak of his forgiving sin was monstrous, and a relic of superstition. Those who thought so had better go to Rome at once. No man could be a mediator. There had been one Mediator and High-priest, who had offered sacrifice once for all. There was no more sacrifice now; that was done with. All that was needed now was faith in Him, and good works, as an evidence that the faith was a living faith.

His sermon was short, and the blessing was pronounced by Mr. Grantham. Then the congregation began to talk; for the people of the Piedmont parish talked after service. It may even be said that they talked enormously—both very fast and very loud, as well as very long. There was so much to say : they had not seen each other for a whole week! And then had they not—as a writer in the *Southern Churchman* had said of country congregations — come to church "to see and be seen?" This was a fearful accusation to bring against the young ladies and gentlemen, but it certainly looked very much like it. The maidens certainly did go to and fro through the aisles, gesticulating, exclaiming, and beaming on all around them. But then that was natural; had not the preacher talked at *them* for an hour, and was it not their turn now?

The elders indulged in friendly greetings outside the church. Here the tall form of old General Lascelles towered above his neighbors, and with his hearty smile, and warm grasp of the hand for everybody, he was a notable figure. He accosted Daddy Welles with the air of an old acquaintance, and pointed to the United States marshal with a smile. The Daddy smiled sweetly in return and nodded.

"You had better be on your guard," said the general. "There is going to be trouble."

"Trouble, did you say, gineral?" Daddy Welles asked, with an innocent air. "Oh no! I hope there won't be any trouble."

"Don't be too certain of it, old friend."

"We can't be certain of anything in this miser'ble world, gineral, onless it's one thing—the have-his-carcass."

But the general shook his head.

"Don't count on that, Daddy," he said, in a low tone. "Any law question that comes up in this business will be decided in the United States District Court, not in our own."

"And does that make a difference, gineral? Ain't the have-his-carcass law in all the courts?"

"There is not much law in the United States District Court, unless it is martial law. Once Virginia was a sovereign State, and her rights were inviolate; now every little judge clothed in the Federal ermine openly sneers at the idea that we have any rights. Only one thing is left —to arrest our old Virginia judges, and issue an order that there shall be no more State courts in the commonwealth, unless negroes preside in them."

"Well, well—but the Virginia people won't stand that long, gineral."

"I hope not. But take care of yourself in the mean while, Daddy Welles."

"I'll try, gineral."

"I am coming to Bohemia to-morrow —to your house. Get our friends together; I want to talk to them."

"About the business?"

The general nodded.

"It will be best not to have any trouble. You see the marshal is here already, and there he is coming up to speak to me."

Daddy Welles did not retire at this intimation; he only smiled. The marshal came up and looked keenly at him.

"I remember you," he said, coldly; "your name is Welles."

"The same, friend."

"So you are a church-goer?"

"I mostly go to meetin' somewheres on Sunday."

"And break the laws all the week, depending for safety on your State courts!"

Daddy Welles smiled, and gazed at the marshal with a look of mild inquiry.

"Is there a law passed in Congress that we're to have no more State courts in Virginia, friend?" he asked.

The marshal frowned. The question was apparently innocent, but was embarrassing.

"And the have-his-carcass—has Congress done away with the have-his-carcass too?"

The marshal uttered a suppressed sound, which very much resembled an oath.

"Nothing of the sort! but the Federal Court has jurisdiction in your case, and you need not depend on it."

"Oh no! I won't depend on it, friend. I s'pose old Virginny 'll have to wait for better times, when the troops won't be sent for to decide law p'ints."

Having thus mildly expressed his hope for the future, Daddy Welles retired, and the marshal bowed to General Lascelles and said,

"I shall apply to you in a day or two for search-warrants, general, as before—in this matter of the illicit distilleries."

The general bowed, and said,

"I shall grant them, of course, sir—though I should think you might have applied to the district judge."

"He is not present."

"And I hope he will stay away as long as possible. Between a judge in a black coat sitting on a bench, and violating our State law, and a marshal acting under orders, with troops to support him, I prefer the marshal and troops—that is intelligible, at least."

The marshal bowed, and said, formally,

"The business is disagreeable; but, as you have said, I act under orders."

The general bowed in reply, and the marshal walked on. Soon afterward the congregation dispersed and returned home—all of them, at least, but a small group which lingered in the quiet church-yard, overgrown with myrtle and shaded by its large sycamores and willows. There was one great weeping-willow, especially, whose tassels reached down and brushed against the tombstones; and the little party, consisting of Harry and the Lefthander and Mouse, were looking at the quiet scene, and musing, before setting out on their return to Bohemia. Harry was thinking of the face of Frances Cary, as she stood, a rose-bud in the midst of rose-buds, in the aisle of the church, and never had she seemed so far away from him as at that moment. The Lefthander, who had seen Mr. Lascelles, wore a very gloomy expression. Mouse alone of the party looked quietly happy—Frances Cary had put her arms around her as she came out of church and kissed her, and Mouse loved her little hostess of Falling Water dearly, and was made happy by the kiss.

The child wandered about, reading the inscriptions on the tombstones. There were a number of little grassy mounds marked by small head-stones. These were the graves of children, but they did not seem to make Mouse sad. She smiled as she read the names, "Little Lucy" or "Our Annie," and said,

"I think it would be nice to be buried here, poppa—don't you?"

"Yes," the Lefthander replied, "it is a very good place."

"Hear the wind in the willow! Maybe the dead people hear it too."

"Doubtful," was his reply; "they don't hear much that is going on. But stop this talking about being buried, Mignon. If they bury you, they'll have to leave room for me not far off from you."

"Of course," said Mouse—"or for me beside you."

"But that won't be here. We'll get up the troupe soon, and go away."

Mouse looked at Harry and smiled.

"I am acquainted with a young gentleman who's not anxious to go away," she observed; then leaning over she whispered, "Forgive me, Harry, I didn't mean to make you blush so!"

After strolling through the old graveyard, carpeted with myrtle, for a little while longer, the party then set out for home, following the road through the Gap.

The Lefthander walked on with his head bent down, and the same moody expression which of late had become common with him. It was an expression of hesitation and doubt — that of the man who is puzzled to determine upon his course in some important matter. The singular part of it was that this expression grew deeper and more intense whenever he mentioned or encountered Mr. Lascelles.

LXV.

JULIET'S SECRET.

HAVING returned from service at the Old Chapel, Mrs. Armstrong proceeded to dine, and then repaired to the drawing-room, whither Juliet followed her.

There was a very great contrast between their expressions. Mrs. Armstrong was restless, moody, evidently displeased, and "out of sorts" generally. From time to time she patted the carpet impatiently, almost angrily, with her small foot in its handsome boot, and the inner extremities of her eyebrows were much too close together to indicate tranquillity. Juliet, on the contrary, had never seemed more composed. Her pretty face, to use an ambitious simile, resembled a rose-tinted evening sky without a cloud upon it. There was not the least shadow in her limpid eyes, and she leaned back in her arm-chair and looked at the fire with the air of a person at peace with all the world.

"It really is unendurable!" said Mrs. Armstrong, at last; "can he call himself a gentleman, I wonder?"

"Who is he, mamma?" said Juliet, with extreme tranquillity.

"Mr. Lascelles! How can he reconcile it with common decency to behave as he does?"

"I am not sure that I understand you."

"At church to-day he did not come near you, or even so much as bow to you. It is disgraceful! Here is the whole neighborhood connecting your name with his own—you are reported to be engaged—and he does not even speak to you!"

Juliet smiled. She had said nothing to her mother of the scene in the woods; but Mrs. Armstrong was quite cognizant of the preference of Mr. Lascelles for Miss Bassick, and was slightly illogical in her present views. If Mr. Lascelles were not Juliet's suitor but Miss Bassick's, why should the lady regard his demeanor as a matter of any importance? For the sake of appearances? Yes, no doubt, for the sake of appearances. Miss Juliet therefore smiled, and as she had a good deal of humor under her calm exterior, said,

"I suppose Mr. Lascelles was moody and unhappy from not seeing Miss Bassick at church. You know when people are in his state of mind they often neglect the little forms of courtesy."

Mrs. Armstrong rose erect in her chair. "Good heavens, Juliet! I really am out of patience!" she exclaimed.

"I would not be if I were you, mamma. You mean with me, I suppose."

"Yes, my dear; I cannot help it. You really seem to have no pride at all."

"We have discussed that before, mamma—don't let us return to it. I will say again, however, that I have a great deal, and that it is a matter of indifference to me whether Mr. Lascelles is polite to me or the reverse. Why should I care?"

"But think, my dear! The whole neighborhood are talking of you. Common decency, I say, would prompt *a gentleman* to act differently. Everybody noticed it, and I saw that hateful Miss Grundy nodding, and smirking, and giggling to her horrid Piedmont friends; they are all low people: she saw Mr. Lascelles pass near you without turning his head, and to-morrow it will be all over the neighborhood."

"Very well, mamma."

Juliet spoke with great composure, as she understood tolerably well what caused Mr. Lascelles to shun her—the very unpleasant meeting in the woods.

"My *dear* Juliet, for heaven's sake don't say 'well, mamma,' to everything!" exclaimed her mother.

"It expresses precisely what I feel," Juliet said. "I mean that I am perfectly well satisfied to have Mr. Lascelles bow to me or not bow, come to see me or not come to see me—though I should very much prefer that, under all the circumstances, he would not do so. As to his manner to me in public, that is really a matter of very little importance, mamma."

Mrs. Armstrong groaned; then she said,

"Fortunately people may think that you have discarded him, and that you have quarrelled on that account."

"I hope they will not. You know I have not discarded Mr. Lascelles—if anything, he has discarded me!"

Juliet smiled sweetly, and added,

"He feels badly, no doubt—I mean, ill at ease with me—as he must see that the atmosphere of Trianon has cooled in some degree."

"So this is the last of everything—the end!" exclaimed Mrs. Armstrong, in a tragic voice.

"It really seems so, mamma, and I am very glad of it. I have a great many reasons for preferring not to receive any more visits from Mr. Lascelles. I have not spoken of these reasons, and perhaps I was wrong in not doing so. Shall I tell you all of them at once, now, and have no more secrets from you?"

"Secrets! Have you secrets from your poor unhappy mamma, Juliet?"

It was a pathetic wail, like the former—here was a new misery.

"Yes, mamma; at least, I have delay-

ed telling you something. Until this moment I have never had secrets, really, or concealed anything. I have only chosen my time to speak as I do now."

"What *can* you mean, my child? Is there anything dreadful coming?" Mrs. Armstrong cried.

"Something very disagreeable, if you think of it as I do."

"What *is* it?"

"I met Miss Bassick and Mr. Lascelles in the woods the other evening—embracing."

"Embracing! I knew it—I knew it was true!"

"It was an accident, and there was an *éclaircissement*—it was unavoidable. Mr. Lascelles is engaged to be married, it seems, to Miss Bassick, and I am obliged, therefore, to give him up, whether I wish to do so or not."

Mrs. Armstrong gasped. Words seemed to fail her. Her lips moved, and probably essayed to utter the phrase "Go on," but there was no sound.

"That is one good reason for not regarding Mr. Lascelles in the light of a suitor," continued Juliet, "and there is another."

She drew from her pocket the letter written by Mr. Ruggles, in which that gentleman characterized Mr. Lascelles as a forger, with one wife living. Juliet read it aloud, and added,

"Of course I do not believe that there is any truth in it. There rarely is any, I suppose, in anonymous letters, as the persons writing them indicate their own characters by not signing them. But still, it is not agreeable, mamma, to receive attentions from a gentleman of whom such things *can* be said by anybody. I meant to send this note to Mr. Lascelles, but thought I would first show it to you."

Mrs. Armstrong took the letter, and read it with an imbecile expression.

"A forger!—one wife living!" she gasped.

"So you see it would be very imprudent for me to marry Mr. Lascelles under any circumstances, mamma."

"Good heavens!"—this was a tragic

expression much used by Mrs. Armstrong—"and the creature is to pollute this mansion again with his presence!"

"Perhaps he will not do so."

"He is coming to-morrow. I requested a private interview at church to-day."

"A private interview, mamma?"

"I meant to demand an explanation," gasped Mrs. Armstrong, exhibiting indications of falling into hysterics—"to have a full understanding with him—and he will be here."

Juliet mused for a few moments, and then said,

"Perhaps it is very well that you did make the appointment. It is due to Mr. Lascelles that he should be informed of the contents of this letter without delay—that is only justice and common courtesy. He will come, and it can be given to him. I need not say who is the proper person to do so."

"The proper person?"

"Miss Bassick. As she is engaged to be married to Mr. Lascelles, this note concerns her more than any one else. She would no doubt object to becoming wife No. 2. I shall therefore give her the note, to be transmitted to Mr. Lascelles, and as you can *now* have no desire to come to an explanation with him, Miss Bassick can take your place, and arrange her own affairs."

Mrs. Armstrong sunk back in her chair, looking so utterly bewildered and helpless that Juliet, who had spoken in an accent of lurking humor and enjoyment of the little comedy to be enacted, felt really sorry for her, and rose and went to her side.

"There, there, mamma, don't take everything so seriously," she said, smoothing her hair gently and pressing her lips to her cheek. She then sat down on the cricket at her mother's feet, and, leaning one arm on the lady's knees, looked up into her face. Her mother bent down and kissed her.

"There was something else to tell you, mamma," said Juliet, coloring slightly.

"Something else?" faltered Mrs. Armstrong.

"Something much more important than anything I have yet told you, mamma. There is a more serious reason than all the rest why I do not wish to marry Mr. Lascelles, and am quite willing that Miss Bassick should, if she wishes."

"What reason?"

"I am engaged to be married to Ellis Grantham," said Juliet, with two blush-roses suddenly blooming in her cheeks.

"Engaged!—to Ellis Grantham!"

"You are not sorry, are you, mamma? Don't say you are sorry—"

Juliet's head sunk a little, and the queen-like young lady suddenly became only a shrinking and pleading girl.

"Don't say you are sorry, mamma!—I love him so much."

Mrs. Armstrong thereupon succumbed and burst into tears. She hugged the young lady to her bosom, kissed her in a wild and tragic manner, and with sobs and gasps said she never could part with her darling—which was singular, as she had been willing to part with the darling to Mr. Lascelles.

"Ellis Grantham!" she exclaimed; "*engaged* to him! Oh, Juliet."

"You know you love him, mamma," Juliet said, in a low tone. "You have said so a hundred times: was it so wrong in your daughter to love him too?"

Juliet smiled as she said this, raising a moist pair of eyes and a pair of blushing cheeks.

"I meant to tell you all about it before, mamma, but there was really very little to tell. You know Ellis came to see us very often, and—and—it happened—I mean, he grew to like me. He did not tell me so, but he told Anna Gray, and made her his confidante, and Anna made no secret of it; you know how intimate we are. When Ellis went away he asked me to correspond with him, and you agreed that I should do so, you remember. That is all, mamma."

Juliet quietly dried her eyes, in an unobtrusive way, with her handkerchief, and looked up with a smile.

"And the engagement took place by letter?" said Mrs. Armstrong, in a dazed way.

"Yes, mamma. It was very foolish in Ellis, as he was coming home so soon. But he begged me so, and said so much about sparing me the pain of a refusal face to face with him, that I gave up, and wrote back that I would marry him if you approved of it. Not now, mamma —when he is ordained; and some day he will become Mr. Grantham's assistant—"

"And you will spend your life here, and never go to Paris!" gasped the poor lady.

"Go to Paris? I don't want to go to Paris in the least, mamma. The Piedmont neighborhood is charming," said this very inconsistent young lady.

"Why, you said it was fearfully dull!"

"I must have been jesting."

"But to give you up—my own, my beloved child!"

"I shall live much nearer to you than I should have lived at Wye."

This reply, which Juliet uttered with a slight smile upon her lips, quite dismounted Mrs. Armstrong's logical artillery.

"Of course, I never will marry without your approval, dear mamma," said the girl, in her sweet, earnest voice, "and I wrote Ellis so. But you will approve of it—won't you? He is so good—and I love him so much, mamma."

When she told her mother good-night that night, Juliet kissed her and said,

"I knew you loved Ellis, mamma, and would not object, and he will love you dearly—but he never can love you as much as I do."

LXVI.

MRS. ARMSTRONG'S GREAT BLOW.

"You will be good enough, if you please, to look for another home, Miss Bassick — I would suggest your friend Miss Grundy's as a congenial retreat. Under all the circumstances, I should prefer your not remaining longer at Trianon."

Mrs. Armstrong uttered these words about an hour after her interview with Juliet, who had gone to her chamber.

The lady and Miss Bassick were seated opposite each other in the drawing-room. It was not Miss Bassick's habit to seat herself in Mrs. Armstrong's presence without being invited, but she had done so on this occasion with an easy air, which seemed to say, "Well, you have sent for me, I am ready to listen to you." Indeed, her whole bearing had changed. She was no longer the submissive companion, but quite a different person. She leaned back gracefully in her red velvet arm-chair, and quietly awaited the coming storm. The storm was coming, she felt, for no doubt Juliet had related to her mother the comic incident in the woods; but then that was unimportant: she had triumphed, since Mr. Lascelles was her *fiancé*. This ill-tempered old woman might rage, but that would do no harm; and it was even with a sort of enjoyment that she anticipated what was apparently approaching.

In response to Mrs. Armstrong's suggestion that she should seek for a new home, Miss Bassick said,

"I will do so with pleasure, madam, as anything is better than to live with a person so very disagreeable as yourself!"

Miss Bassick smiled and looked straight at Mrs. Armstrong as she uttered these words. She evidently expected an explosion, but none took place.

"I am glad there is no difference of opinion, then, in reference to what is best for you in future, Miss Bassick," said the lady.

"There is none at all, madam. Trianon is perfectly hateful to me. I should not like to be married from your house if I could avoid it."

"You are to be married to Mr. Lascelles, I hear."

"Yes, madam — at New-year. The match, I hope, is agreeable to you?"

"Perfectly."

"We will go to Paris in the spring. Until that time Mr. Lascelles will remain at Wye."

Mrs. Armstrong inclined her head and made no reply. Miss Bassick was much disappointed. There was to be no storm after all, then; and that fact greatly diminished the sweets of triumph. She began to grow irritated.

"I have informed you of my approaching marriage," she said, "as an explanation of what Juliet witnessed the other evening—an interview between myself and Mr. Lascelles, when I accidentally met him as I was walking out. He was holding my hand, which I should not have permitted him to do if we had not been engaged. During my conversation with Mr. Lascelles Juliet stole up and listened, which I must say I think was very dishonorable."

Miss Bassick looked at Mrs. Armstrong. Every word she had uttered, and even the omission of *Miss* before Juliet's name, was plainly meant as a provocation.

"I say *dishonorable*," added Miss Bassick, "for it is nothing less than that to lurk and eavesdrop, and go and report what is seen and heard—and a great deal more. Juliet did so on this occasion, though I suppose she will deny it."

"Is it possible?" said Mrs. Armstrong. "I had supposed that Juliet was an honorable person. It is melancholy to have a daughter who could be guilty of such conduct. You must overlook it, Miss Bassick—but you will, no doubt, do so. Yes, poor Juliet—from jealousy, no doubt —must have exaggerated what took place. Indeed, she went so far as to say you were in Mr. Lascelles's arms."

"It is a falsehood—a vile falsehood!" said Miss Bassick, yielding to maiden indignation.

"So you were merely conversing with him: the meeting was accidental, no doubt, like that which took place in the drawing-room that evening."

Mrs. Armstrong smiled, and the smile stung Miss Bassick exceedingly.

"You are all spies!" she cried. "It is disgraceful in persons pretending to good-breeding."

"Don't become excited, Miss Bassick," Mrs. Armstrong said. "Your color is not becoming. You must pardon poor Juliet!—think how much mortified she must be at the preference of Mr. Lascelles

for yourself. You are to be married at New-year? That is not very far off now. Will the ceremony take place in church, and the wedding-supper be at Miss Grundy's? I will make out your account, as you will naturally want money for your trousseau. Let me see, this is the 10th—would it be convenient to you to be with Miss Grundy by the 15th?"

"Yes, madam; I will go at once—and she shall know, and the whole town shall know, why I have left your house."

"You do not refer to the meetings in the woods as the reason?"

"Take care how you insult me, Mrs. Armstrong!" cried Miss Bassick, in a fury.

"Insult you?" said Mrs. Armstrong: "you really are not worth insulting, Miss Bassick. You are perfectly at liberty to injure my character or Juliet's by any means in your power or Miss Grundy's, if you can. Do enjoy yourself as much as possible by maligning me to the common people in Piedmont, and afterward in your more elevated sphere at Wyc. Juliet and I will endeavor to survive it. And now, as that is arranged, Miss Bassick, and we have had a frank talk, suppose we terminate this interview."

"Not until I tell you my opinion of you!" cried Miss Bassick, furiously.

Mrs. Armstrong smiled. She was a very quiet and determined person when she restrained her temper.

"I really don't see what advantage there could be in your doing so," she said; "and I should be tempted to tell you my opinion of yourself, which might not be flattering."

Mrs. Armstrong rose negligently.

"By-the-bye, here is something which Mr. Lascelles ought to see," she said, giving Miss Bassick the anonymous letter. "The writer of this note speaks of him as a forger, with a wife living. It is no doubt a slander, but, of course, he should be informed of the charge. You might give him the note when he comes to-morrow morning. Juliet is going to see her friend Frances Cary, and I am afraid I shall have a headache. You and Mr.

Lascelles will, therefore, have an opportunity to talk over your affairs at your leisure, as you will have the drawing-room entirely to yourselves — which will be more agreeable, I suppose, than the woods."

It was Mrs. Armstrong's great blow. The consciousness that she was going to deliver it had enabled her to pass tranquilly through this very trying interview. It was a cruel *coup*, but the lady struck it without mercy. Had not this creature made herself and Juliet the laughing-stock of everybody? Had not Mr. Lascelles by her intrigues been wiled away and appropriated? Miss Bassick had resorted to trick and deception up to a certain point; then, finding that the game was in her hands, she threw off the mask. She triumphed, and did not take the least trouble to conceal her triumph. What could she expect?

Mrs. Armstrong's revenge was unchristian, and not particularly appropriate to the Sabbath afternoon—but it was sweet. Sweetest of all was the expression of Miss Bassick's face, as she seized the letter and ran her eyes over it. As the twilight had come, she went hastily to the window to read it, nearly turning her back on the lady.

"A forger—married already! It is a falsehood — a base lie!" she said, in a husky voice, in which there was an intonation of fury almost.

"So your wedding will have to be deferred, after all," said Mrs. Armstrong, laughing.

"Married!"

Miss Bassick's pretty brows were knit together, and her eyes were like two coals of fire.

"It is unfortunate, and Mr. Lascelles ought to have mentioned the little circumstance, I think," Mrs. Armstrong said, smiling. "He no doubt lost sight of it, though it seems singular that he should have forgotten it. As this is not Utah, it is not customary for a gentleman to have two wives at the same time. The great objection to marrying Mr. Lascelles is, that the lady who espouses him in second nuptials will occupy a very peculiar position; in fact, she will not be a wife at all—respectable people will not visit her, and, worse even than that, the law would interfere, and make the whole affair exceedingly unpleasant."

Miss Bassick was still glaring at the letter, and did not reply.

"That is your affair, however," Mrs. Armstrong added, laughing a little. "You are quite at liberty to marry somebody else's husband if you wish, as the ceremony is not going to take place at Trianon."

Miss Bassick whirled around like a tigress about to spring. Mrs. Armstrong was sauntering negligently from the apartment.

On the next day Miss Bassick left Trianon.

LXVII.

GENTLEMAN JOE TELLS NELLY THE WIND'S STORY.

BOHEMIA was in all its glory. Not the glory of the summer, when the slopes of the mountain and the banks of Falling Water were clothed in dense foliage full of the songs of birds; nor yet the glory of the autumn, when the fading days touched the forests hour by hour with a deeper yellow and crimson; but the glory, sweeter and sadder if not so picturesque, of the wonderful Indian Summer, which restores to early winter, if not the tender leaflets, at least the faint, sweet charm of the spring days and the childhood of the year.

This magical season had descended upon the little valley of Bohemia; and the remote region, nestling down in the embrace of the mountain, seemed to be steeped in a dreamy languor. Nature remembers and dreams as well as human beings. Look at the silent trees and the rock-ribbed slopes—they are waiting, you would say, for something, and musing over the past days. Sometimes you may hear a low rustling in the few dead leaves, though no wind is stirring. The country people will tell you—and with truth—

that the sound foretells snow. But the trees are really laughing and whispering to each other. That acacia with the lanceolated leaves and the sharp black thorns is in a reverie. Stretch out your finger and touch it—you interrupt it, and it shrinks back. And then the water of the stream yonder in the deep hollow between the high banks—surely you hear it talking to the moss-covered rocks, over which the broad-leaved flags are leaning, waiting as the silent trees wait for something that is coming.

The sunshine was a mild splendor in the air, and just revealed the dim headlands. A faint smoke hovered over them, and in the distance the blue ranges melted away into it. Far up some white clouds were drifting across the delicate blue, and the trailing shadows passed slowly along the side of the mountain—not galloping now, as they used to do in August, but making their way quietly, as though they had the whole day before them, and would arrive in time at some mysterious rendezvous in the mountain gorges.

"They don't laugh at me now—I used to think they were laughing at me," said Gentleman Joe, who was walking along the banks of the Falling Water with Nelly. "I mean the cloud shadows;—look at that one coming. He is going to tell me something."

"Now, Gentleman Joe," said Nelly, looking at the old fellow affectionately, and addressing him as if he were a child, "you promised me you would not talk so about the poor shadows, and the pine-trees and all. How can they tell you anything? They are only shadows, and leaves moving in the wind."

"In the wind? Yes, they move in the wind, my dear," said Gentleman Joe, smiling. "That explains the whole matter; it is not the shadows that really talk, or the leaves either—it is the wind. Did you never hear the voice of the wind? I have heard it often. Sometimes it laughs, then it growls. When it whispers in the tulip-trees, as the bell-flowers are opening in the spring, it is in a good-humor—it is telling the tulips about the south, where it has been travelling, and the orange groves. But in winter it is very different. Have you never listened to it when it was roaring around the gables in the cold, dark nights? It is angry then, and will tear up trees or blow people over precipices if they trifle with it."

"Oh, Gentleman Joe! why *should* you take up all these fancies? Indeed, it is not good for you."

"Fancies? They are not fancies, my dear; and really it does me no harm. I have nothing to say to the wind when it is in a bad humor—I wait. After awhile it gets over that and we have long talks. It has told me a number of strange things in my life. The strangest of all was what it told me only yesterday."

"What did it tell you?"

Gentleman Joe shook his head and fell into a fit of musing.

"It was a very curious story, indeed," he said, after awhile. "Do you think you would like to hear it?"

Nelly hesitated. She did not like to encourage poor Gentleman Joe in his vague wanderings, and was about to say that he had better tell her something else, when he added,

"It is about Crow's Nest, and somebody who once lived there."

"About Crow's Nest?"

"And old times there," said Gentleman Joe, dreamily. "It is a very strange story. If you would like to hear it I will tell you about it, Nelly. I really can't get it out of my mind or understand it—perhaps you may; and then you might tell me, you know, Nelly."

Nelly looked at him closely as he uttered these words. His voice was exceedingly sad. Would it not be a relief to him to unburden his mind? It might be.

"Well, tell me what you thought the wind said, Gentleman Joe."

"Thought? I did not *think* the wind told me. It really told me; and it was not very friendly, either, in the wind—it has made me rather sorrowful, for it is a sorrowful—a very sorrowful story. 'I remember Crow's Nest,' the wind began, 'in very old times. It was part of a great estate which once covered half of Bohemia and extended beyond; but in course of time the Bohemian part, all but the Crow's Nest farm, was sold, and at last there were two brothers who inherited the whole property.' Do you understand that, Nelly?"

"Yes," she said.

"Well, the eldest took one part of the property, and the youngest the Crow's Nest farm. It had a small house upon it—a very small one—but the land was good, and the owner set about improving it. Then he fell in love with and married a young girl of the neighborhood. She was very beautiful, and he loved her dearly; but then she was beneath him, as people say: she was an orphan, and her father had been scarcely more than a laborer."

"Yes, Gentleman Joe."

Nelly was listening with great attention now, and wondering a little at the lucid and connected narrative, divested of everything like extravagance, which the old fellow was presenting.

"That made trouble," he went on, with his head drooping—"a great deal of trouble. Her husband loved her with all his soul, but his fine relations turned their backs on her. They had tried to dissuade him when they heard of his intention to marry her, but as he loved her he only laughed at them, and turned his back on *them*. What was it to the man who loved her so much whether she was a king's daughter or a peasant's? She was herself, which was enough, and he only loved her more dearly when others looked down upon her, as he ought to have done. He was a gentleman—if he had not done so he would not have been a gentleman."

"Yes," said Nelly, in a low tone, thinking of what Frances Cary had said of Brantz Elliot.

"Well, the time passed on," continued Gentleman Joe, "and his family never came to see them or took any notice of them. There was one person who did—his brother, who had never interfered at all in his marriage. He was a very good brother, not at all like the chattering, gabbling women, who rolled their eyes and shook their heads, and would have nothing to do with the poor fellow who had disgraced the family by his low marriage. He and his brother never had an unkind word, but the poor husband was ill at ease. He was suspicious, perhaps, and thought that his brother, too, looked down on his wife. So he grew cool to him—and he, no doubt, saw it, and the visits became fewer and fewer. At last they stopped, and the owner of Crow's Nest was left to himself and his quiet days in Bohemia.

"They were very bright days. He was married to one he loved better than he loved his life. He loved the ground she walked upon. He would take her slipper, sometimes, and kiss it because it had the shape of her foot. You can't understand that. It is the way a man loves when he is in love with a good woman. What she touches or what touches her is sacred and beautiful. As to bad or foolish women —and there are a great number of that sort—the handsomer they are the more disagreeable they are; the very sight of the things they wear is distasteful, since the wearer has given them the shape of her person."

Gentleman Joe looked moody, and a singular expression of disdain quite changed his whole face. Then the vague and dreamy look came back to his face, and he said,

"They were very happy at Crow's Nest, the young husband and the one he loved. What did he care for the people who never came to see him? One face was enough—the face of his wife. Then another face came—there was a little baby that prattled and held out its small rosy arms, and crowed and nestled close, and made its father and mother much happier than they had ever been before. But trouble was coming too—life is full of that. He was not what is called a business man — I mean the owner of Crow's Nest. His head was bad for managing, and his farm went down, and he fell into trouble. But that was really nothing. The world laughs at you and slights you when you are poor and in need; but what does it matter if you can go home and feel the arms of your wife and child around your neck, and see them smile on you? You laugh back at the world then; but it will not do to laugh too much. It is a hard, cruel world, and in the end, if you don't take care, it turns the laugh on *you* and crushes you. You might stand that yourself, perhaps, but there are the others—the helpless ones. It is hard for them. They leave us sometimes, and then they are happier."

Gentleman Joe looked up as he uttered these words. It was either at the clouds or at something or some one he saw beyond them.

"One day she went away from him— I mean the poor man's wife," he continued, in a very low tone. "She was his angel—it was natural, therefore, that she should become an angel of God. She was almost a child when he married her and when she died. A fever carried her off suddenly, and she died in his arms, with her head resting upon his breast."

Nelly sobbed. As to Gentleman Joe, his expression was that of a human being who has shed all the tears he is capable of shedding.

"Well, he longed for death," he said, "but it would not come. A dull stupor followed, and he fell into despair. But Heaven was merciful, after all, since it took away his memory, and his reason with it."

"His reason?"

"Yes, he lost his reason. Poor man, I wonder if he ever got it back! He used to sit in the chair she had sat in, dreaming of old scenes and seeing the face of his dead wife. He was not in his right mind then. He wanted to die, but he did not think of taking his own life. There was his child, and he wished to see his wife again—he will see her!"

He raised his head and looked upward as before, his eyes fixed and full of vague longing. Nelly sobbed, and gazed at him with a startled expression.

"Gentleman Joe, what are you telling me?" she exclaimed.

"The God's truth—just what the wind told me, Nelly. I've nearly done now. Must I go on?"

"Yes, yes!"

"Something had to be done—there was the little one, and the dead mother; they were all three alone. The poor man only moaned, and broke his heart with longing—longing for the lips, and eyes, and the voice he was not going to hear any more. He sat there thinking in this way, or trying to think; but it crazed him. He was waked suddenly. His boy was crying for bread!"

"Oh, how pitiful!" cried Nelly, with streaming eyes; "is it true, Gentleman Joe?"

"True? yes, it is God's own truth. His little boy was about four years old, and could not talk very plain. He said, 'I hung'y, papa!' and he cried, and the corners of his mouth were pulled down; and he put his arms up and hugged me around the neck, and I burst out crying for the first time."

"*You?* You speak of it as if *you* were the poor father, Gentleman Joe!"

"Did I? What could have made me do that, I wonder? I had nothing to do with it — the wind told it to me, and I thought you would like to hear it: it was only yesterday, while I was lying down under the big sycamore yonder. I may have dreamed it, as I was dozing; but I don't think I did. The wind told it, and it wouldn't take the trouble to tell me my own story."

Nelly Welles looked at the speaker with astonishment. What did all this mean? Was the poor victim of fantasy telling her a real history — his history? Could that be possible? He had often referred in his erratic talk to his familiarity with the scenes in Bohemia, around Crow's Nest and along the stream. Could it be possible that *he* was the poor husband and father? and was it only his fantastic imagination, the fancy of his disordered brain, that the wind had whispered the strange story to him, while all the time his own memory was dictating it? Full of wonder, and looking at him with a long, wistful glance, she listened, for the rest of his narrative, feeling vaguely that there would probably be some singular ending to so singular a revelation.

"Is that all?" she said, seeing that his glances were wandering, as if the whole subject had passed from his mind.

"Yes, Nelly — no, that was not all. There was the funeral. She was taken away from him while he sat looking at the floor — he could not move, but he heard the steps of men coming downstairs carrying something."

"Oh me!"

"That was sad for the poor man, but he scarcely felt it, as he was stunned. It was on the same evening that the little one came crying for bread, with his mouth pulled down. Then a neighbor came in, and touched my shoulder, and I saw he was crying. He went and got some bread, and called a servant to bring some milk, and when little Harry had finished eating he stooped down and kissed him. He was the uncle of the child, and a very good man — I could tell you his name. 'It won't do to leave the baby here,' he said, 'I am going to take him home with me.' When he said this the child's father sprung upon him and tore the boy from him. 'You shall not have my child!' he said. 'He is all I have left of her — you shall not take him!' The good neighbor tried to persuade him, but he would not listen to him, and the neighbor went away. 'I will come again to-morrow,' he said; 'it is better for the boy, as he cannot stay with you.' He then left the house, and the father sat down holding his child in his arms and trying to think. He was out of his mind, you see, but he understood one thing. They were going to take his boy from him; they should not do that; he would prevent them. Before morning he took his child in his arms and went away from Crow's Nest."

Nelly sobbed.

"And what became of him and his little boy?" she said.

Gentleman Joe put his hand to his forehead and tried to think. He was so much absorbed in this effort that he did not hear the sound of wheels approaching.

"Where did he go? That is hard, very hard to say."

He smiled sadly—it was a faint sunshine on the old face, but still a sort of sunshine. This sudden change of mood was one of the idiosyncrasies of his fantastic temperament.

"I can hardly tell you where the poor fellow did go, Nelly," he said: "to a great many places—in fact, almost everywhere."

The noise of wheels drew nearer, but either the laughter of the water or a sudden wind which blew from the mountain made the sound inaudible.

"He went on all day with his little boy in his arms," said Gentleman Joe, smiling, "and in the evening met a circus which had halted in a wood to feed the horses. Circus people are very kind, and they gave him plenty to eat. The big fellows danced the boy, and he pulled their beards and laughed. That made friends, and they joined the company, and stayed with it for a great many years, and—"

A carriage came out of the foliage within a few yards of them. It was the Wye coach with General Lascelles in it, on his way to Daddy Welles's, and as it had reached the foot of the ascent, the driver stopped to ask if that was the road.

This question was addressed to Gentleman Joe, but he took no notice of it. He was looking intently at General Lascelles, who was also looking fixedly at him. Gentleman Joe then walked up to the carriage with a bright smile upon his face, and said,

"How do you do, brother? Don't you know me? You have not forgotten Joe?"

General Lascelles looked at the speaker with profound astonishment. Then his face suddenly flushed, and tears rushed to his eyes. His whole frame shook, and with an unsteady hand he opened the door of the carriage and got out, trembling as he did so.

"I am very glad to see you, brother.

Did you think I was dead?" said Gentleman Joe.

General Lascelles, uttering a great sob, put his arms around the poor old fellow and drew him close to him.

"God be thanked!" he said, in a low voice; "this is the happiest day of my life, Joe!"

"Why, you are crying, brother!" said Gentleman Joe, smiling.

LXVIII.

A MEETING OF MOONSHINERS.

HALF an hour after this scene General Lascelles, Gentleman Joe, and Daddy Welles were shut up in the sitting-room of the small mountain-house, and the old master of Wye was listening with deep emotion to the story of his brother's adventures after his departure from Crow's Nest. The poor old ex-clown seemed to have waked up from his long night of hallucination, and evidently recalled now his whole past life and his own individuality. Was this the result of the sudden appearance of the face of his brother, which supplied the missing link in the chain of memory? It is difficult to say. It is always difficult, almost impossible to follow the operations of the mind diseased, and trace out the steps by which it returns to reason. A struggle was plainly going on in the brain of the poor man, as he had called himself; but happiness had evidently already worked an extraordinary change in him. His mind and memory had become lucid, if not strong yet.

The general was soon in possession of all the facts. His brother, as he had told Nelly, had married a young girl of very humble family—she had died, and he had gone away with his boy to avoid a separation from him. The person who wished to take the boy had been Daddy Welles, whose sister had been the wife of Gentleman Joe. When the old wanderer reappeared at Crow's Nest, Daddy Welles had at once recognized him; but it seemed impossible to separate him from his associates, and the attempt had not been made. Nor had Daddy Welles informed General Lascelles of his return. A lurking sentiment of pride deterred the mountaineer. Gentleman Joe's family had looked down upon him for his Welles alliance, and as the Daddy was a proud old fellow, after his fashion, he said nothing now. He liked General Lascelles personally, but would have him discover for himself that his brother and the boy were home again.

This came out during their conversation, and the general shook his head sorrowfully.

"That was a foolish thing for you to do, old friend," he said to Daddy Welles. "A man's brother is his brother, and Joe is the only brother I have. But let that go. Where is Harry, Joe? I am going to take you both to live with me at Wye."

But Gentleman Joe, who was smiling, shook his head.

"We can't leave Mouse, brother. Mouse and the Lefthander are old friends of ours, and we are very happy at Crow's Nest."

"But you can't stay in that cabin, Joe! I will never consent to that."

"It is a very good cabin, and I have been very happy there," said Gentleman Joe, gently.

"Impossible!" the general exclaimed. "Why, the house must be unfurnished. What became of all your effects—I mean the furniture of the house?"

"I really don't know," said Gentleman Joe, serenely.

"They are stored away here," Daddy Welles said; "I took care of them. The land was sold under a mortgage, you know —or perhaps you don't know, Gentleman Joe."

The general reflected, and then consulted with Daddy Welles. It seemed best for the present to leave Gentleman Joe and Harry at Crow's Nest. The furniture could be moved over, and the house made habitable, and in time the wanderers could be persuaded to come and live at Wye.

"I remember Wye; you know we played there when we were boys, brother," old Gentleman Joe said, cheerily. "I love the old place, and would like to see it again, but I never could leave Mouse and the Lefthander."

"Well, don't leave them, Joe; at least for the present," said General Lascelles, rising.

This movement was the result of the appearance of two or three horsemen in front of the house. These were Mr. Barney Jones and other gentlemen of the moonshine fraternity, summoned by Daddy Welles to meet the general, who was coming on this morning to have a talk with them. They dismounted and came into the yard, and the general and Daddy Welles went out and met them. Others were seen coming up the hill. They were a nondescript set, in outlandish costumes, evidently belonging to the class of small farmers and hunters. A glance at the faces was sufficient to show that they were not men of bad character. The sidelong look of the vagabond, conscious of being a vagabond, was wholly wanting. The eyes looked straight into your own, and the erect figures and firm steps were not the figures or steps of tramps or malefactors. Their moonshine business was illegal, certainly, but it was plain that they did not regard it as violating the deeper laws of morals.

General Lascelles was an old acquaintance of most of the moonshine people. He had ridden to and fro through the mountain, and the valley of Bohemia, electioneering for Congress, a long time before, and many of the persons who now greeted him had entertained him and voted for him. He was a popular man with them. His cordial manners and bonhomie had made friends of all classes. It was hard, in fact, to resist General Lascelles when he mingled with a crowd, holding his hand out to everybody, and calling everybody by his name. It was a natural gift, this cordiality; not calculation. He was friendly, and took an interest in people, and they were friendly to him in return.

The general at once proceeded to say what he had come to say. "The moon-shine business," he said, "was illegal, and had better be discontinued. There would be trouble, as the Government was bound to execute the laws, and, if civil process was not sufficient, to call in the military arm. For the law was the law. It might appear oppressive, but it was on the statute-book. He himself was a Virginian, and he was talking to Virginians. They knew him, and it was not necessary for him to say on which side he was. But if troops were sent, as it seemed they would be, there would be fighting if the business went on. That would be bad, for one side would wear blue and the other gray, and it would be better for all parties that Bohemia should not see any more of what took place there in old times. There would be a great deal of hot blood, and more dead men—which would be unfortunate. The best course would be to shut up the stills, and not be at home when the marshal came—"

Here a noise behind the crowd suddenly attracted their attention, and turning round they saw the United States marshal riding up, with three or four companions, to the gate.

General Lascelles ceased his discourse, fixing his eyes on the intruders. He was evidently displeased, and the marshal as plainly more so than himself. He dismounted, and made a sign to the rest to follow him. He then walked into the gate followed by the men, and approached the group of moonshiners.

"What is the meaning of this assemblage?" said the marshal, in an angry tone, addressing Daddy Welles.

"Why, good-day, friend," the Daddy said, cordially; "glad to see you. So you are back agin?"

"I asked the meaning of all this. I recognize in this crowd persons I know to be connected with illicit distilling. What does it mean? I ask you, General Lascelles—you can tell me, perhaps, and will do so if you have a decent respect for the law."

The marshal was growing angry, and spoke imperiously for that reason, perhaps. It was unfortunate, as well as unbecoming, however, that he should have adopted such a mode of address to a person like General Lascelles.

"I have more respect for the law than for some of its officers," said the general, bending his brows. "You ask what the meaning of this assembly is. I ask you in your turn what is the meaning of your presence here, sir?"

"I came to perform my duty."

"What do you mean by your duty?"

"To arrest law-breakers!—I see them all around me."

"By what warrant?"

"My orders are sufficient warrant, and I will not be intimidated, sir! I am not to be intimidated in the performance of my official duty."

"Where are your orders, sir?"

"I am not bound to show them to you, sir—unless you force me to arrest you."

The general frowned.

"I beg you will do so," he said. "Have you orders to read the riot act and fire on the crowd? I am one of them, and I warn you, if you attempt that, we will fire back on you."

"You resist the law!"

"You outrage it. By what authority do you attempt to disperse a meeting of Virginia people? Are we free men or slaves? I have come here to meet my friends, and they have come to meet me. We are talking with each other—is that a violation of law? I notify you, sir, that if you attempt to arrest any one without an express warrant, which you exhibit, it will be at your personal risk. I speak for myself, at least."

The general had not raised his voice, but he evidently meant what he said. A rifle was leaning against the porch by him, and he quietly took it up and cocked it.

"Where is your warrant," he said, "for arresting any person you meet? If it is formal authority I will submit, and test the question in the courts. If you act without authority, and attempt to arrest any one here, you will never leave this spot alive!"

There really seemed to be something in this threat. The visitors of Daddy Welles had brought their rifles with them, and deposited them in the passage of the house. Now they suddenly reappeared, and the crowd was armed in the twinkling of an eye.

"So you, a magistrate, abet the enemies of the law, sir!" shouted the marshal.

"I resist the absurdity of your demand that I shall not visit my friends, sir," retorted the general.

"These people are your friends, then?"

"Yes, they are my friends."

"They are law-breakers, and liable to arrest at any moment."

"Your authority, sir?"

"You yourself promised the search-warrants."

"Yes; why were they not applied for?"

"I visited your house and heard you had driven in this direction, and followed you."

"To make arrests, sir?"

"If necessary. I have the right to demand the warrants now."

Here Daddy Welles interposed.

"Gineral," he said, mildly—very mildly, indeed, for a man fingering a rifle trigger—"if you sign the sarch-warrants you won't mind signing a have-his-carcass too, will you?"

The marshal scowled at the Daddy, but said nothing. He had grown much calmer after some moments' reflection, and was really as much averse to any trouble as General Lascelles. This did not arise from a want of nerve—the marshal was quite a brave man; but he was really a very good-hearted man, and felt that he had acted precipitately.

"Well, sir," he said, at length, "I will not ask for the warrants to-day; I have searched this house, and I see it would be a farce to repeat the search this morning—I should do so at all hazards if I thought it my duty."

"You would be right," said the general.

"And you are right, sir, in intimating that a general order to arrest suspicious people is too loose—I acknowledge that.

It is my duty to inform those around me, however, that the illicit distilleries will be suppressed by military force, if necessary, and the persons engaged in the business arrested and brought to trial in the Federal courts."

"Without a have-his-carcass!" sighed Daddy Welles.

The marshal looked at Daddy Welles with a grim smile on his lips, and said,

"I'll get hold of you yet, you cunning old fox! Fox and goose now, and I am the goose, it seems. But in the long run the goose will get the better of the fox."

Having brought himself to take this philosophic view of the circumstances, the marshal scowled at the moonshiners, bowed stiffly to General Lascelles, who punctiliously returned his salute, and rode away with his associates.

Soon afterward the moonshiners dispersed also, the general renewing his advice to them to shut up the stills, and either leave home for a short time or remove all traces of their occupation. A vague murmur was the only reply to this advice: it was not plain what they were determined to do; and leaving the matter in this ambiguous condition, they retired.

The general, looking after them as they rode off, said to Daddy Welles,

"They are a hard set to manage—they will go their own gait, as the Scotch say. What will they do, Daddy Welles?"

"Well, I reckon they'll be guided by circum'unces, gineral," returned the Daddy.

"You mean they will fight."

"They mought, if they're pushed too close."

"It will be unlucky—and you will be one of the fighting men?"

"To be sure!" said Daddy Welles, cheerfully, "if there's fighting; but that's not likely. I'm gittin' old, now, and I'm a peaceful man, gineral; but you must make allowances for us poor mounting folks, that have wintered and summered the Yankee troopers in Bohemia. We don't like 'em much."

"Well, you and your friends had better get over that. Don't you remember what General Lee said to the lady who wished her sons to be educated to hate the Yankees?"

"What was that, gineral?"

"He said, 'Don't teach your sons to hate the United States, madam—we are all *Americans* now!'"

"Did the gineral say that?"

"Yes."

"Well, I thought he was a good old *Virginian*," said Daddy Welles, thoughtfully; "leastways *I* am, and I don't reckon I'll ever be anything else—I'm too old. But, then, a man can't tell; maybe some o' these days I'll git to be an *American*, as you call it. I'll try, but it'll be a mighty hard job, gineral."

General Lascelles laughed with evident enjoyment of these unpatriotic views of Daddy Welles.

"Well," he said, "you are right. The separate sticks in the fagot remain sticks, in spite of all. They are harder to break bound together, but they are not a solid block. Enough of politics, Daddy. I am going to take Joe with me now, and go over to Crow's Nest and see my nephew Harry!"

The intonation of his voice was joyful. The old face flushed, and he said, as he had said before,

"This is the happiest day of my life!"

"You are right, brother," said Gentleman Joe, with a cheerful smile. "I don't think I ever saw the sun shine so bright as it does to-day!"

"Well, come on, old fellow! We are going to look up Harry."

Gentleman Joe shook his head.

"We are not likely to find him at Crow's Nest, brother."

"Why not?"

"He has gone to see his sweetheart, I reckon."

"His sweetheart!—has Harry a sweetheart?"

"Mouse says so. She is very pretty. Her name is Frances Cary."

"Frances Cary! Has Harry fallen in love with Frances Cary?"

"I really don't know, but something or

other takes him in that direction every day or two—maybe to catch a sight of her; you know young men are given to that, brother."

"Well!" the general exclaimed. "But it wouldn't be a bad match, Joe! Well, well—but there is the carriage. Come, get in; I know the road. Come to Wye, Daddy, and tell me if anything happens —this moonshine business weighs on my mind."

And with a grasp of the Daddy's hand General Lascelles got into his carriage, followed by Gentleman Joe, and directed old James to drive to Crow's Nest by the way of the ford.

LXIX.

A FORTUNATE VICTIM OF MISFORTUNE.

It was late in the afternoon on this same day when Brantz Elliot rode up to the mountain-house on his return from Piedmont.

He had ridden to the village to engage his seat in the stage, as he intended, on the very next day, to return to New York. This resolution had been forced upon him at last. There was evidently no hope of inducing Nelly to marry him. The girl was more determined than ever that she would not take a step which would result in his unhappiness, and he found it utterly impossible to change her resolution.

Brantz Elliot had been thus compelled to accept his fate, and tried to accept it calmly; but it was a hard task. He loved Nelly Welles now with all the strength of his being, and had set out to engage his seat in the stage under the profoundest depression. Nelly had seen his face as he went away, and retired to her room, and indulged in a hearty cry. It was hard for her to give him up—very hard indeed. The future without the young man seemed a weary blank; but it was of his happiness that she was thinking. If her action seems fanciful, and her motive exaggerated, let us respect it — there are not so many instances of it.

She was looking out of an upper window when he rode up, her head leaning upon her hand. She was almost afraid to look at his sad face, but she could not resist the temptation. There was about him the nameless charm that surrounds the person who is beloved.

"Oh, if I was only worthy of him!— if it would not be so unequal!—if he was poor, as we are, and would not be ashamed of me!"

Brantz Elliot rode up and dismounted. His face was not all sad. What did it mean? He came into the house humming a song—he was actually laughing, too! Daddy Welles met him at the door and greeted him cheerfully, and Brantz Elliot, instead of sighing, cried,

"I'm as hungry as a hawk, Daddy! Is there any dinner for me? I hope you haven't eaten everything in the house."

Is there something in male hunger which appeals to the female heart? One would say so. As soon as Brantz Elliot went to his chamber to make his toilet, as he always did after riding, Nelly slipped down-stairs, set the table with rapid and skilful hands, placed a cold ham and whatever else the cupboard contained upon it, arranged his seat—the one he liked best—and retired quietly to the sitting-room opposite, where she was reading with much interest in a tattered newspaper when Brantz Elliot came down-stairs.

As soon as he had finished his dinner he went into the sitting-room and lit a cigar.

"I know you don't object to smoke, Nelly," he said.

"Oh no!"

"Smoking is a good thing. It drives away dull care, and is a dead shot for the blue-devils!"

It was a long time since Brantz Elliot had spoken in that tone. His voice laughed like his lips, and he was plainly in the most joyous mood imaginable. This was a mystery to her, and caused her a pang. But if he was not unhappy at leaving her, it was all the better.

"I am glad you are in good spirits," she said, trying to speak cheerfully.

14

"Riding always makes me gay," he said, laughing, "like walking. And that reminds me that I ought to walk over and see my friends at Falling Water before I leave Bohemia. It is a beautiful afternoon. Would you like to go and see your dear Frances?"

He was laughing still. What did it mean? Nelly felt like crying.

"I don't feel well this afternoon," she murmured.

"Then the stroll will be good for you. Do come, Nelly. I shall be so lonesome."

"I don't think—"

"Well it is wrong to think, so you are perfectly right! Say you'll go, without thinking about it. There never was such an evening. Look at that faint new moon yonder, like a silver skiff following the sun as he is setting. The air is as mild as summer. It is not more than a mile or so to Falling Water; and I'll bring you back soon after dark, Nelly."

Nelly tried to resist, but had not the courage to do so. The temptation was too great. It was their last evening together; she would not hear his voice any more very soon; so she yielded, and they set out for Falling Water.

They always remembered this walk afterward. Certain scenes become the frames in which the pictures of memory are set, and are never separated from them. The faint new moon was sailing through light clouds, tinted with orange by the sunset, and the stream which ran beside them seemed to laugh and prattle to them as they followed the path along its banks. The sycamores were leafless now, and there was no verdure but that of the cedars and evergreen-pines along the little watercourse and on the slopes; but the air was so calm and soft that it was difficult to realize that the season was not June.

"This is the very path we took that day when you fell into the water, Nelly," said Brantz Elliot. "Have you forgotten that day? I have not. That was the only time I ever kissed you—and I began to love you after that!"

Nelly's head sunk in spite of herself, and her bosom heaved. She was only conscious of one thing—that if she attempted to speak she would burst into tears.

"It was not so strange that I should love you after being nearly drowned with you, Nelly!" he said. "A man likes a girl better after going under with her, and not expecting to see daylight any more. Here is the log. It is another one—the mountain people were obliging enough to throw it across to get to Piedmont this way—I wonder if it will break with us again."

They were already crossing.

"Take care!" said Brantz Elliot, who was holding her hand; "if you fall in again, I'm not sure I'll jump after you! But I would, too—the water is shallow now, and there's no danger!"

Nelly was in a maze. What was the meaning of her companion's tone? It was one of actual hilarity. Could he speak in that manner if he was really depressed at the prospect of leaving her? She colored slightly. Then she drew away the hand which he was holding, ostensibly to raise her skirt and avoid treading upon it. A moment afterward they were over, and following a path covered with a deep carpet of brown pine tags, which wound through a thicket in the direction of Falling Water.

There is nothing more picturesque than a path winding away before you, either across fields or through woodlands. It seems to beckon and say, "Come, I will lead you home to your bright fireside, where smiles and fond arms are awaiting you." It may run through lonely scenes and gathering darkness, but that is nothing. You have only to follow it, and it will take you home—if you follow it.

Sometimes, if you have a companion and are talking, you do not follow it; you unwittingly take a side-path, as Nelly and Brantz Elliot did. This obliqued in a gradual and very sneaking manner to the left; they continued to pursue it, gradually ascending, until it ended at last on the summit of the high ground south of and above the ford, at Lover's Leap, where Mr. Ruggles had been conducted by the Lefthander.

"Why, we've taken the wrong path, Nelly!" exclaimed Brantz Elliot; "but it is not important—we have not far to go back, and it was worth making a mistake to see this view."

Was it a mistake? Nelly asked herself. Brantz Elliot knew the country perfectly.

"I have been here before," he said, laughing, "but perhaps you have not. This is Lover's Leap, where some forlorn lover, they say, put an end to himself. I'm glad I'm not like him. Let me show you where they say he leaped off."

He took Nelly's hand and drew her toward the edge of the precipice—a sheer descent of about fifty feet to the water. A single pine-tree grew from the rock—it was that under which the Lefthander had taken his seat. Far down beneath them the current broke in foam over the rocks in its channel.

Nelly looked down and then drew back, clinging to Brantz Elliot's hand, and drawing him with her.

"It makes me dizzy," she said, in an agitated voice; "come back!"

"I am not going to jump over," he said.

"You might fall."

"I wouldn't like to fall *now*, Nelly."

She looked up quickly. His whole voice had changed in an instant to deep earnestness. As their eyes met Nelly blushed—he was looking at her with so much tenderness that her heart throbbed as she caught the glance.

"I have something to say to you, Nelly—do you know what it is?" he said. "It is not what I have said to you so often before. You can't guess what it is. It is a misfortune—a great misfortune, as the world would call it—and has filled me with delight."

She looked at him with a startled expression, murmuring,

"A misfortune—to you?"

"Yes and no. There are misfortunes which are blessings. I am ruined! Here is the letter announcing the fact. I got it to-day."

"Oh! can it be true?" she exclaimed. "Ruined! What is the meaning of it?"

"It means having a dishonest uncle for your guardian. My father died while I was in Europe, leaving his affairs in the hands of my uncle. He delayed settling the estate, alleging pretexts for the delay. As I had perfect confidence in him, and was amply supplied with money when I called for it, I did not press the matter; and now the whole story has come out. My father's executor, my uncle, was what unceremonious people call a scoundrel."

Nelly was quite overcome by this sudden announcement, and seemed much more agitated than her companion.

"But you are not *ruined*—how could you be ruined?" she murmured, scarcely knowing what she said.

"Well, the process was very simple—my uncle stole the money," replied Elliot. "He disposed of my father's stocks and mortgaged his real estate, and speculated in Wall Street with the proceeds—and lost everything. This letter from him, written as he was leaving for Europe, acknowledges the whole transaction, and begs me not to expose him."

Nelly made no reply. Her heart was beating so that it could be heard almost. An immense tenderness filled her bosom for the man she loved so dearly in his trouble.

"So you see I am a poor fellow, without a dollar in the world, almost, Nelly," said Brantz Elliot. "There is a little remnant only, to keep me from starving—not near enough to enable me to live in Fifth Avenue."

His voice laughed again as he spoke, and he took both Nelly's hands, and looked into her eyes.

"But it will enable me to buy a small tract here in Bohemia, which will give me a living. I could build a small Swiss *châlet*, and hunt to my heart's content; but then I would die of *ennui* if I lived by myself, Nelly."

He drew her toward him as he spoke, and put his arms around her neck. She was blushing and trembling.

"You will have me now, won't you, Nelly?"

Poor Nelly! She could not make the least bit of a reply to him, her heart was beating so. But she leaned her cheek upon his breast and looked up, and their lips met—which was, perhaps, as good a reply as any other.

LXX.

MR. LASCELLES REFLECTS DEEPLY AND WRITES A NOTE.

THE parting between Miss Bassick and Mrs. Armstrong was not pathetic. Indeed, the performance was quite business-like, and not indicative of yearning affection on either side. Having informed Mrs. Armstrong, with some *hauteur*, that she would be glad to have paid her what was due her, and to be sent to Miss Grundy's, where she proposed hereafter to reside, Miss Bassick proceeded to pack up her goods and chattels, and at the appointed hour descended, canary-bird cage in hand.

Mrs. Armstrong was in the drawing-room, and advanced politely to bow to her; but Miss Bassick probably regarded this interchange of civilities as a vain show, and not wishing, apparently, to be hypocritical without necessity, passed coolly by, not so much as turning her head, and, still clinging to her canary, got into the carriage, which drove away.

As to Mrs. Armstrong, she came out and looked after the vehicle when it disappeared. A heavenly smile illumined her visage, and she drew a long breath. "Thank heaven, she is gone!" said the excellent lady.

As Miss Bassick had despatched a note to Miss Grundy on the evening before, all was ready for her, and the friends rushed into each other's arms and went through the kissing ceremony. Then Miss Bassick sat down and wrote a little note on scented note-paper, which she addressed "Mr. Douglas Lascelles, at Wye," and requested Miss Grundy to mail. This commission Miss Grundy, in a high-ly delighted state of mind, fulfilled with her own hands; and all the way to the village post-office she was reflecting with profound satisfaction that she would have a paying lodger, and would be initiated into all the secrets of Trianon.

As Miss Bassick had a quiet little chamber, propitious to meditation, she availed herself of Miss Grundy's absence to indulge in that amusement, probably reflecting that on her friend's return it might be impossible.

The emergency demanded meditation, but swift decision, too. Mr. Lascelles was coming, and she must make up her mind what to do before his arrival. The anonymous note had excited a very great fury in Miss Bassick. Could it be true? Seated in an easy-chair, and knitting her brows, she reflected deeply. It might be true. Mr. Lascelles was very young when he went to Europe—the world was full of mercenary adventuresses, ready to snap up young heirs—she must know before proceeding further. It would be a blunder to marry some one else's husband, as Mrs. Armstrong had very justly observed. If he had a wife in Europe, Mr. Lascelles would be unable to endow his new bride with all his worldly goods; and in the event of his death her position would be embarrassing, inasmuch as she would not be anybody's widow.

It was true, this unlucky rumor, or it was not true. If it were not true, then all embarrassment ended at once. If it were true—what then?

Miss Bassick's pretty eyebrows came close together. Having no mamma or other adviser, she had to do her own thinking. There were marriages and marriages. Mr. Lascelles might have been a minor, and the marriage void. The laws of different countries as to matrimony were conflicting. She might be giving herself a great deal of unnecessary uneasiness. . . .

In the evening Mr. Lascelles made his appearance, and Miss Bassick received him in an elaborate toilet in the small drawing-room. There were to be no endearments, apparently. Miss Bassick extricated her hand from his own in an instant, went and closed the door, and then, sinking into a seat, burst into tears, covering her face with her hands. It is true, she was looking at Mr. Lascelles through her fingers. . . .

An hour afterward Miss Bassick's blushing face sought its place of refuge in Mr. Lascelles's waistcoat, and the momentary cloud of calumny had been dissipated into thin air. He *had* formed a temporary connection of a certain sort, he was sorry to say, with a person in Europe; but the matter had long lost its importance, and was nothing in law. He was well assured that no risk would ensue either to himself or Miss Bassick; and, if she adhered to her word, they would be married in three days, in an adjoining village, and then go to Wye and announce the fact to everybody.

In this world it is not difficult to convince people who wish to be convinced. Miss Bassick asked nothing better, and subsided with sniffs and blushes upon the waistcoat.

The waistcoat did not seem altogether quite as ardent to receive her as was its wont. It did not repel her, but it did not smile and hold out its arms to her, to use a mixed figure. In fact, Mr. Lascelles seemed, so to say, a little chilled. His sentiment toward Miss Bassick might be as pronounced as ever, but the situation of things began to impress him, perhaps, as involving enormous risks. He was going to marry without the knowledge or consent of his family, and, besides this—   .

He was uncomfortably silent and *distrait*. Did he realize that the passing moments were to decide his whole future—that before him, a step in advance, the path he was following branched in two different directions—that a good deal would depend upon which of the two paths he turned into? That conviction comes suddenly to every human being at some period of their lives; and it seemed to have come to Mr. Lascelles at the pres-

ent moment. A vague instinct told him that danger was lurking near him; and, with such impressions occupying the mind, the very sweetest face becomes a bore.

Thus it happened that when Mr. Lascelles took leave of Miss Bassick it was rather coolly. Her quick eye noted the fact perfectly, and it filled her with sullen anger and uneasiness. But then Miss Bassick was a very good actress. It was not necessary always to show one's real feelings. Her handsome face assumed an expression of sad sweetness, and she sighed gently; then the door closed, and Miss Bassick went to her chamber, flushing with anger. Luckily Miss Grundy, who had been seated on the steps attempting to listen, thought it best to retire silently to avoid misconception.

Mr. Lascelles rode forward through the night toward Wye. He went along slowly, and was evidently buried in thought. He had lit a cigar, but it speedily went out, and he was scarcely conscious of throwing it angrily away.

It was early when he reached home, and he went at once to his chamber. Here he sat down and wrote:

"It is necessary for me to see you— for many reasons. Meet me at the bridge on the stage-road at sunset to-morrow evening. A simple 'yes' to the servant taking this will be enough.   D. L."

He called a confidential servant, gave him the note and instructions where to find the Lefthander, and then went downstairs.

General Lascelles had just arrived from the mountain.

LXXI.

A HAPPY FAMILY.

GENERAL LASCELLES entered. For years no one had seen the old statesman look so happy—and all around him were speedily in possession of the cause of this happiness.

It was an affecting recital. This man, whose voice had thundered above crowds or in senates, faltered now as he told the strange story of the discovery of his brother; and the honest eyes filled with tears in response to the tears in the eyes around him.

Mrs. Lascelles exhibited very deep feeling, and Anna cried quietly. This good family had but one thought—that God had given back to them those whom they loved; and it was decided that preparations should at once be made at Wye to have Gentleman Joe and Harry come and live there for the remainder of their lives.

"One good thing, my dear, in having a wife like yourself," said General Lascelles, cheerily, "is to know in advance what one can expect. I knew very well you would be ready to love and cherish my dear Joe. He must not leave us any more—nor Harry either, unless somebody takes him away from us."

"Who will do that, my dear?" Mrs. Lascelles said, in a puzzled tone.

"Well, I should not be very much surprised if the capture was effected by a Miss Frances Cary."

"Frances Cary!"

"My pet, you know, madam. She wished me to remain at Falling Water tonight, but I was afraid that you might be jealous. I told her how improper it was to be so free and easy with a married man, but she only laughed—the customary reply of maidens to all arguments."

"But—"

"The possible capture of nephew Harry you mean. Well, it really is a very romantic story, and was told me by Joe. It seems Harry was a circus-boy, and drew Frances from under the feet of some horses; he also shot the panther, killed some time since, when he was about to spring at Frances. Romantic, you see—but what would the world be without romance? Then the poor fellow was sick, and pity sways the feminine heart; so, to cut short my story, Harry has fallen in love with Frances, and as she blushed and tried to laugh when I recommended him to her good graces, perhaps she thinks

she ought to reward him for all his heroism."

"I hope she will!" exclaimed Anna.

"I really don't know. Your dear sex are past finding out. It is your privilege to startle us by the unexpected. As an illustration, Ellis Grantham and Miss Juliet Armstrong—she is at Falling Water—are plainly engaged to be married. He came to see her, and I am informed they make no secret of it."

Mr. Lascelles had come in behind the general, and looked quickly at him.

"Ah, there you are, Douglas! You hear what I say, and you have been distanced."

"I confess what you say is news to me," said Mr. Lascelles, moodily; "but nothing in this world is surprising, sir. I thought we were to have the honor of an alliance with Mr. Grantham's family ourselves."

He glanced at Anna, but as that young lady only laughed, he said no more.

"You saw the moonshiners, I suppose, sir?"

"Yes, all but the big Lefthander, as they call him."

Mr. Lascelles drew a long breath of relief and sat down. Then the incidents of the day continued to be discussed until a late hour. The family had not been so happy for a long time—the only moody member of it was the man seated apart, with his brows knit, and his eyes on the floor, communing with his conscience, and goaded by it.

LXXII.
A MAN OF THE BOHMERWALD.

INSTEAD of attending the meeting of moonshiners at the house on the mountain, the Lefthander had taken Mouse by the hand on that morning and they had rambled away into the woods, which accounted for the fact that General Lascelles had not found them at Crow's Nest.

The Lefthander had resolved to leave the moonshine fraternity. His motive for this was a double one. There would probably be trouble soon, and something might happen to him—that is, to Mouse. As to personal apprehension, that was something wholly alien to the character of the man. Fear was a sentiment almost, if not quite, unknown to him; but if he were arrested, it would be a terrible thing for the child, who had now become the sole thought of his life. She seemed to be dearer to him every day. He watched her with the long glance of the mother whose existence is bound up in her babe. The strength of this sentiment in the ponderous nature was phenomenal, but natural too. The athlete, with his huge muscles and rugged strength of body and mind, had his soft side, open to tender emotions, and the child touched him there; and the effect was wonderful. She had slowly acquired a strange influence over him, awakening in his rude nature all that was soft and pure. This had begun some time before. He had given up drink, which had once been his vice; now he meant to dissolve his connection with the moonshiners and their illicit business, which was a breach of the law, and therefore wrong, he said, whether it was morally wrong or not. What the Lefthander intended to do was to go away from Crow's Nest, and take his companions with him. They would form a little troupe, and go about the country, or he would settle down quietly somewhere with Mouse. It was an attractive thought to him, but strangely enough, whenever it occurred to him now, his face clouded over, and he fell into the deepest depression.

He had gone away into the woods with Mouse on this morning in a thoughtful mood, holding her hand in his own. A walk would do her good, he said; she was growing too white; and, indeed, Mouse was more aerial than ever. This did not arise from drudgery at her household duties, which sometimes pulls down people. There was no real drudgery. A poor woman who lived in the hills behind Crow's Nest came every day to look after things and relieve the child. But something seemed to have made Mouse thinner and more delicate. When the Lefthander spoke of it she laughed, but this did not change things. "You are too white, Mignon," he said; "you must go out more, and get some roses into your face again."

They went up the banks of the stream, a considerable distance above the Lover's Leap, and reaching a bluff covered with brown pine-tags, sat down upon them and looked out across the little valley. Bohemia was sleeping tranquilly in the mild Indian summer weather. Now and then the long tassels of the pines above them uttered a low sigh, which passed on as the wind passed, and died away in the distance toward the south, in the direction of the Hogback. The Lefthander, sitting with his hands clasped around his knees, looked thoughtfully at the opposite mountain, which swam in a faint mist.

"It is better," he said, at length. As he uttered these words his face began to flush slowly, and his eyes half closed; a sudden moisture had come to them which resembled tears.

"What is better, poppa?" said Mouse, who was looking down and listening to the laughter of the Falling Water, which came up like a joyous murmur from beneath them.

"It is better that you should have something more like a home than you have now," he said; "and you shall have it."

"A better home? What do you mean, poppa? I'd like to know how I could have a better home."

"That will be easy," said the Lefthander; "and the time has come for it. You had a home once—there is another that you are going to soon."

Mouse listened with utter astonishment, looking at his face; but he turned away from her.

"Listen, Mignon," he said, speaking in a voice so deep and tremulous that it penetrated to the child's heart. "It is not right for you to grow up in this way. It has been on my mind for a long time. I was never satisfied at the circus—do you remember that I told you I was tired of it? I was not tired of it for myself. I liked the rough life of the ring, and to rove around, and drink, and risk breaking my neck—that suited me; but it did not suit you."

"You mean you left the circus on my account, poppa. But it was best for you too. We are happier."

"Yes, we are happier, my Mignon—a great deal happier. You were growing, and would be a young girl soon; it would not do for you to live in the midst of circus men and women, hearing things sometimes that you ought not to hear. I did not mean you should, so I gave up that, and brought you away. Yes, we are happier, but—"

"What *can* you mean, poppa?"

"You ought to have a home, Mignon. If something happened to me you would have nobody in the world to look after you. And then men will not do: some good woman ought to have charge of you—that would be better. I can arrange that."

"Arrange what, poppa?"

"Finding a home for you. Did I never tell you that some of your mother's family came to America? There are a great many European people in this country. I can trace your mother's relatives and place you with them, Mignon. You would have a home then."

"Oh no, no!" exclaimed Mouse, turning quickly and fixing her moist eyes upon him.

"A happy home, with womanly hands to do little things for you, and people to care for you. I could come and see you now and then—it might not be so often, but—"

Mouse threw her arms around his neck and burst into tears, looking up at him. The huge breast on which she was leaning rose and fell.

"It would be better—" was all he could say.

"No, it would not be better!" the child cried, passionately. "It would make me so unhappy that I would die, without *you!* Go away from you? What made you ever think of such a thing, poppa?

Don't say any more about it, for I am not going—you shall not leave me—how could I live without you, poppa?"

She clung closely to him, sobbing and crying as if her heart would break.

"But," he said, in a low voice, "you cannot go on living as you are living now, Mignon. You must be educated, and go to church, and have little girls to play with, my own poor little Mignon—my snow-drop!" He spoke with exquisite softness and tenderness. "How can a father see his child growing up without the care that children ought to have? There are bad fathers, perhaps, who do not think of their little ones much. God makes such people, as he makes monsters. But a good father—one that has a little girl—how can he let her run wild and not be cared for and happy? You have the right to be cared for, Mignon—you are like your mother. I will find your relations, and then you will have a home. No doubt they are well-to-do, and you will have nice clothes to wear and good food, and, if you are sick, loving hands to do things for you. Think how it would be if you were sick here at Crow's Nest!"

But it was of no avail whatever. The eloquence of the Lefthander produced no impression. Mouse only clung closer to him, exclaiming, "No, no! I will never leave you—and you shall not leave me, poppa! How *could* I live without you?"

This was the end of the discussion. The Lefthander gave it up—either hopeless of bending the child's resolution or unable to control his emotion. She had never seen him so much moved. His face was flushed, and his eyes were wet. At last a single tear rolled down and fell on the child's face. It was probably one of a very few shed by the Lefthander during the whole of his life.

LXXIII.

UNDER THE ICE.

ALL that evening, after his return to Crow's Nest, the Lefthander was evidently revolving something in his mind, and did not utter a word. When the next day came he was still pondering, and his strong features betrayed an emotion which his companions had never witnessed in him before. Every movement indicated that a conflict was going on. After sitting down and smoking for some moments he would rise and walk to and fro, with his eyes fixed upon the ground; then he would raise his head and look suddenly toward Mouse. At such moments his face filled with blood, and his expression was heart-breaking.

About noon he put on his hat and walked down the hill. Having reached the road, he turned to the left, as if he meant to go toward Piedmont, and went some steps. Then he turned back and stood still for some moments. Then he wheeled round quickly and began walking rapidly in the direction which he had at first taken. As he did so, a mounted servant came over a knoll in front of him and drew rein, looking at him. It was the confidential servant sent by Mr. Lascelles; and as he was a most intelligent negro, and the Lefthander's person had been described by his master, he delivered the note to him. The Lefthander took it and read it. He then turned to the man and said "Yes," after which the servant rode away.

Toward the afternoon the Lefthander kissed Mouse, and said quietly that he was going to see Colonel Cary on some business. This was true; as, after following the road to the bridge for some distance, he turned into a path and reached the house of Falling Water. Mr. Cary was at home, and the Lefthander spent an hour with him in the library. Then he came out again and went in the direction of the bridge, which he reached as the sun was sinking and throwing long shadows across the valley.

Mr. Lascelles was already at the rendezvous. He had dismounted, and was standing, with the bridle of his horse in his hand, upon the bridge. As the Lefthander approached slowly, with his long and firm tread, Mr. Lascelles looked at him with a certain wariness which indicated that he was on his guard, and expected that their interview would be a critical one. His face was a little pale—perhaps sallow would be the better word. In fact, Mr. Lascelles had not slept much, his affairs having reached a crisis which produced a tension of the nervous system. He was, however, perfectly cool, as he was a person of strong will. He waited until the Lefthander had come to the spot where he was standing, and then said,

"I have been waiting for you, but, as you waited for me the last time, we are quits."

"We are quits," repeated the Lefthander, in his customary tone of phlegm.

"I called to see you some time since, but you were not at home. We are here alone together at last, and can talk together. It is not necessary to use ceremony. I have come on business. What is the price of the papers?"

"You mean your letters to your wife and the record of your marriage?"

"Yes."

"The papers are not for sale."

Mr. Lascelles exhibited no indication of any emotion whatever at these words.

"That means that the price will be high," he said. "It would save time if you would state the amount."

The Lefthander looked at him attentively.

"Then you think I am bargaining," he said; "but I am not. I will not sell the papers."

"Are you in earnest?" Mr. Lascelles said, retaining his coolness, but knitting his brows slightly. "Men act from intelligible motives in this world; are you an exception? I offer to buy what is valueless to you. You are poor, and no doubt need money. It is an exchange of what can be of no use to you for a sum of gold which will be of use to you. Why do you refuse? There is always a motive, as I have said, in men's actions—what is yours?"

The Lefthander did not reply for an instant; his face flushed slightly.

"Yes, I have a motive," he said, in a moment. "You might guess at it, perhaps."

"I cannot imagine any."

"There are other motives besides love of money which affect people. There is a thing called hatred—have you thought of that?"

"Then you hate me, and think that by keeping possession of these papers you will be able to gratify your hatred?"

"Why not?" the Lefthander said, quietly. "I have reason to hate you."

"What reason?"

"Then you really do not know?"

"Know what?"

"That I loved Mignon."

Mr. Lascelles greeted this announcement with a look of astonishment that was plainly unaffected.

"*You* loved Mignon?"

"Yes—better than the young American who married and deserted her."

Mr. Lascelles did not speak for a moment; his face was growing sullen and threatening, but he evidently made a great effort to preserve his coolness.

"So you cared for her?" he said.

"It is not the word," returned the Lefthander, in his deep voice. "I *loved* her with my whole strength—my brains and my heart. You did not know that; you say—now you will begin to understand some things. I was sick, and she nursed me. I began to love her, and she would have married me but for one thing. A young American came to hunt in the mountain and made her acquaintance. He was richly dressed, and had a smooth tongue, which deceives women. Besides, he loved her, or thought that he did, for when he found that she was a pure girl, and would not listen to his unworthy proposals, he married her."

Mr. Lascelles made no reply, but the dark and sullen expression of his face deepened.

"That was the first act of the play— the young American thought it was a comedy when it was a tragedy, or soon grew to be one. I am not speaking of the young man Karl Ottendorfer's feelings — you knew him, but gave no thought to him. He was wretched enough — but that is no matter; I am speaking of *her.* The young American soon grew weary of her, and found that he had business at Rome. Fortunately he had been absent for a short time before that, and had written to her."

Mr. Lascelles set his teeth together, but made no reply.

"The letters were written while he still loved her, and were such as a husband writes to his wife. Afterward he did not write any letters—when he went away on the business which took him into Italy. In fact, he neither wrote a line to her nor ever saw her any more. He deserted her!"

Mr. Lascelles moved restlessly under the harsh words, as a horse moves under the spur, and growled,

"I did not mean—to—desert her. There would be no end reached now by blackening my name. Where are the letters, and how did they come into your possession?"

"They came into my possession in a natural manner. You deserted your wife —her parents died, and she had no other friend but myself. I watched over her day and night. I had long ceased to love her as a lover—she was a saint to me; and I have knelt at her bedside and kissed her little feet when she was so white and weak that I thought the angels were coming for her."

He raised his head and looked up as he spoke, as though he saw the angels. The man of the Bohmerwald was suddenly revealed in him.

"White—and weak?" said Mr. Lascelles in a low voice, looking down at the water running under the bridge. He was leaning on the railing and had turned half away.

"Women are white and weak in her situation. She had just given birth to her child."

"To her child!"

"To her child. For a month she grew weaker, and as white—as white as the snow-drops of the Bohmerwald. Then a day came at last when they called her— the angels—and she went."

Mr. Lascelles started, turning his head quickly.

"She did not die!—she is not dead!"

Was it the voice of the cold man of the world that uttered these words? There was in his accent a quick anguish, as though some weapon had pierced him.

"She is not dead!" he repeated. "Mignon is not dead!"

"She died in my arms, and I followed her to the grave and saw her laid under the snow. The child was left. I took the child, and have been a good father to her. I promised her mother that I would be a good father; and I have kept my word to the woman I loved."

"Dead!" came in a low, trembling voice from his companion; "dead! Mignon *dead?* Can that be?"

"She is dead—the flowers have grown out of her bosom for years. I took her child and left Bohemia and came to this country."

"Dead!"

The word constantly recurred in the same tone. The sound fell like the dull, harsh blow of the clod on a coffin. In the silence which followed nothing was heard but the washing of the water against the trestle-work of the bridge. Once something like a groan issued from the pale lips of the man looking down into the water.

"I am sorry!—sorry is not the word. I did not know she was dead—you would not tell me—if breaking my heart would bring her back, it might break!"

The hard crust of the man's nature was heaving and cracking.

"I loved her," he said, in a low, deep voice, in which there was something hopeless. "Yes, I deserted her—and I was mad. I would give my life to see her face!"

The Lefthander drew a medallion from his breast. It was held by a chain.

"Here she is!" he said.

Mr. Lascelles seized the medallion, and drew it close to his face. As it was held by the chain it was necessary that he should come close to his enemy; but he seemed to have lost sight of him. He opened the medallion, and saw the picture of a young girl—a plain photograph—taken probably by some wandering artist in the Böhmerwald. The face was full of an inexpressible modesty and sweetness. In every feature could be traced the likeness to Mouse.

Mr. Lascelles looked long at it, and his frame shook; his eyes filled with fiery tears, and from his lips escaped, in a long, hopeless groan, the single word,

"Mignon!"

Suddenly the Lefthander closed the medallion and put it back in his breast. It might have been supposed that he was jealous. This sole remaining memorial of the woman whom he had loved was his property.

"I will not ask you to give me that picture," said Mr. Lascelles, in a trembling voice; "but I will give you all I possess for it."

"The world could not buy it from me!" said the Lefthander, coldly.

"I can understand that. I never knew you. I know you now. Where is my child?"

The voice had altered suddenly. From the depths of an agony of despair this man caught, as it were, at this support to keep his heart from breaking, and his voice shook.

"She is living. You have seen her."

"Seen her?"

"She saw and talked with you at Crow's Nest when you came one day."

"That child—that is *my* child?"

"She is Mignon Lascelles, since you are her father! I did not mean to tell you that; but something might happen to me, and it is necessary for me to tell you."

"Yes, yes!"

"But leave her to me: I love her so that I cannot live without her. I meant to follow you and kill you once—I hated you so; but I do not wish to kill you now, and will forgive you all you have ever done to me if you will give me Mignon."

"No!"

"You will not? You take her? You have the right to do that."

The Lefthander knit his black brows and groaned. Suddenly he said,

"Listen! There will be no trouble about the papers; they are in a bag at Mr. Cary's — all. You have only to go with me, and I will deliver them to you. All I ask in return is that you will give me Mignon."

"Give you my child? No!—I do not want the papers now. My child is all that is left of the woman I love. I say *love!* — not *loved!* Yes, I deserted her, and thought I had forgotten her. Since she is dead I know better."

"Give me Mignon!"

The voice was beseeching. The giant had become a suppliant.

"I cannot give you Mignon. I can offer you my hand, and thank you for not killing me, as you had a right to do. Keep the letters and marriage record—I do not want them now. I will come to Crow's Nest to-morrow—not to-night. I have business to-night."

Before the Lefthander was aware of it Mr. Lascelles had gripped his hand, mounted his horse, and was galloping toward Piedmont.

LXXIV.

MOUSE CHOOSES.

THE Lefthander went away in the direction of Crow's Nest, with his chin nearly resting on his breast. An unutterable gloom possessed him. He was going to lose Mignon! The long doubt was over. He had hoped that her father would disown her: he claimed her; and thenceforth he, the Lefthander, was alone in the world.

He went on groaning. He would see her soon, for nearly the last time. He had a great thirst of the heart to see her, and take her in his arms and say, "I love you more than your real father can ever love you!"

He reached Crow's Nest as the twilight was deepening into dusk. In front the valley of Bohemia was asleep. Not a breath of air stirred the few leaves of the trees, and a crescent moon was floating through fleecy cloud-waves, bound for the haven of the sunset.

Mouse saw him coming and ran to meet him, and put her arms around him.

"Why, poppa! what is the matter? You do not look happy," she said.

"Not happy? That is your fancy, Mignon. How can I be unhappy when you are by me?"

But Mouse shook her head, and said,

"Something troubles you, poppa.— What's the use of loving people if we can't see when they are happy or troubled?"

"And do you love me really—just a little, my own Mignon?"

"Love you! What do you mean, poppa? How could I ever live without you?"

"Are you sure of that? Suppose you had to go away from me, Mignon. Yes —let us suppose a thing. Say I was not your father — and that your real father was living."

"My real father! Why, what father could I have but my own poppa?"

"Such things happen. You read curious things in the newspapers sometimes, and when the story-tellers put them in stories people say they are improbable. Sometimes little ones like you are brought up by strangers, then you think they are father and mother. Say that this was true of you, and your real father, as I said, was living; then suppose he came one day and said, 'Give me Mignon, you have no right to her.' You may think the idea foolish, but — tell me — what would you say?"

Mouse had begun to laugh at the romantic case supposed by the Lefthander, but something in his deep voice quite suppressed her tendency to mirth.

"I don't know what you mean, poppa," she said, earnestly; "but I know what I would say if they came to take me from you."

"What would you say?"

"Well, I would not *say* anything. I would show them what I meant by what I did."

"What would you do?"

"I would do this."

The child put both arms around the Lefthander and nestled close to him.

"You would not leave me, then, Mignon?"

"Leave you?"

"I mean you would not, even if there were other people who wanted you, who could make your life pleasanter to you? Let me tell you what I mean, little one—there is something I ought to say to you." His voice had grown deep and full of sudden emotion—he drew long breaths.

"I am poor, and your life is a hard one. Suppose, once more, that I was not your father, and your real father was a rich man. Suppose you had only to choose which you would stay with—the poor man or the rich one. Suppose your real father could give you pretty dresses, and nice things of every sort, while the other one could not do that—he could only give you his love. Which would you choose?"

Mouse looked at him in utter astonishment at his fantastic speech. What could he mean? Her mind was in a maze.

"Are you in earnest, poppa?" she said, with a look of bewilderment.

"Yes, Mignon; in dead earnest. It is my fancy to ask you — tell me — would you leave me or stay with me?"

"I would stay with you, and be your Mignon to the last day of your life!" exclaimed the child. "You are my father, and I love you more than everything in this world!"

Mouse nestled still closer, and leaned her small face against his own; the little white cheek was like a snow-drop against the bearded face.

"The very idea of leaving you — or your leaving me — I would rather die!" she said.

The Lefthander raised his head and looked upward. His lips were moving, and he seemed to be praying.

Suddenly hoof-strokes were heard approaching rapidly from the direction of the ford. The Lefthander turned his head and saw Daddy Welles coming on at a long gallop, with his rifle in his hand. In a moment he had reached the spot, and said to the Lefthander,

"Be on the lookout, friend; the troops will be in Piedmont to-night."

LXXV.

THE DEAD AND LIVING.

MR. LASCELLES had ridden on toward the Gap. At first he went at a gallop; then he slackened his pace, and finally came down to a walk. With knit brows and a face full of unutterable things, he went along looking down and reflecting.

He was going to see Miss Bassick, but he did not think of her once. He was far away from Virginia, and living in past years. He had gone back to the time when he was young, and had loved with his heart; he had deserted the woman thus loved, and she was dead now. It was enough to break the heart to think of it—but she was dead. As long as he could think of her as living, and as having probably formed a connection with some Bohemian boor, his heart was at rest, and he thought that he cared nothing for her. It had been a youthful *liaison*, to be regretted, perhaps, but not mourned over. She had forgotten him, no doubt, and he was thus at liberty to forget her—the past would be the past for both of them, and fall like a funeral pall over their dead loves.

Now things were different, he found. She had not forgotten him, and had not married again—she was dead—and dead from his desertion! There was no one there on the lonely mountain - road to argue with—he was alone with his own heart. He had killed her, and the thought drove him to despair. His love for her had been very different from his sentiment toward Miss Bassick; there was as much difference between the two sentiments as between sunshine and darkness. He had really loved his little bride of the Bohmerwald, and had been happier with her than he had ever been before or since; and thinking now of what had followed, he lost sight of everything—of worldly views, the inequality of their position, and every obstacle—and cursed his own frivolous temperament and love of change, which had made him leave her, slowly forget her, and never return to her. He had loved her, he felt that, now that he knew she was dead. The flowers of memory grow on graves. He remembered every feature of her face, her smile, the light in her blue eyes, the touch of her hand, and his frame shook.

His face, as he rode on slowly, was not a pleasant spectacle. Pain, physical or mental, writes itself on the eyes and lips, as the storm writes itself on the face of a landscape. In an hour this man seemed to have lost his identity. A great agony had transfigured him.

As he got to the top of the mountain he suddenly put his hand into his breast-pocket and drew forth Miss Bassick's picture, which hung upon a silken guard around his neck. There was enough light to see by, and he looked long at the face, with its physical beauty and provoking smile. The face seemed ugly to him—the cheeks painted. The smile he had admired so was immodest, not the smile of a pure maiden. The eyes of a woman ought not to look at a man as the eyes of the picture looked at him. The truth came to him as a night landscape lives in the quick lightning-flash—he understood all now. The senses had usurped the seat of love; darkness had swallowed up the dawn.

Then he thought of Mignon and his child, and a sob followed the thought. His own Mignon was dead, but had left a little Mignon to love. As to doubting the Lefthander's statement, that never entered his mind. He felt that every word was true, and now remembered what indeed had impressed him vaguely on his visit that day—the likeness between the child and his Mignon. Oh yes, this was his child, and he meant to cherish her for her mother's sake, if not for her own. He would acknowledge all!

It was very little: he would have courage to do it. Yes, he would do what was yet in his power to right a great wrong. She was dead—his Mignon of the Bohmerwald—but she would smile on him then! As he thought of that he remembered her smile, and the faint light in the blue eyes as she came to meet him, with her white arms held out to him. He heard her little sigh of pleasure, and the caressing voice that greeted him. The picture of Miss Bassick fell from his hand, and but for the guard would have dropped into the road. A single tear rolled down his cheek. It was so hot that it seemed a wonder it did not burn what it fell upon.

Suddenly thrusting the picture back into his pocket he broke into a gallop; and, as if seeking to outrun his thoughts, went at full speed down the mountain. He did not go toward Wye, but kept the main road to Piedmont, and dismounted at last before the small house in the suburbs occupied by Miss Grundy.

Miss Bassick had heard the hoof-strokes of his horse, and came to meet him in the drawing-room. Never had he seen her look more provokingly beautiful, or fuller of physical attraction. Her eyes melted; her lips pouted, and seemed asking to be kissed; her white arms moved vaguely, as though ready not only to be clasped but to clasp.

Miss Bassick had, in truth, determined to dissipate that *distrait* mood and rather chill preoccupation which she had observed and raged at in their last interview. She closed the drawing-room door and came up to him, leaning toward him. Her face and body said, "Take me!"

Mr. Lascelles sat down.

For a moment Miss Bassick stood looking at him, and it taxed her powers of acting to the very utmost to conceal the internal rage which had suddenly taken possession of her.

"One would really say that monsieur had seen a ghost, he looks so woe-begone," she said, with satirical, almost bitter emphasis.

"I have," said Mr. Lascelles.

"A ghost! Indeed!"

"I have seen my wife."

Miss Bassick felt as though she were suddenly choking.

"Your wife!"

"They were right when they told you I had a wife."

"And—you have—*seen her?*"

"Her ghost, I said. My wife is dead!"

Miss Bassick drew a great breath of relief, and said, in the same satiric tone, "I congratulate you, if you wish to be congratulated."

"Congratulate me?"

He looked sidewise at her. His glance was like the lunge of a steel blade.

"As you please: it is indifferent to me. Choose your own sentiment for the occasion."

The intonation of contempt in his voice suddenly enraged her. The profound dissimulation of her character gave way to passion.

"One would say that your sentiment, whatever it is, excludes common courtesy."

"If I am discourteous I beg you will excuse it, madam. I am fatigued—nearly ill."

She refused to accept the explanation. Bitter resentment mastered her.

"That scarcely accounts for your tone —it is an insult!"

"I do not mean to insult you."

"People who—love, speak in a different tone. If you love me no longer, tell me so."

He hesitated, looking at her. Her face was hot with anger.

"You exact the truth, then?" he said.

"Yes."

"You force me to speak. I would avoid doing so. Well, to be frank — I think we have deceived each other."

"Deceived! Speak for yourself, sir."

"I will do so. I never really loved you."

"This is an insult!—an outrage!—it is unworthy of a gentleman!"

"Perhaps; and I am not so sure that I am a gentleman."

He spoke in the cold, dull tone which he had preserved from the beginning.

"I have done that in my life," he went on, "which a gentleman could hardly have done. I have married a pure woman who loved me, and deserted her. I was a coward—not a gentleman—have it as you will, madam. But I have seen her face to-night, and it comes between all other loves. She is dead years ago, but reaches out her hands from the grave and they chill me."

Miss Bassick had not seated herself. Her superb figure towered above him in an attitude which would have done honor to the mythological Furies.

"And you think I am to be treated in this manner—you dare to treat me so!"

He shook his head. His dull, mournful eyes, full of hopeless anguish, had never changed their expression.

"It is little to me to dare anything," he said. "I have seen to-night what hardens my nerves — strong nerves, for that matter, which have never shrunk yet. To speak plainer still: I thought I loved you, and I do not love you. All ends here between us, and needs must end. It is best to tell you that."

He took the picture and laid it on the table.

"This is your property. You have nothing that I desire to have returned to me."

He rose and stood facing her, as though conscious, for the first time, of the discourtesy in seating himself.

"You will pardon me—I was fatigued, and scarcely aware that you were standing."

Suddenly the fury appeared in all the force of her rage.

"You are a common person, sir!—a low person!—you shall repent this!"

The taunt did not affect him. The threat even afforded him a dull satisfaction, and a bitter smile came to his lips.

"Do you mean by poison, or a suit for breach of promise, madam?"

He looked around him, and saw pen, ink, and paper on a table near.

"That is your due, and, if you wish, we need not go into court. As you wish, I say—it is indifferent to me."

She made no reply. Did she understand his meaning, and not resent it? He seemed to think so. He went to the table, and wrote a check for a considerable amount. He then left it lying on the table and rose. As his gloves were lying by him, he took them and slowly put them on. Then he took his hat, and made Miss Bassick a bow.

"Farewell, madam!" he said.

As he spoke it required all Miss Bassick's self-control to prevent herself from springing at him.

"Coward!" she cried, in a voice so hoarse and furious that it cut like a whip.

"I was a worse coward once," he said, "and only act my nature. Farewell, madam!"

And he went out of the apartment and, mounting his horse, rode away. Miss Bassick remained standing in the middle of the room, looking after him. Her face was the face of a fury. She raised the little handkerchief in her hand and tore it with her white teeth. As she stood thus, trembling with rage, she resembled a tigress about to spring; but, after all, the business woman was under the tigress.

From the door through which he had disappeared her eyes passed to the table. The check was lying there, and she went and took it up and looked at it.

Was there balm in it? Her face grew calmer; an expression of fierce satisfaction even took the place of her fury. She folded up the paper, put it like a love-token in her bosom, and slowly went up to her chamber.

Mr. Lascelles had ridden away, absorbed in gloomy thought, but something suddenly drew his attention to the world around him.

As he passed by the tavern, which was full of lights, he observed figures in blue uniforms swarming in the bar-room, and heard the clash of spurs and sabres. Among the blue figures he noticed others clad in citizen's dress—the marshal whom he had accompanied to the mountain, and his revenue collectors; also the figure of no less a personage than Mr. Ruggles, who seemed engaged in fraternizing and imbibing liquids with his blue friends. The troops were United States cavalry, refreshing themselves with strong potations after a long march that day; and Mr. Lascelles had no difficulty in deciding in his mind what brought them.

"Who are these people, Tom?" he said to a stable-boy passing with a lantern.

"De Yankee cabblery, Mas' Douglas, come to stirminate de moonshine people," was the grinning response. "De marshal heself in dar—gwyne to set out early."

Mr. Lascelles rode up close, leaned over and counted the number. There were twenty-five men. He then rode away toward Wye.

LXXVI.

BLUE COATS IN BOHEMIA.

THE moment had come at last when the issues between the Government and the moonshiners seemed about to be decided by an appeal to arms. All the morning the marshal was fretting to get to saddle. But delays will take place in the best arranged programmes. It was important to surprise the moonshine people, for which reason the troops had been timed to reach Piedmont at midnight. They were to have set out at dawn, but many of the horses had cast their shoes on the march and limped. It would not do to attempt the rocky mountain-roads without replacing the shoes, and it was not until past noon that this was accomplished.

Then the search-warrants were not obtained yet, and the marshal was obliged to go to Wye for them, as General Lascelles was the nearest magistrate. There was a stormy interview. The general protested against the employment of troops; but the marshal replied, stiffly, that he obeyed his orders, and galloped away with the warrants in his pocket.

The troops were already on the march, as the officer had seen them leave Piedmont before his departure for Wye. A prompt irruption into Bohemia he hoped would take the enemy unawares, and resolving that he would make an end of the business this time, the marshal hastened on from Wye toward the Gap.

He caught up with the troops and revenue-officers at the foot of the mountain on the opposite side. The cavalry numbered twenty-five, and were regulars commanded by a lieutenant. Two or three of the marshal's subordinates rode at the head of them, carrying black leather satchels slung from their shoulders for the transaction of business.

"Well, lieutenant, that is your road to the left," the marshal said to the commandant of the troop. "It leads to the home of a man who is the real leader of these people—an old fox named Welles. He looks peaceful, but is not to be trusted. He was a furious bushwhacker during the war, and from what I can learn is willing to have it open again. Keep your eye on him particularly, and warn your men to be ready to fire if necessary. There is his house."

The cavalry, preceded by the revenue-officers, defiled up the road leading to the house on the mountain, the hoof-strokes of the horses clashing on the rocky pathway. It was a very unusual sound in the peaceful valley. A long time had passed now since Bohemia had seen the blue cavalry, and the valley bathed in the mild sunshine of the Indian summer day seemed to be listening. Did it remember? It had witnessed such scenes in the "wild war days" of the past. Was it going to look again on men dyeing the red autumn leaves with a redder tint than before?

If there was to be any fighting, it was not going to take place just yet. Daddy Welles was not at home, and his aged helpmate, in response to the marshal's statement that he should search the premises, expressed her perfect willingness. The search was made, but resulted in nothing. There was no spirit of any description about the abode of Daddy Welles, and the marshal bowed curtly, and remounted his horse.

"This is a specimen of what we are to expect," he said, "at all the houses we search. These people have been notified, and have removed all traces of their occupation. Luckily, they can't remove the stills so easily, and we are apt to discover some of them before the day is over."

He looked up at the sun, which was sinking toward the west, and added,

"Why have we lost so much time? These December days amount to nothing. It will be bad to be caught by night in this detestable country. It is bad enough in broad daylight—but there's nothing to do but to go on. Put your column in motion, lieutenant."

The young lieutenant, who wore a dandy uniform, and was smoking a cigar, gave his orders in a nonchalant voice, and the troop began to descend the mountain with the revenue-officers in front.

"I am going to the house of a man named Barney Jones next," said the marshal; "a small detachment may be sent to a place called Crow's Nest—but I think there's nothing there. To be plain, I expect to find nothing and nobody anywhere. The rascals are forewarned, and have escaped into the mountain—and to say that troops are not necessary to deal with such people! They are outlaws, and may even resist. I advise you to keep your men well together, lieutenant, and look out for a brush—you may have it."

"All right," returned the lieutenant, puffing at his cigar. "It is my trade to brush or be brushed, and I'll attend to that; I only wish it was under other circumstances. This infernal moonshine business is no better than police duty, and I didn't go through the hazing at West Point for that."

"It is a part of the duty of the army, sir," said the marshal, somewhat offended.

"Is it? Well, the army does seem to be looked to in these days to do a little of everything. It has now and then occurred to me that the authorities might apply to somebody else. Leave us to go after the Indians, who are interesting animals to deal with, and if you want a police force to operate in the States, enroll a battalion of black coats out of the swarm of civil employés—they ought to smell a

15

little powder if any is to be burnt—it would enlarge their ideas. But that don't suit them."

The nonchalant tone of the lieutenant betrayed his opinion of civilians, and the marshal was much offended. He would, perhaps, have made some reply indicative of his opinion as to the results of the military movements against the Western Indians, but at that moment the vidette in front was heard halting some one. They could not see who this some one was, as a dense wall of rock rose between them and the stream from the direction of which the sound came. The marshal spurred forward, and saw that the person halted was Mr. Lascelles.

LXXVII.

THE LAST GREETING.

As the troop of horsemen had obliqued from the Gap into the mountain-road, a man had passed the rear of the column at a gallop, and this man was Mr. Lascelles.

Some of the troop turned their heads, and possibly wondered where this horseman was going at his long gallop; but as that was none of their business they dismissed him from their minds, rightly concluding that a soldier's business is to obey orders, not think.

Mr. Lascelles crossed the bridge, turned into the road leading by Falling Water, and went on at a headlong gallop. The mournful composure of the rider was in vivid contrast with the quick movements of the animal. The horseman seemed scarcely aware that he was being borne along. Profound and absorbing thought made him unconscious of surrounding objects. He was thinking, in fact, of the Böhmerwald, and of the face there once, when he was young in heart and hope, and all the harsh and jarring emotions of his present life had been unknown.

Did he think, too, of that other face, resembling the face of his Mignon, which he was going to see? Passionate love and regret drove him on, as his flying animal was driven by the spur. One emotion only possessed and quite mastered him at length—he would see her soon! He had come up out of the depths of his soiled love to the pure air again. The face yonder in Piedmont, with its physical beauty, its lasciviousness and fury, had disappeared. He was going to see his child: and with that single thought heaven entered his breast.

At Falling Water he stopped and went in. Mr. Cary was in the library.

"I have come for a moment only—I am in haste," he said, grasping his host's hand.

"Welcome," Mr. Cary said. "What is it moves you so? You speak to a friend."

"I know that. I have no time, and come to the point. You have a travelling-bag, intrusted to you by the person known as the Lefthander."

"Yes, intrusted to my safe-keeping."

"Keep it safely. It contains the evidence of my marriage in Europe. I was married there, and deserted my wife. I did not know that I had deserted my child, too. My child is the little one at Crow's Nest; she is Mignon Lascelles—I pray you to remember that."

"Mignon Lascelles!—is it possible?"

"She is my child."

He went to the table where the family Bible lay, and rested his hand upon it.

"She is Mignon Lascelles. In the presence of God and of Jesus Christ, in whom I believe as the Son of God, the child is mine — she is Mignon Lascelles. You will remember that?"

"Yes, yes—why do you make this solemn declaration?"

"To forestall events — whatever may happen. Life is uncertain. My child's future is now certain. I may share it' and direct it—I may not be permitted to do so. It is the same, since she can want nothing now."

With a hurried grasp of Mr. Cary's hand he went out, without saying anything more, and mounted his horse. Resuming the gallop, he went on toward Crow's Nest, reached the low fence at the foot of the hill, leaped it, threw his bridle over a bough, and hastened to the house.

Mouse met him on the threshold. The little mamma had wound her hair into a Grecian knot behind, and the delicate outline of the head had a womanly air that was charming. The man looking at her shook. It was his Mignon of the Bohmerwald.

He came up to her, and could scarcely control the passionate longing to clasp her to his heart. He thought that would frighten her—the long look of the human being who sees nothing and thinks of nothing but the face his eyes rest upon, and longs to devour with caresses.

"Your father—is he here, little one?" he said.

Was it the voice of Mr. Lascelles? No one would have recognized it. It was music, and melted into cadences of exquisite tenderness.

"He is not here, sir," said Mouse, not at all afraid of one who spoke in that tone to her; "he has gone to the mountain." ·

"I thought so—I came to tell him—but I will tell him in time."

He turned his head and looked across the valley, listening. The sun was sinking, and long shadows ran across Bohemia. In the red light he could see the cavalry slowly descending the path from the mountain-house.

"There is time," he said, in a low tone; and addressing Mouse,

"You are all alone here, my child?"

"Yes, sir."

"You are not afraid?"

"Oh no, sir!"

"Not afraid of me? You were afraid when I was last here. Do not be afraid of me; we ought not to fear those who love us."

He looked at her with inexpressible tenderness, and said,

"Will you tell me your name?"

"Mignon Ottendorfer, sir."

"Your father is the Lefthander?"

"Yes, sir."

"And you love him?"

"Love poppa? Oh yes, indeed, sir! How could I help loving him?"

"Well, I, too, love him. He is a brave man, and a better man than I am. I am called a gentleman—it is he who is the true gentleman. I am going to see him now—there is no time to lose. Is your name Mignon, my child? I knew a Mignon once and loved her, and she loved me; but she is dead, now. You are so much like her—oh! so very much like my Mignon, my child."

He sobbed, and stooping down took the child in his arms and held her to his heart, and covered her face with kisses.

"You are so like my Mignon!—the same eyes, and the very lips: oh, so very much like my own Mignon, my own child!"

He drew her closer, and leaned down and laid his pale cheek on her forehead. She could feel his heart throbbing and his tears on her cheek. One of his arms was around her neck, he placed the other hand on her hair and raised his eyes. Then he pressed a last, long kiss on her lips, and, with a sob which shook his whole frame from head to foot, went out, and, mounting his horse, rode rapidly in the direction of the ford.

He had hoped to reach the mountain in advance of the cavalry. It was too late. As he went at full speed up the narrow road from the ford he came suddenly on the vedette sent out in advance, and was halted.

LXXVIII.

THE ADVANCE INTO THE GORGE.

THE marshal spurred forward, followed by the young lieutenant, and saw Mr. Lascelles.

"You, sir?" he said, stiffly, for he was in a very bad-humor.

"Myself!" was the cold reply. "Is it forbidden to ride on the Virginia highway? Why am I halted—I may say, arrested?"

"You are not arrested, sir," the marshal replied, apparently conscious of the justice of the protest.

"I am halted."

The young lieutenant interposed, laughing, and said,

"That was by *my* order, sir. No offence to you in particular, my dear Mr.— You have not told me your name."

"Lascelles."

"Well, you've fallen a victim to general orders, my dear Mr. Lascelles. You see we are temporarily on the war-path, and in the enemy's country. I don't mean that the late little unpleasantness between the sections is still in progress—and Heaven forbid that a democrat like myself should look on old Virginia as an enemy now. My great-grandmother was an F. F. V., and I'm an unworthy scion. But what the devil—excuse me—brings you here to this infernal Hades, so to call it? It's dark enough now when the sun is setting."

"I came for my pleasure."

The deep and mournful voice affected even the mercurial young West Pointer.

"For your pleasure? That's strange," he said; "but every man to his fancy. You will pardon me for saying that I think your taste is devilish bad. It gives *me* no pleasure at all to be here, I assure you; but there's no accounting for tastes in this miserable world. Forward the column!" he added, turning in his saddle and calling out to the men. He then added to his companion, with a gay laugh,

"Happy to know you, Mr. Lascelles. We are going after the moonshine people, and I'm glad to have your company. Try a cigar?"

Mr. Lascelles bowed but declined, whereupon the young lieutenant lit his own. With his gauntleted hand resting gallantly on his hip, he rode on with Mr. Lascelles beside him.

"Yes, we are on the way to annihilate the wretches that make bad whiskey," said the gay youth. "They deserve it, too; if it was good, the case would be different. Here we are in battle array, and we'll probably have an infernal row

—I heard a preacher in New York use that word 'infernal,' and therefore consider it scriptural! Yes, we'll come on the moonshiners, and I'm told they mean to fight. All right, that's my trade. But this sort of thing is not much to my taste. Here they are—tag, rag, and bobtail, Mr. Lascelles: collectors, revenue-commissioners, and detectives—for there's a detective along. He's that villanous-looking fellow in the black coat yonder—Ruggles by name. I wish he was at the devil! Do try a cigar—they are excellent."

Again declining the friendly offer of his companion, Mr. Lascelles looked over his shoulder. There, in fact, at the head of the column, some distance in rear, was Mr. Ruggles. He was not present willingly, and had come only under compulsion. Recognized by the marshal, he had been drafted for the expedition: and there he was — probably resolved to disappear at the first crash of carbines.

All at once the marshal said, pointing in front,

"There is the house of the man Jones. It is useless to search it, but we may as well go through the form. We will not find the man."

The marshal was quite correct in his surmise that Mr. Barney Jones would not be "at home" on that evening. It was evidently not one of his receiving days. A hard-featured woman, with a baby in her arms, and a series of tow-headed young ones, rising above each other with a regularity which implied that the matron was a fruitful vine, appeared at the door, and confronted the visitors. Was Mr. Jones at home? No, Mr. Jones was not at home. Where was he to be found? They might find that out for themselves, if they could. He was, likely, huntin' somewhere, and shot off his gun at a ventur' in the woods often. It was dang'rous to be ridin' round in the mounting when Barney Jones was a-huntin'.

"As I expected," the marshal said; "any search would be a mere farce."

"I think it would," said the lieutenant, indifferently. "We had better go on or go back. If I am consulted I'll say go back, as I'm getting devilish hungry and thirsty; but that's no matter. If you are anxious to go on, and interview Mr. Barney Jones, I'm ready."

"Go on? Of course I shall, sir!" the marshal said; "and I will call your attention to the fact, sir, that your orders are to assist in these arrests!"

"I don't think you'll make any, from present appearances," returned the young officer; "but give your orders. I brought along my overcoat, and wish there was a flask in the pocket. But if we meet any of the moonshiners they may have the politeness to offer us a drink."

The column moved on, and entered the gorge extending up to the Hogback. The sun was sinking, and the long red rays pierced the glades like spears, and fell in vivid crimson on the rocks, covered with variegated mosses. From in front came the low sigh of the pines in the depths of the gorge; from the rear no sound was heard but the measured hoof-strokes of the troopers.

Bohemia was waiting, and expecting something—you could see that.

- - -

LXXIX.

FAREWELL TO BOHEMIA.

BOHEMIA was in all its last and crowning glory.

Not the glory of the fresh spring mornings, when the violets first come and the buttercups star the glades and the fields; nor yet the glory of the summer days, when the clouds drift on the blue sky, and the green foliage of the forest is alive with singing birds; nor the autumn glory of splendid colors and dreamy hours, when the heart dreams of other hours, and sees the faces that have gone many a year into the dust; but the glory of the last moments of the Indian summer—the Nurse of the Halcyon which cradled the Greek fancy—this had come now, and the year was bidding farewell to Bohemia, and expiring in a dream of beauty.

There were few leaves clinging to the trees—the winds had swept them. They lay on the ground, and formed a deep yellow carpet. Here and there a cedar, forming a perfect cone, stood out like a sentinel from a background of rocks, and over rock and cedar, and under the great pines, trailed the autumn creepers with bright crimson berries, glittering like coral beads in the light of the sunset. That sunset light made the glory more glorious. It was dashed on rock and tree, and lit up the gorge with a sombre splendor: the wild pines, the dark depths, the figures of the troopers, and the sky above. You would have said that it had come to salute Bohemia for the last time, and that thereafter her glory would be a dream.

The column was in the gorge, and was advancing over a narrow bridle-path, when the young lieutenant ordered "halt!"

"I saw the gleam of a gun-barrel on that height yonder," he said to the marshal. "As we're about to proceed to business, let us act in a business-like manner."

He sent forward an advance-guard of three men with instructions. These were to keep a keen lookout on the bluffs above, and if fired upon return the fire, and fall back upon the column.

"You won't have far to fall back," added the young fellow. "I'll be close behind you."

The advance-guard went in front, and disappeared around a bend in the road. The spot was wild beyond expression, and lofty heights extended like walls on either side as the column proceeded. Beyond the tops of the trees could be seen the long blue line of the Blue Ridge on the left; and on the right rose the bristling and threatening crest of the Hogback.

"I begin to think the moonshiners are going to fight, Mr. Lascelles," said the lieutenant, lighting a fresh cigar. "I saw the man with the gun as plainly as I see you. There are probably some stills in the vicinity here—it is the very place for them; and I think the moonshiners, like good patriots, are going to die by their altars and fires!"

A shot rung out as he spoke from the direction of the vanguard; and then a rattling volley followed, and the men were seen coming back at a gallop.

"Well," said the lieutenant, coolly, "what's up?"

The report was that they had been fired upon—apparently from a barricade in the mouth of a small gorge debouching into the main one.

"I think it probable there's a barricade, which is not a bad thing to fight behind," said the lieutenant, smoking and reflecting. "Well, I'm going to charge it, as a matter of course. I'll have some saddles emptied, I rather suppose, but that's to be looked for."

"It is unfortunate," said Mr. Lascelles; "it would be better to have no bloodshed."

"Vastly preferable, I allow, but the devil of the thing is to avoid it. I'm not speaking for myself; I'm engaged to a pretty girl, but she'll have to take her chances for a wedding. This is my business—and after all, too, it's the business of these good fellows on both sides. So here's for a charge!"

"A moment," said Mr. Lascelles; "you ought to summon them to surrender."

"Useless—but it would be more regular."

"I'll take the summons."

"You!"

"Certainly, with very great pleasure."

"You'll be shot!"

"No. They might shoot one of your men in his uniform, but they will not shoot me. I am in citizen's dress, and will raise my white handkerchief."

"That is true—but suppose you're shot. You have nothing to do with this business. I like your face, Mr. Lascelles, though it's rather mournful. You were cut out for a soldier, but then you are a civilian. Well, do as you choose."

"I will go, then, and deliver your summons. You will wait?"

"Yes, but be quick. Night is coming."

"If I am not back in ten minutes it will be because they refuse. Then you can charge."

He put spurs to his horse, and, without troubling himself to display the white handkerchief, went at a swift gallop forward into the gorge.

The shadows grew deeper as he went, and the overhanging banks more densely wooded. He was penetrating to the most mysterious depths of the gorge.

Suddenly a voice called "Halt!" and he saw the gleam of gun-barrels behind a barricade of felled trees. He paid no attention to the order, and reaching the barricade leaped to the ground.

LXXX.

THE BARRICADE.

THE Lefthander was standing on the top of the barricade, with a carbine in his hand. It was he who had ordered "halt," but he did not raise his weapon. He had recognized Mr. Lascelles, and quietly waited.

Behind him were grouped nearly a dozen rough-looking figures armed to the teeth; among these were Daddy Welles, Barney Jones, and Harry Vance. Under low drooping boughs in rear of the barricade was a rude door in the rock. Behind this door, which the pine boughs brushed, was the still.

The barricade itself was constructed of felled trees, and about breast-high. Behind this the moonshiners were obviously going to fight.

Mr. Lascelles threw his bridle over his horse's neck, and mounted the barricade.

"They are coming," he said to the Lefthander, "and I have come to summon you to surrender."

"To surrender? We will not surrender," said the phlegmatic athlete.

"I knew that, and so that's done with. They will charge you in ten minutes; but there will be time to say what I came to say to you. I have been to Crow's Nest."

He took the Lefthander by the arm and drew him aside. For some moments the group of moonshiners saw the two men engaged in low, earnest talk. Then they saw them grasp hands and come back toward the group.

As they did so the troopers charged the barricade.

A volley met it in the face, and the horses, wild with fright, wheeled and retreated in disorder.

"Halt!" the lieutenant's voice was heard shouting, as he whirled his light sabre. "Form column in rear!—I'll soon attend to this."

The men stopped, and fell into column again just beyond range of the fire of the barricade.

"Dismount and deploy skirmishers! Advance on both flanks and in front! I'll be in the centre."

And throwing himself from his horse, he formed the line of skirmishers. Then, at the ringing "Forward" of the game young fellow, the skirmishers closed in steadily, firing as they did so on the barricade.

All at once the quiet scene was turned into the stage of a tragic drama. Nature was pitiless and serene; the red crowns were rising peacefully from the summits of the trees; a crow was winging his way toward the sunset on slow wings; it was a scene to soothe dying eyes, if the light needs must disappear from them.

In ten minutes it had disappeared from more than one on both sides. The moonshiners were evidently determined to fight hard, and only give way when they were forced to do so. The crack of the sharpshooters was answered from behind the barricade, and the gorge was full of smoke and shouts as the assailants closed in.

They did so steadily, like good troops, and at last rushed upon the barricade. There a hand-to-hand fight followed, and it was a weird spectacle in the half gloom. In the shadowy gorge the figures were only half seen as the light faded, and the long thunder of the carbines and shouting rolled through the mountain, awaking lugubrious echoes in the mysterious depths.

The moonshiners fought desperately, but the fight was of no avail. They were outnumbered, and, after losing some of their best men, scattered into the mountain. Among those who thus escaped were Daddy Welles, Barney Jones, and Harry Vance. The parting salutes from their carbines were heard from the heights as they retreated; and the barricade was in possession of the cavalry.

The young lieutenant leaped on the felled trees, and stood there looking around.

"A good work—constructed by soldiers," he said; "and they were game, too."

He was tying up his arm with a white handkerchief. A bullet had passed completely through the fleshy part, and it was bleeding.

He leaped down into the barricade. Suddenly he stopped—he had nearly trodden upon something: it was the body of Mr. Lascelles. A bullet had passed through his forehead, and he was quite dead. The shot had been fired from behind a rock by the man whom he had lashed that day in the Wye woods—his bitter enemy.

At three paces from the body of Mr. Lascelles lay the Lefthander—dead. Three other moonshiners were dangerously wounded, and were leaning against the barricade. They closed their eyes, as though to avoid seeing the blue uniforms. They were probably troopers of the old battles of Ashby, and accepted their fate like soldiers, not complaining.

As to the faces of Mr. Lascelles and the Lefthander, they were quite tranquil. They had died, in fact, with little pain, and perhaps willingly. Each had muttered the same name as the light faded, and they went into the darkness. This name was "Mignon."

LXXXI.

THE SONG OF AN ORIOLE.

SINCE these scenes some years have passed, and Bohemia and the Wye neighborhood are much changed. Piedmont is looking up, and Bohemia is threatened with a railroad — merciless disenchanter of the modern age.

As to the moonshiners, they seem to have disappeared, and the old trouble with these excellent people has ceased. No one connected with them is disturbed, and Daddy Welles is at peace with all men. If he ever longs for a chance shot at anybody, he never says so, and passes his old age in his mountain lodge in smiling content.

Not far from his house, and on the very summit of the Blue Ridge, stands a sort of Swiss *châlet* or hunting-lodge, in which Mr. and Mrs. Brantz Elliot pass a large part of the year. Having had restored to him a considerable portion of the property appropriated by his uncle, Mr. Elliot has his house in New York, where he spends the winter; but the whole summer and autumn are passed on the mountain, where he and Nelly are not at all lonely, as they have two fine boys, who afford them society.

Gentleman Joe lives at Wye with his brother, General Lascelles; and Mr. Harry Lascelles, his son, at Falling Water with his wife and father-in-law, Mr. Cary. They were married about a year after the scenes in Bohemia, but Frances would not consent until he had promised her not to take her away from her father. She is even more beautiful than before, and more like the cabinet picture in the library— the portrait of her mother. Harry manages the estate, and hunts, and is devoted to his wife; and every Sunday they attend church at Piedmont, where Mr. Ellis Grantham generally preaches. He has returned with his wife from a year of Indian missionary service in Idaho, and is the assistant of his father, whose health is growing feeble. But the old foe of ritualism is cheerful and happy. A little girl, with Juliet's eyes, flourishes her spoon from her high chair, and requests to be helped first; and Mr. Grantham, Sr., while elaborating his "History of Ritualism," hears the pattering of small feet up-stairs, and is thankful for them. There is a great deal of going to and fro between the parsonage and Trianon, where Mrs. Armstrong makes out to sustain existence in spite of her loneliness. It is true, she drives out almost every day, and consumes hundreds of paper-bound novels. Miss Bassick is a loss, as she has no one to scold—but then she never could bear to look upon that serpent again.

The serpent disappeared from Piedmont soon after the unfortunate issue of her affairs. No one knew whither she went, but the rumor was brought that she had become one of the *corps de ballet* of a theatre in New York. There was still another rumor that she had appeared in a breach of promise case at the capital; but as the jury decided that it was only an attempt to levy blackmail, they dismissed it, and Miss Bassick vanished from all eyes.

The peaceful little neighborhood of Piedmont is thus quiet, and lives its life contentedly under the shadow of the mountain, far off from the noisy world. The days follow, and resemble each other, and glide from Sunday to Sunday without events. Sometimes religious services are held in the Old Chapel, sleeping quietly on the wooded slope of the mountain. The winds sigh or laugh in the leaves of the great oaks there, and the weeping-willow murmurs as it murmured on that morning when Mouse listened to it, and the Lefthander said it would be a good place to be buried.

He is buried there, not far from Mr. Lascelles. His wish was remembered and observed, and Mr. Grantham read the burial-service. When some busybody questioned the propriety of admitting an outlaw into the sacred precincts, Mr. Grantham was greatly offended, and said, "He is a man — are you more?" And that was the end of it.

There is another grave close by that of the Lefthander. The small head-stone has on it the single name "Mignon." After the Lefthander's death she was taken to Wye, and guarded with the fondest affection. Mrs. Lascelles and Anna Gray were quite wrapped up in her, and the old general could not bear her out of his sight—for her parentage was known, through Mr. Cary, and she was all that was left of his dead son. But all was of no avail. The poor child had loved the Lefthander with her very heart of hearts, and her health slowly failed after his death. Grief seldom kills, but it weakens, and then disease finds the citadel ready to totter. Mouse lingered until they had some violets to place on her white bosom, and then she went to the Old Chapel to sleep by the Lefthander.

This is sad, and it is not well to leave a sorrowful impression upon those who listen to a narrative — since life is sad enough already without that. Fortunately Piedmont resounds once more with rejoiceful music. The Unrivalled Combination has come back to visit the borough again. The triumphal entry is a triumphant affair, and the crowds shout and hurrah, and Mr. Manager Brownson waves his black hat and bows. And then the great domes of canvas rise on the same old ground, and the crowds rush in, and the band roars, and the barebackers appear, and the world of Piedmont is a world of enjoyment. The circus means to remain until the afternoon of the next day, and the tired performers therefore sleep late—all but one of them.

She is a woman, who rises at daylight, and goes out into the silent streets and toward the mountain. She has made inquiries as to some events and personages connected with the last visit of the company to Piedmont, and informed herself. She takes a path which obliques to the left from the road leading to the Gap, and just as the sun is rising reaches the graveyard around the Old Chapel.

It is difficult to recognize the laughing and brilliant Clare de Lune in the plainly-dressed woman, with the heaving bosom and eyes wet with tears. She finds the grave she is looking for under the long tassels of the weeping-willow, and the small stone with "Mignon" engraved upon it close beside it, and bends down, and cries, and calls to them to come back to her.

"He told me to be a good girl, and I have been a good girl—and he is dead!" she sobs.

All at once the sun rises and the whole world is full of light. From the top of the weeping-willow the song of an oriole bursts forth. Clare de Lune raises her eyes and listens, and understands, perhaps.

THE END.

25 BOOKS FOR $5.00.

HARPER'S HALF-HOUR SERIES.

SPECIAL INDUCEMENTS TO PRIVATE BUYERS:

A Selection of Twenty-five Volumes, with Paper Covers, in a Box, for Five Dollars.

HISTORY.

CENTS

Afghanistan. By A. G. Constable 15
Constantinople. By James Bryce 15
The Turks in Europe. By E. A. Freeman... 15
The Spanish Armada. 1587-1588. By Alfred
   H. Guernsey............................. 20
The Jews and their Persecutors. By Eugene
   Lawrence............................... 20
University Life in Ancient Athens. By W.
   W. Capes............................... 25
Modern France. By George M. Towle...... 25
The Four Georges. By W. M. Thackeray ... 25
English History. Early England, up to the
   Norman Conquest. By Fred. York-Powell.
   With Four Maps........................ 25
English History. England a Continental
   Power, from the Conquest to Magna Char-
   ta, 1066-1216. By Louise Creighton. With
   a Map................................. 25
English History. Rise of the People and
   Growth of Parliament, from the Great
   Charter to the Accession of Henry VII.,
   1215-1485. By James Rowley, M.A. With
   Four Maps............................. 25
English History. Tudors and the Reforma-
   tion, 1485-1603. By M. Creighton, M.A.
   With Three Maps 25
English History. Struggle against Absolute
   Monarchy, 1603-1688. By Bertha M. Cor-
   dery. With Two Maps.................. 25
English History. Settlement of the Con-
   stitution, 1689-1784. By James Rowley,
   M.A. With Four Maps 25
English History. England during the Amer-
   ican and European Wars, 1765-1820. By O.
   W. Tancock. With Five Maps. 25
English History. Modern England, 1820-1874.
   By Oscar Browning, M.A................ 25
Half-Hour History of England. By M.
   Creighton.............................. 25
The Origin of the English Nation. By E. A.
   Freeman 25

DOMESTIC SCIENCE.

Food and Feeding. By Sir Henry Thomp-
   son................................... 20
The Youth's Health-Book................. 25
Cooking Receipts. From *Harper's Bazar*... 25
Healthy Houses. By Fleeming Jenkin,
   F.R.S. Adapted to American Conditions
   by G. E. Waring, Jr. 25

FINANCE.

CENTS

Hints to Women on the Care of Property.
   By Alfred Walker...................... 20
Labor and Capital Allies—Not Enemies. By
   Edward Atkinson 20
The A B C of Finance. By S. Newcomb,
   LL.D 25

BIOGRAPHY.

Some Recollections of Rufus Choate. By
   Edwin P. Whipple...................... 15
Oliver Cromwell. By Knatchbull Hugessen. 20
Gaspard De Coligny. By Walter Besant ... 25
Warren Hastings. By Lord Macaulay 25
Life and Writings of Addison. By Lord Ma-
   caulay 25
Lord Clive. By Lord Macaulay............ 25
Frederic the Great. By Lord Macaulay..... 25
The Earl of Chatham. By Lord Macaulay.. 25
William Pitt. By Lord Macaulay.......... 25
Samuel Johnson. By Lord Macaulay....... 25
John Hampden.—Lord Burleigh. By Lord 25
   Macaulay 25
Sir William Temple. By Lord Macaulay.... 25
Machiavelli.—Horace Walpole. By Lord Ma-
   caulay 25
John Milton.—Lord Byron. By Lord Ma-
   caulay................................ 25
Goldsmith. —Bunyan. — Madame D'Arblay.
   By Lord Macaulay..................... 25
Lord Bacon. By Lord Macaulay 25
Peter the Great. By John Lothrop Motley. 25

FICTION.

The Sunken Rock. By Geo. Cupples........ 15
The Bar-Maid at Battleton. By F. W. Robin-
   son.................................. 15
The Awakening. By Katharine S. Macquoid 15
Lady Carmichael's Will, and other Christmas
   Stories............................... 15
The Sorrow of a Secret. By Mary Cecil Hay 15
A Dark Inheritance. By Mary Cecil Hay ... 15
Our Professor. By Mrs. E. Lynn Linton.... 15
The Romance of a Back Street. By F. W.
   Robinson 15
Irene Macgillicuddy...................... 15
Kate Cronin's Dowry. By Mrs. Cashel Hoey. 15
Othello the Second. By F. W. Robinson.... 20

Published by HARPER & BROTHERS, New York.

☞ *Any twenty-five of the above volumes, in paper covers, will be sent by mail (in box), postage prepaid,
to any part of the United States, on receipt of Five Dollars. The volumes sent
separately at their advertised prices, postage free.*

☞ *"Harper's Half-Hour Series" will be supplied in cloth for fifteen cents a volume in addition to the
prices of the respective volumes in paper covers.*

FRANKLIN SQUARE LIBRARY.

HISTORY AND BIOGRAPHY.

POETRY.

ANECDOTES.

TRAVEL AND ADVENTURE.

FICTION.

FICTION—*Continued.*

CENTS

Within Sound of the Sea. By the Author of "Iseulte," &c................................ 10
The Last of Her Line. By Eliza Tabor..................... 15
Vixen. By M. E. Braddon...... 15
Within the Precincts. By Mrs. Oliphant..................... 15
All or Nothing. By Mrs. Frances Cashel Hoey..................... 15
The Grahams of Invermoy. By M. C. Stirling..................... 15
Coward Conscience. By F. W. Robinson..................... 15
The Cloven Foot. By M. E. Braddon..................... 15
Quaker Cousins. By Agnes Macdonell..................... 15
The Sherlocks. By John Saunders..................... 15
That Artful Vicar. By the Author of "The Russians of To-day," &c..................... 15
Under One Roof. By James Payn..................... 15
"For a Dream's Sake." By Mrs. Herbert Martin..................... 15
Lady Lee's Widowhood. By Captain Edward B. Hamley, R.A..................... 15
Basildon. By Mrs. Alfred W. Hunt..................... 15
John Halifax, Gentleman. By Miss Mulock..................... 15
Orange Lily. By May Crommelin..................... 10
John Caldigate. By Anthony Trollope..................... 15
The House of Lys. By General W. G. Hamley..................... 15
Henry Esmond. By W. M. Thackeray..................... 15
Mr. Leslie of Underwood. By Mary Patrick..................... 15
The Green Hand. A Short Yarn. By George Cupples..................... 15
Dorcas. By Georgiana M. Craik..................... 15
The Gypsy. By G. P. R. James..................... 15
Moy O'Brien. A Tale of Irish Life. By "Melusine"..................... 10
Framley Parsonage. By Anthony Trollope..................... 15
The Afghan's Knife. By Robert Armitage Sterndale, F.R.G.S..................... 15
The Two Miss Flemings. By the Author of "Rare Pale Margaret," &c..................... 15
Rose Mervyn. By Anne Beale..................... 15
Adventures of Reuben Davidger. A Tale for Boys. By James Greenwood..................... 15
The Talisman. By Sir Walter Scott, Bart. Illustrated..................... 15
The Pickwick Papers. By Charles Dickens..................... 20
Madge Dunraven. By the Author of "The Queen of Connaught"..................... 10
Young Mrs. Jardine. By Miss Mulock..................... 10
Cousin Henry. By Anthony Trollope..................... 10
Sense and Sensibility. By Jane Austen..................... 15
The Bertrams. By Anthony Trollope..................... 15
The Fugitives. By Mrs. Oliphant..................... 10
The Parson o' Dumford. By George Manville Fenn..................... 15
High Spirits. By James Payn..................... 15
The Mistletoe Bough for Christmas, 1879. Edited by M. E. Braddon..................... 10
The Egoist. By George Meredith..................... 15
The Bells of Penraven. By B. L. Farjeon..................... 10
A Doubting Heart. By Annie Keary..................... 15
Little Miss Primrose. By Eliza Tabor..................... 15
Donna Quixote. By Justin McCarthy..................... 15
Nell—On and Off the Stage. By B. H. Buxton..................... 15
Sweet Nelly, My Heart's Delight. By James Rice and Walter Besant..................... 10
Sir John. By the Author of "Anne Dysart"..................... 15
The Greatest Heiress in England. By Mrs. Oliphant..................... 15
Queen of the Meadow. By Charles Gibbon..................... 15
Friend and Lover. By Iza Duffus Hardy..................... 15
Cousin Simon. By the Hon. Mrs. Robert Marsham..................... 10
Mademoiselle De Mersac. By the Author of "Heaps of Money"..................... 15
Barbara; or, Splendid Misery. By M. E. Braddon..................... 15
A Sylvan Queen. By the Author of "Rachel's Secret," &c..................... 15
Tom Singleton. By W. W. Follett Synge..................... 15
The Return of the Princess. By Jacques Vincent. Translated by L. E. Kendall..................... 10
A Wayward Woman. By Arthur Griffiths..................... 15
Two Women. By Georgiana M. Craik..................... 15
Dalreen. By F. Frankfort Moore..................... 15
For Her Dear Sake. By Mary Cecil Hay..................... 15
Prince Hugo. By the Author of "My Heart's in the Highlands"..................... 15

MISCELLANEOUS.

The Russians of To-day. By the Author of "The Member for Paris," &c..................... 10
The People of Turkey. By a Consul's Daughter and Wife..................... 15
Haverholme; or, The Apotheosis of Jingo. A Satire. By Edward Jenkins..................... 10
Impressions of Theophrastus Such. By George Eliot..................... 10

PUBLISHED BY HARPER & BROTHERS, NEW YORK.

☞ HARPER & BROTHERS *will send any of the above works by mail, postage prepaid, to any part of
the United States, on receipt of the price.*

WILKIE COLLINS'S NOVELS.

Armadale.	The New Magdalen.
Basil.	The Woman in White.
Hide-and-Seek.	Antonina.
Man and Wife.	Poor Miss Finch.
No Name.	The Queen of Hearts.
After Dark, and other Stories.	My Miscellanies.
The Dead Secret.	The Law and The Lady.
The Moonstone.	The Two Destinies.

16 volumes, 12mo, Cloth, $1 25 per volume.

Complete Sets, $18 00.

W. M. THACKERAY'S WORKS.

Vanity Fair.	The Virginians.
Pendennis.	The Adventures of Philip.
The Newcomes.	Henry Esmond, and Lovel the Widower.
Barry Lyndon, Hoggarty Diamond, &c.	Four Georges, English Humorists, Round-
Paris and Irish Sketch-Books, &c.	about Papers, &c.
Book of Snobs, Sketches, &c.	Catherine, Christmas Books, &c.

Illustrated. 11 volumes, 12mo, Cloth, $1 25 per volume.

Complete Sets, $12 00.

GEORGE ELIOT'S NOVELS.

Adam Bede.	Middlemarch. 2 vols.
Daniel Deronda. 2 vols.	Scenes of Clerical Life, and Silas Marner.
Felix Holt.	The Mill on the Floss.
	Romola.

9 volumes, 12mo, Cloth, $1 25 per volume.

Complete Sets, $10 00.

CHARLOTTE BRONTË'S NOVELS.

Jane Eyre.	The Professor.
Shirley.	Villette.

Illustrated, 12mo, Cloth, $1 00 per volume.

Complete Sets, $3 50.

PUBLISHED BY HARPER & BROTHERS, NEW YORK.

JOHN ESTEN COOKE'S WORKS.

ry St. John, Gentleman,

Of "Flower of Hundreds," in the County of Prince George, Virginia. A Tale of 1774–'75. By JOHN ESTEN COOKE. 12mo, Cloth, $1 50.

is story depicts the social life of Virginia in the of Governor Dunmore, and is full of happy, ef- | fective touches. The characters are well introduced, and the scenes of Old Virginia are finely sketched.

ther Stocking and Silk;

Or, Hunter John Myers and his Times. A Story of the Valley of Virginia. By JOHN ESTEN COOKE. 12mo, Cloth, $1 50.

is unique story of Virginia life quietly winds ray to the heart of the reader by its simple hes of nature, its gentle pathos, and the admir- | able harmony and fidelity of its coloring. The author has a rare perception of the capacities of character for dramatic effect.—*N. Y. Tribune.*

. Grantley's Idea.

By JOHN ESTEN COOKE. 32mo, Paper, 25 cents.

lively story.—*N. Y. Tribune.*
graceful novel.—*Rochester Express.* | A sprightly story.—*Chicago Interior.*
A bright Virginian tale.—*Worcester Spy.*

ofessor Pressensee, Materialist and Inventor.

A Story. By JOHN ESTEN COOKE. 32mo, Paper, 25 cents; Cloth, 40 cents.

is written in a vigorous and entertaining style. . Y. *Evening Mail.* | It is full of action and incident, and is charmingly told.—*Philadelphia Item.*

ries of the Old Dominion.

From the Settlement to the End of the Revolution. By JOHN ESTEN COOKE. 12mo, Cloth, $1 50.

r. Cooke has the manner of an entertaining *ra-nur* as well when he is telling stories to his boys | and others—to whom this book is dedicated — as when he is writing for older folk.—*N. Y. World.*

e Virginia Bohemians.

A Novel. By JOHN ESTEN COOKE. 8vo, Paper, 75 cents; Half Bound, $1 00.

The work is in Mr. Cooke's best style, abound-in vivid pictures of the mountain scenery, | sketches of quaint native character, and local descriptions of great freshness of coloring."

PUBLISHED BY HARPER & BROTHERS, NEW YORK.

⁂ HARPER & BROTHERS *will send any of the above works by mail, postage prepaid, to any part of the United States, on receipt of the price.*

HARPER'S MAGAZINE, One Year,
HARPER'S WEEKLY, One Year
HARPER'S BAZAR, One Year
HARPER'S YOUNG PEOPLE, One Ye

Singularly good as the *Magazine* has been from the
first, it has been of the progressive and cumulative sort, ...
numbers than a beauty and amplitude of illustration and ...
tools greater than any which have preceded them. The ...
in its editorial articles the vigor and ability, the best ...
which its readers have learned to expect ; while its illus...
very charmingly the life of the day, and a large amount ...
and profitable reading is found in its pages. The *Bazar*
as often ... to the needs ...
feminine world ... *Harper's Young People*—the latest from ...
periodicals—is a handsome 16-page weekly, well filled and ...
and amusable, adapted to interest and instruct the ...
journal.

The Volumes of the *Weekly* and *Bazar* be
first Numbers for January, and the Volumes of ...
with the Numbers for June and December of e...

Subscriptions will be ... with the
each Periodical current at the ... of receipt ...
cept in cases where the subscriber ...

Remittances should be made by Post
Order or Draft, to avoid chance of loss.

Address   HARPER & BROTH
FRANKLIN SQU